S0-BXX-975

EndNote®

...Bibliographies & More Made Easy™

Search bibliographic databases on the Internet
Organize references, images and PDFs in a snap
Construct your paper with built-in templates
Watch your bibliography, table and figure list appear as you write!

THOMSON

™

ISI RESEARCHSOFT

EndNote®

Macintosh Version 7

COPYRIGHT

© 1988-2003 Thomson ISI ResearchSoft, all rights reserved worldwide. No part of this publication may be reproduced, transmitted, transcribed, stored in a retrieval system, or translated into any language in any form by any means, without written permission from Thomson ISI or Thomson ISI ResearchSoft.

Trademark Information:

EndNote is a registered trademark of Thomson ISI. Cite While You Write is a trademark of Thomson ISI. Apple and Macintosh are registered trademarks of Apple Computer, Inc. MACWINSOCK™ is licensed from Altura Software, Inc. WASTE text engine (c) 1993-1998 Marco Piovanelli. Palm OS and HotSync are registered trademarks of PalmSource, Inc. Palm, Palm Powered, and the HotSync logo are trademarks of Palm, Inc. Microsoft and Windows are registered trademarks of Microsoft Corporation. All other product and service names cited in this manual may be trademarks or service marks of their respective companies.

NOTICE REGARDING LEGAL USE OF DOWNLOADED REFERENCE DATA

EndNote gives you the capability to import references from online databases and store them in your personal EndNote libraries. Some producers of online reference databases expressly prohibit such use and storage of their data, others charge an extra fee for a license to use the data in this way. *Before you download references from a database, be sure to carefully check the copyright and fair use notices for the database.* Note that different databases from the same provider may have varying restrictions.

Table of Contents

Chapter 5   **Entering and Editing References**

Chapter 6   **Searching Remote Databases with EndNote**

Chapter 9   Term Lists

Chapter 10   **Using EndNote with Microsoft Word**

Chapter 11   Scanning and Formatting RTF Files

Chapter 15   Bibliographic Styles

Chapter 1

Welcome to EndNote

Chapter 1   Welcome to EndNote

Introducing EndNote

Welcome to EndNote—the complete reference solution!

♦ EndNote is an online search tool—it provides a simple way to search online bibliographic databases and retrieve the references directly into EndNote. (EndNote can also import data files saved from a variety of online services, CD-ROMs, and library databases.)

♦ EndNote is a reference and image database—it specializes in storing, managing, and searching for bibliographic references in your private reference library. You can organize images—including charts, tables, figures, and equations—and assign each image its own caption and keywords.

♦ EndNote is a bibliography and manuscript maker—it formats citations, figures, and tables in Microsoft® Word with the Cite While You Write™ feature. Watch the reference, figure, and table lists grow as you insert citations in your manuscript. Microsoft Word templates guide you through the exacting manuscript requirements of publishers.

You can also create bibliographies using RTF Document Scan with other word processors.

See "What's New in EndNote 7" on page 6 for a list of the most recent features added to EndNote.

About This Manual

This manual assumes that you know how to use your word processor and the basics of working with the Macintosh System. For help on these topics, consult your computer owner's guide or your word processor manual. The following representations for key combinations are used:

Instruction	Explanation
⌘+O	While holding down the ⌘ (COMMAND) key, press the O key.
⌘+SHIFT+T	While holding down the ⌘ (COMMAND) key and the SHIFT keys, press T.

This complete EndNote manual is also available as a PDF file in your EndNote folder.

You can also consult the online Help file. From EndNote's *Help* menu, select *EndNote Help* to view the various topics.

Customer Services

Register Your Copy of EndNote

If you haven't done so already, please mail, fax, or email your registration to ISI ResearchSoft (go to www.endnote.com/encontact.asp). You also have the opportunity to register during installation. Even if you purchased EndNote directly from ISI ResearchSoft, do not assume that you are registered. Registered users receive:

♦ free technical support

♦ special upgrade offers

♦ notification of new EndNote versions that are compatible with the latest version of your word processor

Customer Service

Contact Customer Service for non-technical questions such as registering your software, ordering new copies or upgrades of EndNote, quantity discounts, referrals to dealers, and general product, billing, or payment information.

Sales Information

Mail: ISI ResearchSoft
              2141 Palomar Airport Road, Suite 350
              Carlsbad, CA 92009 U.S.A.
Phone: (760) 438-5526 (country code is 01)
Fax: (760) 438-5573 (country code is 01)
Web/Email: http://www.endnote.com/encontact.asp

Customer Service (Orders, Billing, and Shipping)

Mail: ISI ResearchSoft
              3501 Market Street
              Philadelphia, PA 19104 U.S.A.
Phone: (800) 336-4474 (country code is 01)
Fax: (215) 386-2911 (country code is 01)
Web/Email: http://www.endnote.com/encontact.asp

Technical Support

Contact Technical Support if you encounter problems while using EndNote. Before contacting us, have a clear description of the problem and know the version of your copy of the Macintosh operating system, EndNote, and your word processor. (To find the EndNote version, start EndNote and choose *About EndNote* from the EndNote menu.) Also have your EndNote serial number available.

Our hours are Monday–Friday, 8:00 am – 5:00 pm Pacific Time.

Mail: ISI ResearchSoft
800 Jones Street
Berkeley, CA 94710 U.S.A.

Phone: (408) 987-5609 (country code is 01)

Fax: (510) 559-8683 (country code is 01)

Web/Email: http://www.endnote.com/encontact.asp

Technical support tips are also available on the EndNote Web site and through the endnote-interest email forum (see below).

International Customer and Technical Support

For customer support or technical support outside of North America, please visit our Web site to check for a local distributor.

Go to http://www.endnote.com, click on *Contact Us*, and then click on *International Distributors* to find a local distributor.

The EndNote Web Site

The EndNote Web site (www.endnote.com) contains technical support tips, utilities for data transfer, and information about the latest versions of EndNote. You can also find updated styles, filters, connection files, and other related documents at this site. Go to the Web site and look under *Support and Services*.

To easily locate incremental updates available on the Web site, go to the *Help* menu in EndNote and select *EndNote Updates*.

The *EndNote-Interest* Email Forum

If you wish to join an ongoing email forum of EndNote users like yourself, go to the EndNote Web site at www.endnote.com, click on *Support and Services* and then scroll down for instructions on how to subscribe to the *EndNote Interest List*.

There are two types of subscriptions: The first delivers the endnote-interest messages individually, so that every time a user sends a message to endnote-interest, it is redirected to each member of the list. The second option, which we recommend, is to subscribe to the endnote-interest-digest—a daily compendium of endnote-interest messages. In general, ISI ResearchSoft does not answer questions posted to endnote-interest, but lets users answer each other's questions. Contact ISI ResearchSoft directly for a guaranteed response from technical support staff.

What's New in EndNote 7

Bibliography Tools

♦ Create a subject bibliography with topic headings for easily producing *curricula vitae* and reading lists. See "Creating Subject Bibliographies and Subject Lists" on page 319.

♦ Scan documents and create a bibliography using RTF Document Scan for compatibility with word processors such as OpenOffice, FrameMaker, AppleWorks, NisusWriter and more. See "Scanning and Formatting RTF Files" on page 289.

♦ Use Macintosh OS X Services in other applications to Find Citation(s), Insert Citation, and run an RTF Document Scan. See "Using Macintosh Services" on page 294.

Cite While You Write

♦ Locate and insert charts or tables in Microsoft Word—now the reference, figure, and table lists are easily maintained for manuscript submission. See "Finding and Inserting Figures and Tables" on page 271.

♦ Place figures and tables stored in EndNote anywhere in a Microsoft Word document to create reports and more in a snap. See "Placing Figures and Tables" on page 275.

♦ Highlight text in a document and use Find Citation to find references for citing instantly. See "Finding and Inserting from Highlighted Text" on page 244.

♦ Preview and edit in-text citations throughout an entire document. See "Editing Citations" on page 258.

New Database Features

♦ Identify references containing an image easily with a new icon displayed in the reference list. See "The Library Window" on page 76.

♦ Navigate within an EndNote record using "Go to" to locate any word or phrase. See "Finding Text in a Reference" on page 95.

♦ Edit standard import filters (for example, RIS, Tab delimited, or ISI CE) to easily move data between applications.

♦ Import/Export a reference list in XML format.

Connectivity

♦ Access an EndNote library on a Palm™ handheld device—mobilize your library. See "Using EndNote With Palm OS Handhelds" on page 501.

♦ Locate full text faster by connecting to your institution's online resources with OpenURL links. See "Finding Related Online References" on page 203.

♦ Connect to more online resources and create bibliographies in over 1000 styles.

Chapter 2

Installing and
Upgrading EndNote

Chapter 2   Installing and Upgrading EndNote

Before You Install EndNote

Please read the requirements section below before you proceed with the installation.

Requirements

EndNote is distributed on a CD, so you need a CD-ROM drive to install the program.

System Requirements:

This version of EndNote requires OS X, version 10.1.5 or later.

In the Finder, choose *About This Mac* from the *Apple* menu to find your system version.

Hardware Requirements:

◆ At least a Power Macintosh G3.

◆ A hard drive with at least 62 MB of free space.

◆ A minimum of 64 MB of available memory (RAM).

◆ In order to use EndNote's *Connect* command, an Internet connection is required. To use the *Open Link* command to access a web site, you also need a web browser installed.

NOTE: Make sure that your computer meets the system and hardware requirements before continuing. If necessary, contact the distributor, dealer, or store where you purchased EndNote to arrange for a full refund. If you have any problem obtaining a refund, contact ISI ResearchSoft directly. You must do so within 30 days of purchase.

Installation Options

Are you upgrading EndNote?

You do *not* need to uninstall any earlier version of EndNote to upgrade it. EndNote 7 is installed into a new EndNote 7 folder. See "Upgrading from an Earlier EndNote Version" on page 16. Back up custom styles, import filters, and connection files as well as any Word documents that use Cite While You Write before you remove the old program.

Do you plan to use EndNote to format citations in your word processor documents?

Cite While You Write in Microsoft Word

EndNote's Cite While You Write commands are available for Microsoft Word X.

These Cite While You Write functions put an EndNote submenu of commands on Word's *Tools* menu. They also allow EndNote to format citations and create a bibliography for the document that is open in Word. You can format, unformat, and re-format a single document—without ever exiting your word processor.

If Microsoft Word X is installed on your computer, the appropriate Cite While You Write files are installed automatically when you run the EndNote installation.

Keep in mind that in order for Cite While You Write to install properly:

♦ Microsoft Word X must be correctly installed on your computer *prior to* installing EndNote.

♦ The EndNote installer must be able to locate the Word startup folder. You need to have full read and write access to Word's startup folder in order to install EndNote commands.

RTF Documents

For word processors other than Word, write your paper, insert in-text citations, then save to an RTF file to use EndNote's RTF Document Scan feature and format the citations and bibliography. See Chapter 11 for details.

Do you plan to use EndNote for Palm OS on your Palm handheld device?

If your computer has software installed to allow synchronizing with a Palm OS® handheld device, the EndNote installation program will ask whether you want to install EndNote for Palm OS.

Requirements for running EndNote for the Palm Operating System include:

♦ Handheld device from Palm, Inc. (e.g. Tungsten series, Zire series, m series)

♦ Palm Operating System 4 to 5.2

♦ Communication port for HotSync operations

♦ 4 MB RAM

See "Using EndNote With Palm OS Handhelds" on page 501 for information about how to install and use EndNote on a handheld device.

EndNote Installation

Follow these instructions to install the EndNote program. If you are upgrading from an earlier EndNote version, first see "Upgrading from an Earlier EndNote Version" on page 16.

Installing EndNote

To install EndNote:

1. Make sure no applications are running.

2. Insert the EndNote CD into your CD-ROM drive.

3. Double-click the *EndNote 7 Installer* icon, read the information regarding this version of EndNote, and click *Continue* to proceed with the installation.

4. By default, the Install Location is set to use (or create) an EndNote 7 folder in the Applications folder of your startup drive. If necessary, you can direct the installer to put the EndNote 7 folder elsewhere using the options in the Install Location section of the installation dialog.

5. The *Full Installation* option is selected automatically. Using this option, all of the files that are provided with EndNote are installed. Choose the *Custom Install* only if you are low on disk space or if you want to install only specific components.

   If you would like to do the full installation, simply click *Install* and the installation begins. If you would like to customize your EndNote installation, see "Custom Installation" on page 15.

Once the installer is finished you are ready to get started using EndNote! See "Checking Your Installation" on page 17 to make sure both the EndNote program and Microsoft Word support were installed correctly.

NOTE: If you use a non-English version of Word, see page 18.

Installed Files

The full EndNote installation includes:

♦ *EndNote 7* application

♦ *EndNote Read Me* text file containing late-breaking news

♦ *EndNote Manual.pdf* electronic manual

♦ *EndNote 7 Help* folder
Double click the *EndNote 7 Help* file in the finder, select it from EndNote's *Help* menu, or click the *Help* key on your keyboard while using the EndNote program. Clicking the *Help* key brings up a context-sensitive topic.

♦ *Examples* folder
This folder contains example files to follow the Guided Tour in Chapter 3, and to experiment with while learning EndNote.

♦ *Styles* folder
This folder contains the full collection of over 1000 bibliographic formats (styles).

♦ *Connections* folder
This folder contains hundreds of connection files to connect to and search online bibliographic databases.

♦ *Filters* folder
This folder contains hundreds of import filters used when importing text files downloaded from online bibliographic databases.

♦ *Terms* folder
This folder contains the three journal abbreviation term lists: Chemical, Medical, and Humanities. These three lists contain thousands of journal names and standard abbreviations. Import a list into your library's Journals term list to use the abbreviations in your bibliographies.

♦ *Spell* folder
This folder contains various language or discipline-specific dictionary files for spell checking.

♦ *Cite While You Write* folder
This folder contains the Cite While You Write files for Microsoft Word X. They integrate EndNote commands into Word's *Tools* menu.

♦ *Templates* folder
This folder contains Microsoft Word templates to accurately and quickly set up your papers for electronic submission to publishers.

◆ *Services* folder
This folder supplies RTF Document Scan commands for the *Services* menu of other software applications.

◆ *Palm* folder
This folder contains a Palm Read Me file and an ENPalm Installer file to install EndNote for Palm OS, which allows you to keep an EndNote library on a Palm handheld device.

Custom Installation

If you are short on disk space, you can use the *Custom Install* option to install a minimal version of EndNote. You can also use *Custom Install* to re-install specific components (such as specific output styles) after the EndNote program has already been installed.

To do a custom installation:

1. Make sure no applications are running.

2. Insert the EndNote CD into your CD-ROM drive.

3. Double-click the *EndNote 7 Installer* icon, then click *Continue* to proceed with the installation.

4. By default, the Install Location is set to use the EndNote 7 folder in the Applications folder of your startup drive. If necessary, you can direct the installer to a different location using the options in the Install Location section of the installation dialog.

5. The *Full Installation* option is selected automatically; change to the *Custom Install* option in the top left corner of the installation screen.

6. Select the components you want to install and click *Install*.

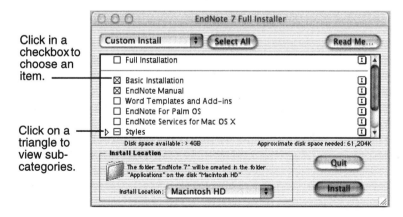

Click in a checkbox to choose an item.

Click on a triangle to view sub-categories.

Most of the components are described under "Installed Files" on page 14.

The *Basic Installation* option installs the basic components necessary to run EndNote (the EndNote 7application, Microsoft Word support, examples, four basic styles, and a demonstration set of connection files). The collections of styles, filters, and connection files are *not* installed.

EndNote's *Full Installation* installs the complete collections of styles, filters, and connection files. You may want to install just certain portions from the collections (for example, the Life Sciences journal styles, or the Ovid connection files). Choose the *Custom Install* option, select the appropriate collection (styles, filters, connections), and then select the desired sub-category.

Additional styles, filters, or connection files can be installed at any time. Simply run the installer, select *Custom Install*, and select the desired files.

Upgrading from an Earlier EndNote Version

Installing EndNote 7 on a computer that already has an earlier version of EndNote installed does not change what is in your old EndNote folder. The EndNote 7 Installer creates a new folder called "EndNote 7" and installs the updated EndNote 7 files in that folder.

After installing EndNote 7, you will have two folders, with each containing an EndNote program. Copy your libraries from your old EndNote folder to your new EndNote 7 folder.

If you have any customized styles, filters, or connection files, you should also copy them to the Styles, Filters, or Connections folders in the EndNote 7 folder. EndNote 7 includes a full collection of updated files, so unless you have specially customized a file for your needs, there is no reason to copy the old files.

Once you have removed your customized files and libraries from the old EndNote folder, and EndNote 7 is up and running, you can drag the remaining items in the old EndNote folder to the Trash. Be careful not to delete any libraries, papers, or other items that you need.

NOTE: To see what features have been added to EndNote, see "What's New in EndNote 7" on page 6.

Cite While You Write Users

If you have a Microsoft Word document that was formatted with an earlier version of EndNote, we recommend that you first make a backup of the file. Then, use the new version of EndNote to format the document again. From Word's *Tools* menu, choose *EndNote 7* and then *Format Bibliography*. This updates the document to work with EndNote 7.

File Compatibility

EndNote Libraries: EndNote 7 is fully compatible with all libraries from earlier versions of EndNote and EndNote Plus for DOS, Windows, and Macintosh. See "Transferring Libraries Across Platforms" on page 89 for details.

EndNote Styles: EndNote 7 can use styles created by EndNote versions 2-6; however, EndNote 7 styles cannot be used by versions earlier than EndNote 4. When opening an EndNote style prior to version 4, EndNote 7 opens it as a new untitled style which you may save with a new name. The original style remains untouched so that you may still use it with older EndNote versions.

NOTE: Customized reference types, temporary citation markers, and display fonts are all carried over from earlier versions of EndNote for use with EndNote 7.

Checking Your Installation

To run EndNote, double click the EndNote 7 icon found in the EndNote 7 folder.

EndNote 7.0

A dialog will ask you to open a reference library file. Choose *Cancel*.

To check the version number of EndNote, go to the EndNote menu and choose *About EndNote*. Click the splash screen to clear it.

Checking Support for Microsoft Word

To see whether Cite While You Write is correctly installed, start Word X and click on Word's *Tools* menu. You should see EndNote's Cite While You Write commands on an *EndNote 7* submenu.

EndNote 7 submenu on the Tools menu in Word X

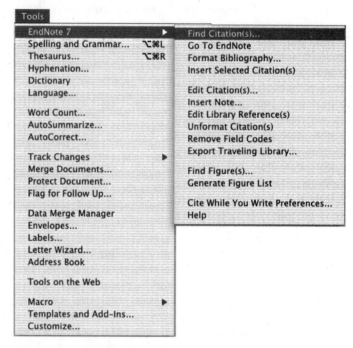

If you do not see these commands, Word support was not correctly installed. Most likely, the installer could not find the correct folder location to install the Cite While You Write files. You can try to reinstall EndNote. You may need to install the files manually as described under "Manually Installing Support for Word X" on page 19.

If you limited your installation of Word with a Custom Installation, and attempting to use Cite While You Write results in a Visual Basic error, you need to reinstall Word using the Full Installation option.

Non-English Versions of Word

The EndNote installer uses English terms for the various target folders in the installation (such as "Word Startup Folder"). If you are running a version of Word localized for a different language, you will most likely need to install Word support manually as described next.

Manually Installing Support for Word X

If you install Microsoft Word X *after* installing EndNote 7, or if you have a customized startup folder for Word, you should either reinstall EndNote or do a Custom install to copy just the word processor files. However, there may be a case where you need to install Cite While You Write support manually.

First, determine the path of Word's Startup Folder:

By default, Word X uses this path for the startup folder:

```
Microsoft Office X:Office:Startup:Word
```

However, Word's startup folder location could have been changed. If you are unsure which startup location is being used, or to change the startup location:

1. Start Microsoft Word.

2. From the *Word* menu, choose *Preferences*.

3. Select the File Locations item and look at the "Startup" line to see the path for the designated startup folder.

4. If the Startup line is blank, or if you would like to change the startup folder location, select the Startup line, click *Modify*, select the desired folder, and save your changes.

5. Quit from Word.

Next, copy Cite While You Write files to Word's Startup Folder:

From this folder:

```
EndNote 7:Cite While You Write:Word X
```

copy these files:

```
EndNote 7 CWYW Commands
EndNote 7 CWYW Word X
```

to Word's Startup Folder, which is typically this:

```
Microsoft Office X:Office:Startup:Word
```

Check your installation as described under "Checking Support for Microsoft Word" on page 18.

Then, copy Manuscript Templates to Word's Templates folder:

Copy the template files from this folder:

```
EndNote 7: Templates
```

to the folder:

```
Microsoft Office X:Templates:EndNote
```

Updating EndNote Files

You can update EndNote 7 with free incremental program enhancements, including the latest output styles, filters, and connection files.

To update your copy of EndNote:

1. Open a connection to the Internet.

2. From EndNote's *Help* menu, select *EndNote Updates*. Your browser will direct you to an EndNote web page where you can download the latest files.

We continually update output styles, filters, connection files, and Microsoft Word templates. The latest versions are included with program updates, but you can also download the latest files at any time from our website at www.endnote.com.

Uninstalling EndNote

Before you remove EndNote, back up your libraries and any other files you have created or customized.

To uninstall EndNote:

1. Make sure no applications are running.

2. Insert the EndNote CD into your CD-ROM drive.

3. Double-click the *EndNote 7 Installer* icon, then click *Continue* to proceed.

4. On the installation dialog, select "Uninstall" from the drop-down list in the upper left corner and click the *Uninstall* button.

NOTE: Uninstall removes the last files installed. If you installed the full program, and then later re-installed only a subset of files (such as output styles), only the later subset will be uninstalled. You will need to manually uninstall the full program as described next.

To manually uninstall EndNote:

1. Start by dragging the entire EndNote 7 folder to the trash.

2. To remove Cite While You Write files, remove these EndNote files from Microsoft Word's Startup folder (typically `Microsoft Office X:Office:Startup: Word`):

        EndNote 7 CWYW Word X
        EndNote 7 CWYW Commands

3. To remove Manuscript Templates, remove the EndNote folder found in the Microsoft Office X: Templates folder.

4. To remove EndNote preference files, go to the folder:

   `Users:[your folder]:Library:Preferences`

   and delete the folder: `EndNote` ƒ

There may be several copies of EndNote preference files; one for each user account.

Chapter 3

The EndNote Guided Tour

Chapter 3   The EndNote Guided Tour

Introduction to the Guided Tour

This Guided Tour introduces you to the basics of using EndNote for storing references and writing papers. The Guided Tour is not designed to show you everything about EndNote, but it does provide a quick summary of some important features.

Part I: Introduction to an EndNote Library

In this section, you learn how to start EndNote, open a reference library, set a default library to open automatically, and select, open, and close a reference. These skills prepare you for the rest of the Tour.

Part II: Entering and Managing References

This section illustrates how to enter references, insert images in references, search for references, and print references from an EndNote library.

Part III: Using EndNote While Writing a Paper

This section describes how to cite EndNote references while writing a paper with Microsoft Word X. You will learn how to insert citations and figures, and have EndNote generate a bibliography plus figures and tables for the paper. (If you use a different word processor, see Chapter 12.)

Part IV: Creating a Subject Bibliography

This section shows you how to create and print a bibliography grouped by keywords, where the keywords appear as headings.

Part V: Searching Remote Databases

This part of the tour demonstrates how to use EndNote to search remote databases and library catalogs available online. This feature requires that you have a connection to the Internet.

Are You Ready?

At this point we assume that both EndNote and your word processor are installed on your computer. If you have not installed EndNote, please follow the instructions in Chapter 2 before continuing.

The Guided Tour uses sample files that are installed in the Examples folder in the EndNote folder. These example files include a sample EndNote reference library called Paleo Library and a number of image files.

Part I: Introduction to an EndNote Library

This part of the Guided Tour covers the basics of working with EndNote. In particular, you will learn how to:

♦ Start EndNote and open a library.

♦ Select a default library to open automatically.

♦ Select and open references in the EndNote library.

♦ Close references.

♦ Quit from the EndNote program.

Start EndNote

To start the EndNote program and open the sample library:

1. Open the EndNote 7 folder. By default, the EndNote 7 folder is installed in the Applications folder on your hard drive.

2. Double-click the EndNote program icon.

EndNote 7.0

A dialog appears, prompting you to open a reference library.

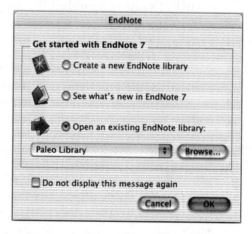

NOTE: If you have set a default library to open automatically, that library will open instead of the dialog shown above. If this happens, close the library, choose *Open* from the *File* menu, and continue with step 4.

---

3. Select "Open an existing EndNote Library and click *Browse*.

4. Select the Examples folder that was installed in the EndNote 7 folder and click *Open*. Then, select the Paleo Library and click *Open*.

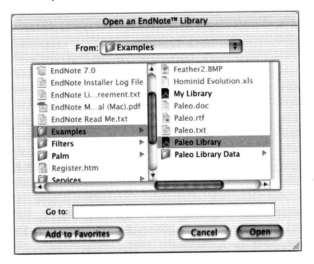

NOTE: You can open a library from within EndNote by choosing *Open* from the *File* menu.

The Library Window

When you open the Paleo Library you see the **Library window** listing all of the references that the library contains:

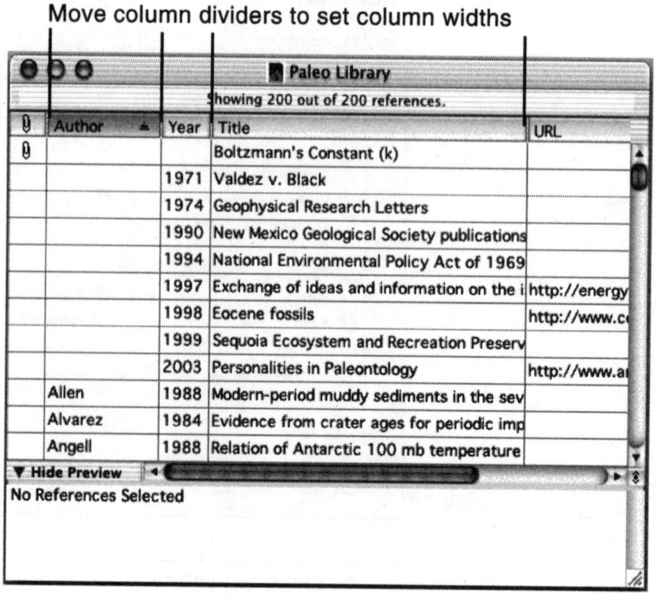

Move column dividers to set column widths

The Library window displays a multi-column list. By default, the first column shows a paper clip for references that include attached graphics, figures, or files. Then, the first author's last name, the year, the title, and the URL are displayed for each reference. The information displayed here in the Library window, as well as the font used for the display, can be changed using the EndNote Preferences. Chapter 4 provides more information about customizing the Library window.

You can browse through your reference library by first selecting a reference, and then using the scroll bar, the scroll arrows, or the PAGE DOWN, PAGE UP, HOME, END, and ARROW keys.

Preview References

You can easily see more detail about a reference by highlighting the reference and viewing the Preview pane at the bottom of the Library window.

To preview a reference:

1. For this example, click on the reference titled "Geophysical Research Letters."

The preview pane uses the current **output style** to display the selected reference as it will be formatted for a bibliography.

2. To select a different output style to apply to the reference, go to the main toolbar and select *Numbered* from the drop-down list of output styles.

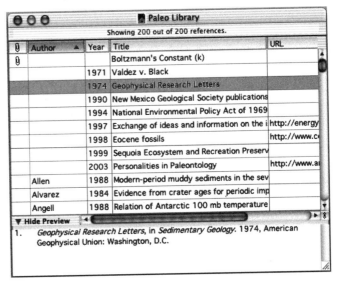

Only one reference is displayed in the preview pane at a time. If multiple references are selected, only the first one is displayed. The format of the reference in the preview pane can be changed at any time by choosing a different output style.

When the preview pane is showing, a *Hide Preview* button is available at the bottom of the window. You can click *Hide Preview* to hide the preview pane if you wish. The name of the button will toggle to *Show Preview*.

Sort the References

References can be easily sorted by clicking on the column heading (such as Author, Year, or Title).

To change the sort order:

1. Click the Year column heading to see the references sorted in ascending order based on the year of publication.

2. Click the Year column heading again (a second time) to reverse the sort order and see the references sorted in *descending* order.

3. Now, click the Author column heading to return the sort order of the library to an alphabetical list sorted by the author names.

Set a Default Library

You can assign a library to open automatically every time you start EndNote. You will find it useful to set the Paleo Library as your default library for now. Later, when you create your own library, you can set it as the default library.

To set a default library:

1. From the *Endnote* menu, choose *Preferences* and click *Libraries*.

2. Click *Add Open Libraries*. You should see the Paleo Library listed at the top of the window.

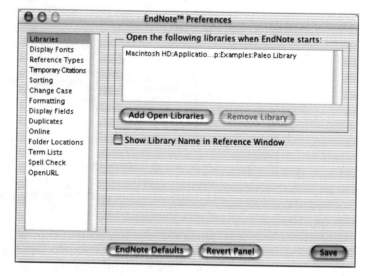

3. Click *Save* to save this change.

4. While you could make changes to other EndNote preferences, for now you can click the red close button to leave the Preferences dialog.

Select and Open a Reference

To work with specific references you must first select them in the Library window.

There are different ways to select a reference such as clicking on the reference using the mouse, using the arrow keys, or typing the first few letters of the field by which the library has been sorted.

To see how this works, click *once* on any reference to select it. If you have arrow keys on your keyboard, press the UP or DOWN ARROW to select the previous or next reference. When the library is sorted by author name (as it should be now), you can also select a reference by typing the first few letters of the author's last name.

To quickly find and display a reference:

1. Select the first Argus reference in the list by typing "arg" without pausing between letters.

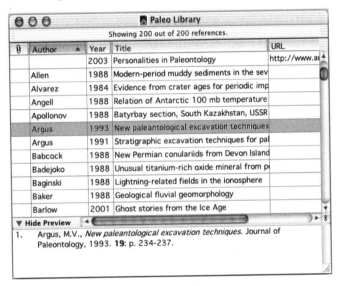

Now that the reference is selected, there are a number of things you can do with it, such as view its contents, copy, cut, delete, or edit it. For now, just open the reference to view the contents.

2. Open the selected Argus reference by pressing the RETURN key or by using the *Edit* command on the *References* menu. You can also open a reference by double-clicking on it in the Library window.

The Reference window opens to display all of the information associated with the reference.

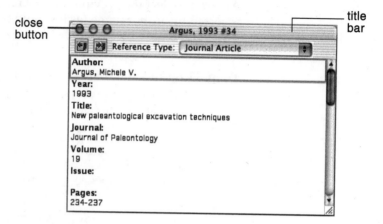

close button

title bar

This is where you enter or edit information for a reference. The citation information is displayed at the top of the Reference window in the title bar, "Argus, 1993 #34." This information is used by EndNote to match citations in a paper to references in a library.

To view the rest of the reference, use the mouse to scroll down the Reference window, or press the TAB key to move forward from one field to the next. Press SHIFT+TAB to move backwards through the fields.

The window may also be resized by clicking and dragging the lower right window corner. To reposition the window, click on the title bar and drag the window to the desired location.

Close the Reference

Close the reference by clicking the close button in the upper left corner of the Reference window. You can also choose *Close Reference* (⌘+W) from the *File* menu. EndNote automatically saves all changes to a reference when the Reference window is closed.

This concludes Part I of the Guided Tour. If you do not plan to continue with the Guided Tour, quit from EndNote by choosing *Quit EndNote* from the *EndNote* menu (⌘+Q). Otherwise, continue with the tour.

Related Sections

The following chapters provide more information about topics mentioned in this part of the Guided Tour:

◆ Learn how to change the display of the Library window in Chapter 4.

◆ The Preferences panels provide numerous ways in which you can customize your version of EndNote. See Chapter 18 for more information about working with the preferences.

Part II: Entering and Managing References

In this part of the Guided Tour you will learn how to:

♦ Enter references into a library.

♦ Insert graphics and files into references.

♦ Search for a subset of references.

♦ Print an annotated bibliography.

In this part of the tour, you are going to enter references: first a typical book reference, and then references that contain images.

Next you will search for a set of related references and print them, as though to share the information with a colleague.

Open the Paleo Library

If EndNote is not already running, start it and open the Paleo Library, as shown in Part I of the Guided Tour.

Create a New Reference

There are various ways to add references to an EndNote library:

♦ Type the reference information into the Reference window.

♦ Connect to an online bibliographic database and retrieve the references directly into EndNote, as demonstrated in part V of this tour and described in Chapter 6: "Searching Remote Databases with EndNote".

♦ Import text files of references that have been downloaded from online bibliographic databases or CD-ROMs as described in Chapter 7: "Importing Reference Data into EndNote".

This example demonstrates how to type reference information into EndNote.

Once a library is open, you can add a new reference to it:

1. From the *References* menu, choose *New Reference* (⌘+N). An empty Reference window opens with the words "New Reference" displayed at the top.

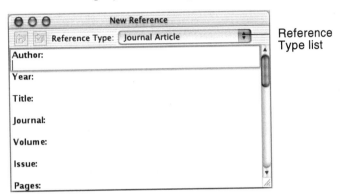

Reference Type list

New references appear as journal articles (unless you change the default setting) but can be changed to any other type of reference using the *Reference Type* list at the top of the Reference window. For this example, create a Book reference.

2. Click the *Reference Type* list and choose *Book*.

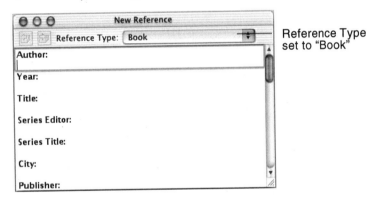

Reference Type set to "Book"

You are now ready to enter reference information, beginning with the author names. Author names can be entered two ways: either "First Middle Last" such as "Carol Margaret Jacobson" or "Last, First Middle" such as "Jacobson, Carol Margaret." Individual author names *must* be entered one per line.

3. With the cursor in the Author field, type:

    Jacobson, Carol

As you type, EndNote will suggest names similar to the one you are entering. This is EndNote's way of using **term lists** to facilitate the process of entering new references.

4. The name you are entering, Carol Jacobson, is a new author in this library, so keep typing until you complete the name and then press the RETURN key.

   The name appears in red text to indicate that it is a new name in the Author term list for this library. When you close or save the reference, it will be added to the Author term list and the red text will change to black. You can read more about term lists (and how to turn these options on or off) in Chapter 9.

5. Now enter the second author's name:

   `Roe, Jennifer`

   This author is already in the Paleo Library, so as you start typing the last name, you will see EndNote complete the name for you.

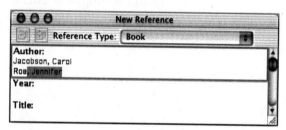

6. Press the TAB key to accept EndNote's suggested author name, and move to the Year field. In the Year field, type:

   `1999`

   Continue entering the reference as shown below, using the TAB key to move to the next field, and SHIFT+TAB to move to the previous field, if necessary. You can also use the mouse to click in the desired field. If information is not provided for a particular field, leave that field empty.

   Title: Impacts of meteorites on Earth

   City: New York

   Publisher: Blackcourt Press

   Number of Pages: 100

Abstract: The impact of a meteorite hitting earth millions of years ago may have led to the extinction of some marine life.

close button ——————

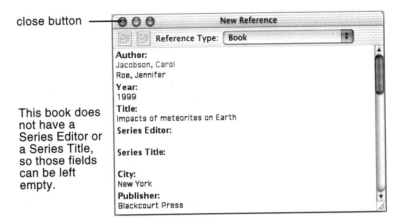

This book does not have a Series Editor or a Series Title, so those fields can be left empty.

No extra punctuation (such as parentheses around the year) or text styles (such as bold or italic) are entered into the reference. EndNote adds the necessary punctuation and text style changes to the references when it creates a bibliography.

7. Close the Reference window by clicking the close button, or by choosing *Close Reference* (⌘+W) from the *File* menu.

All information is automatically saved when you close a window. Your new reference should now appear in the Library window.

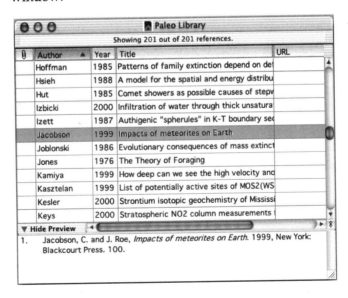

Enter References That Contain Images

EndNote helps you organize both reference information and images. Three reference types–Figure, Chart or Table, and Equation–are available specifically for cataloging graphics and files, although you can add Images and Captions to any reference type.

In this section, you are going to enter a journal reference that includes a graphic.

To enter a reference that includes a graphic:

1. From the *References* menu, choose *New Reference* (⌘+N). An empty Reference window opens with the words "New Reference" displayed at the top. The Reference Type should appear as *Journal Article*.

2. Enter the reference as shown below, using the TAB key to move to the next field, and SHIFT+TAB to move to the previous field, if necessary. You can also use the mouse to click in the desired field. If information is not provided for a particular field, leave that field empty.

   Author: Tiberius Rex

   Year: 1995

   Title: The scale and the feather--a suggested evolution

   Journal: Paleontology

   Volume: 23

   Issue: 9

   Pages: 23-45

   Keywords: Feathers
   Evolution
   Birds

   Abstract: This article discusses the evolution of bird feathers from reptilian scales.

3. Scroll down to the bottom, where you can see the Image and Caption fields.

4. From the *References* menu, select *Insert Picture* to display a file dialog.

5. On the file dialog:

   a. Navigate to the folder: Applications:EndNote 7:Examples.

b. Highlight the file titled **Feather2.BMP**.

c. Click *Open* to insert the file into the Image field.

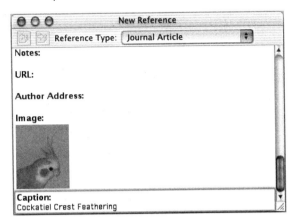

The graphic appears as a thumbnail in the reference. EndNote copied the file to a DATA folder stored with the Paleo library, and linked the copied graphic to this reference.

6. In the Caption field, enter:

   ```
   Cockatiel Crest Feathering
   ```

   Always enter a caption for your image. It assists in locating images, and it labels figures in your Microsoft Word documents.

7. Click the close button to close and save the reference and return to the library window.

Next, enter a reference that includes an attached file:

1. From the *References* menu, choose *New Reference* (⌘+N). An empty Reference window opens.

2. Click the *Reference Type* list and choose *Chart or Table*.

3. Enter the reference text as shown below.

   Created By: Milkirk, Marie

   Year: 2002

   Title: Hominid Timeline

   Image Source Program: Microsoft Excel

   Date: May 9

   Keywords: Evolution
   Hominids
   Timelines

4. From the *References* menu, select *Insert Object*.

5. On the file dialog:

   a. Navigate to the folder: Applications:EndNote 7:Examples.

   b. Highlight the Microsoft Excel file titled Hominid Evolution.xls.

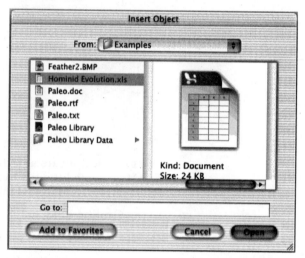

   c. Click *Open* to insert the file into your new reference.

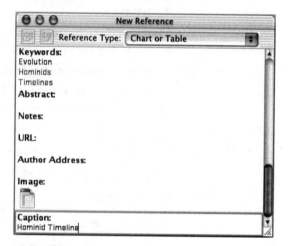

The file appears as an attachment in the image field. EndNote copied the file to the DATA folder stored with the Paleo library, and linked the copied file to this reference.

6. In the Caption field, enter:

   `Hominid Timeline`

7. Click the close button to close and save the reference and return to the library window.

To easily locate the references containing images:

Click on the Image column heading (the paper clip) once to sort records containing images at the bottom of the list, and then click it again to move them to the top of the list.

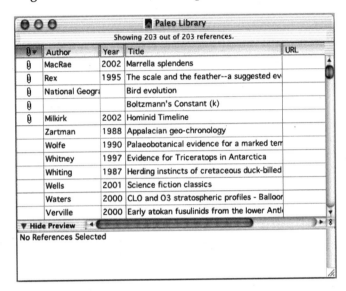

You can double-click on an individual reference if you would like to view the complete reference. When you are done viewing a reference, click the close button to close it.

Click the Author column heading to again order the list by author names. Sort in ascending (A to Z) order.

Search for a Set of References

Now you are ready to print a list of references that you want to share with your colleague. Let's assume you want to generate a list of all references about extinction that were published in 1990 or later.

To search for references:

1. From the *References* menu, choose *Search References* (⌘+F).

2. Type `extinction` as the first **search item**.

The words *Any Field* above "extinction" mean that EndNote will find references that have the word "extinction" in any field. Now set up the second search item to find references from 1990 or later.

3. From the **field list** in the second search item, choose *Year*; from the **comparison list**, choose *is greater than or equal to*; and type `1990` as the search term.

4. Notice the option between the two search items is set to "Or". Click "And" to set up the search to find all references about extinction that are also published in 1990 or later. The Search window should now look like this:

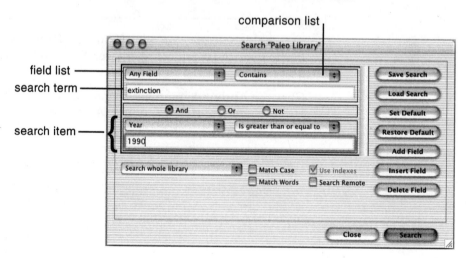

5. Click the *Search* button to begin the search. In a moment, EndNote displays the search results.

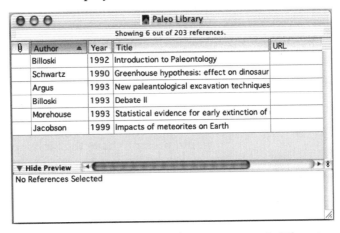

The top of the Library window should now read, "Showing 6 out of 203 references."(You are looking at the same Paleo library as before, but EndNote has restricted the view to display only the results of the search.)

Now that you have located all of the desired references, you are ready to print them for your colleague.

Select a Style That Includes Abstracts

EndNote's output styles (or just **styles**) represent the rules for creating bibliographies for a variety of journals and other publications. The styles determine how your references look when you print, export, preview, or create bibliographies.

We have provided a style called *Annotated* that includes the contents of the Abstract field with the formatted reference. Select this style to print the references with abstracts:

◆ On the Main toolbar, select *Annotated* from the output style list to print the references with abstracts.

If you do not see the *Annotated* style in the output style list, you can select any style and go on to the next step. Any bibliographic style can be modified to make an annotated bibliography. See Chapter 15 for more information about modifying and selecting styles.

Print the Found References

Now that you have selected a style, you are ready to print the bibliography.

To print a bibliography:

1. From the *File* menu, choose *Print*. A standard print dialog appears.

2. Click *Print* to begin printing.

You can also use the *Export* or *Copy Formatted* commands to create a word processing document with these references if you would prefer to have the bibliography on disk rather than on paper. See Chapter 12 for more information about creating independent bibliographies.

♦ To show all references again in the library window, go to the *References* menu and select *Show All References*.

This concludes Part II of the Guided Tour. Part III demonstrates how to write a paper and cite references and figures in Microsoft Word. If you do not use Word, skip Part III and move on to "Part IV: Creating a Subject Bibliography" on page 60.

If you are finished working with EndNote for now, go to the *EndNote* menu and choose *Quit EndNote* to close the EndNote program.

Related Sections

Sections in the manual related to this portion of the tour:

♦ If you are eager to begin creating your own library, see Chapter 4.

♦ Chapter 5 provides more detail about typing references into your library and inserting images.

♦ For information about connecting directly to online bibliographic databases and retrieving references into EndNote, see Part V of this tour and Chapter 6.

♦ If you will be importing references that have been downloaded from an online or CD-ROM database, see Chapter 7.

♦ More information about searching the EndNote library can be found in Chapter 8.

♦ Read Chapter 12 about creating reference lists directly from your EndNote library.

Part III: Using EndNote While Writing a Paper With Microsoft Word

NOTE: Continue with this part of the tour only if you use Microsoft Word X. If you use a different word processor, or if you have an older version of Word, turn to Chapter 11 to learn how to cite EndNote references and create bibliographies in your papers.

EndNote's Cite While You Write feature inserts EndNote commands into Word's *Tools* menu to give you direct access to your references while writing in Microsoft Word. The Cite While You Write commands enable EndNote to do bibliographic formatting to the document that is currently open in Word.

In this part of the Guided Tour, you will learn how to:

♦ Use a manuscript template to set up your paper.

♦ Insert EndNote bibliographic citations into your paper and create a bibliography.

♦ Insert EndNote figure citations into your paper. (This section uses the image references that were inserted while following Part II of the Guided Tour.)

Open the Paleo Library

If EndNote is not already running, start it and open the Paleo Library, as shown in Part I of the Guided Tour.

EndNote looks for matching references in the currently open libraries. While EndNote can automatically start and open your default library when needed by Word, opening the library first assures you that you are citing references from the appropriate library.

Create a New Document with the Manuscript Template Wizard

Manuscript templates make it easy to set up your paper for electronic submission to a publisher. For this example, pretend you are writing a paper about evolution that you plan to submit to the publishers of *Nature*.

To create a new Word document:

1. From EndNote's *Tools* menu, choose *Manuscript Templates*.

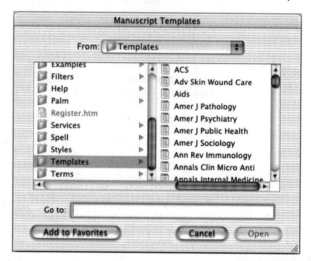

2. From the list of Word templates, highlight the **Nature** file and click *Open* to start the manuscript template wizard.

NOTE: The first time you launch the manuscript template wizard, you may receive a notice about macros. Accept macros to continue with the wizard. Select *Always trust macros from this source* to avoid future alerts.

---

3. On the opening window, click *Next*.

4. Enter a full title for this paper:

    `Theories About Evolution`

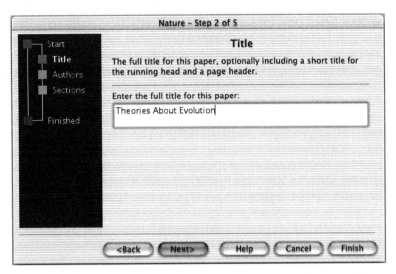

5. Click *Next* to display a list of contributing authors. In this case, the list is blank.

6. To enter the author of this document, click *Add Author*. If you have not yet added any author names for manuscript templates, the Authors on File list will be blank.

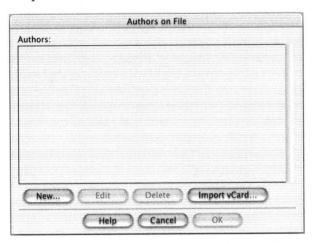

7. Click *New* to add an author to the list.

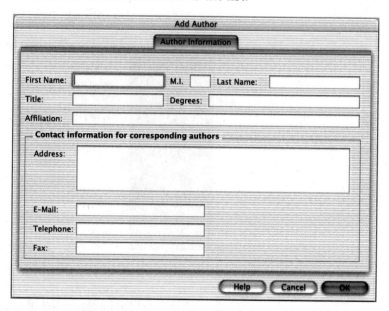

8. Enter your name and contact information, and then click *OK*. Your name appears in the Authors on File list.

9. Highlight your name, as an author of the current document, and click *OK*.

10. Select the check box next to your name, indicating that you are a corresponding author, and click *Next*.

11. The Sections window lists the document sections required by Nature. (The Section list varies greatly between publishers.) Normally you would simply click *Next* to accept all sections.

For this tour, you can deselect some of the sections as indicated in the window below, and then click *Next*.

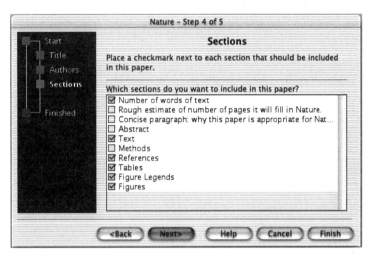

12. Click *Finish* to complete the manuscript wizard and display the new Word document.

As you scroll through the paper, you can see where the template wizard inserted the title and author information you provided, and where you need to insert additional information.

In the example below, the author's name and contact information was inserted by the template wizard in the font and style required by *Nature*. You would need to select each bracketed area and enter the appropriate information required by *Nature*.

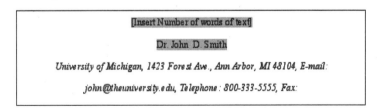

Cite EndNote References

Next you are going to start entering text and citations. For this tour, you are going to enter minimal information.

To start writing your paper and insert citations:

1. Scroll down the document to the area that says Insert Text here, and highlight the line.

[Insert Text here]

2. Enter text as though you were writing your paper:

   The fossil in question was generally regarded to be the 220 million year-old remains of tyrannosaurus. Several years ago, however, this hypothesis was overturned by the discovery of yet another species.

   Now you are ready to insert a citation.

3. From the *Tools* menu, go to the *EndNote 7* submenu and then *Find Citation(s)*.

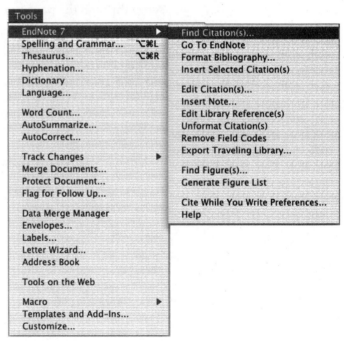

4. The EndNote Find Citations dialog appears. Type the author name "Morehouse" in the "Find" box and click *Search*.

EndNote lists the matching references. In this case, a single reference matches the search.

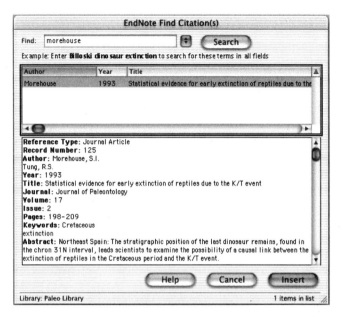

5. Click *Insert* to insert the selected reference as a citation.

   EndNote not only inserts a citation, but Instant Formatting formats it in the numbered Nature style.

6. Add more text to the paper:

   It is now the undisputed progeny of the species at hand.

7. From the *Tools* menu, go to the *EndNote 7* submenu and then *Find Citation(s)*.

8. Type the date "1987" into the find box and click *Search*. EndNote lists the matching references.

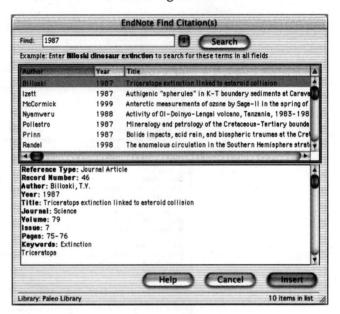

9. Scroll down the list of matching references, select the reference by the author Turnhouse, and click *Insert*.

EndNote not only inserts the citation, but Cite While You Write technology formats it and adds it to the bibliography at the end of the paper. Your document text should now look like this:

> The fossil in question was generally regarded to be the 220 million year-old remains of tyrannosaurus. Several years ago, however, this hypothesis was overturned by the discovery of yet another species. It is now the undisputed progeny of the species at hand.

10. Scroll down the document to view the References list formatted with the Nature output style:

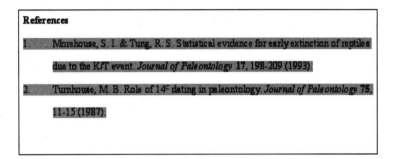

NOTE: In these examples, each of the Cite While You Write citation and bibliography fields is shaded. This is set with Microsoft Word's Field Shading option, which you can turn on if you find it helpful. The shading is for on-screen help only, and does not print.

11. Assume that you have finished inserting citations in your paper. From Word's *File* menu, choose *Save* to save your document.

Confirm the Bibliographic Style

You can format your citations and bibliography as many times as you like, changing the output style and various other layout settings each time.

To confirm the bibliographic style used for formatting:

1. From Word's *Tools* menu, go to the *EndNote 7* submenu and choose *Format Bibliography*.

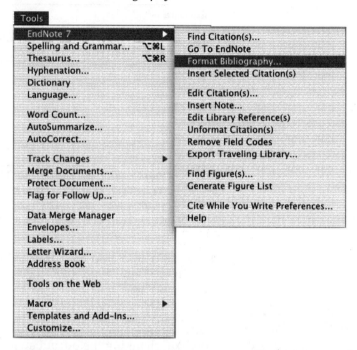

A Format Bibliography dialog appears, where you can select a bibliographic style.

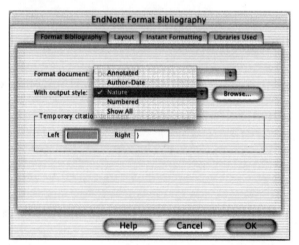

Styles contain instructions for how EndNote should format the citations and bibliography. For this example, the manuscript template automatically selected the *Nature* style, which inserts citation numbers and a bibliography at the end of the paper.

2. For this example, leave "With output style" set to *Nature*.

3. Click *OK* to leave the dialog.

   EndNote automatically updates the existing citations and regenerates the bibliography. If you had changed the bibliographic style, those changes would be reflected in the paper.

In the future, if you need to make changes to the paper such as adding or deleting citations or text, just make the necessary edits or additions in your paper. If you want to change the output style or bibliography layout settings, choose the *Format Bibliography* command again. EndNote will reformat the in-text citations and generate a new bibliography based on your changes.

NOTE: Do not directly edit citations or the bibliography. Any changes will be lost when you *Format Bibliography* again.

Insert Figure Citations

Next you are going to insert two figure citations—one inserted and numbered as a figure, and one inserted and numbered as a table. This section uses the references inserted in Part II of the Guided Tour.

All figure citations are inserted in the same way; the EndNote reference type determines whether it is inserted and numbered as a figure or a table. Images found in the *Chart or Table* reference type are inserted as tables, while images found in any other reference type are inserted as figures.

To find and insert figure citations:

1. First, add more text to your paper:

   ```
   As researchers look at evidence, even the
   crest on the modern Cockatiel provides insight
   into the evolution of feathers.
   ```

   Now you are ready to insert a figure citation.

2. From the *Tools* menu, go to the *EndNote 7* submenu and then *Find Figure(s)*. The EndNote Find Figures dialog appears.

3. Type the search term "bird" in the "Find" box and click *Search*.

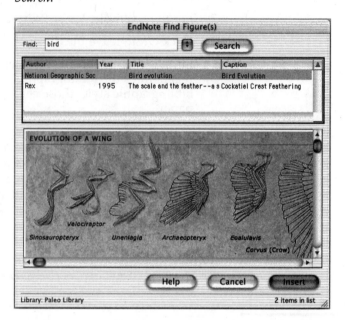

EndNote lists only references that match the search text *and* contain an image. As you highlight a reference, the graphic stored within the reference is displayed below the reference list.

You can use your mouse to move the column dividers to set column widths and to drag the lower right corner of the window to adjust the size of the window.

4. Select the reference with the Caption "Cockatiel Crest Feathering," a reference inserted earlier in this guided tour, and click *Insert* to insert the figure citation.

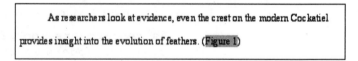

5. Next enter the text:

       While exploring the evolution of dinosaurs and birds, it becomes clear that *Homo sapiens* have occupied earth for a relatively short period of time.

Now you are ready to insert a reference to the Microsoft Excel file we inserted into an EndNote reference earlier in this guided tour.

6. From the *Tools* menu, go to the *EndNote 7* submenu and then *Find Figure(s)*. The EndNote Find Figures dialog appears.

7. Type the text "hominid" in the "Find" box and click *Search*.

   EndNote displays a single matching reference. The file attachment icon shows that the figure is in a Microsoft Excel document.

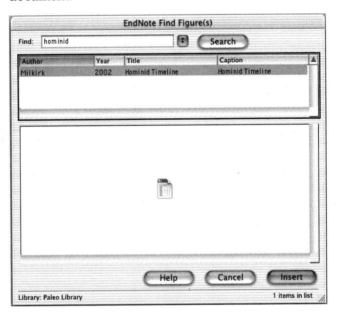

8. Click *Insert* to insert the citation.

NOTE: The Excel file may load quite slowly, and you may find that you need to start Excel before inserting the figure citation.

The image was found in the *Chart or Table* reference type, so it was added to Word and numbered as a table.

> As researchers look at evidence, even the crest on the modern Cockatiel provides insight into the evolution of feathers. (Figure 1)
>
> While exploring the evolution of dinosaurs and birds, it becomes clear that *Homo sapiens* have occupied earth for a relatively short period of time. (Table 1)

9. Scroll through the document, and you will find that EndNote used Word bookmarks to place the images under labeled Tables and Figures sections as required by *Nature*.

10. You may need to resize the Hominid Timeline to fit on the page. Click on the image, and then hold down the **Shift** key while you drag a corner of the figure to resize it proportionally.

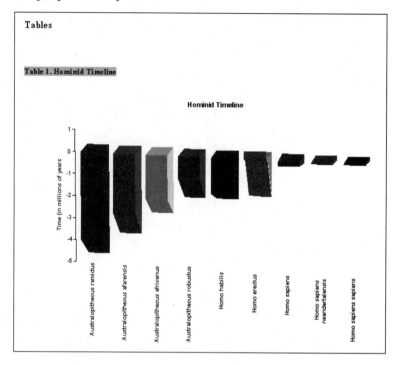

Tables

Table 1. Hominid Timeline

11. You can also reduce the size of the Cockatiel Crest Feathering graphic.

Figures

Figure 1. Cockatiel Crest Feathering

As you are working, remember to often *Save* your document. You can continue adding text, bibliographic citations, and figure citations to the paper, and EndNote will continue adding to the References list, Figures list, and Tables list!

That completes this section of the Guided Tour. Quit from Microsoft Word by choosing *Quit* from the *Word* menu.

If you do not want to continue with the next part of the Guided Tour (Creating a Subject Bibliography), go to the *EndNote* menu in EndNote and choose Quit EndNote to close the program.

Related Sections

The following chapters provide more information about topics mentioned in this part of the Guided Tour:

◆ This process of citing references and figures and creating bibliographies with Cite While You Write is covered in Chapter 10.

◆ More than 1000 styles are installed in EndNote's Styles folder. To see a list of them organized by discipline, choose *Output Styles* from the *Edit* menu and select the *Style Manager*. See "Accessing Styles in Other Places" on page 369 for information on how to access other styles.

Part IV: Creating a Subject Bibliography

In this part of the Guided Tour, you will learn how to:

♦ Generate a list of references grouped by subject.

♦ Change the layout of a subject bibliography.

You can create a list that groups references under any EndNote field or combination of fields—such as journal title or publisher. However, the most common use is to group references by subject with terms from the Keywords field.

Open the Paleo Library

If EndNote is not already running, start it and open the Paleo Library, as shown in Part I of the Guided Tour.

Select the References to Include

The first step in creating a subject bibliography is determining which references you want to include. For this example, we will include all references in the library.

To select the references to include in the subject bibliography:

1. First, make sure all references are displayed in the reference list. From the *References* menu, select *Show All References*. If that command is not available, all references are already included in the list.

2. Go to the *Edit* menu and choose *Select All* to highlight all of the references in the library.

   If no references are selected, EndNote assumes that all references should be included in the subject bibliography. If references are selected (highlighted), EndNote will use only those references to generate a subject bibliography.

   By selecting all references, you are sure to include them all in the bibliography.

Select the Subject Fields and Terms

Next, you will select a subject field and the terms from that field to use as subject headings.

To select a subject field and terms from that field:

1. From the *Tools* menu, select *Subject Bibliography* to display a list of the EndNote fields by default field name.

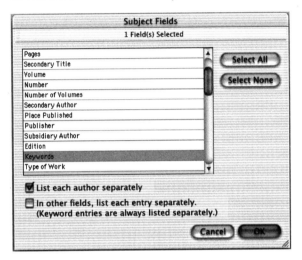

2. Highlight the *Keywords* field.

You can click on individual fields to select any combination and number of fields, but the most common selection is the single Keywords field to create a subject bibliography.

Neither of the check boxes at the bottom affect a list by keyword. Terms in the Keywords field are always listed as separate headings.

3. Click *OK* to display the terms found in the Keywords field of the selected references (in this case, every Keyword found in library).

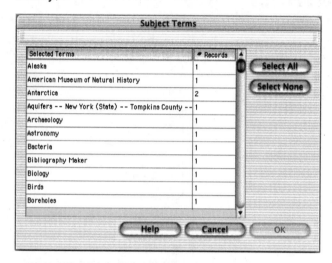

4. While you could select specific terms as headings, for this example you will select all keywords. Click the *Select All* button.

    It can be helpful to *Select All*, and then click on the few terms that you do not want in order to deselect them.

5. Click *OK* to format the subject bibliography on the screen.

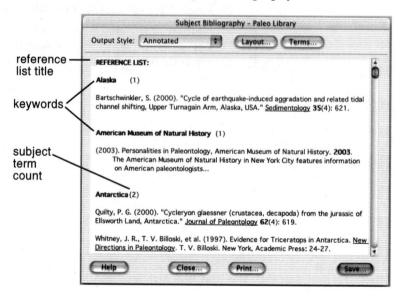

A reference list title appears at the top of the bibliography. Formatted references display beneath each keyword heading. Next to each heading, a term count indicates how many references contained the keyword.

Change the Layout of the Bibliography

You have a subject bibliography, but is the layout of it quite what you want? For this exercise, you will change the output style, enter a different reference list title, and remove the term counts.

To change the layout of your subject bibliography:

1. First, use the Output Style list at the top of the window to select a different output style for the formatted references. In this case, select *Author-Date* and EndNote will update all of the references in the bibliography to reflect the new style.

    You could choose *Select Another Style* to choose from the 1000+ output styles provided with EndNote.

2. Click on the *Layout* button to modify the layout and style of your subject bibliography.

3. On the References tab, change the Reference List Title to "References:". This is the title that prints at the top of the bibliography.

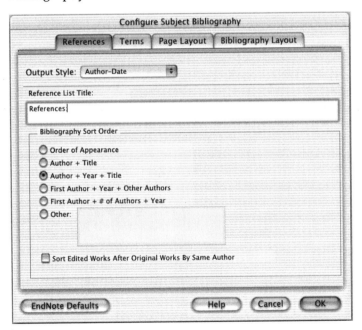

You could also use this tab to change the sort order of the formatted references that appear beneath each subject heading.

4. Click on the Terms tab, and look under the Reference List section.

For a subject bibliography, it is important to select the *Subject Terms and Reference List* button. In this case, *Subject Terms and Reference List* should already be selected.

The *Subject Terms Only* button would print only a list of subject headings, and not the formatted references.

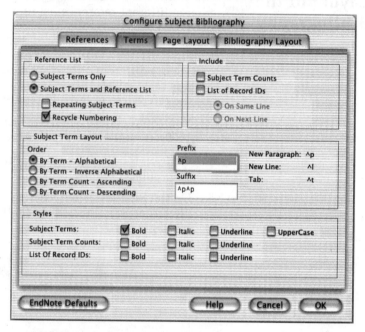

Notice that the Recycle Numbering box is selected. This restarts numbering under each subject heading when you select an output style that numbers references.

5. Under the Include section, click to clear the Subject Term Counts box.

This tab also controls the sort order of the subject terms and the styles applied to subject terms, subject term counts, and the list of record IDs (record numbers) if they are selected to print.

6. Click on the Bibliography Layout tab. The Author-Date output style did not insert a blank line between formatted references. To force a line, use the second drop-down list to

insert an "End of Paragraph" marker in the text box labeled "End each reference with."

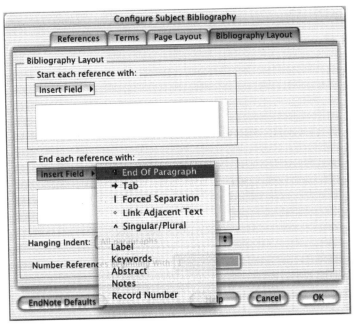

7. Click *OK* to save changes to all of the Layout tabs.

8. At this point, you can do any of the following:

   ♦ Click *Print Preview* to display a formatted page view of the subject bibliography. (Macintosh OS version 10.1.5 requires that you first click *Print* to display the Print dialog, and then click *Preview*.) Click *Close* to dismiss the Preview window when you are done viewing it. You could click *Layout* again to fine-tune your settings.

   ♦ Click *Print* to send a copy of the bibliography to your printer. The Print dialog appears. Verify settings and click *OK* or *Print*.

   ♦ Click *Save* to save a copy to a file that you can open with your word processor. A file dialog appears for you to name the file and choose the file type (text, RTF, or HTML). Verify settings and click *Save*.

9. Click *Close* to dismiss the Subject Bibliography window and return to the library reference list.

This concludes Part IV of the Guided Tour. Part V walks through searching a remote database. If you are finished working with EndNote for now, go to the *EndNote* menu and choose *Quit EndNote* to close the EndNote program.

Related Sections

The process of creating and printing subject bibliographies or subject lists is covered in Chapter 13.

Part V: Searching Remote Databases

This brief tutorial guides you through the basic steps of connecting to a remote database, searching the database, and saving the references that you want to keep. In order to complete this Guided Tour, you must be at a computer with access to the Internet (either dial-up or a direct network connection).

About the PubMed Database

For this guided tour, we will be connecting to PubMed, the National Library of Medicine's online public access version of their MEDLINE database. PubMed is the **remote database** we will be searching; the National Library of Medicine is the **information provider**.

For Users With "Dial-up" Internet Connections

If you use a modem and a phone line to connect to the Internet, as opposed to a direct network connection, this section pertains to you.

Connecting: Most setups for dial-up connections are configured to automatically dial your information provider and connect to the Internet when you use an application that requests an online connection (as EndNote's *Connect* command does). However, some setups, such as America Online, require that you establish an online connection (sign on) *before* choosing EndNote's *Connect* command.

Disconnecting: EndNote will not disconnect your Internet connection at any point. You need to shut down your connection when you have finished using EndNote's *Connect* feature.

NOTE: America Online users must have version 3.0 or later in order to use EndNote's online features.

Open the Paleo Library

If EndNote is not already running, start it and open the Paleo Library, as shown in Part I of the Guided Tour.

Connect to a Remote Database

The first step in searching a remote database is connecting to it, so that is how we will begin.

To connect to the PubMed Database:

1. With EndNote running, go to the *Tools* menu, select the *Connect* submenu, and select *Connect*. (The *Connect* menu will eventually list the databases to which you have connected in the past. You may customize this list using the Connection Manager. See page 130.)

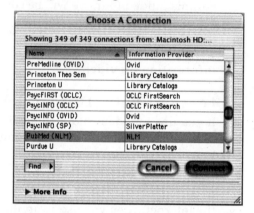

NOTE: This window displays all of the connection files available in your Connections folder. Use the *Find* button to quickly view various categories of databases to help you locate the one that you need.

2. Select the *PubMed* connection file (you can start typing the file name to quickly jump to it in the list), and click *Connect*.

By selecting that connection file, you have directed EndNote to connect to the National Library of Medicine's PubMed database. If for any reason the connection *cannot* be successfully established, EndNote alerts you with an error message and closes the connection. See "Troubleshooting Connections" on page 522.

When the connection has been successfully established, EndNote opens a **Retrieved References window** for the PubMed Database, and displays the Search window. Note that the "Search Remote" check box is automatically selected. EndNote is ready to search the remote database.

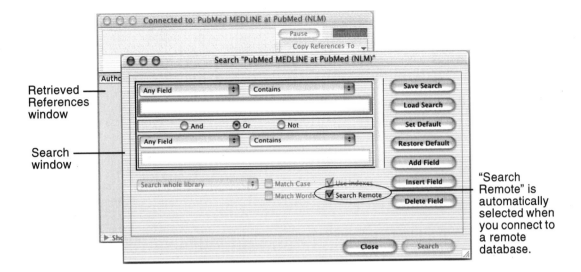

Retrieved References window

Search window

"Search Remote" is automatically selected when you connect to a remote database.

NOTE: If you previously set a default configuration for the Search window, the search field lists display the fields you selected as your defaults. If one of these fields appears italicized in the Search window lists, that indicates it is not a valid option for the remote database.

Search the Database

The next step is to enter the search term(s) to find the references you need. Searching a remote database is very similar to searching an EndNote library, with a few exceptions. (See "Available Search Options" on page 135.)

Let's say you are interested in information about corrective eye surgery, such as LASIK.

To enter the search term(s) and perform the search:

1. Enter "lasik" into the first search item and verify that the field list in that item is set to *Keywords (MeSH)*. The comparison list for remote searches is always set to *Contains*.

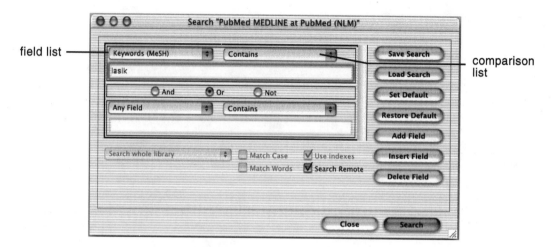

field list ——

comparison list

2. Click *Search*.

   EndNote sends the search request off to the remote database (PubMed, in this example), and a summary of the search results is displayed:

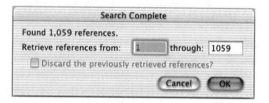

   The dialog displays the number of references that were found to match your search request, and gives you the option to retrieve them.

NOTE: PubMed is updated regularly, so you may find a different number of references than illustrated here.

   If the result set seems too big, you can always refine the search to get closer to exactly those references you want. Let's refine this search by looking for just those references that include mention of a "high diopter."

3. Click *Cancel*, and you are returned to the Search window.

4. Click in the second search item and type "high diopter".

5. Set the field list in that second search item to *Any Field*.

6. Change the setting between the first two search items to "And."

Choose the "And" option.

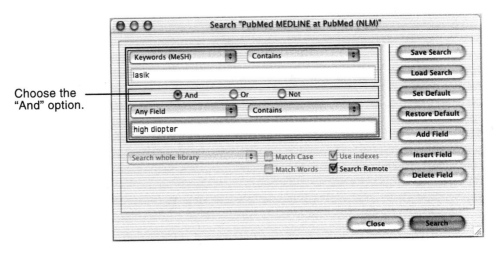

7. Click *Search*.

This time only 8 references were found.

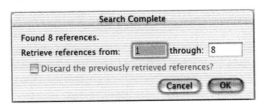

8. Click *OK* to retrieve the matching references.

The references are downloaded and appear in the Retrieved References window for the PubMed Database connection.

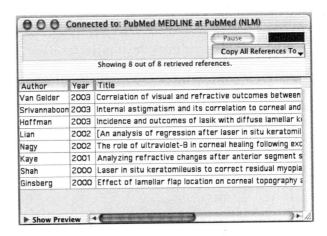

You can halt a retrieval in progress by clicking the *Pause* button at the top of the Retrieved References window, or by pressing ⌘+PERIOD or the Escape key (ESC).

Save the References

At this point you can peruse the retrieved references to see which ones you would like to keep. Save the references you want by transferring them into one of your own EndNote libraries.

The selected references can be copied to an open library using drag-and-drop or the *Copy* and *Paste* commands. You can also copy references directly to a library that is open, to a library that is closed, or to a new library using the *Copy References To* command, as described below.

For this example, we will save two of the retrieved references to EndNote's sample Paleo library.

To save your retrieved references:

1. Select two of the references displayed by holding down the ⌘ key and clicking on the individual references. (SHIFT-click to select a range of references.)

2. Click the *Copy # References To* button and select *Choose Library* (the # indicates the number of selected references).

3. In the file dialog that appears, open the Examples folder in the EndNote folder, choose Paleo Library, and click *Open*. The references retrieved from the PubMed Database are copied to the library.

That's all it takes! When you close the Retrieved References window for PubMed, EndNote alerts you that the references in the Retrieved References window will be discarded. Because you have already saved what you needed, you may click *Discard* and close the window.

Where to Go From Here

This concludes the tutorial for using EndNote's *Connect* command.

♦   See Chapter 6 for details about establishing connections, searching for references, and retrieving references.

♦   Read "Selecting a Connection File" on page 128 to learn about the connection files that are available with EndNote.

♦   See "Troubleshooting Connections" on page 522 if you encountered any problems establishing a connection.

Chapter 4

Introducing the EndNote Library

Chapter 4   Introducing the EndNote Library

The EndNote Library

An EndNote **library** is a collection of references, each containing the information required to create a bibliography. Additional information such as keywords, notes, and abstracts can also be stored in these references. This chapter provides an overview of the EndNote library, including instructions for opening and creating libraries, and navigating within a library.

Important Points About Libraries

Listed below are some important points about the EndNote library. Detailed information about each of these items follows.

♦ Each library can reach a record number limit of 32,767 or a maximum size of 32 MB (whichever comes first). Once a record number is assigned, it cannot be used again in that library. So, if you import 30,000 records, then delete all but 1000 of them, you cannot enter more than another 1000 records into that particular library.

♦ There is no limit to the number of libraries you can create, assuming that you have the disk space to store them. We recommend that you keep all the references you cite in your papers in one main library.

♦ You can select default libraries to open automatically when EndNote is started.

♦ You can open more than one library at a time.

♦ Libraries created with the DOS or Windows versions of EndNote can be used by the Macintosh version of EndNote, and vice versa (see page 89 for more information on transferring libraries across platforms).

♦ Each library is a separate file that can be independently moved, copied, renamed or deleted using the Macintosh Finder

♦ The icon for an EndNote library file looks like this:

Paleo Library

♦ The Library window can be resized and the display font can be changed to any font or size that you prefer.

♦ The Library window displays a multi-column list. By default, the first column shows a paper clip for references that include attached graphics, figures, or files. Then, the first author's last name, the year, the title, and the URL are displayed for each reference. You can change the displayed fields with the *Display Fields* preference.

♦ If your library includes images, they are stored in a [library name] DATA folder which is in the same folder as your library. Remember to move, copy, rename, or delete the associated DATA folder along with the library.

Back Up Your Libraries

Your EndNote library becomes increasingly valuable to you as you add references to it. Consequently, it is imperative that you back up your libraries, along with any other important documents. You can use the *Save a Copy* command to save a copy of your library to a removable disk (or elsewhere) for safe keeping. If your references include images, remember to also back up the DATA folder. See Appendix A for more information about making backup copies of your files.

The Library Window

When you first open a library with EndNote you see a **Library window**, showing the references you have entered. Each reference is displayed on a single line showing first a paper clip if a graphic or file is attached to the record, then the first author's last name, the year of publication, as much of the title as will fit in the window, and the URL.

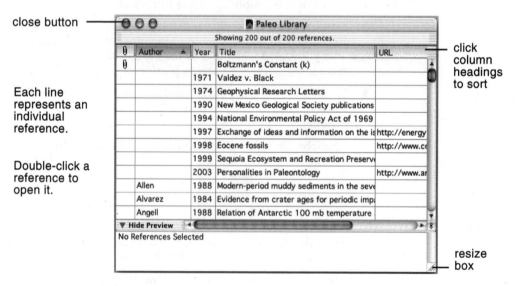

close button

Each line represents an individual reference.

Double-click a reference to open it.

click column headings to sort

resize box

Navigating in the Library Window

There are a number of ways to browse through your references.

♦ Scroll through the list of references in the Library window by clicking in the vertical scroll bar with the mouse.

♦ The ↑ and ↓ keys move up or down from the currently selected reference, or if nothing is selected they select the last or first reference in the library, respectively.

♦ You can quickly sort the references by clicking on a column heading. For example, click *Year* to sort by year. A second click will change the order of the sort from ascending to descending.

♦ Typing a letter selects the first matching reference. The matching depends on the order in which the library is sorted. If the library is sorted by the Author field, typing a letter selects the first reference in which the author's last name begins with that letter. For example, typing the letter "Z" selects the Zartman reference in our Paleo Library since Zartman is the first author's name to begin with a "Z." Type several letters and the selection jumps to the first name that begins with those typed letters. Letter matching starts over after a half-second pause.

♦ On extended keyboards, the HOME and END keys go to the first or last reference respectively; PAGE UP and PAGE DOWN move up or down a screen of references.

♦ To find specific references, choose *Search References* from the *References* menu. (See Chapter 8 for more information.)

Showing a Reference Preview

Click the *Show Preview* option at the bottom of the Library window to hide or display the preview pane. (Click the triangle next to the words "Show Preview.") When the preview is showing, click the triangle again to hide the preview pane. You could also select *Show Preview / Hide Preview* from the *Tools* menu.

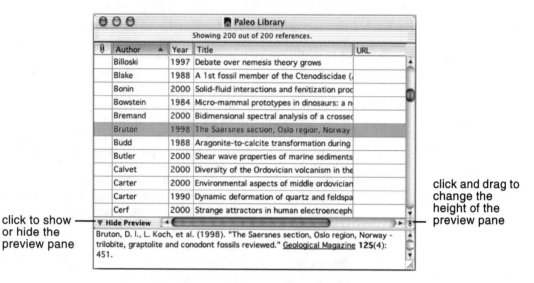

click to show or hide the preview pane

click and drag to change the height of the preview pane

The preview displays the selected reference in your current style. If multiple references are selected, it displays just the first one in the selection. The preview is not editable; to edit the reference, double-click it in the Library window.

Choosing the Current Style

Since the preview uses the current style, it's important to know how to set that style. To select your current style:

♦ On the Main toolbar, use the *Output Styles* list to select a new style.

♦ Or, from the *Edit* menu, choose *Output Styles* and select a style in the list. The check mark next to a style name indicates that it is the current style.

If you do not see the style that you want on the toolbar or in the *Output Styles* menu, do not worry. Hundreds of styles are provided with EndNote and are available via the Style Manager. Choose *Open Style Manager* from the *Output Styles* menu, and mark the style or styles that you would like to be available in your *Output Styles* menu. You should now be able to choose the style that you need from the *Output Styles* menu. (For more information about using the Style Manager, see "The Style Manager" on page 364.)

You can also add styles to the menus using the *Select Another Style* option from the style list on the toolbar. Simply choose *Select Another Style*, select the style, and click *Choose*.

Resizing the Preview Pane

To change the height of the preview pane, click on the bar that separates the preview from the rest of the Library window, and drag up or down. (When the cursor is over this area, it changes to indicate that you are in the right place to resize the pane.) You may also click in the resize box to the right of that bar and drag it up or down to resize the preview.

Previewing Multiple References

The preview pane only displays a preview for one reference at a time, formatted according to the current style.

To preview multiple references:

1. Select (highlight) the references in the Library window.

2. From the *Edit* menu, choose *Copy Formatted* to copy the formatted references to the Clipboard.

3. Use the *Edit>Show Clipboard* command from the Finder to view the contents of the Clipboard, or Paste the formatted references into a word processor document.

Using the Preview to Display Notes or Abstracts

You may find it useful to configure the Library window such that the main window displays bibliographic data (such as author, year, title, and journal), and the preview pane displays just notes or abstracts. That would allow you to browse through your references in the Library window without having to open individual references to see more about them.

To configure the display of the Library window fields, see "Changing Display Fields" on page 81. To get the preview to display just the notes or the abstract, you will need to create a custom style to include just those fields (see page 317).

You can use the *Show All* style to display all reference fields in the preview pane.

Resizing the Library Window

Like most windows in EndNote, the Library window can be resized by clicking in the **resize box** in the lower right corner of the library, and dragging to the desired size.

EndNote remembers the new size of the Library window as well as its location on the screen so the next time you open it, the library appears with the same dimensions and in the same location as when you last closed it. Each EndNote library can have its own unique dimensions and screen location.

Library Display Font

Choose a different font and size for the text displayed in the Library window by using EndNote's preferences. The list of references in the Library window uses the Library Display Font. The Preview uses the General Display Font. Changes made to the display fonts apply to all EndNote libraries opened on that computer.

To change the Library Display Font:

1. From the *EndNote* menu, choose *Preferences*.

2. Click the *Display Fonts* option.

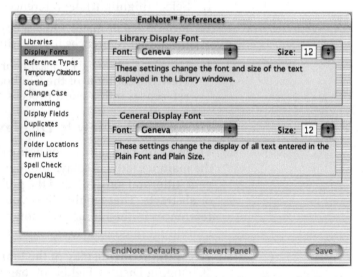

3. Select a different display font and/or size from the *Font* and *Size* lists.

4. Click *Save* to save the changes, and then close the Preferences window by clicking in the close button in the upper left corner.

Changing the display fonts does not affect the font EndNote uses when it creates a bibliography. EndNote uses the font of your paper for the bibliography.

Changing Display Fields

In the Library window, EndNote defaults to showing first a paper clip if a graphic or file is attached to a reference, then the Author, Year, Title, and URL fields. You may display other fields, change the order of the fields displayed, or change the names used for the column headings in the Library window.

To customize the Library window display:

1. From the *EndNote* menu, choose *Preferences*.

2. Click the *Display Fields* option in the list.

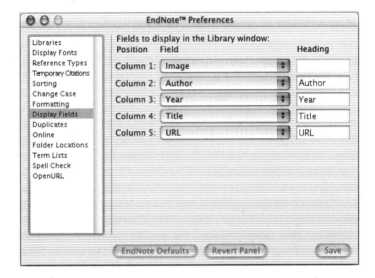

3. Choose the desired field from the Field list. You may select up to five fields to be displayed in the Library window. Select *Unused* instead of a field name if you want to show fewer than five fields.

4. By default, the column heading in the Library window will be the same as the Generic name of the field. If you would like to change the name for the Library window display, you may do so by entering a new name in the Heading section next to the chosen field.

5. Click *Save* to save the changes, and then close the Preferences window by clicking in the close button in the upper left corner.

These settings apply to all libraries.

The Library Window Sort Order

The references listed in the Library window are automatically sorted by the first author's last name, the year, and the order in which they were entered (the record number). This sort order can be changed by choosing *Sort References* from the *References* menu (see "Sorting the Library" in Chapter 8) or by clicking the column headings. When you sort a library, that sort order is retained even after you close and reopen a library.

When you sort the library, all alphabetical sorting is carried out according to the rules of your Macintosh system (such as U.S. or Swedish) unless you specify a different language in the *Sort Order* dialog.

The library sort order is in effect only when the library is showing all of the references. EndNote displays the results of a search in the order in which they were found. Similarly, after importing references, EndNote displays the newly imported references in the order in which they were imported. This behavior greatly enhances the speed of these two functions. Choosing *Show All References* (⌘+M) from the *References* menu returns all of the references to the Library window and lists them according to the last sort order specified.

NOTE: "Sort Order: Bibliographies and Multiple Citations" on page 402 describes how to set the sort order for a bibliographic style. See "Sorting" on page 480 for information about having EndNote ignore certain words or names when sorting references.

Creating Libraries

Although you can create as many libraries as you like, we strongly recommend that you keep all of your references together in one main EndNote library. Having all of the references you need in one place avoids unnecessary complexity when you are writing papers, creating bibliographies, or moving files between computers. Instead of making different "specialty" libraries, you will find it more useful to create one library and use the Keyword and Label fields together with EndNote's *Search* and *Sort References* commands to help you organize and categorize your references.

Creating a New Library

To create a new library:

1. From EndNote's *File* menu, choose *New*.

   EndNote presents a dialog prompting you to name and save the new library:

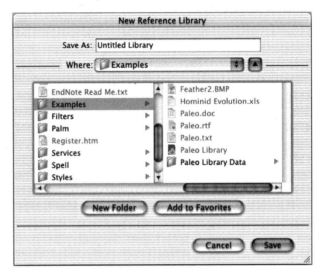

2. Enter a name for your new library.

3. Using the folder menu, choose the location where you would like to save the library. For simplicity, we suggest that you save your EndNote libraries in the EndNote 7 folder, which is typically located in the Applications folder.

4. Click *Save* and the new library appears as an empty EndNote library, showing "0 out of 0 references."

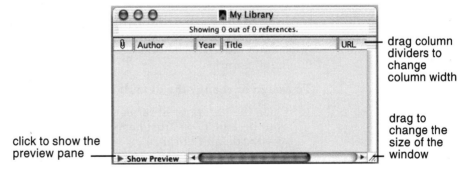

Now that you have created a new library, you can begin entering references into it. The following chapters illustrate the different ways to add references to an EndNote library:

- Chapter 5, "Entering and Editing References," discusses how to enter individual references manually.

- Chapter 6, "Searching Remote Databases with EndNote," describes how to connect directly to online databases and retrieve references from them.

- Chapter 7, "Importing Reference Data into EndNote," shows you how to import references that you have previously downloaded from online bibliographic databases.

If you have just created a library that will be the main library that you use, you can set it to open automatically every time you start EndNote by setting it to be your "default library" (see page 84).

Save a Copy of a Library

EndNote automatically saves changes to your library as you work with it, so there is no *Save* or *Save As* command for the library. You can, however, use the *Save a Copy* command to create an exact copy of your library.

To create a copy of your library:

1. With a library open, choose *Save a Copy* from the *File* menu.

2. Name the new library and choose where to save it.

3. Click *Save* and EndNote creates a copy of the library.

The new library does not open, it is simply saved to disk. EndNote leaves your original library open as it was before the command was chosen.

NOTE: If images are included in the library, the *Save a Copy* command also creates an image folder for the new library and copies all images to it.

Setting a Default Library

EndNote allows you to specify the libraries that you want to open automatically when EndNote starts up. We call these the "default" libraries.

To assign or change the default library:

1. Open the library or libraries that you would like to set as your default. (You must have a library open in order to set it as your default library.)

2. From the *EndNote* menu, choose *Preferences* and select *Libraries*.

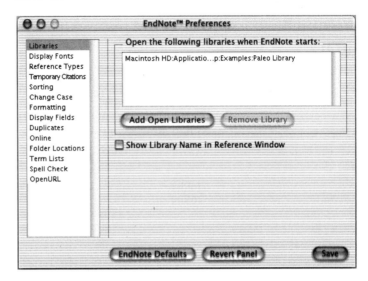

3. Click *Add Open Libraries* and all of the currently open libraries will be added to the list of default libraries that should open every time EndNote starts.

4. Click *Save* to save your changes, and then close the Preferences window by clicking in the close button in the top left corner.

Removing Default Libraries

To remove a library from the list of default libraries:

1. From the *EndNote* menu, choose *Preferences* and select *Libraries* from the list of options.

2. Select the library that you would like to remove from the list of default libraries and click *Remove Library*.

3. Click *Save* to save your changes, and then close the Preferences window by clicking the red close button in the top left corner.

Opening, Closing, and Deleting Libraries

Opening a Library

To open a library when the EndNote program is already running, choose *Open* from EndNote's *File* menu and select *Open Library*. (If you have previously opened a library, EndNote will list that library below the *Open Library* command; you can simply choose the library to open it directly, and skip the dialog shown below.)

When you choose the *Open Library* command, EndNote displays a dialog similar to this:

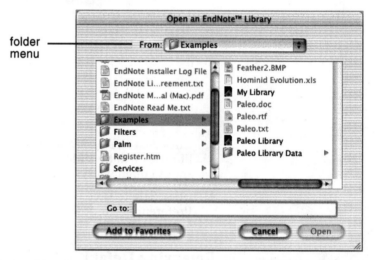

If your library is listed in the dialog, select it and click *Open*. If your library is not listed there, then it is probably saved in a different place on your hard drive or removable disk.

To locate a library:

1. From the *Folder* menu, choose *Desktop* and open the drive on which your library is stored.

2. Select the folder that contains your library and click *Open*. (If your library is within several folders, continue to open each folder until you locate the library.)

3. When you see your library, select it and then click *Open*.

Opening a Library from the Finder

You can also open a library by double-clicking its icon in the Finder. The icon for an EndNote library looks like this:

Paleo Library

Multiple People Opening One Library

EndNote does not perform "record locking" functions that would allow multiple users to *edit* one library at the same time. However, multiple users can *access* one EndNote library simultaneously as long as the library is restricted to *read-only* or *locked* status. This will allow the user to perform searches, copy information to their documents, and format their papers.

The simplest way to set up an EndNote library for shared network access is to use the network's system of file permissions to control the type of access allowed for users and groups. Except for the person who posts the database, grant all users read-only access.

One person should be assigned the responsibility for maintaining and updating the library at a separate location; this user should be granted full access to the file. Then, periodically post the updated library on the network for all other users, with read-only access.

One quick way of making your library "read-only" is to select it in the Finder, choose *Get Info* from the *File* menu, and click the "Locked" checkbox. When it is locked, multiple people can browse the file, but no one can edit it.

Closing a Library

To close a library, do one of the following:

♦ Choose *Close Library* from the *File* menu.

♦ Type ⌘+W when the Library window is active.

♦ Click the close button in the top left corner of the Library window.

♦ Hold down the OPTION key when clicking the red close button of a library to close all open Library windows.

EndNote automatically saves the information in your library when you close each reference. As a result, closing the library does not invoke the familiar "Save changes?" question. Instead, the Library window simply disappears, as all changes have already been saved.

Closing a library does not quit the EndNote program. If you want to quit from EndNote, simply choose *Quit EndNote* from the *EndNote* menu and any open libraries are saved and closed automatically.

Deleting a Library

Delete unwanted libraries by dragging them to the Trash in the Macintosh Finder.

Paleo Library

Recovering a Damaged Library

Occasionally computer files get damaged. If an EndNote library gets damaged, you may get an error message when trying to open it or work with the references. The best way to protect yourself from damaged files is to make regular backup copies of your important documents (see Appendix A). If you do not have a backup copy of a damaged EndNote library, you can use the *Recover Library* command to repair the damaged file.

To repair a damaged EndNote library:

1. Close the library if it is currently open.

2. From the *Tools* menu, choose *Recover Library*. Read the information about the Recover Library command, and click *OK*.

3. In the dialog that appears, locate and select the library that needs to be repaired, and click *Open*.

4. EndNote creates a copy of the library with the suffix "-Saved" added to the name. For example, if you were repairing a library called "References" the original library would remain untouched and a new, repaired library called "References - Saved" would be created in the same location.

Once the new library has been saved, you should be able to open it and use it in place of the damaged library.

NOTE: The *Recover Library* command does not create a new DATA folder. If your library contains images, either rename the recovered library to the original library name or rename the DATA folder to match the new library's name.

Differences Between Saved Libraries & the Original

The purpose of the *Recover Library* command is to recover as many references from the original library as possible. This means that it may also recover references that had previously been deleted from the library, but not yet purged from the file itself. If there are more references recovered in the saved library than existed at the time the original library was damaged, it means that EndNote was able to reconstruct references that had recently been deleted. These references must be deleted again.

Term lists are not recovered with the library. Consequently, you will need to rebuild each term list by choosing *Define Term Lists* from the *Tools* menu, highlighting the list, and then clicking *Update List* to fill the term list with the terms used in your library.

Often the file size of the "saved" copy of the library will be smaller than the original. This is normal and not cause for concern.

Transferring Libraries Across Platforms

EndNote 7 can read libraries created in any version of EndNote for Windows or Macintosh.

If you plan to email a library to someone, and your library contains images, remember to send all of the images found in your library's DATA folder. While you cannot attach an entire folder to an email, you can attach each file separately, to be placed in a DATA folder. Or, use a program (such as WinZip or Stuffit) that can zip your library and DATA folder into a single file to send via email.

NOTE: To copy a library to your Palm handheld device, see "Using EndNote With Palm OS Handhelds" on page 501.

From Windows to Macintosh

Libraries created with EndNote for Windows can be used by EndNote for Macintosh. No conversion is necessary.

1. If you are on a network, simply copy the library from the PC to the Macintosh. Otherwise, use the Windows Explorer to copy the library to a CD or Zip disk. Use your Macintosh to copy the library from the CD or Zip disk to the Macintosh.

NOTE: If images are included in the library, make sure you also copy the DATA folder found in the same folder as the library.

---

2. In the EndNote program on the Macintosh, choose *Open* from the *File* menu and select *Open Library*.

    As long as the library has the ".enl" extension, EndNote can display it. If the library does not have the ".enl" extension as part of the file name, EndNote will not recognize it.

3. Select the library and click *Open*.

    Once the library has been opened in EndNote on a Macintosh, it maintains the EndNote Macintosh icon and can be opened just like any other library created by EndNote on the Macintosh.

From Macintosh to Windows

Any library created by EndNote on a Macintosh can be used by EndNote for Windows. No conversion is necessary, however you should change the name of the library to include the ".enl" extension (for example, Medicine.enl).

1. If you are on a network, simply copy the file from the Macintosh to the PC. Otherwise, use a file transfer utility to move the library from the Macintosh to a CD or a Zip disk and then to the PC.

    NOTE: If images are included in the library, make sure you also copy the DATA folder found in the same folder as the library.

    ---

2. Start the EndNote program in Windows. (If you see a dialog prompting you for a reference library file, choose *Cancel*.)

3. Select *Open* from the *File* menu, and choose *Open Library*. Use the "Look in" list to navigate to the location of the library you want to open. If your library does not have the extension ".enl" or "*.lib" it will not appear in the dialog. If that is the case, select *All Files *.** from the file type list at the bottom of the dialog, and you should be able to see your library.

4. Select your library and click *Open*.

Chapter 5

Entering and Editing References

Chapter 5   Entering and Editing References

Introduction

There are various ways to add references to an EndNote library. This chapter explains how to type information into EndNote, edit EndNote references, and insert graphics and files.

See Chapter 6 for information about connecting to remote bibliographic databases and retrieving references directly into EndNote. Chapter 7 describes how to import references from a variety of sources using EndNote's *Import* command.

Important Points About References

Here is an overview of important aspects of EndNote references:

◆ Each EndNote reference stores the information required to cite it in a bibliography. Keywords, notes, abstracts, URLs and other information can be stored in a reference as well.

◆ Each reference added to a library is automatically assigned a unique record number that never changes for that reference in that particular library. EndNote uses these numbers to format papers. You cannot change these record numbers.

◆ Each library can reach a record number limit of 32,767 or a size of 32 MB (whichever comes first). Once a record number is assigned, it cannot be used again in that library. So, if you import 30,000 records, then delete all but 1000 of them, you cannot enter more than another 1000 records into that particular library.

◆ Each field in a reference can grow to accommodate roughly 8 pages of text (32,000 characters), with a total limit of about 16 pages (64,000 characters) per reference.

◆ Twenty-six **reference types** are already defined (such as Journal Article, Book, Conference Proceedings, etc.). Three additional Unused reference types are available so you can define your own.

◆ The **fields** (Author, Title, Year, etc.) displayed for each reference type can be modified or deleted. New fields can also be added, up to a total of 40 fields per reference.

◆ The text of the references should remain as "plain text" unless a special font, size, or style of text is required for a specific term or character.

◆ The font used to display the text in the references can be changed using the *General Display Font* preference.

◆ You can insert one graphic or file attachment into the Image field of a record.

♦ References are automatically saved when they are closed; however, you may save a reference while editing the reference using the *Save* command in the *File* menu.

The Reference Window

The **Reference window** displays the contents of the reference. Each part of the reference is stored in its own field, and the type of reference is displayed below the title bar:

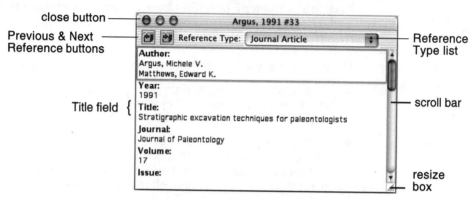

close button

Previous & Next Reference buttons

Title field {

Reference Type list

scroll bar

resize box

Argus, 1991 #33

Reference Type: Journal Article

Author:
Argus, Michele V.
Matthews, Edward K.

Year:
1991

Title:
Stratigraphic excavation techniques for paleontologists

Journal:
Journal of Paleontology

Volume:
17

Issue:

♦ The **Reference Type** list displays the type of reference that you are viewing, such as a journal article or a book.

♦ Click the *Previous Reference* or *Next Reference* buttons to close the current reference and open either the previous or next reference (based on the order the references appear in the Library window). All changes to the open reference are saved when you click these buttons.

♦ Resize the Reference window by clicking the **resize box** and dragging the window to the desired size. EndNote remembers the size and location of the last reference that you closed, so the next time you open a reference it will appear with the same dimensions and in the same location.

♦ Click the close button to close the reference, or type ⌘ +W (or OPTION-click the close button to close all references at once). All changes are saved automatically when a reference is closed.

♦ Click in the scroll bar with the mouse to scroll through the information in the Reference window.

♦ Press the TAB key or ⌘ +↓ to move to the next field and select its contents. SHIFT+TAB or ⌘+↑ selects the previous field.

♦ The first author's last name, the year, and the EndNote record number appear at the top of the Reference window in the title bar. This is the same information that is used for the temporary citations in word processing documents.

◆ Click the **zoom box** in the top corner to expand or minimize a Reference window. Click it again to restore the window to its original size.

The *Window* Menu

Any open library or reference is listed in EndNote's *Window* menu. The title of each open Reference window (that is, the author, year, and record number of a reference) appears in the *Window* menu, and it can be selected to bring that reference forward on the screen.

Previous and Next Reference Commands

When a Reference window is open, use the *Previous Reference* and *Next Reference* commands in the *References* menu to quickly browse through your references. The Reference window also includes buttons to move to the previous or next reference.

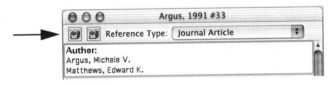

When you choose one of these commands (or click the buttons), the content of the References window changes to display the information for the previous or next reference listed in the Library window.

This command has the same effect as closing the reference that is currently displayed and opening another reference, so any changes to the currently opened reference will be saved before EndNote switches to display another reference.

Finding Text in a Reference

When you have a reference that contains a significant amount of text, such as long abstracts or notes, it can get hard to find things!

To jump to specific text within a reference with the Go to command:

1. Open a reference.

   The *Go to* command works on the currently open reference. If more than one reference is open, it works on the topmost reference.

2. From the *References* menu, select *Go to*.

   You could also use Control+Click to select *Go to* from the context-sensitive menu, or use the keyboard command noted on the *References* menu.

3. Type the text you want to locate and click next (or press Return).

   You can type a maximum of 255 characters. The Go to dialog also includes a drop-down list of recently searched terms.

EndNote will jump to the text and highlight it within the reference. You can use *Go to* again to find the next occurrence, or click *Cancel* to dismiss the Go to dialog.

Changing the General Display Font

By default, any text that you type or edit in EndNote is displayed in 12 point Geneva font. You can change this to another font and/or size using the *General Display Font* option in EndNote's preferences.

The General Display Font changes the font used to display all other text that is typed into EndNote (such as in the Reference or Style windows). The General Display Font is also used for most of the previews and information panels in EndNote, as well as for bibliographies that are printed, exported, or copied directly from EndNote.

Changes made to the display fonts apply to all EndNote libraries opened on that computer. They do not affect the font used when you are formatting bibliographies in a word processing document. The normal font of the document is used for that. Changing the General Display Font simply changes the font that EndNote uses for its "Plain Font" and "Plain Size" settings. Deliberate font changes that you have made in your references are not affected by the display font.

To change the General Display Font:

1. From the *EndNote* menu, choose *Preferences* and click the *Display Fonts* option.

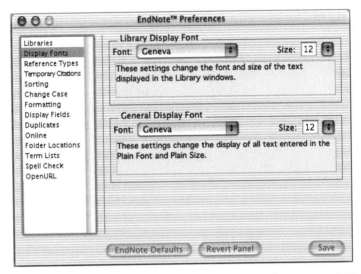

2. In the "General Display Font" section, use the *Font* and *Size* menus to choose the font and size for text displayed throughout EndNote.

3. Click *Save* to save your changes, and then close the Preferences window by clicking the close button.

Selecting References

To work with individual references (for example to copy, open, export or edit them), first select them in the Library window. The simplest way is to click on a reference in the Library window. That reference is then highlighted to indicate it is selected.

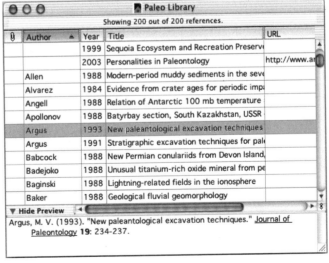

Click any reference to select it.

You can also select a reference by typing the first few letters found in the field by which the library is currently sorted. For example, if the library is sorted by the author field, type the first few letters of an author's last name to select the first reference by that author. If the library is sorted based on title, type the first few letters of the title of the reference that you want to select. (When typing the letters to match a title, articles such as "a," "an," and "the" are skipped.)

To select multiple references:

◆ Hold down the COMMAND key (⌘) while clicking on individual references. Press the COMMAND key and click on a *selected* reference to deselect that reference and retain the rest of the selection.

◆ Select a range of references by clicking on the first reference, then press the SHIFT key and click on the last reference of the range.

◆ You can also select a range of references by holding down the mouse button and dragging the mouse vertically across a range of references.

◆ Choose *Select All* from the *Edit* menu (⌘+A) to select all of the references showing in the Library window. When all the references are selected, the *Select All* command changes to *Unselect All*.

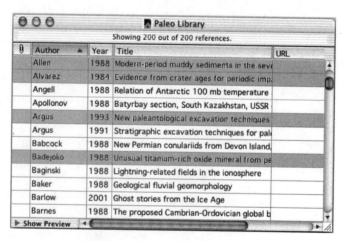

See "Showing and Hiding References" on page 175 in Chapter 8 to learn how to display only the selected references, or temporarily hide the selected references from view.

Opening, Closing, Saving, and Deleting References

Opening References

Once you have the references selected, any of the following actions opens them (a maximum of 10 references at a time):

♦ Double-click the selected reference(s).

♦ Press Return.

♦ Choose *Edit References* (⌘+E) from the *References* menu.

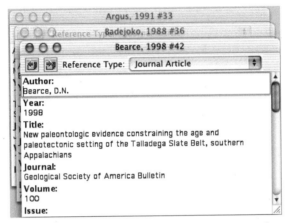

You can stop a series of selected references that are in the process of opening by pressing the Escape key (ESC) or ⌘-PERIOD.

The Reference window that opens for each of the references is where you enter and edit the reference data. Modify this text just like you would edit a word processing document: select the incorrect text and retype it, or delete and add text as necessary. Important information about entering reference data follows.

Closing References

To close a currently open reference, do any of the following:

♦ Click in the close button on the Reference window.

♦ Choose *Close Reference* (⌘+W) from the *File* menu.

♦ Close all open references with just one click by pressing the OPTION key when clicking the close button.

♦ To close one reference and view the next or previous reference in the library, use the *Next Reference* and *Previous Reference* commands in the *References* menu (or the buttons in the Reference window). See page 95 for details.

NOTE: All data in a reference is automatically saved when you close the Reference window.

Saving References

To save a reference that you have just created, or to save any changes made to an existing reference:

♦ Close the reference(s) as described above, or

♦ Choose *Save* (⌘+S) from the *File* menu.

If you quit from EndNote while Reference windows are open, the references are closed and saved automatically.

Reverting References

The *Revert Reference* command in the *File* menu discards all changes made to a reference since it was last opened or saved. *Revert Reference* is not available after you close the reference.

To remove the very last change made to a reference, use the *Undo* command in the *Edit* menu before closing or saving a reference.

Deleting References

Delete references from a library by selecting them in the Library window and choosing one of the following commands:

♦ *Delete References* (⌘+D) from the *References* menu,

♦ *Cut* (⌘+X) from the *Edit* menu, or

♦ *Clear* from the *Edit* menu.

Delete References and *Clear* serve the same function of removing the references from the library. *Cut* also removes the references from the library, but it stores them temporarily on the Clipboard so that you can paste them into another library. (Information on the Clipboard is replaced with whatever you *Cut* or *Copy* next.)

All three commands have you confirm that you want to remove the references from the library. You cannot undo these operations, so be sure you want to delete the selected reference(s) before dismissing EndNote's warning.

NOTE: If you delete a reference, you delete its record number in that library forever. Even if you paste the reference back into the same library, it is assigned a new, unique record number. This may cause incompatibilities with older papers that have citations that use old record numbers. We strongly recommend that you do *not delete references that have been used in papers* that you might want to reformat later, and keep backups of your libraries!

Creating a New Reference

Overview

To add a new reference to an open library:

1. From the *References* menu, choose *New Reference* (⌘+N). This opens an empty Reference window:

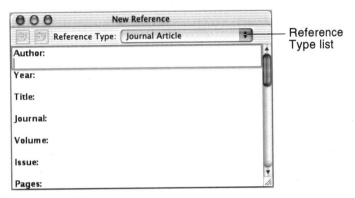

2. Choose a reference type from the *Reference Type* list at the top of the window.

3. Enter the bibliographic data into each of the fields in the reference according to the rules outlined later in this chapter. When you are finished, close the reference to save it and add it to the library.

The rest of this chapter goes into more detail about how to enter references into EndNote.

Changing the Default Reference Type

By default, new references appear as Journal Article references. You may change this using the *Default Reference Type* option in the Preferences panel.

1. From the *EndNote* menu, choose *Preferences*.

2. Click the *Reference Types* option in the list.

3. At the top of that *Reference Types* preferences panel, click the *Default Reference Type* list and choose the reference type that new references should use.

Choosing a Reference Type

When you create a new reference, that reference is assigned the default reference type. If you want to add a different type of reference, click the *Reference Type* list at the top of the Reference window, and select the reference type that you need.

Normally, you should select the reference type before entering information in the reference. However, you can change the reference type at any time, and the information you have entered is retained and transferred to the corresponding field for the new reference type.

In addition to determining how the reference is formatted in the bibliography, the reference type determines which fields appear in the Reference window. For example, a Journal Article reference would have fields for Journal, Volume, and Issue, whereas a Book would have fields for Editor and Publisher.

Customizing Fields and Reference Types

Fields can be removed, added, or renamed. You can also create entirely new reference types. See Chapter 14 for instructions on removing, adding, or modifying fields for each reference type.

Tips for Choosing the Right Reference Type

Use **Book** for books written by one or more authors, and use **Edited Book** for books edited by one or more editors (whether they are books in a series or not).

Use **Book Section** for references to parts of edited or non-edited books (a chapter, for example, or one article in a published conference proceedings).

The **Conference Proceedings** reference type is best used for unpublished proceedings. Articles that are published as part of the comprehensive conference proceedings should be entered as **Book Section** references.

Use the **Electronic Source** reference type for citing material from a Web page or FTP site. If you are citing a journal article that appears both online and in print, most style guides prefer that you use the print information and cite it as a regular journal article. Email discussions should be cited as **Personal Communications**, just like any other correspondence.

Use the **Chart or Table** reference type if you want to include an image and later insert that image as a table in Microsoft Word. Images in all other reference types will insert into Word as figures, which are listed and numbered separately from tables.

Entering References

Bibliographic information (as well as keywords, notes, and other relevant information) is entered into separate **fields** in each EndNote **reference**. By storing the pieces of bibliographic data in different fields, EndNote can later rearrange the elements to conform to various bibliographic formats (such as APA or MLA).

Special bibliographic formatting and punctuation should *not be included* when you enter reference data into EndNote. For example, you do not need to put quotes around titles, italicize journal names, or include the abbreviation "Vol." along with volume numbers. Enter only the raw data, and leave the formatting to EndNote.

NOTE: There are a few exceptions to this punctuation rule, notably in the Author, Editor, and Edition fields. Read on for details.

Using Term Lists with Data Entry

EndNote uses **term lists** for the Author and Editor names, Journals, and Keywords. Term lists can also be created for other fields. These lists are updated automatically as you enter new terms into these fields. The benefit of this is that the term lists also help with data entry. If you begin to enter a name, journal or keyword that you have used before in that library, EndNote will complete the term for you to speed up data entry:

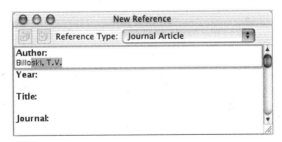

To accept a term that EndNote has suggested, simply press RETURN, TAB, or click in the next field. Terms that are new (that is, those that do not already appear in the corresponding Author, Journals, or Keyword term list) appear in red text.

A more complete discussion of EndNote's term lists is provided in Chapter 9.

NOTE: Both the "Auto-Update" and "Auto-Complete" term list features described here may be turned off using the *Term Lists* settings in the EndNote preferences.

Author and Editor Names

The following information about Author and Editor fields applies to the following "Generic" field names: Author, Secondary Author, Tertiary Author, and Subsidiary Author.

It is best when author and editor names are entered *one name per line*, although you could also delimit them with a semicolon, slash, or backslash. If an author's name is too long to fit on a single line, just let it wrap to the next line as you type it.

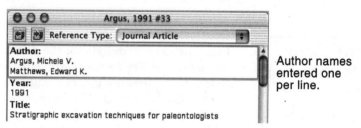

Author names entered one per line.

The Authors term list (which maintains a list of terms used in the Author fields) can be set up to recognize semicolons (;), slashes (/), backslashes (\), and returns as the delimiters that separate individual author names. If you would prefer to use other punctuation to separate your author names, you may change these settings using the *Define Term Lists* command from the *Tools* menu. See Chapter 9 for details.

Author names can be entered either with the last name followed by a comma and the first name, or the first name followed by the last name. Both are correct. However, note that if you have the "Suggest Terms as You Type" feature of the term lists turned on, EndNote suggests author names based on the assumption that the names are being entered with the last name first.

EndNote can abbreviate first and middle names, so for maximum flexibility enter whole names whenever possible. If you are entering initials instead of full names, be sure to type a period or a space between initials, (for example "Fisher, J.O." or "J O Fisher"), otherwise EndNote interprets the initials as a single name: "Jo."

See "Author List (Bibliography and Footnotes)" on page 395 for information about how EndNote can format author names in bibliographies. For more information about term lists, see Chapter 9.

Using "et al." or Similar Abbreviations

Enter all author names for a particular reference. EndNote will truncate the list of authors with "et al." or "and others" as required by the bibliographic style. If you do not know all of the authors' names, then the last author should be "et al." or "and others" followed by a comma.

Anonymous Works

If a reference has no author, you should leave the Author field blank. Do not enter "Anonymous." The style that you use to format the bibliography determines how anonymous references are treated.

Note that if a work is published with "Anonymous" printed on the title page, most style guides request that "Anonymous" be entered as though it were the author name.

Corporate Authors

When entering corporate authors, put a comma after the name:

```
U.S. Department of Agriculture,

Apple Computer Inc.,
```

Be sure that you do not have any commas in the name because all text before the comma is interpreted as a last name.

Complex Author Names

For multiple-word last names, like Charles de Gaulle, enter the name with the last name first, such as:

```
de Gaulle, Charles
```

Entering a name this way ensures that both words "de" and "Gaulle" will format as the last name.

Enter authors with titles, such as "Jr." or "III", as Last, First, Title. For example, "Alfred Smith Jr." must be entered as:

```
Smith, Alfred, Jr.
```

NOTE: See the *Sorting* section of the EndNote preferences if you do not want EndNote to include prepositions (such as de, van, von, etc.) when it alphabetizes references in a bibliography (page 480).

Year

Normally, you should enter the four numbers of the year of publication, as in 2002. When appropriate, you may enter in press, or in preparation, or some other notation.

Titles

The following information about Title fields applies to the "Generic" fields Title, Secondary Title, Tertiary Title, and Alternate Title.

Enter titles without a period or any other punctuation at the end. Do not press the RETURN key while typing titles into EndNote; allow long titles to just wrap to the next line. Although the EndNote styles can change the capitalization of titles, it is best to capitalize the title in the same way you would like it to be capitalized in your bibliographies.

Journal Names

The Journal field is automatically set up to work with the Journals term list. This means that the Journals list is updated as you add new journal names to your references, and EndNote will use this list to facilitate data entry by suggesting journal names as you enter them into the Journal field. See Chapter 9 for more information about term lists and turning these options off.

The Journal field (in the Journal Article reference type) can be used with the Journals term list to allow for multiple formats of a journal name to be used in your bibliographies, depending on the format required (see page 224 for details). When the different forms of the journal name are entered into the Journals term list, then all it takes to change the format of your journal names in a bibliography is one change in the style used (see "Journal Names" on page 386). All of the appropriate substitutions are made when the bibliography is created.

EndNote includes predefined term lists for medical, chemistry, and humanities journals. If you would like to use these lists, you should import them into your Journals list as described in Chapter 9.

The Alternate Journal Field

The Alternate Journal field is most useful when importing or retrieving references from an online source that provides two forms of each journal name (full and abbreviated). By importing both, you can easily update the Journals term list and use the correct form of the name without having to enter it yourself (see page 223).

If you do not import from sources that include an alternate journal name, this field is probably not necessary for you to have in your Journal Article references. You can remove it by editing the Reference Types table (see page 350).

Pages

Page ranges can be entered as complete (1442-1449) or abbreviated (1442-9) ranges. The style used to create the bibliography can change the page numbers to be either full or abbreviated page ranges, or show just the first page (see the "Page Numbers" section in Chapter 15).

Do not use commas in the Pages field for page numbers in the thousands.

Edition

The text of the Edition field is not modified by EndNote for your bibliographies, so be sure to enter "1st," "2nd," and so on for this field if that is what you need in your bibliography.

Date

Enter dates as you would like them to appear in your references; EndNote does not reformat dates.

Entering Dates for Record Keeping

You can use the Label, Notes, or any of the Custom fields to enter a date for your own record-keeping purposes (such as a record entry or modification date, or any date other than the publication dates). If you plan to sort your references by these dates, or search for a range of dates, enter the numerical version of the date instead of the name of the month because EndNote does not interpret dates and would therefore sort months alphabetically. For example, enter "1998/5/21" instead of "May 21, 1998." Enter the year first, followed by the month and the day, so that the references can be sorted first by year, then month, then the day.

Short Title

Use the Short Title field to enter abbreviated versions of the regular title which should be used as part of an in-text citation or a footnote citation. This is a common request for many of the humanities styles which use a shortened form of the title in the citation to help identify which reference is being cited. For example, MLA typically lists just the author name and the specifically cited pages in the in-text citation:

(Perin 141)

But if there are multiple works by that author, MLA requires that the title, or a shortened form of it be added to the citation. If the full title of the reference is fairly long, such as "Burning the Midnight Oil: Tales from Working the Night Shift," you should enter an easily recognizable form of the title that starts with the first word on which the normal title would be sorted. For example:

(Perin, *Burning* 141)

If an EndNote style is configured to use the Short Title field, and that field is empty for a particular reference, the normal Title field is used instead.

Original Publication

Use the Original Publication field to enter any information about the original publication that you need to be included in the cited reference. For example, when citing a republished book you might want to include the original publication date, as well as any other supplementary information about the original publication (such as place published and publisher). Enter this information just as you would want it to appear in your formatted bibliography reference (including text styles and punctuation).

Reprint Edition

Use the Reprint Edition field for references that were originally published under a different title. The field should include the original title and year to indicate that this reference is a reprint of an earlier publication. Enter this information exactly as you would want it to appear in your formatted reference (including text styles and punctuation).

NOTE: This field is not intended to be used to indicate whether or not you have a reprint of the article on file. You may use one of the custom fields for that.

Reviewed Item

Use the Reviewed Item field for articles or chapters that are critical reviews of books, cinema, art, or other works. The contents of the Reviewed Item field varies depending on the type of review that you are citing, but typically you should enter the title of the reviewed work and the primary person responsible for it (author, artist, performer, etc.). Additional information about a production or performance may also be included. Enter the information exactly as you want it to appear in the formatted references (including punctuation and text styles).

ISBN/ISSN

ISSN (International Standard Serial Number) and ISBN (International Standard Book Number) are codes used to identify a particular publication. An ISSN number would refer to an entire journal (such as the Journal of Virology), and an ISBN would refer to a particular book.

This field is not used by default for all reference types, but it is available in the Generic list of EndNote fields. It is most useful if you are importing reference data or retrieving references directly from an online source. These numbers help to identify a specific publication if you needed to order it or locate it. See page 350 for information about adding fields to your reference types.

Call Number

The Call Number field is used to store library call numbers. These are the codes that help you to locate a particular publication on the shelves in your library. When available, the EndNote connection files import the call number information into this field. If you do not plan to use this feature, you may remove the field (see page 350).

Label

The Label field can be used for many purposes, such as special in-text citations or reprint numbers.

Some citation styles require that citations include only part of the author's name, such as [SMIT 90]. EndNote cannot create this citation for you, but if you type "SMIT 90" into the Label field and use the Label field in your style's citation template, EndNote will insert the Label field into the citation.

If you do not need the Label field for citation purposes, it can be used as an additional field for categorizing references or storing reprint numbers. (Do not use EndNote's record numbers to number reprints because these numbers change when references are moved to different libraries. EndNote's record numbers cannot be assigned or changed by the user.)

Keywords

Use the Keywords field to store keywords that you want to associate with the reference. You can restrict a search to just the Keywords field, so the terms you enter into this field can be used to later retrieve the references when using EndNote's *Search* command.

The Keywords term list (which maintains a list of terms used in the Keywords field) can be set up to recognize semicolons (;), slashes (/), backslashes (\ ), and returns as the delimiters that separate individual keywords. If you would prefer to use other punctuation to separate your keywords, you may change these settings using the *Define Term Lists* command from the *Tools* menu. See Chapter 9 for details.

Notes and Abstract

The Notes and Abstract fields, like all other fields, can hold up to 32,000 characters which is equivalent to about 8 pages of single-spaced text. Use the Notes field to store personal reminders, such as the location of a quotation in a book or the quotation itself. Use the Abstract field for a brief description of the contents of the work.

URL (Uniform Resource Locator)

Even if you're not familiar with the acronym "URL" (Uniform Resource Locator), you probably know about the World Wide Web. The URL is simply the term for the address used to locate a specific piece of information using your Web browser. The URL for the EndNote home page provides a typical example of how a URL should be entered:

```
http://www.endnote.com
```

When a correctly formatted URL is entered into this field, the *Open Link* command in the *References* menu can be used to launch your Web browser and take you to that site. Adding any other information along with the URL may keep the *Open Link* command from successfully finding the desire site.

Some online reference databases include a URL for the full text of an article online. When importing or retrieving references directly from these sources, the URLs can import directly into this field to take advantage of the *Open Link* command. You can also store a URL to related information on the Web or other relevant material.

You can also use this feature to store the path to files on your hard drive (such as graphics and word processing documents). Use the *Link To* command in the *References* menu to select the file for which you would like to insert a link. This is a good trick for linking graphics or other files on your hard drive to a reference in your EndNote library. Selecting the *Open Link* command when this reference is open or selected in the library will then use the appropriate application to open the linked file.

This field is unique in how it interacts with the *Open Link* command in that the *Open Link* command automatically checks this field to find a URL or a file to launch. See "Linking References to Files and Web Sites" on page 201.

Clickable URL Links

EndNote automatically recognizes URLs if they are entered with the correct prefix (such as "http://" or "ftp://") in any field. When recognized, they become clickable Web links and appear as blue and underlined text. Simply clicking on one of these links will open your Web browser and go to the address given. This feature is not specific to the URL field.

Image and Caption

The Image field may have a different name depending on the reference type. It may be labeled Image or have a custom label assigned by you. The Image field can contain a graphic or an object (file attachment). For information about entering images, see "Inserting Images" on page 117.

The Image field is included by default for all reference types, but it is available in the Generic list of EndNote fields so you can remove it from any reference type.

NOTE: Each reference can contain only one graphic or file attachment.

A related Caption field appears directly under the Image field in a reference. Use this field for a short description of the image or file.

Cite While You Write allows you to insert the image and its caption into a word processing document. See "Inserting and Formatting Figures and Tables" on page 270. Use the *Chart or Table* reference type if you want to include an image and later insert that image as a *table* in Microsoft Word. Images in all other reference types will insert into Word as *figures*, which are listed and numbered separately from tables.

Font, Size, and Style

EndNote is designed to produce bibliographies that automatically use the font and size of the text in your word processing documents. Normally, when you type text into an EndNote reference, it is entered in EndNote's Plain font, size, and style, which means that your references follow the font settings in your paper.

If any fonts, sizes, or styles other than Plain are entered into your library, they will appear in your bibliography regardless of the font of your paper. For example, you can italicize species names, add a superscripted number, or enter Greek characters such as β.

To apply font or text styles, select the text to be changed then choose the desired font, size, or style from the *Edit* menu.

NOTE: If the *Font*, *Size*, and *Style* options are dim, it is either because you are not in an editing window (such as a Reference or Style window), or you have not selected (highlighted) any text to change.

Plain Text

The *Plain Text*, *Plain Font*, and *Plain Size* commands in the *Edit* menu remove overriding fonts, text sizes, or text styles from the selected text in a reference or a Style window.

When EndNote creates a bibliography, text in Plain Font and Plain Size uses the font and size of your paper. To use these commands, first select the text you want to change, and then choose *Plain Text*, *Plain Font*, or *Plain Size* from the *Edit* menu.

The default font used to display EndNote's "Plain Text" is Geneva 12 point, but it can be changed using the *General Display Font* option in the *Display Fonts* section of the EndNote preferences. (Choose *Preferences* from the *EndNote* menu and click the *Display Fonts* option.) The General Display Font setting changes the font in which the references are displayed but does not affect the font of a bibliography created for a word processing document.

Keyboard Commands

A full set of key commands is available so that you can enter references without using the mouse. For example, to create and enter a new reference without touching the mouse: type ⌘+N to add a new reference, type the bibliographic information using TAB or SHIFT+TAB to move forward or backward between the fields, and then press ⌘+W to save and close the reference.

Key Command	Function
⌘+N	creates a new reference
⌘+CLICK	to select more than one reference
SHIFT+CLICK	to select a range of references
⌘+E	opens selected reference(s)
⌘+W	closes the active window
⌘+OPTION+W	closes all windows of the same type as the active window
TAB	selects the next field
SHIFT+TAB	selects the previous field
When text is selected:	
⌘+T	sets the text style to Plain
⌘+L	selects the Plain font
⌘+B	turns bold on and off
⌘+I	turns italic on and off
⌘+U	turns underline on and off
⌘++	turns superscript on and off
⌘ +-	turns subscript on and off
⌘+]	makes text larger
⌘+[	makes text smaller

Use the ARROW keys to navigate within a field.

The EndNote menus display equivalent key commands next to many menu commands.

Cut, Copy, Paste Text in the References

The *Cut, Copy,* and *Paste* commands in the *Edit* menu can be used to move text from one field in a reference to another field by selecting and copying or cutting the text and then pasting it in the desired location. You can also *Copy* and *Paste* text from a field in an EndNote reference to your word processor. Similarly, you can *Copy* text from a word processing document and *Paste* it into a reference. If it is important to paste the text along with the fonts and text styles, use the *Paste with Text Styles* command in the *Edit* menu. The regular *Paste* command does not include font, size, or text style information when pasting into EndNote from another program. Avoid pasting unwanted fonts and text styles into EndNote references because those fonts and text styles will carry through into future bibliographies.

Using "Drag-and-Drop" Within a Reference

Text may also be moved around within a reference by selecting the text and then dragging and dropping it in a new location. When text is moved this way *within* a reference, it is moved from one location to another. When it is dragged from one reference to another reference or to another program (such as your word processor), it is *copied* and therefore not removed from the reference.

To drag-and-drop text: First select the text of interest. Then click on the selection, and keep the mouse button pressed while you drag the text to another location. When the cursor is positioned in the right place, release the mouse button to "drop" the text there.

Copying and Pasting Complete References

In addition to copying and pasting text between fields, EndNote can *Copy* and *Paste* entire references between libraries.

To use the *Copy* and *Paste* commands:

1. Select one or more references in the Library window (hold down the COMMAND (⌘) key to select multiple references or the SHIFT key to select a range of references). Do not open the references.

	Author ▲	Year	Title	URL
	Allen	1988	Modern-period muddy sediments in the seve	
	Alvarez	1984	Evidence from crater ages for periodic imp:	
	Angell	1988	Relation of Antarctic 100 mb temperature	
	Apollonov	1988	Batyrbay section, South Kazakhstan, USSR	
	Argus	1993	New paleantological excavation techniques	
	Argus	1991	Stratigraphic excavation techniques for pal	
	Babcock	1988	New Permian conulariids from Devon Island,	
	Badejoko	1988	Unusual titanium-rich oxide mineral from pe	
	Baginski	1988	Lightning-related fields in the ionosphere	
	Baker	1988	Geological fluvial geomorphology	
	Barlow	2001	Ghost stories from the Ice Age	
	Barnes	1988	The proposed Cambrian-Ordovician global b	

Paleo Library
Showing 200 out of 200 references.
Show Preview

2. Choose *Copy* (⌘+C) from the *Edit* menu and those references are copied to the Clipboard.

3. Open another EndNote library and choose *Paste* (⌘+V) from the *Edit* menu to paste directly to the Library window. The references you copied are pasted into the library and sorted correctly with the existing references.

Copying references using drag-and-drop:

An easy way to copy references between libraries is to use the drag-and-drop functionality. Simply select the references you want to copy, click on any part of the selection, and use the mouse to drag them to another open library. Release the mouse button when the cursor is over the destination library, and all of the select references will be copied into the library.

If you need to copy all of the references in one library to another library, you can also use the *Import* command to directly import one library into the other (see Chapter 7).

NOTE: Any time you copy a reference and paste it into another library, or import a reference into another library, the reference is assigned a new record number in the destination library.

Entering Several Articles from the Same Source

Use a reference "template" to facilitate entering a series of references that have some information in common (such as various sections from one book, or a number of papers presented at the same conference). The template you create is an incomplete EndNote reference with just the common information entered into it.

To create a reference template:

1. From the *References* menu, choose *New Reference*.

2. Enter all of the bibliographic information that the references have in common (such as the year, book title, publisher, and city for different sections from one book).

3. Close the reference when you are finished. It remains selected in the Library window.

4. Choose *Copy* (⌘+C) from the *Edit* menu to copy it.

5. Use the *Paste* (⌘+V) command to paste the reference several times, to create as many partially-filled references as you need. You should paste directly to the Library window—do *not* open a new reference and choose *Paste*.

6. Select all of the partially-filled references that you just created and edit them (double-click them, press RETURN, or type ⌘+E to open up to 10 selected references at one time).

Complete each of the individual references. Close each reference as you complete it.

Entering Special Characters

Symbols

Use the *Symbol* font in the *Edit>Font* menu to type various Greek letters. If you have *Key Caps* installed in your Apple menu, you can use that to see other examples of characters available with a particular font, and when pressing the OPTION key. For example, with the Symbol font:

Type:	a	to get:	α
	b		β
	m		μ
	p		π
	y		ψ

Diacritical Characters

Diacritical marks can be applied to the appropriate letter by pressing the OPTION key and the key that activates the accent mark. The accent mark will be applied to the next key pressed after this sequence. For example, typing OPTION-U then releasing those keys and pressing the letter "o" will produce: ö. The Cedilla is a unique character, therefore it cannot be used for any other letter.

Examples of Key Commands for Entering Diacritics

Character	Key Sequence	Example
Grave Accent	OPTION-`-(a letter)	lòuvre
Acute Accent	OPTION-E-(a letter)	école
Umlaut	OPTION-U-(a letter)	Büblingen
Circumflex	OPTION-I-(a letter)	maître
Tilde	OPTION-N-(a letter)	mañana
Cedilla	OPTION-C	façade

Inserting Images

EndNote extends the organization of reference information by including the ability to embed graphics and files in an EndNote library and link them to papers. You can insert a graphic, figure, or file into the Image field of any EndNote reference.

NOTE: While the Image and Caption fields are included by default for all reference types, you can remove them at any time if you don't intend to use them and they are just taking up space. See "Adding, Deleting, and Renaming Fields" on page 350.

Once you have an image in your EndNote reference, Cite While You Write allows you to insert the image and its caption into a word processing document. See "Inserting and Formatting Figures and Tables" on page 270 for more information about using images with Cite While You Write.

Selecting the Appropriate Reference Type

You can insert a graphic, figure, or file into the Image field of an EndNote reference. Depending on the reference type, the field may be labeled Image or have a custom label assigned by you.

By default, the Image and Caption fields are included in all reference types. So, while a reference to a journal may contain primarily bibliographic information, you can also include an illustration that appeared with the journal article.

The Figure, Chart or Table, and Equation reference types can be used specifically to catalog images and files, and may contain minimal reference information.

NOTE: Images in the Chart or Table reference type are inserted into Word as tables, and are labeled and numbered separately from the figures found in all other reference types.

To add or remove the Image and Caption fields from a reference type, go to the *EndNote* menu, choose *Preferences*, and select *Reference Types*. For more information about modifying reference types, see "Adding, Deleting, and Renaming Fields" on page 350.

Inserting Graphics

Notes about inserting graphics:

◆ Always use the *Insert Picture* command to insert graphic files. If you simply *Copy* and *Paste* a graphic, System settings are used and you could ultimately lose colors and other attributes from the original file.

◆ Each EndNote reference can contain only one graphic or file attachment. If you insert a second graphic or file, it will *replace* the first one. The previous image is deleted from the DATA folder. See "Storing and Sharing Image Files" on page 121 for more information about the DATA folder.

◆ After inserting a graphic, you should always type Caption text into the Caption field, particularly if you intend to later insert the figure into a Word document. The Caption will label the graphic in the figure list at the end of the Word document. The Caption also helps you search for the image.

◆ You can insert a graphic only into a reference that contains the Image field. If you need to add the Image field to a reference type, use the Reference Types preferences panel as described on page 476.

To insert a graphic into the Image field:

1. With the reference open for editing, go to the *References* menu and choose *Insert Picture*. (The *Insert Picture* command is also available on the toolbar.)

2. In the file dialog, locate the graphic file and *Insert* it. EndNote recognizes *at least* these graphic file types:

   ◆ Bitmap - BMP
   ◆ Graphics Interchange Format - GIF
   ◆ JPEG File Interchange Format - JPEG
   ◆ Portable Network Graphics - PNG
   ◆ Tag Image File Format - TIFF

The graphic appears as a thumbnail within the reference.

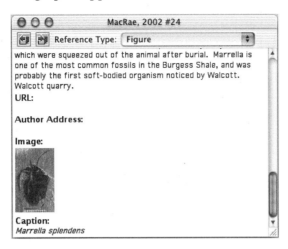

Double-clicking on the thumbnail will launch an associated application to open the graphic file, with the same effect as if you had double clicked the file on your computer desktop.

Inserting Files

Notes about inserting files:

♦ Each EndNote reference can contain only one graphic or file attachment. If you insert a second graphic or file, it will *replace* the first one. The previous image is deleted from the DATA folder. See "Storing and Sharing Image Files" on page 121 for more information about the DATA folder.

♦ After inserting a file, you should always type Caption text into the Caption field, particularly if you intend to later insert the figure into a Word document. The Caption will label the file in the figure list at the end of the Word document. The Caption also helps you search for the file.

♦ You can insert a file only into a reference that contains the Image field. If you need to add the Image field to a reference type, use the Reference Types preferences panel as described on page 476.

To insert an object, or file, into the Image field:

1. With the reference open for editing, go to the *References* menu and choose *Insert Object*. (The *Insert Object* command is also available on the toolbar.)

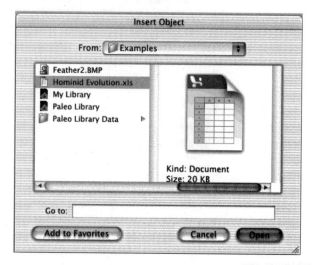

2. Locate the file and *Insert* it. EndNote recognizes *at least* these formats:

   ♦ Audio files (WAV, MP3)
   ♦ Microsoft Access files
   ♦ Microsoft Excel files
   ♦ Microsoft Power Point files
   ♦ Microsoft Project files
   ♦ Microsoft Visio files
   ♦ Microsoft Word files
   ♦ Multimedia files (MOV, QuickTime)
   ♦ PDF files
   ♦ Technical drawing files
   ♦ Text files (.TXT, .RTF, HTML)

The file will appear as an attachment, with the program icon and filename.

Entering a Caption

A related Caption field appears directly under the Image field in a reference. Use this field for a short description of the image or file. The Caption field allows you to easily search for images.

If you insert an EndNote image into a Word document with Cite While You Write, the corresponding caption appears either above or below the image in your paper (the placement is determined by the current output style).

NOTE: The Caption field is a text-only field. URLs or paths and filenames are not hot linked when entered into this field.

Opening the Image File

Double-clicking on a graphic or attachment icon in the Image field of a reference will launch an associated application (determined by the file type and your operating system) and open the file for viewing or editing. It is the same as if you had double clicked on the image file on your computer desktop. Any changes to the file are saved for this EndNote reference.

Storing and Sharing Image Files

When you insert an Image, EndNote does this:

◆ If it doesn't already exist, EndNote creates a folder, specifically for images, in the same folder as your EndNote library. It gives the folder the same name as your library, plus DATA. For example, for the Paleo.enl library, the folder where images are stored is titled Paleo.data

◆ EndNote copies the image file and places it in the DATA folder. The file is specifically linked to a single EndNote reference.

NOTE: Simply putting an image into the DATA folder does not link it into a reference. You must use the *Insert Picture* or *Insert Object* command.

If you move your library to a different computer, or if you want to share your library with someone, remember to copy the DATA folder along with the library so that images are included.

Editing Image Files

To edit an image stored in an EndNote reference, open the reference and double click on the image icon. This launches an associated application to open the file for editing. See "Opening the Image File" on page 121.

Editing changes are made to the file stored in the library's DATA folder for this reference, and not to the original image file that was inserted.

NOTE: Never rename image files within the DATA folder. EndNote assigns each image a unique name that helps link it to a specific reference.

Deleting or Replacing Image Files

To delete an image from an EndNote reference:

1. Open the EndNote reference, scroll to the Image field, and select the image icon.

2. Press the Delete key.

Deleting an image from the reference also deletes it from the DATA folder.

NOTE: If you insert the same image in two different references, EndNote stores two copies of the image in the DATA folder. Deleting the image from one of the references will not affect the other reference.

To replace an image in an EndNote reference, you can do one of these:

♦ Open the EndNote reference and *Insert* the new image. The existing image is deleted from the DATA folder and is replaced with the new image.

♦ Delete the old image from the reference, and then *Insert* the new image.

Spell Checking

To begin using EndNote's spell checker, you must have an open record as the active window. If the active window does not display an open record, the spell check command is disabled.

If text is highlighted in the active record, that selection is checked first, and then you are prompted to check the rest of the record. If there are other open records, you are then prompted to check those records.

EndNote's spell checker can check spelling accuracy in all fields except the Author fields (Author, Secondary Author, Tertiary Author, and Subsidiary Author) and the URL field.

Starting Spell Check

To start spell checking:

1. Open the record(s) you wish to check.

2. (optional) If you want to check only a portion of the text, highlight only that text.

3. From the *Tools* menu, select *Spell Check*.

NOTE: These are other ways to start spell checking: Click the Spell Check toolbar button or press Control, click the mouse, and select *Spell Check* from the contextual menu.

---

4. If EndNote finds a word that is not found in the selected dictionaries, it displays a Check Spelling dialog.

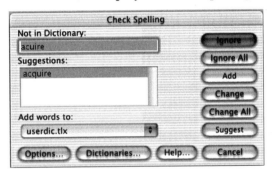

The Check Spelling dialog works just like a spell checker in a word processor. For a complete description of each button on the Check Spelling dialog, click the *Help* button.

Spell Check Options and Dictionaries

You can access Spell Check Options and Dictionaries in two ways:

♦ From the *EndNote* menu, select *Preferences*. At the bottom of the left column, click on *Spell Check*. An *Options* button and a *Dictionaries* button appear.

♦ Start Spell Check. When EndNote detects a misspelled word, the Spell Check dialog appears. An *Options* button and a *Dictionaries* button are available on the dialog.

For information about the Spell Check Options and Dictionaries preferences, including a list of dictionaries supplied with EndNote, see "Spell Check" on page 488.

Chapter 6

Searching Remote Databases with EndNote

Chapter 6   **Searching Remote Databases with EndNote**

Introduction to Searching Online Databases

Using EndNote's *Connect* and *Search* commands, you can search online bibliographic databases just as easily as you can search an EndNote library on your own computer! And to make it even easier, the results of your searches appear as EndNote references—ready for you to store in your own EndNote library.

How Does It Work?

EndNote is able to provide access to these remote sources using an information retrieval protocol called "**Z39.50**." Z39.50 is widely supported by libraries and information providers around the world as a convenient method to access their library catalogs and reference databases.

EndNote stores the information necessary to connect to and search these online databases in individual **connection files**. Pre-configured connection files are provided for a number of these sources. If necessary, you can also customize or configure your own connections to Z39.50-compliant databases (see Chapter 17).

NOTE: If the online database that you access is not available on a Z39.50 server, EndNote will not be able to connect directly to it. We suggest that you submit a request for Z39.50 compatibility to your librarian or the institution that provides access to the database. You can still import references downloaded from non-Z39.50 databases. See Chapter 7 for instructions.

What EndNote's Searching Offers

EndNote's search interface provides a simple way to do basic searches on EndNote libraries and remote databases. The same Search window is used for both purposes. This removes the need to learn a separate program to access the online databases or go through the extra steps of saving the references to a text file and importing them into EndNote.

This search interface is not intended to replace the advanced search options that may be available using the search interface offered by your information provider. There may be times when you want to use the information provider's search interface (for example, to take advantage of a thesaurus of search terms) and then import those references into EndNote. This is still an option using EndNote's *Import* command (see Chapter 7). But once you know the terms that you want to use in your searches, being able to retrieve the necessary references directly from EndNote is a very fast and efficient approach.

Quick Overview

The process of searching a remote database is very similar to searching an EndNote library. Here are the basic steps involved, more detailed descriptions of these steps are provided throughout this chapter. Also see page 67 (in the Guided Tour chapter) for a detailed demonstration of how to use this feature.

To retrieve references from a remote database:

1. From the *Tools* menu choose *Connect* and select the *Connect* command from the submenu.

2. Select the database that you would like to search, and click *Connect*.

   When the connection has been established, an empty Retrieved References window opens and EndNote's Search window appears, ready for you to enter a search.

3. Enter your search request into EndNote's Search window, and click *Search*.

4. EndNote searches the database and displays the number of references that were found to match your search criteria. Click *OK* to retrieve the references.

5. Once the references appear in the Retrieved References window, you may browse through them and transfer to your EndNote library the ones that you want to keep.

Selecting a Connection File

Before a remote source may be searched, you must first connect to it by selecting the corresponding **connection file**. The connection file tells EndNote which online database you want to search, where to find it online, and what search options are available for it.

Access-Restricted Databases

EndNote comes with pre-configured connection files to free reference databases and library catalogs as well as databases that require payment and/or authentication for access. Most of the databases offered by the commercial information providers (Ovid, OCLC, DIMDI, SilverPlatter, etc.) require an account for access. There are, however, numerous databases that are available at no cost to you, and no account is required (see "Free Databases" on page 130).

NOTE: To gain access to a restricted database, you will need to contact the information provider directly to set up an account. ISI ResearchSoft does not control access to any of the sources.

When you attempt to connect to a restricted database, by default EndNote prompts you to enter your user ID and/or password. If you have a user ID and/or password supplied by the data provider that hosts the restricted database, simply enter the necessary information, and click *OK* to log on. (Depending on the database you are accessing, the passwords and IDs may be case-sensitive.)

If you do not have a user ID and/or password, but instead have authenticated access to a database either by IP address recognition (for example, your computer is on your university campus or company network and has an IP address that is recognized as authenticated by the data provider's server) or through a proxy server, it may be possible to configure the connection file and your Network Preferences so that you do not need to enter a user ID and password.

If you have access to a restricted database by IP address recognition, you may need to edit the connection file so that it does not prompt you for a user ID and/or password. In EndNote, select *Edit>Connection Files>Open Connection Manager*. Locate the connection file for the database you wish to access, select it, and click *Edit*. Click on *Connection Settings* and uncheck the User ID and Password boxes under "Login Information Required." Select *Save* from the *File* menu to save your changes, and then close the connection file.

If you have access to a restricted database via a proxy server, you must make sure that your Network Preferences are properly configured, because EndNote uses these settings. Enter the address and port number of your proxy server under the System Preferences/Network/Proxies tab. (See "Troubleshooting Connections" on page 522 for information about proxy servers.)

Free Databases

Two major databases that do **not** require passwords are the PubMed database from the National Library of Medicine, and the Library of Congress. Many of the general library catalogs are also unrestricted. Additional connections may be available at the EndNote Web site (http://www.endnote.com/support/enconnections.asp).

Databases Not Requiring an Account

Description	Information Provider/Category
PubMed (MEDLINE and pre-MEDLINE) references from the National Library of Medicine	NLM
Most university library catalogs	Library Catalogs
Books at the Library of Congress	Library of Congress

Picking Your Favorite Connection Files

EndNote provides hundreds of connection files for a variety of sources. To peruse the list of available connection files in EndNote's Connections folder, choose *Connection Files* from the *Edit* menu, and select *Open Connection Manager*.

Click column headings to sort the list.

Click to search for files.

Click to display details about the selected file.

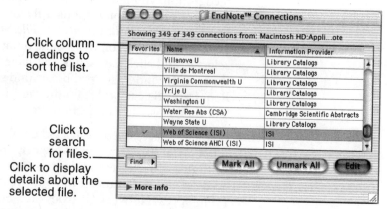

When you have found a connection file that you'll want to use in the future, click in the Favorites column next to it to mark it as a favorite.

All marked files appear in a submenu of the *Connect* command, giving you easy access to those files you use most often.

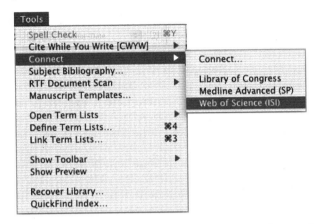

This step is not required; you can always choose the *Connect* command to pick a connection file that is not listed in the menu.

Use the following features in the Connection Manager window to locate the connection file(s) that you want to use:

♦ Click *Find* and EndNote displays the list of information providers (categories) used for all of the connection files. Choose one to restrict the list to show just that set of files. That will help you to find the one you want, or choose *Mark All* to mark the entire subset.

♦ Click the *Find* button, and choose *by Name* to search for a connection file by the name of the database.

♦ Click the column headings to sort the connection files by name or by information provider. Clicking the same column heading a second time will change the sort order from ascending to descending. Click again to set it back to ascending order.

♦ If you know the name of the connection file that you want to use, you may start typing it and the first file that matches what you type will be selected.

♦ Click the *More Info* triangle button at the bottom of the dialog to display additional information about the selected connection file.

NOTE: For information about editing connection files or creating new ones, see Chapter 17.

What if Your Database Isn't Listed?

If a connection file hasn't been provided for the database that you want to search, contact your librarian or information provider to see if their database is available on a Z39.50 server. If it is, you should request the information required to set up a Z39.50 client for that database. See "Steps to Create a New Connection File" on page 466 for more information.

Adding Connection Files

The Connection Manager displays all of the connection files in the selected connections folder. If you have received a connection file from a colleague or librarian or downloaded one from the Web, simply copy it into your Connections folder in your EndNote folder, and it will appear in the Connection Manager.

If necessary, you can designate a different Connections folder:

1. Choose *Preferences* from the *EndNote* menu, and select the *Folder Locations* option.

2. In the "Connection Folder" section, click *Select Folder* and select the folder that contains the connection files that you want to use.

3. With the folder open and selected, click *Choose*.

4. Click *Save* and close the Preferences window.

NOTE: New and updated connection files are posted on the EndNote website (http://www.endnote.com) as they become available.

Searching a Remote Database

The first step to searching a remote database is to connect to it. Once the connection has been made, you're able to use EndNote's Search window to search the remote database.

Establishing the Connection

If you have connected to a particular database before, or if you have selected a database as one of your "favorites" (see page 130) it will appear in the submenu of the *Connect* command. This saves you a few steps in the process of using the *Connect* command.

To connect to a remote database:

♦ From the *Tools* menu, choose *Connect* and then select the desired database if it is listed there. That will start the connection.

♦ If the database you want to search is not listed with the *Connect* command, choose *Tools>Connect>Connect*, select the desired database, and click *Connect* to make the connection.

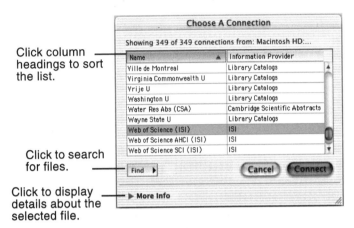

Click column headings to sort the list.

Click to search for files.

Click to display details about the selected file.

(This Connection dialog is very similar to the Connection Manager described on page 130, but it does not provide the options to edit connection files or mark them as favorites.)

When a successful connection has been made, the Retrieved References window appears and the Search window is automatically opened with the "Search Remote" setting selected. You are now ready to begin searching the database.

The connection to the remote database is maintained until you close the Retrieved References window or, after a period of inactivity, the connection automatically times out. If you are using a dial-up Internet connection (with a modem), EndNote does not disconnect you after it closes a connection to a remote database.

NOTE: If you have any difficulty establishing a connection, see "Troubleshooting Connections" on page 522.

Remote Database Searching (Overview)

Searching a remote database is essentially the same as searching your own EndNote library. After establishing a connection:

1. Enter your search term(s) into EndNote's Search window.
2. Choose the appropriate search options.
3. Click *Search* to send the search request to the remote database.

A few significant differences between searching a remote database and an EndNote library are described in this section. See "Searching for References" on page 176 for general information about using the Search window.

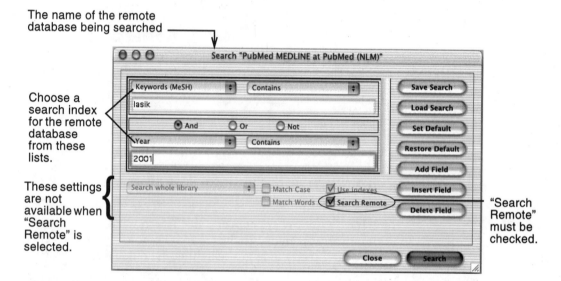

The name of the remote database being searched

Choose a search index for the remote database from these lists.

These settings are not available when "Search Remote" is selected.

"Search Remote" must be checked.

The Search Remote Option

The "Search Remote" checkbox must be selected in order to submit a search to the remote database. Turn this option off to search only the references that are in the Retrieved References window, instead of searching the entire remote database.

If you change the focus of your search from a remote database to an EndNote library (by clicking on a Library window, or by closing the Retrieved References window), this "Search Remote" option is automatically dimmed because it does not apply to an EndNote library. If you then switch back to have the Retrieved References window as the focus of a search, the "Search Remote" option will be available again.

Available Search Options

Once you are connected to a remote database and the "Search Remote" option is selected, certain elements in the Search window change from the settings that are available for EndNote library searches.

- The search options menu at the bottom of the window is dimmed when searching a remote source. You are always set up to search the entire remote database whenever "Search Remote" is chosen.

- The Match Case, Match Words, Use Indexes, and Set Default options are unavailable for remote database searches.

- The options available in the search menus (such as *Author, Title,* or *Keywords*) vary with each database and they are not the same as searching the fields in an EndNote library (see "Searching EndNote Fields vs. Remote Database Indexes" on page 137).

- The comparison list for each search item is always set to *Contains.*

Boolean Searches

Multiple search terms can be combined using the boolean operators And, Or, and Not. EndNote constructs a search from the top to the bottom of the search window, finding the search results of the first two items, then combining that result set with the third search item, and so on.

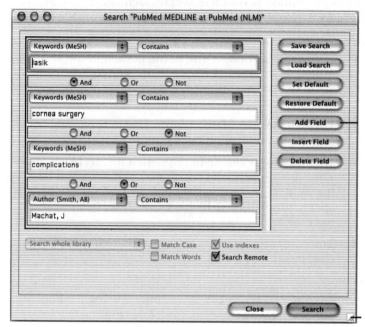

Click *Add Field* to append a new search item to the list.

Click and drag the corner to view more search items at one time.

For example, the search shown above could be written as:

```
(((lasik AND cornea surgery) NOT complications)
OR Machat, J)
```

First EndNote looks for references about LASIK and cornea surgery, then any references about complications would be omitted from that set, and finally all references by "J. Machat" would be added.

Keep in mind that "OR" broadens your search by adding together two result sets; "AND" narrows the focus of the search by looking for the intersection of references found; "NOT" also narrows the search by omitting the results for one term from the current result set. See Chapter 8 for more information about the *Search* command.

Searching EndNote Fields vs. Remote Database Indexes

When searching a remote database, you are *not* searching the specific fields in each record, but rather the available search indexes for that database. The search menus in EndNote's Search window list only available indexes for the remote database, so you won't see all of the generic EndNote field names listed as you do when searching an EndNote library.

The connection file for a particular database stores the names and settings for the search options listed in the search menus. See "Search Attributes" on page 463 if you are interested in changing the pre-configured options.

Understanding Search Results

When searching a remote database, the search menus display a list of available search *indexes* supported at the remote site. These are not *fields* in the remote database, but rather sets of search terms and synonyms designed to facilitate your searches.

It is not uncommon to search for a term in an index and notice that the exact term appears nowhere in the retrieved reference(s). For example, you might search for "heart attack" in the Title index of a medical database and find references that do not include "heart attack" in the Title field but, instead, they use the term "myocardial infarction." This apparent discrepancy can be attributed to the search index of the remote database, which has mapped the common term "heart attack" to its scientific equivalent "myocardial infarction."

It is also not uncommon for some of these databases to index personal names that appear in the titles or keywords along with the author names. For example, a search of the Library of Congress for "Charles Dickens" in the Author index displays books *about* Dickens as well as those written by him. This form of indexing is most commonly seen with library book catalogs and not with the scientific reference databases. Sometimes you can restrict the searches to books *by* that particular author by setting up a search to find (for example) "Charles Dickens" in Author, NOT "Charles Dickens" in Keywords.

These search indexes are maintained by the providers of the databases and are not controlled by EndNote.

Remote Database Search Limitations

Some of the search options have additional limitations that you wouldn't encounter when searching an EndNote library. For example, some databases prohibit searching for a year alone. The year can be specified only to limit a search (these are called "limit fields"). In such a case, a search for 1997 as the year would be denied, but searching for Smith as an author *AND* 1997 as the year (thereby limiting the results of the author search), would be allowed.

If you have set up a search that is not accepted by the remote database, an error message will describe the source of the problem as specifically as possible. (See "Troubleshooting Connections" on page 522.) Keep in mind that these restrictions are set by the information provider, not EndNote.

Documentation from the information provider may help to clarify what search options are available.

Changing the Focus of the Search

The target of the search is the remote database (represented by the Retrieved References window) or EndNote library that is active (forward-most) when the *Search* command is chosen. (If you haven't yet connected to the remote database or opened a library, you will need to do so before you can search it.) To change the focus of a search from one currently open database to another, choose the desired source from the *Window* menu or click on its window, and then choose the *Search* command (⌘+F) from the *References* menu.

The available search options differ among the various remote databases, as well as between remote databases and EndNote libraries. When you change the target of a search, the options in the Search window change automatically. As a result, it is possible to set up a search for a particular remote database that is *not* supported when searching an EndNote library, the retrieved references, or a different remote database.

If a previously selected option in the search menus is not available for the new target, it appears italicized in the search menu to show that it is not a valid option.

When switching the focus of your search from one source to another and back again, the original search setup is retained as long as you haven't changed any settings in the Search window.

Running Multiple Searches

If references are in the process of being retrieved when you submit another search to the *same* remote database, the new search cancels the retrieval of the previous search. However, simultaneous searches of *different* remote sources do not interrupt each other's search and retrieval.

Retrieving and Saving References

After a successful search, EndNote alerts you to the number of references that were found. You have the option of retrieving all of the references or a specific range of references. (The order of the retrieved references reflects the way they were returned from the server—this is not necessarily alphabetical, chronological, or in order of relevance.)

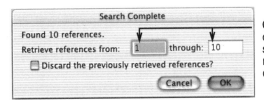

Change one or both of these numbers to specify the range of references to be downloaded.

Choosing *OK* brings the Retrieved References window forward and EndNote begins to retrieve references into it.

Changing the range of references to be retrieved is useful if you want to check the results of your search before downloading the entire set of references. For example, if your search found 50 references, you may want to retrieve only references 1-10, then check those references, and either continue downloading or change your search criteria. To continue downloading, submit the search again, then request only references 11 through 50. You can also use the *Pause* button at the top of the Retrieved References window to halt the retrieval. Click *Resume* if you want to continue.

If you discovered that you should refine your search to get better results, it's helpful to look at the keywords of the references you have downloaded to see if there are terms there to help you refine your search strategy.

If references have already been downloaded into the Retrieved References window, this dialog (shown above) gives you the option of deleting them with the "Discard the previously retrieved references?" checkbox. Choosing that option deletes all of the references in the Retrieved References window (whether they are "showing" or not). Newly retrieved references are appended to the references already showing in the Retrieved References window.

The Retrieved References Window

References downloaded from a remote database are displayed in a temporary holding place called the Retrieved References window. When you connect to multiple remote databases, each one is represented by its own Retrieved References window.

Use the Retrieved References window to browse through the references you have found. Open the references to review their contents just as you would for a reference in an EndNote library: by double-clicking, or selecting the reference(s) and choosing *Edit* from the *References* menu, or pressing RETURN. Use the *Search, Sort,* and *Show/Hide Selected References* commands to help you review the search results. The preview pane can also be used to preview a formatted version of the selected references. You can even use the *Change Field* command to add a comment to the retrieved references. (See Chapter 8, "Managing References" for information about these database commands.)

Retrieved references that you want to keep should be transferred to a new or existing library as described on page 142.

Features of the Retrieved References window

♦ The window's title bar displays the name of the remote database to which you are connected.

♦ The **message area** at the top of the window shows the progress of the reference retrieval or the number of references currently displayed.

♦ The *Pause* button lets you pause or resume the reference retrieval. Pressing the Escape (ESC) key or ⌘+PERIOD also stops retrieval.

♦ As with a normal EndNote Library window, the center region contains the (retrieved) references.

♦ An animated logo at the top of the window indicates exchange of information with the remote database.

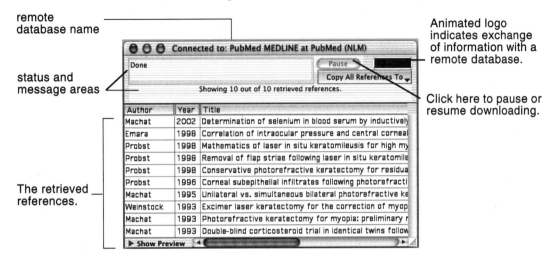

remote database name

Animated logo indicates exchange of information with a remote database.

status and message areas

The retrieved references.

Click here to pause or resume downloading.

Differences Between the Retrieved References Window and a Library

Although a Retrieved References window mimics many of the features of an EndNote Library window, it is **not** a place where you permanently store references. Consequently, features such as the QuickFind index, term lists, and the ability to add references are not available when working with references in the Retrieved References window.

Retrieved references are not assigned record numbers until you save them into an EndNote library. As a result, you cannot cite references from this window in a paper—they must be saved to an EndNote library first.

Term lists are specific to individual EndNote libraries, therefore term lists (and their auto-completion and auto-update features) are not available for references in the Retrieved References window. However, when you transfer references to a library, the new terms are added to that library's term lists (as long as the auto-update preference has not been turned off).

Saving References to a Library

The Retrieved References window is a temporary holding bin for the results of a remote search. They need to be transferred to the library of your choice using any one of the following methods:

♦ If the destination library is open, you can drag-and-drop selected references from the Retrieved References window to the destination library. Select the desired references, then click on any part of the selection, keep the mouse button pressed, and drag the selection to another Library window. The selected references will be copied to that library.

♦ Select the references that you want to save, and click the *Copy References To* menu at the top of the window. Choose the option to copy them to any currently open library (names of open libraries are listed in the menu), to a new library, or to an existing library that is not already open. If no references are selected, all of the references are transferred. Pressing the OPTION key changes the *Copy References To* option from copying the selection to copying all showing references.

♦ Selected references may be copied by choosing *Copy* from the *Edit* menu, and then pasted into another library by opening the desired library and choosing *Paste* from the *Edit* menu.

NOTE: EndNote does not check for duplicates when you use any of the methods above. If you transfer your references from the Retrieved References window to a temporary library, you can use the *Import* command to import that library into your main library and check for duplicates in the process. See Chapter 7 for details. You may also use the *Find Duplicates* command in the *References* menu.

NOTE: Each library can reach a record number limit of 32,767 or a maximum size of 32 MB (whichever comes first). Once a record number is assigned, it cannot be used again in that library. So, if you import 30,000 records, then delete all but 1000 of them, you cannot enter more than another 1000 records into that particular library. When importing records, we recommend that you import into a temporary new library, determine which ones you want to keep, then move those records into your permanent library.

The Connection Status Window

The Connection Status window provides detailed information about a connection and EndNote's interactions with the remote database and server. This window is useful to help you or to help EndNote Technical Support assist you in tracking down the source of a problem with a remote database.

View the connection status information by choosing *Show Connection Status* from the *Window* menu to display the Status window. When that window is open, this command changes to *Hide Connection Status*, which closes the Status window.

The Status window displays information for all of the current connections. A menu at the top of the Status window lets you view either the record data for each reference or the status messages returned from the server of the remote database.

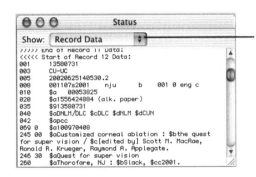

Click to change the view between Record Data and Status Messages.

The data shown here is in MARC format. This format is described on page 443.

NOTE: The Connection Status window displays the last 32K of text written to the log file. If you need to see more than that, you can open the Connect.log file in a word processor after closing the Retrieved Reference window(s).

The Log File

All messages and retrieved references for a given EndNote session are recorded in EndNote's log file. By default, the log file is called "Connect.log" and is saved in the same folder as the EndNote program. An existing log file is overwritten the first time EndNote establishes a connection after being started.

You may choose a different name and / or location for the log file using the Online settings in the Preferences window. To do so, choose *Preferences* from the *EndNote* menu and select the *Online* option from the list. Click *Choose* in the "Connection Log" section to name the new log file and choose where to save it.

You may also choose not to create a log file by unchecking the "Use Log File" option. This will slightly speed up the retrieval process. However, without a log file you will not be able to scroll back through the record data or status messages after you change the *View* setting in the Connection Status window.

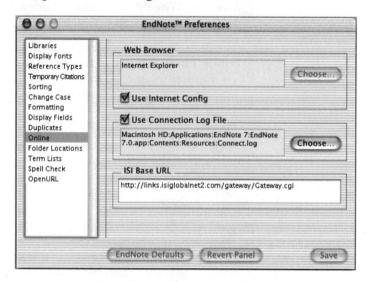

Importing a Log File

The log file is just a regular text file. It can be viewed using a word processor and even imported, if necessary, using the connection file. In this sense, you can think of the log file as a back up for the references that you have retrieved in a particular EndNote session. You can verify that EndNote retrieved the reference data correctly by browsing through the log file in your word processor and comparing the unmodified data to what came through in your EndNote references. If necessary, you can change the filter settings in your connection file and re-import the references (without re-connecting to the remote database).

To import a log file using the filter options of a connection file:

1. Open a library into which you want to import the log file.
2. Choose *Import* from the *File* menu.
3. Click *Choose File* and select "Connect.log." (Substitute the name of your log file if you have changed the default name.)
4. Choose *Use Connection File* from the *Import Options* list in the Import dialog
5. Select the desired connection file and click *Choose*.
6. Now you should be back in the Import dialog with both the file and the import option set. Click *Import*.

NOTE: The connection file and filter file for the same database are most likely configured to import very different reference formats. Normally a connection file is configured for MARC data, whereas a filter is set up for tagged data. Because the output formats are so different, you should not use a filter file to import a log file from the same database—instead, choose the connection file as the import option.

Searching the ISI *Web of Science*

The ISI *Web of Science* is the Web interface for access to the ISI Citation Databases, which cover over 8,000 international journals in the sciences, social sciences, and the arts and humanities. Through ISI Links, the *Web of Science* also offers navigation to electronic full-text journal articles, genetic information, and chemical and patent databases.

Search the *Web of Science* just as you would search any other remote database. Your search results are copied directly to the EndNote library of your choice.

Once the records are in EndNote, you can click on an EndNote record's URL to jump back to the original *Web of Science* online record. Various options are available to you online, such as viewing a list of related references.

Full Record Charges

Web of Science requires a paid subscription. You may have an online subscription with username and password, or you may have access to a local *Web of Science* server.

Users of Previous Versions of EndNote

If you used a previous version of EndNote, many of your preferences were saved when you upgraded to EndNote 7. However, if you want the ability to link back to *Web of Science* records, you must update the Base URL. From the *EndNote* menu, select *Preferences*. Then select *Online*, and click the *EndNote Defaults* button to update to the latest Base URL.

Locally Mounted *Web of Science* Servers

You must use *Web of Science* version 4.3.2 or later. To access your local *Web of Science* server, first contact your network administrator for the server address (URL) plus the path to your institution's copy of the ISI Gateway V2.5 software.

To search a locally mounted Web of Science server, you must open the appropriate Web of Science connection file, click on

Connection Settings, and update the Server Address and Custom fields with your local server address and ISI Gateway software path.

To link back to Web of Science records once they are in EndNote, you must change the Base URL to your local server address. From the *EndNote* menu, select *Preferences.* Then select *Online,* and enter your local server address as the Base URL.

Chapter 7

Importing Reference
Data into EndNote

Importing Reference Data into EndNote

Retrieving References Directly from Online Databases

If you have access to a library catalog or bibliographic database that supports the Z39.50 protocol, you can use EndNote as a tool to search and retrieve references directly from that database into EndNote. You do not need to use EndNote's *Import* command at all; you use the *Connect* command instead. This is by far the easiest way to get data into EndNote because it involves no intermediate steps. The direct retrieval of references is not covered in this chapter. See Chapter 6 for information.

There are many sources of bibliographic data that can be used to help you create your EndNote library. To avoid re-typing this data into EndNote, we have provided several means by which you can get references into EndNote:

♦ Import references saved or downloaded from CD-ROMs or online data services (for example, Ovid, SilverPlatter, or ISI)

♦ Import text files that conform to a particular format (such as the Tab-delimited or EndNote Import format). These files can be created by you or generated from other databases.

♦ Import text files exported from other bibliographic software programs

Once you have a file in the proper format and you know which import option or filter to use, the import instructions are the same for all of these types of data. This chapter covers the basic import instructions first, and then goes into detail about how to get your data files in the right format and choose the correct import option.

NOTE: Although we try to provide many flexible ways to get data from other sources into EndNote, we do not claim that EndNote can import data from all sources. In some cases, you may have to write your own import filter (see Chapter 16), or you may need to manipulate the data in a word processor before it can be imported. If none of these tools helps you to import your data, tips on how to quickly copy and paste data into EndNote are described on page 170.

NOTE: Each library can reach a record number limit of 32,767 or a maximum size of 32 MB (whichever comes first). Once a record number is assigned, it cannot be used again in that library. So, if you import 30,000 records, then delete all but 1000 of them, you cannot enter more than another 1000 records into that particular library. When importing records, we recommend that you import into a temporary new library, determine which ones you want to keep, then move those records into your permanent library.

General Importing Instructions

To import a text file or an EndNote library into an EndNote library:

1. Open the library into which you want to import the references.

2. From the *File* menu, choose *Import*.

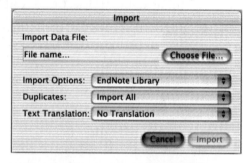

3. Click the *Choose File* button to locate and open the file you want to import. All files, except for EndNote libraries, must be plaintext files. Select the file and click *OK*.

4. Select the appropriate import option from the *Import Options* list. Import options are described on page 151.

5. Select an option from the *Duplicates* list:

   ◆ *Import All*
   Imports all references, including duplicates.

   ◆ *Discard Duplicates*
   Imports all references except duplicates.

   ◆ *Import into Duplicates Library*
   Duplicate references are imported into a library called File-Dupl, where "File" is the name of the library into which you are importing.

By default, a reference is considered a duplicate when the Author, Year, Title, and Reference Type match a reference already in the library. See page 484 if you would like to change the duplicates criteria.

6. Choose a *Text Translation* option if necessary.
This option allows you to specify the text encoding of the file you import.Choose *No Translation* for text files created on a Macintosh or if a Macintosh text option was used by the source from which you downloaded the data. Choose *Latin-1* for text created on a computer other than the Macintosh, including Windows and UNIX. The *ANSEL* option should be used only for MARC format files. If you do not know the encoding of the file, try *No Translation* first, then try *Latin-1* if diacritical characters are not imported correctly.

7. Click *Import* to import the file.

When the import is complete, only newly imported references display in the Library window. This is a perfect time to add a keyword to each imported reference with the *Change Field* command (page 195), or to peruse the imported data to make sure it imported as expected.

To return all of your references to the library display (including the newly imported ones), choose *Show All* from the *References* menu.

NOTE: When you import an EndNote library, images are not included. References that contain images do remember the link to the image field. After importing, you can copy image files from the original library's DATA folder to the destination library's DATA folder so the images will link and appear correctly in the destination library. See "Storing and Sharing Image Files" on page 121 for more information about the DATA folder.

Import Options

EndNote's import options include:

♦ **EndNote Library**
Used to import one EndNote library into another.

♦ **EndNote Import**
Used to import text files that have been downloaded from online databases or exported from EndNote using the EndNote format. See page 167 for more information.

♦ **Refer/BibIX**
Used to import text files exported from the Refer or BibIX

programs. The EndNote import format is based on the Refer/BibIX format.

♦ **ProCite**
Used to import text files that have been exported from ProCite (Macintosh or Windows) in the default comma and quote delimited format.

♦ **Tab-Delimited**
Used to import text files in which the fields within a single reference are separated by tabs. For details see page 162.

♦ **Reference Manager (RIS)**
Used to import text files exported from Reference Manager, Reference Update, Reference Web Poster, or any other source that uses the RIS format.

♦ **ISI-CE**
Used to import text files downloaded from the ISI *Web of Science* and other ISI sources.

NOTE: See "Searching the ISI Web of Science" on page 145 for information about directly retrieving *Web of Science* records.

♦ **EndNote Generated XML**
Used to import EndNote's proprietary XML format.

♦ **Multi-Filter (Special)**
A special option for importing files that include references from multiple sources (see "Identifiers" on page 435).

♦ **Various import filters**
EndNote includes hundreds of import filters configured to import data from a variety of online databases. Most likely, the first time you import a file, you won't see the import filter that you need in this list. Choose *Other Filters* from the *Import Options* list to find the filter that matches the source of the data you want to import. Import filters that you have recently used or chosen as your favorites will be listed in the Import Options list in the Import dialog.

The table on page 156 provides more information about the download formats that work with these filters. See page 154 for information about how to choose the filters to appear in the *Import Options* list.

♦ **Use Connection File**
EndNote provides the option of using a connection file as an import filter. This is useful if you need to import the Connect.log file generated by using EndNote's *Connect* command to search a remote database. The Connect.log file

should include all of the references from your previous session. See Chapter 6 for more information.

NOTE: See Chapter 16 for information about creating and modifying import filters. All of the import filters (except EndNote Generated XML) can be modified.

Importing References Downloaded from CD-ROMs and Online Databases

If you have access to an online bibliographic database, a university catalog, or a bibliographic database on CD-ROM, you can probably use EndNote's import filters to import text files saved or downloaded from these sources. EndNote filters are configurable so they give you the flexibility to import the reference data you need, and eliminate data you do not need.

There are two main things you need to know in order to correctly import downloaded references into EndNote:

◆ How to download the data in the right output format.

◆ Which import filter to use to import the data into EndNote.

This section describes these two items. The table on page 156 summarizes a number of common sources of bibliographic data, the instructions for downloading tagged files, and the EndNote import option to use to import the references into EndNote.

Getting Data in the Right Format

To import text with any of the EndNote filters, the data must be consistently "tagged," with each tag starting on a new line, and the file saved as a plain text file. Here are two examples:

```
AU- CRAMER, -Z.O.
TI- AQUATIC MACROPHYTES AND LAKE ACIDIFICATION
PY- 1993
SO- ENVIRONMENTAL-POLLUTION. VOL. 5, NO. 2, PG.54-79
DE- LAKES, ACIDIFICATION, ENVIRONMENTAL EFFECTS,
    MACROPHYTES, ECOLOGY, PLANT PHYSIOLOGY
```

```
Author:    Cramer, ZO
Title:     Aquatic macrophytes and lake acidification
Year:      1993
Source:    Environmental Air Pollution. Vol. 5(2) pp.54-79
Keywords:  lakes--acidification--environmental effects--
           macrophytes--ecology--plant physiology
```

NOTE: If data is inconsistently tagged, or poorly delimited, it may not be possible to import all the data accurately. See page 415.

Choosing the Correct Import Filter

Once you have captured and saved your data file in the appropriate format, you should identify the proper EndNote filter to import the data. There are hundreds of filters included with EndNote, each designed to read a specific tagged format from a specific information provider.

♦ To see a complete list of available filters, choose *Import Filters* from the *Edit* menu, and select *Open Filter Manager*.

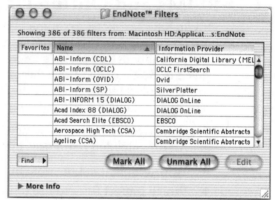

Use the *Find* button in the middle of the Filter Manager window to find all filters for a particular information provider or to search for a filter by name. When you have located the filters that you want to use, mark them as your favorites by clicking in the Favorites column to the left of the filter name. You can also mark all of the filters currently showing after using the *Find* option by clicking *Mark All*. Once a filter is marked as a favorite, it will appear in the Import Options list in the import dialog.

NOTE: There are many more databases and services that provide data than there are filters included with EndNote, so in some cases you may need to write your own filter or modify one of ours. See Chapter 16 for information about creating and modifying filters. You can also check our Web site periodically for new and updated filters (http://www.endnote.com).

Comparing a Filter to a Data File

If you are uncertain whether a filter matches a data file that you have downloaded, you can compare the format from your downloaded data file to a filter. To do so, select a filter in the Filter Manager, and click the *Edit* button. When the Filter window opens, select the *Templates* option in the list at the left of the window to display the tags recognized by that filter.

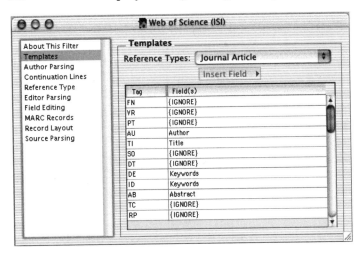

The tags and templates in the filter should match the data in the file you want to import. See Chapter 16 for information about editing filters.

Changing the Filter Folder

By default, all filters provided with EndNote are grouped in the Filter folder in the EndNote folder. These are the filters displayed when you open the Filter Manager.

To access a different set of filters with the Filter Manager:

1. From the *EndNote* menu, choose *Preferences*.

2. Choose *Folder Locations*.

3. In the Filter Folder section, click *Select Folder*.

4. Locate the folder that contains the filters you would like to use, select it, and click *Choose*.

5. Click *Save* to save your changes to the Folder Location preferences, and close the Preferences window.

NOTE: When you select a filter folder, only the filters at the top level of that selected folder are listed in the Filter Manager. Filters in sub-folders (folders within the selected folder) will not appear.

Summary of Output Formats and Corresponding Import Options

A subset of the supported services are listed here with their recommended output formats. At the time this manual was printed, these were the current format options for each information provider listed in the table. If you find that these formats have changed, please check the documentation from your information provider or contact us.

Copyright Issues and Fair Use of Downloaded Data
EndNote gives you the capability to import references downloaded from online databases into its libraries. Some producers of online reference databases expressly prohibit such use and storage of their data, others charge an extra fee for a license to use the data in this way. Before you download references from a database, be sure to carefully check the copyright and fair use notices for the database. Note that different databases may have varying restrictions, even from the same information provider (such as DIALOG or Ovid).

Output Formats and Corresponding Import Options

Information Provider	Recommended Download Format	Import Option
BioMedNet's free Medline service	At the bottom of the results list, click the *Download* button. Choose *EndNote 3.1 or later* as the format, and click *Get All* or *Get Selected Refs*. The References are sent directly to EndNote and you are prompted to pick the library into which you want the references to be imported.	Direct Export - the *EndNote Import* option is chosen automatically. (See page 161.)
California Digital Library Web Site **(formerly MELVYL)**	1. Click the *Display* button to display your references. 2. Click *Download*. 3. Change the "Citation Format" to "Tags Long". 4. Click *Download Now*.	Various filters for California Digital Library (Melvyl) databases are provided in EndNote's Filters folder.

Output Formats and Corresponding Import Options

Information Provider	Recommended Download Format	Import Option
California Digital Library via Telnet **(formerly MELVYL)**	If you are using your communication software's option to capture text, type "DISPLAY ALL TAGS LONG AB CONT" for searches on the database. To send the search results to your e-mail address, type "MAIL ALL TAGS LONG AB TO JOHN_DOE@BERKELEY.EDU". Save references e-mailed to you as a "Plain Text" or "Text Only" file.	Various filters for California Digital Library (Melvyl) databases are provided in EndNote's Filters folder.
Cambridge Scientific Abstracts	From the CSA search results screen, click *Save/Print/Email*. On the "Save/Print/Email" screen, select: Record Format: Full Record Save File Format: Mac Click *Save*. Your Web browser asks where to save the file. If your Web browser lets you save in different file formats, make sure you save as a "Text Only" (*.txt) file.	Various filters for Cambridge Scientific Abstracts databases are provided in EndNote's Filters folder.
CAS SciFinder	Save references in the "Tagged Format" (*.txt).	SciFinder (CAS) filter
Current Contents on Disk (CCOD) - Mac	Save references in "EndNote" format.	EndNote Import
Current Contents on Disk (CCOD) - Windows	Save references in "EndNote" format.	ProCite
DIALOG OnLine	Set your communication software's option to capture text. Use Dialog's Format 5 with "tag" appended to the TYPE command -- type "s1/5/1-20 tag". You must be using the command line mode to obtain Format 5; if in doubt how to do this, contact Dialog's tech support.	Various DIALOG filters are provided in EndNote's Filters folder.
DIMDI	Use the DLOAD command with report D1 (e.g. DLOAD REPORT=D1).	Various DIMDI filters are provided in EndNote's Filters folder.
EBSCOhost	Save results in "Bibliographic Manager format".	Various EBSCO filters are provided in EndNote's Filters folder.

Output Formats and Corresponding Import Options

Information Provider	Recommended Download Format	Import Option
HealthGate - MEDLINE	At the "HealthGate Search Results" screen, select the desired references to download. At the bottom of the screen, choose "Download references for importing into bibliographic management software", then click on the *Retrieve Selected References* button. You will be prompted by your Web browser to save the file to your computer.	MEDLINE (HealthGate) filter
Information Express Alerting Service	Save references in the "EndNote" format.	EndNote Import
INIST	1. Click the *Enregistrer* button. 2. Select the records you wish to download. 3. Under "Quels champs?" choose "Tous les champs." 4. Under "Include" choose "Numéro de notice et nom de la base de données" and "Libellés abrégés." 3. Click the *Sauvegarde de notices* button	Various INIST filters are provided in EndNote's Filters folder.
ISI CD (Citation Indexes)	From the *File* menu, choose *Save Records*. In the Save Records dialog, choose the *NLM Medline* format from the *Export Format* menu.	ISI Citation Indexes filter
ISI *Web of Science*	When viewing your marked references, click *Export* to have the references exported directly to EndNote. (See "Direct Export from Web Pages" on page 161.) You may also choose *Save to File* to save the references to a text file and import them into EndNote.	ISI-CE
Knowledge Finder	Place document in the Save file, and select the document. Choose *Export Selected Documents* from the *File* menu.	Various Knowledge Finder filters are provided in EndNote's Filters folder.
Medscape	After selecting the desired records and adding them to your clipboard, click the *Save or Email Clipboard* link. Save or email your clipboard in PC or Mac MEDLARS format as a plain text (*.txt) file.	MEDLINE (Medscape) filter

Output Formats and Corresponding Import Options

Information Provider	Recommended Download Format	Import Option
NERAC	Save your file as plain text (*.txt).	NERAC
OCLC FirstSearch - Web	Mark those references to be saved and click *Export*. At the next page, choose EndNote and then click *Export*. EndNote will prompt you to select a filter.	Various OCLC filters are provided in EndNote's Filters folder.
Ovid Web	After selecting the references you wish to download, click *Citation Manager*. Choose the following options: Fields: Complete Reference Citation Format: Reprint/Medlars (or Direct Export, if available) Click the *Email* or *Save* button. Save the file as plain text (*.txt).	The appropriate Ovid filter will be selected automatically when using *Direct Export* option. If you are using Ovid's multiple database searching, you must select the *Direct Export* citation format.
Ovid for Windows	Select the *Options* button from within the "Save Documents" dialog box. From the list of options, choose the Output Format, then click *OK*. On the next screen, choose *Reprint Format*.	Various Ovid filters are provided in EndNote's Filters folder.
ProQuest	Use the *E-Mail Article* button to send records to your email account. Then save as "Plain Text."	Use the appropriate ProQuest filter.
PsycINFO at www.apa.org	After marking the records you wish to download, choose *Full PsycINFO Record* then click the *Display Marked Records* button. Select the text, then copy and paste it into a text editor, saving the file it as plain text (*.txt).	Use the PsycINFO (APA) filter.
PubMed	Display your search results in "MEDLINE" format by choosing *MEDLINE* from the popup list between the *Display* and *Save* buttons. Click *Save* to save the references to a text file.	PubMed (NLM) filter

Output Formats and Corresponding Import Options

Information Provider	Recommended Download Format	Import Option
Reference Update v5X	Select *Reference Listings* from the *Output* menu, and choose the following options: Device: ASCII File - No Printer codes (be sure to enter the path and file name for the output file.) Output Format: Medline Click *Print* to create the output file.	ISI Reference Update-Medline filter
SilverPlatter WebSPIRS, Version 5	Once you've obtained your search results, click *Save*. Select the following "Save Records" options: Which fields?: All fields Include: Record number and database name Field labels: Short labels. Click the *Save Records* button. Use your Web browser to save the page as "Text Only" (do not save in HTML format).	Various SilverPlatter filters are provided in EndNote's Filters folder.
STN	Set your communication software's options to capture text to a file. Type the command "Display All".	Various STN filters are provided in EndNote's Filters folder.
UnCover (Ingenta)	Using your e-mail software, save references e-mailed to you as a "Plain Text" or "Text Only" file.	Reveal (Carl UnCover) filter
Wilson	Select the following options Destination: Choose *e-mail* or *save*. Include: Record numbers and full-text links (optional). Format: Choose *text*.	WilsonWeb

Direct Export from Web Pages

Certain Web sites contain a download button that will send your search results directly to EndNote, pick the correct import option, and start the import process automatically. All you need to do is choose the EndNote library into which the data should be imported. This "direct export" or "direct download" method does away with the additional steps of saving the references to a text file, and then importing that file with the appropriate filter. Many online databases, such as Highwire Press, Ovid, OCLC, ProQuest, the ISI *Web of Science*, and more, provide a direct export of references into EndNote.

Creating Structured Text Files that EndNote Can Import

What do you do if your data is *not* in a format that EndNote can automatically import? You can do one of several things (or even a combination these options):

♦ Rearrange the reference data using your word processor so that it is in a format that EndNote can import (as described in this section).

♦ Copy and paste each piece of data from its source into the proper fields in EndNote, as described on page 170.

♦ Enter the data manually by typing it into EndNote as described in Chapter 5.

Creating a file that EndNote can import can be a lot of work if your data is in an arbitrary or inconsistent format. If you only have a few references to import (less than 30 or 40), it might be faster and easier to re-type them or copy and paste the references than to try to put them into a format that EndNote can import.

However, if you have a very large bibliography, it might save time to first manipulate the data in a word processor as best you can, and then import the references into EndNote and clean up the references there. Even if the imported data doesn't come through perfectly, it can be rearranged with EndNote's various commands, drag-and-drop, and copy and paste.

This section describes two different formats that you can put your data into such that it can be imported into EndNote:

♦ A *tab-delimited* format (best if your data is in a database or spreadsheet that can export to a tab-delimited file)

♦ A *tagged* format (best for when your data is in a word processor document and looks like a bibliography)

Creating a Tab-Delimited Format

The *Tab-delimited* import option can import text files in which each reference is separated by a paragraph mark (¶), and the fields within a reference are separated by tabs. Most databases or spreadsheets can export a tab-delimited text file.

Preparing the Data Before Exporting

♦ **Author Names:**
Before you export data from a database or spreadsheet into a text file, we recommend that you separate multiple author names with a semicolon (;) or two forward slashes "//", such as: McCartney, P.//Harrison, G.//Lennon, J. If you cannot easily do this in your database, you can do it after exporting, or manually edit the data after it is in EndNote.

♦ **Reference Types:**
If possible, you should make sure that each of your references includes a field indicating the reference type. Use EndNote's Reference Type names so that EndNote is able to recognize the formats. If you have only one type of reference (such as Journal Articles), it is not necessary to do this—the import settings can indicate that all references should be imported as journals by default.

If you cannot label each reference with the appropriate Reference Type name, you should export your data into separate files based on reference type. This makes it easy to preserve the original reference types of the references when importing the data files into EndNote.

Preparing the Data File for Import

Once the tab-delimited file(s) are generated, you must open each file in a text editor or word processor and add two lines to it. These lines tell EndNote what the default reference type is for the data, and how the data should be interpreted.

First Line: The Default Reference Type

The first line of the file must define the default reference type for the entire file. The format for the first line is an asterisk immediately followed by a valid EndNote reference type, followed by a paragraph mark (¶). For example,

*Journal Article <¶>

If you could not make separate files based on reference type, you can specify each reference type individually within one file. In this case, your first line must be the "*Generic" reference type. Then you can set up an additional column called "Reference

Type," and under it, have the actual EndNote reference type names. For example:

```
*Generic <¶>
Reference Type  <tab>  Author              <tab>  Year  <tab>  Title     <tab>  Secondary Title <¶>
Journal Article <tab>  Jones, J// Smith, S.<tab> 1994  <tab>  Easy Pie  <tab>  J. of Eating     <¶>
Book Section    <tab>  Woo, W. //Lee, L.   <tab>  1995  <tab>  Rain Hats <tab>  J. of Clothing   <¶>
Report          <tab>  Carlos, C.//Luis, R.<tab> 1991  <tab>  Cat Talk  <tab>  J. of Animals    <¶>
```

NOTE: The "<tab>" and "<¶>" characters are used to indicate where an actual tab and paragraph mark should be entered; the literal text "<tab>" and "<¶>" should not be typed.

Second Line: EndNote Field Names

The second line of the tab-delimited file must contain the actual field names used by EndNote into which you want the data imported. The order of the fields names does not matter, as long as they correspond to the order of the data in the rows beneath them and correspond to the names of the default reference type.

For example, if your default reference type is "*Journal Article," then the field names in the second line of your file will be those of the Journal Article reference type:

```
*Journal Article<¶>
Author            <tab>  Year  <tab>  Title     <tab>  Journal        <tab>  Volume <¶>
Jones, J// Shoe, S <tab> 1994  <tab>  Easy Food <tab>  J. of Eating   <tab>  1        <¶>
Woo, W //Lee, L    <tab> 1995  <tab>  Rain Hats <tab>  J. of Clothing <tab>  2        <¶>
Carlos, C//Luis, L <tab> 1991  <tab>  Cat Talk  <tab>  J. of Animals  <tab>  3        <¶>
```

NOTE: The field names must be separated by tabs, and a paragraph mark must follow the last field name.

Additional Considerations

♦ Only ANSI or ASCII text files can be imported. This means no font styles or text styles can be preserved during import.

♦ All field names and reference type names in the file must be identical to those in EndNote. See page 354 for a listing of all of the reference types and field names. If you have custom reference types, you may check them by choosing *Preferences* from the *EndNote* menu, selecting *Reference Types*, and clicking the *Modify Reference Types* button.

♦ Multiple author names should be separated by semicolons (;) or by two forward slashes (/ /).

♦ Fields cannot contain tabs or paragraph marks. Let the lines of data "wrap" to the next line.

- Leading and trailing spaces are removed during importing.

- No upper/lower case conversion is made during importing.

- A reserved field name called "Unused" may be used for data that you do not want imported into EndNote.

Errors While Importing Tab-delimited Files

When you are ready to import this file into EndNote, choose *Import* from the *File* menu, and select *Tab-Delimited* as your import option. See "General Importing Instructions" on page 150 for detailed instructions on importing.

If EndNote cannot import a record or a field within a record, it will alert you to the error. There are three basic alerts:

- Bad Default Reference Type — The default reference type that you specified in the first line of the file is not a valid EndNote reference type name.

- Bad Field Name — A field name that you entered in line 2 of the file is not a valid EndNote field name.

- Missing Reference Type Information — There is no default reference type specified for the file and there is no reference type field defined for the references.

If you get one of these error messages during the import process, open the import file in your word processor, correct the problem, save the file as a text file, and try again.

Creating a Custom "Tagged" Format

If you have a large bibliography that you would like to import into EndNote, it may be possible to use your word processor's *Find* and *Replace* commands to insert descriptive tags in front of some of the fields of data so that EndNote can accurately import the references. In addition to adding tags, you also need to make a filter to read your tags. (See page 167 for information about using a predefined EndNote Import format if you would rather not create your own filter.)

This section outlines the basic steps to convert a bibliography into a tagged text file.

Step I. Save a Copy of Your File

♦ Open your bibliography in a word processor and save a copy of the file with a new name (this is your backup).

♦ Remove everything but the reference data from the file.

Step II. Add Descriptive Field Tags

Use your word processor's *Find* and *Replace* commands to search for unique delimiters between fields, and insert paragraph marks and descriptive field tags in front of specific fields. For this example, we will show a very simple case where only the start of each reference is tagged, and the filter does the rest of the work. This works well for reference lists that have clear delimiters separating the individual components of the reference (author, year, title, etc.). In some cases, you may have better results making additional replacements in the text file before importing. The more tags you add to your data, the greater degree of accuracy you can get with the import filter.

Suppose your references look like this:

```
Jones, M. C. and Harrison, G. (1990) "Planet X"
Icarus. Vol. 3 no. 4, pp. 11-23.

Billoski, T.V. (1990) "Greenhouse hypothesis"
Extinction. Vol 2 no. 1 pp. 12-18.
```

The process of converting this bibliographic format to a tagged format would be something like this:

♦ Search for 2 paragraph marks (since the references are separated by 1 blank line), and replace with two paragraph marks and a tag "XX-" followed by a space.

The result is a tagged data file that looks like this:

```
XX- Jones, M. C. and Harrison, G. (1990) "Planet
X" Icarus. Vol. 3 no. 4, pp. 11-23.

XX- Billoski, T.V. (1990) "Greenhouse
hypothesis" Extinction. Vol. 2 no. 1 pp. 12-18.
```

Once you have made all the changes to tag as much of the data as necessary, save the file (as a plain text file), and create an import filter to match the tags and formats of the references.

Step III: Create a Filter

Using EndNote, create a new filter to read your data file (see Chapter 16 for instructions on how to create a filter). The template of a filter for the above data file would look like this:

Tag	Field(s)
XX-	Author (Year) "Title" Journal. Vol. Volume no. Issue, pp. Pages

Step IV: Clean Up the Data

After you set up your file with tags and create a filter to import it, you should test and refine the filter by importing into a new library. Once your filter is working as you would like it, you can use it to import the data file into your real EndNote library.

If you can't get the filter to import everything exactly as you want, you may have to do some manual editing to correct this either before or after importing the data into EndNote. You might find it useful to import into a test library, then use the *Change and Move Fields* commands in EndNote's *References* menu and the *Change Text* command in EndNote's *Edit* menu to clean up the data. Then, transfer these references to your real library with drag-and-drop, copy and paste, or the *Import* command.

Creating a Tagged "EndNote Import" File

The EndNote Import format is a tagged format based on the rules of Refer/BibIX format. In this format, each field of data (i.e., Journal, Volume, or Title) is preceded by an identifying tag: a percent sign (%) followed by a single capital letter. Entire references are separated by one blank line:

```
%0 Book
%A Geoffrey Chaucer
%D 1957
%T The Works of Geoffrey Chaucer
%E F. N. Robinson
%I Houghton
%C Boston
%N 2nd

%0 Journal Article
%A Herbert H. Clark
%D 1982
%T Hearers and Speech Acts
%B Language
%V 58
%P 332-373

%0 Thesis
%A Cantucci, Elena
%T Permian strata in South-East Asia
%D 1990
%I University of California, Berkeley
%9 Dissertation
```

Author Names in the EndNote Import Format

◆ Author names use the %A tag. This tag should repeat for each author, with the names listed one per line:

```
%A Jones, Mary
%A Simon, Jeff
```

◆ Author names can appear either as:

Geoffrey Chaucer   **or**   Cohen, Sarah

◆ Either initials or full names are accepted.

Defining Reference Types

EndNote has two ways of setting the reference type for each of the imported references.

♦ One method is to specify a reference type by using %0 (zero) and the reference type name.

Using this method, you can precisely specify the reference type, and not rely on the appearance of certain tags, as described below. The default reference types are listed below. If you have created any custom reference types, then your EndNote data files should use those names instead.

%0 Generic	%0 Journal Article
%0 Book	%0 Book Section
%0 Manuscript	%0 Edited Book
%0 Magazine Article	%0 Newspaper Article
%0 Conference Proceedings	%0 Thesis
%0 Report	%0 Personal Communication
%0 Computer Program	%0 Electronic Source
%0 Audiovisual Material	%0 Film or Broadcast
%0 Artwork	%0 Map
%0 Patent	%0 Hearing
%0 Bill	%0 Statute
%0 Case	%0 Figure
%0 Chart or Table	%0 Equation

♦ If you do not state the reference type using the %0 tag in each record, then EndNote uses the following rules to assign reference types to the imported references:

Tags Present in the Reference	Reference Imports As This Reference Type
J and **V**	Journal Article
B	Book Section
R but not **T**	Report
I without **B**, **J**, or **R**	Book
Neither **B**, **J**, **R**, nor **I**	Journal Article

EndNote Tags and Corresponding Fields

The table below shows the tags recognized in the EndNote Import format, and the corresponding EndNote field into which each tagged item is imported.

Tag	EndNote Generic Field Name
%A	Author
%B	Secondary Title (of a Book or Conference Name)
%C	Place Published
%D	Year
%E	Editor / Secondary Author
%F	Label
%I	Publisher
%J	Journal Name
%K	Keywords
%L	Call Number
%M	Accession Number
%N	Number (Issue)
%P	Pages
%S	Tertiary Title
%T	Title
%U	URL
%V	Volume
%X	Abstract
%Y	Tertiary Author / Translator
%Z	Notes
%0	Reference Type
%1	Custom 1
%2	Custom 2
%3	Custom 3
%4	Custom 4
%6	Number of Volumes
%7	Edition
%8	Date
%9	Type of Work
%?	Subsidiary Author
%@	ISBN / ISSN
%!	Short Title
%#	Custom 5
%$	Custom 6

%&	Section
%(	Original Publication
%)	Reprint Edition
%*	Reviewed Item
%+	Author Address
%^	Caption

Copying and Pasting References from a Document into EndNote

If you have a bibliography that is too inconsistent or difficult to parse using your word processor (as suggested in "Creating a Custom "Tagged" Format" on page 164), you can use the *Copy* and *Paste* commands as an alternative method for getting your data into EndNote and still avoid a lot of re-typing. For example, let's say you have a paper with a bibliography entry such as:

```
Blocker, C. E., R. H. Plummer and Richard C.
Richardson. The Two Year College: A Social
Synthesis. 1965.
```

To transfer the references into EndNote:

1. Open the list of references in a word processor.

2. Select a reference and copy it using the *Copy* command in your word processor's *Edit* menu. (Some word processors allow you to triple-click a paragraph to select the whole thing at once. That might be a useful shortcut for quickly selecting a reference.)

3. Open your EndNote library, and choose *New Reference* (⌘+N) from the *References* menu to create a new reference.

4. Put the cursor in the Title field of the new reference and choose *Paste* from the *Edit* menu.

This will paste the entire reference into the Title field of the Reference window. From here, you can drag-and-drop (or cut and paste) the individual pieces of data into their proper fields. Be sure to remove extraneous punctuation, and make sure author names are each on a separate line. Follow the guidelines for entering references in Chapter 5. See page 476 for information about setting a default reference type for new references.

Importing References From Other Bibliographic Software Programs

If you wish to convert references from another bibliographic program into EndNote, consult the chart below for instructions.

Conversion Utilities at the EndNote Web Site

In some cases, you may be directed to download a conversion utility or instructions from the EndNote Web site at:

`http://www.endnote.com`

Follow the "Support and Services" link from the home page to display the EndNote Technical Support page.

If you do not have Internet access, contact EndNote technical support for assistance.

Unsupported Databases

If your program is not on the chart, see page 162 for instructions on setting up a tab-delimited file for importing into EndNote. If your database does not offer a tab-delimited export option, contact technical support for other suggestions.

Software:	Basic Conversion Instructions:
Bookends and Bookends Pro	Export from Bookends or Bookends Pro using the "ProCite" format, and import the resulting file into EndNote using the *ProCite* import option.
BibTex	User-contributed utilities and instructions for converting BibTex files are available from the EndNote Web site at: http://www.endnote.com. Go to the "Support and Services" section and browse the FTP site.
Citation 6 and WordPerfect Citation	Conversion utilities are available from the EndNote Web site. Go to the "Support and Services" section and browse the FTP site for the "citation" folder.
EndNote Library	Use the *EndNote Library* import option in the import dialog. Note that the records from the library being imported will be assigned new record numbers.
NoteBook II Plus and NoteBuilder	Conversion utilities are available from the EndNote Web site. Go to the "Support and Services" section and browse the FTP site for the "notebook" or "notebuilder" folder.
Papyrus 6 and 7	Conversion utilities are available from the EndNote Web site. Go to the "Support and Services" section and browse the FTP site for the "papyrus6" or "papyrus7" folder.
ProCite	For the Macintosh and DOS versions, use the default export settings to export from ProCite. For the Windows version, export from ProCite using the comma-delimited export option. Use EndNote's *ProCite* import option to import the resulting file.
Ref-11	Conversion utilities are available from the EndNote Web site. Go to the "Support and Services" section and browse the FTP site for the "ref11" folder.
Reference Manager	You can export the references in RIS format, and import them using EndNote's *Reference Manager (RIS)* import option.
Refer/BibIX	Use the *Refer/BibIX* import option to import a Refer or BibIX text file.

Chapter 8

Managing References

Chapter 8   Managing References

Showing and Hiding References

When working with references in your EndNote library, you can view all of the references or just a subset. Here is an example of an EndNote library showing only 10 of the 200 references in the library. Notice the words "Showing 10 out of 200 references" at the top of the Library window.

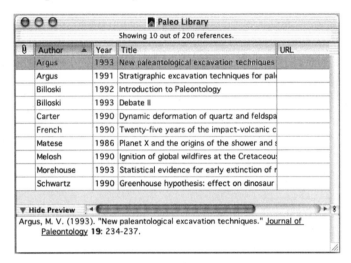

Working with Showing References

Many EndNote commands (such as *Search References, Change Field, Change Text, Sort, Print,* and *Export*) can be instructed to work with just those references that are "showing" in the Library window. Here are a few examples of operations that you can do with the showing references:

♦ Restrict the *Search References* command to search only the showing references.

♦ Add the results of a new search to the currently showing references, as a way to combine search results.

♦ Use the *Change Text,* and *Change Field,* and *Move Field* commands to modify only the showing references.

♦ Use the term lists' *Update List* command to scan only the showing references for new terms.

♦ *Print* or *Export* just the showing references.

One way to view just a subset of references is to use the *Search References* command as described later in this chapter. The *Show Selected References* and *Hide Selected References* commands in the

References menu provide another convenient way for you to control which references are showing in the Library window.

Using Show Selected

Use the *Show Selected References* command to restrict the references showing in the Library window to only the selected references.

To use the *Show Selected References* command:

1. Select the references of interest (hold down the COMMAND (⌘) key and click the references with the mouse, or hold down the SHIFT key to select a range of references).

2. Choose *Show Selected References* from the *References* menu. The references that you had selected will now be the only ones showing in the Library window.

3. After completing the work you need to do with the showing references, choose *References>Show All References* (⌘+M) to display all references in the Library window.

Using Hide Selected

The *Hide Selected References* command is similar to the *Show Selected References* command except that it temporarily hides the selected references in the Library window from view.

To use the *Hide Selected References* command:

1. Select the references that you want to temporarily hide.

2. Choose *Hide Selected References* from the *References* menu.

3. After you have completed your work with the showing references, choose *Show All References* (⌘+M) from the *References* menu to return all of the references to the Library window.

Searching for References

EndNote provides a powerful and flexible *Search References* command that enables you to locate specific references or groups of references. For example, you can choose a very general search, one that scans the entire library, or you can limit your searches to specific fields (such as Author or Keywords). You can also create more complex searches using a variety of operators such as *And, Or, Not, Greater than, Less than,* and others.

You can use the *Search References* command to search EndNote libraries as well as remote databases that are available online. See Chapter 6 for information about remote database searches.

The Search Window

To begin a search, choose *Search References* (⌘+F) from the *References* menu. The **Search window** appears, displaying two empty **search items** (you can add more if needed).

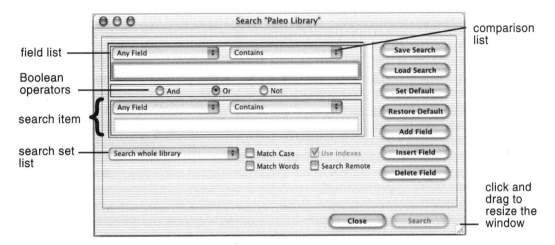

Quick Overview of the Search Window

Functions are described in more detail in the sections that follow.

Search Set List

Use the search set list to specify the set of references to search and how the search results should be combined with other references in the Library window. By default, EndNote searches the entire library and displays only the results of the search.

Search Item and Search Term

A search item includes the field to be searched (from the *Field* list), the comparison operator, and the text to be found (the "search term"). Use the buttons at the bottom of the Search window to add, insert, or delete new search items.

Field List

The field list allows you to restrict your search to a particular field such as Author, Year, or Keywords or all fields. By default, the *Field* lists are set to search *Any Field* (meaning that *all* fields will be searched). See page 182.

Comparison List

Choose an item from the comparison list to indicate how the search term should relate to the field(s) being searched. For example, EndNote can find references in which the Journal field

Contains "science" or it can find references in which the Journal name actually *Is* "science." See page 182.

Boolean Operators

The "And," "Or," and "Not" radio buttons between the search items indicate how the search items are to be combined. By default, these operators are set to "Or." See page 184.

Search Remote

The "Search Remote" option is available when the target of the search is a Retrieved References window for a remote database. This setting lets you switch from searching the entire remote database to the subset of references in the Retrieved References window. See Chapter 6 for more information about remote searches using the *Connect* command.

Match Case

By default, EndNote ignores capitalization when searching for text in a library. For example, a search for the text "paleontology" also finds "Paleontology."

When the "Match Case" option is checked, EndNote finds only those records in which the search term is capitalized exactly as you typed it in the Search window. For example, if your search term is "AIDS" and you select "Match Case", EndNote ignores the word "aids" and finds only the acronym "AIDS."

Match Words

With "Match Words" selected, EndNote finds only exact matches to the search term, rather than partial-word matches. For example, a search for the term "state," with the "Match Words" option selected, finds references with the word "state" while ignoring words like "statehood" or "understated."

Use Indexes

Selecting "Use Indexes" allows EndNote to take advantage of the built-in Author index and optional QuickFind index, resulting in faster searches. See page 189 for more information.

Set Default and Restore Default

Use the *Set Default* button to save the configuration of all of the items in the Search window except for the search terms. Click *Restore Default* at any time to return the window to that configuration. See page 180 for more information.

Save Search and Load Search

If you frequently use the same search or configurations of the Search window, you can save these searches and later load them when you need them. See page 187 for more information.

Search Command Tips

Canceling Searches

Pressing COMMAND-PERIOD (⌘+.) cancels a search in progress.

Matching Partial Words

Unless you have selected the "Match Words" or "Use Indexes" options, EndNote matches partial words when searching for text (both right- and left-truncation are enabled). Consequently, you can search for just the root of a word and find all related terms. This is a good tactic for general subject searches.

Diacritics (Accents)

Diacritical marks can be used in searches. Letters such as é, ü and î match those letters exactly. Thus, a search for "résumé" will not find "resume." See "Entering Special Characters" on page 116 for information about entering diacritics.

Searching with Multiple Libraries Open

The *Search References* command searches one library at a time. If you have more than one library open, only the front-most library will be searched. To avoid confusion, the name of the library to be searched is displayed in the title bar of the Search window.

The Year Field

When searching in the Year field, you can enter just the last two digits of any year in the 20th century and EndNote will find all references published in that year. A search for "94" retrieves all references published in 1994, where as the same search not using indexes retrieves references from the 1940s and 1994.

Finding Empty Fields

EndNote can search for empty fields. Simply choose the desired field from the Field list, and choose *Is* as the comparison operator, and leave the search term blank. Click *Search* and EndNote finds references in which the chosen field is blank.

Cleaning Up Search Results

After executing a search, there may be a handful of references that you want to exclude from the search results. Select those references and choose *Hide Selected References* to hide them from the set of found references and display exactly the references that you want. Often this is much easier than trying to refine your search.

Viewing the Opposite of Your Search Results

Let's say that you have searched for all of the references written by Billoski or Hall, so you are currently viewing only those references. Now, you would like to view the references *not* written by those authors. Instead of doing another search:

1. From the *Edit* menu, choose *Select All* (⌘+A) to select all of the Hall and Billoski references.

2. From the *References* menu, choose *Show All References* (⌘+M) (notice that the original selection is maintained).

3. From the *References* menu, choose *Hide Selected References*.

   You are left viewing only those references that were not previously showing in the Library window, that is, all references *not* written by Hall or Billoski.

Setting and Restoring Defaults for the Search Window

Use the *Set Default* button to save the current configuration of the Search window as your default. The default configuration will appear whenever you first open the Search window.

The layout of the window (such as the number of search items and the shape of the window) is saved, as are all of the operators, field names, and the Match Case and Match Word settings. The search terms are not saved.

Click the *Restore Default* option in the Search window to clear out all of the search terms currently entered in the Search window, and reset all of the settings back to the default configuration.

Simple Searches

To find all references that contain a particular term:

1. From the *References* menu, choose *Search References* (⌘+F).

2. Type the desired text into the first search item. This example uses the word "triceratops" as the search term.

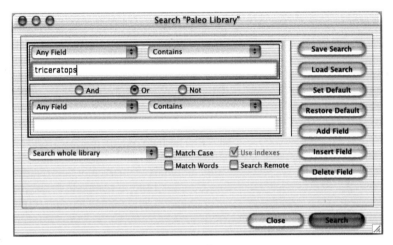

3. Click *Search* to begin the search.

   If no references in the library match your search request, EndNote beeps and displays "No matching references were found." Otherwise, all matching references are displayed in the Library window:

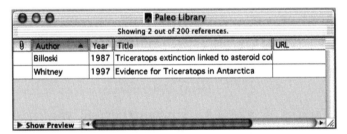

4. When you are finished working with the found references, choose *Show All References* (⌘+M) from the *References* menu to restore all references to view, or choose *Search References* (⌘+F) from the *References* menu to start another search.

NOTE: After completing a search, EndNote displays the same library that you were viewing before the search, however only the references that match your search requests are showing.

Restricting Searches to Specific Fields

By default, the *Search References* command looks for a match for the search term in any of the fields in your references. This is what the phrase "In Any Field" indicates. Use the *Field* list in the Search window to narrow your search by changing *Any Field* to a specific field.

For example, to find references published in 2002, restrict the search to the Year field to avoid finding entries that include "2002" in the abstract, title, or elsewhere.

The search is restricted to the *Year* field.

NOTE: The field names in the *Field* list are EndNote's "Generic" field names. For example, *Author* represents Reporter, Editor, Artist or any other variations of the Author field used in the different reference types. See Chapter 14 for a complete list of Generic field names and their corresponding field names in each reference type.

Using Comparison Operators

Comparison Operators

The "comparison operators" are used to indicate how the search term relates to the chosen field in that search item. For example, if you have a search item that looks like this:

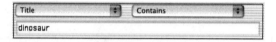

You will be searching for references where the Title (the search field) *contains* (the comparison operator) dinosaur (the search term). The comparison operators function as follows:

- ◆ **Contains:** finds all references where the search field includes the search term.

- ◆ **Is:** finds all references in which the entire content of the search field is exactly the same as the search term.

- ◆ **Is Less Than:** finds all references in which the search term is less than the contents of the search field.

- ◆ **Is Less Than or Equal To:** finds all references in which the search term is less than or identical to the contents of the search field.

- ◆ **Is Greater Than:** finds all references in which the search term is greater than the contents of the search field.

♦ **Is Greater Than or Equal To:** finds all references in which the search term is greater than or identical to the contents of the search field.

For all of the "Greater Than" and "Less Than" comparisons, the comparison is either numerical or alphabetical based on the nature of the term. When the fields have both numbers and letters, numbers are considered "less than" letters, and empty fields are ignored.

NOTE: Comparison operators other than "Contains" cannot be used when searching remote databases.

Examples of Symbols in Searches

Field	Comparison Operator	Search Term	EndNote finds:
Year	Is Greater Than	1990	all references published after 1990.
Year	Is Less Than	1990	all references published before 1990.
Year	Is Greater Than or Equal to	1995	references published during or after 1995
Title	Is Less Than	A	all references where titles start with a number.
Author	Is Less Than or Equal to	C	all references with authors whose last names begin with A, B, C, or a number.
Author	Is Greater Than or Equal to	S	all references with authors whose last names begin with S-Z.
Title	Contains	hawaii	all references with "hawaii" in the title
Title	Is	hawaii	all references with "hawaii" as the exact title
Abstract	Is		all references with no abstract

Combining Search Items with "And," "Or," and "Not"

You can combine search items in EndNote using the Boolean operators "And," "Or," and "Not" to produce the following effects:

And   finds references that match the preceding search item(s) and the following search item. "And" narrows search results.

> **Example:** A search for "triceratops" *And* "extinction" finds only those references that mention both terms.

Or   finds references that match either the preceding search item(s) or following search term. "Or" broadens the search.

> **Example:** A search for "triceratops" *Or* "extinction" finds all references that include either term.

Not   finds all references containing the preceding term(s) and then omits references that contain the subsequent term. "Not" narrows search results.

> **Example:** A search for "triceratops" *Not* "extinction" finds all references including "triceratops," excluding any triceratops references that mentioned extinction.

You can use the Boolean operators ("And," "Or," and "Not") in sequence with as many search items as necessary to build your search strategy.

Items in combination searches are executed from the top to the bottom of the Search window. For example, if you have entered four search items in the Search window, EndNote carries out the search by combining the results of the first two items with the third search item. Those results are combined with the fourth search item to produce the final search results.

For example, the search below could be represented as:

(((confidentiality *and* insurance) *not* medicare) *or* Qualler, J)

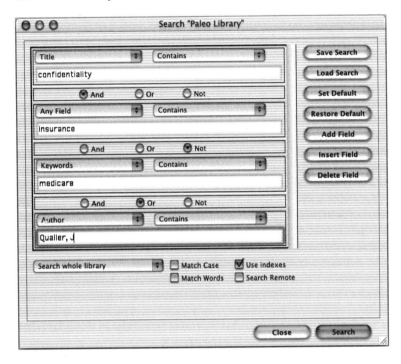

Adding or Deleting Search Items

You can add or delete search items using the *Add Field, Insert Field,* and *Delete Field* buttons on the Search window.

Add Field   adds a new search item to the end of the list.

Insert Field   inserts a new search item immediately before the selected search item.

Delete Field   removes the selected search item.

The selected search item is identified by the highlighted border around the search term box. Move between search items by pressing the TAB key to go forward and SHIFT+TAB to go backwards. You can also click with the mouse in the desired search item to select it.

Combining Results from Separate Searches

By default, EndNote searches the entire library and then displays *only* the results of the search in the Library window. To search only a subset of references, or to combine your search results with other references, choose one of the following options from the Search Set list in the Search window.

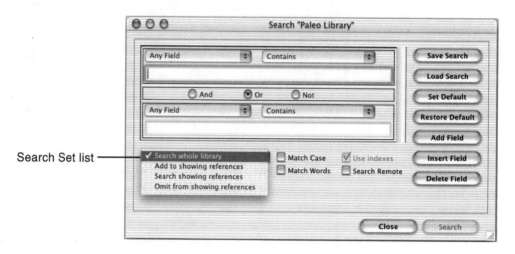

Search Set list

Add Search Results to Currently Showing References

Choose *Add to showing references* if you want to search the whole library and add the results of your search to a subset of showing references. For example, if you have already found a group of references written by Komar in 1998, and now you want to add, all references written by Billoski in 1997:

1. From the *References* menu, choose *Search References* (⌘+F).

2. Enter "Billoski" in Author *And* "1997" in Year.

3. From the Search Set list, choose *Add to showing references*.

4. Click *Search* and you should see the combined results of the two searches.

Search Only the "Showing" References

Select the *Search showing references* option in the Search dialog to restrict a search to only those references that are currently displayed in the Library window.

This is useful to narrow the results of a previous search, or to search a set of references that you have just imported from another library or online database.

Omit Search Results from Showing References

Choose the *Omit from showing references* option to hide the results of a search from the references that are showing in the Library window. This is a convenient way to locate all references that *do not* include a particular term or to narrow the results of a previous search. For example, to find all references *not* about extinction:

1. With all of the references showing in the Library window, choose *Search References* from the *References* menu.

2. Choose *Omit from Showing References* from the Search Set list in the Search window.

3. Type "extinction" into the first search item, leaving the *Field* list set to *Any Field*.

4. Click *Search*.

EndNote displays every reference except those that contain the word "extinction."

Saving Search Strategies

The *Save Search* and *Load Search* buttons at the bottom of the Search window allow you to save the settings currently in the Search window and recall them for later use. Most of the options in the Search window are saved, including the search terms; however, the target of the search (the EndNote library or remote database) is not saved, nor are Match Case and Match Words.

To save a search:

1. Configure the Search window as you would like.

2. Click the *Save Search* button in the Search window.

A dialog appears, prompting you to name the search strategy. Enter or edit the name and click *Save*. The search files are saved by default in Users: [Your Folder]: Library: Preferences: EndNote *f*: Searches. You may save them elsewhere if you prefer, but EndNote will open to this Searches folder when you choose to Load a saved search.

To load a saved search:

1. With the Search window open, click the *Load Search* button near the bottom of the window.

2. In the dialog that appears, select the search strategy that you would like to use, and click *Open*.

3. The contents and settings of the Search window change to reflect the saved search. Click *Search* to initiate the search.

Using EndNote Database Indexes

For each of your reference libraries, EndNote can maintain special "indexes" for high-speed searching. EndNote automatically maintains an Author index. In addition, you have the option of setting up a special QuickFind index for the Keywords field or for all of the fields in your library.

Searching With Indexes

Setting Up a Search to Use Indexes

Check the "Use Indexes" box in the Search window to make use of the indexes during searches of EndNote libraries. With this option selected, EndNote finds references almost instantly when searching the indexed fields, even in very large libraries.

The "Use Indexes" option in the Search window is available only if you are searching specifically in an indexed field (for example, select *Author* from a search item's *Field* list). The "Use Indexes" option must be checked for EndNote to use the indexes during the search.

You can combine an indexed search with other search items, but the speed applies only to the indexed item(s), meaning that the overall search is subject to the regular unindexed speed. Take advantage of the speed of the indexes by searching the indexed fields alone and by entering only one word per search item.

Differences Between Indexed and Non-Indexed Searches

Speed is not the only difference between indexed and non-indexed searches. Indexed searches differ from normal searches in that they match partial words only from the *beginning* of the word (right truncation). For example, a search for "physics" will not find "geophysics." Searching an indexed library finds only words; punctuation and other symbols are not found.

Author Searching

If you need to search for first names or initials (without the last name), turn off "Use Indexes." Indexed author searches should be used when searching for the last name of the author.

Though the Library window only displays the last name of the first author for each reference, EndNote finds all authors cited in a reference whether or not they are listed first.

Sort Order of Indexed Search Results

In a simple EndNote search, without the "Use Indexes" option selected, the search results appear sorted by author and year. When you use the indexes, search results do not conform to a particular sort order. You can always use the *Sort References* command in the *References* menu to sort your search results by any combination of fields.

NOTE: Turning the "Use Indexes" option on or off from inside the Search window does not alter or delete your indexes.

QuickFind Indexes

Important Points About QuickFind Indexes

♦ Once you create a QuickFind index, it is maintained as you add, delete, or modify the references in your library. As a result, it takes longer to save new and edited references because they need to be saved *and* indexed. Similarly, deleting records also takes more time, since it requires removing data from the index.

♦ Creating an "All fields" index for a large reference library takes considerable time, so you might want to have EndNote index your library at a time when you do not need to use your computer (for example, let it index overnight).

♦ An "All fields" index for a library with extensive abstracts and notes can double or triple the size of a library; a Keywords field index may only add 10% to the size of the file. Be sure that you have plenty of extra space on your hard disk when creating an "All fields" index.

♦ Once a library has been enlarged, it will *not* immediately shrink back to its original size if you change indexes. The size will be reduced over time as EndNote adjusts the storage of data in the file to reuse or release the unused space.

♦ We recommend that you make a back up copy of your EndNote library before creating a QuickFind index. For instructions see Appendix A.

Creating a QuickFind Index

Be sure to read "Important Points About QuickFind Indexes" before you create a QuickFind index for your library.

To create a QuickFind index, open your library and choose *QuickFind Index* from the *Tools* menu.

By default, the option for "No QuickFind index" is selected. If you select either "All fields" or "Keywords field" and click *OK*, EndNote will create the index and maintain it unless one of the other options is specified. When you change these settings, or choose the "No QuickFind Index" option, the previous index becomes inaccessible.

Finding Duplicate References

In order to help locate duplicate references, EndNote offers a *Find Duplicates* command. This command searches the references that are currently showing in the Library window to identify duplicates (based on the duplicate criteria specified in the preferences—see page 484).

To find all of the duplicate references in a library:

1. With the Library window open, choose *Show All References* from the *References* menu.

2. Choose *Find Duplicates* from the *References* menu and EndNote displays all duplicate references in the library.

By default, references are considered duplicates if they have the same reference type (such as Journal Article or Book), and the Author, Year, and Title fields are identical. The criteria for detecting duplicates can be changed using the *Duplicates* settings in EndNote's Preferences dialog. See page 484 for details.

References which *seem* identical may not show up as duplicates if the information in the fields EndNote checks is slightly different or if the reference types are different. When trying to determine how references differ, it is helpful to know exactly how EndNote compares them.

Author:	Compares last name and first initials (even if the first or middle name are written in full). Capitalization is not important.
Year:	Compared exactly as entered.
Title:	Leading articles "A," "An," or "The" are ignored but punctuation is included. Capitalization is not important.
Reference Type:	Compared exactly as entered.

Deleting Duplicates

When EndNote displays the duplicates that it has found in a library, it selects all references except for the earliest entry. For example, if you have three of the same references for a journal article, all three will be displayed, but the one that was entered into your library first will not be selected. (References with the lowest record numbers are the ones that were entered first.)

With all but the original references selected, you may choose *Delete References* from the *References* menu (or *Cut* from the *Edit* menu) to remove the duplicates from your library.

We strongly suggest that you check the duplicate references before deleting them. A more conservative approach to just deleting the selected duplicates would be to choose *Show Selected References* from the *References* menu. That displays only the references that are candidates for deletion. You may then peruse them to verify that you would like to delete them all. Once you are comfortable that these are the references to be deleted, you may choose *Select All* from the *Edit* menu, and then *Delete References* from the *References* menu.

WARNING: Before deleting duplicates, check the record numbers to be sure that you are not deleting references already cited in a paper. Use the *Display Fields* settings in EndNote's preferences to display record numbers in the Library window (see page 483). Move Reference windows and adjust their size in order to compare them side-by-side.

Changing Text in References

Global editing commands make it easy to keep your reference data consistent: *Change Text* is available from the *Edit* menu, while *Change and Move Fields* is available from the *References* menu.

The *Change Text* command searches for text in your library, and either deletes that text or replaces it with other text that you specify. The *Change Field* command modifies any field in your library by either inserting text at the beginning or end of the field, replacing all contents of the field with different text, or deleting the contents of the field. The *Move Field* command moves the entire contents of a field to a different field.

NOTE: Be sure that you have a current backup of your library; these operations cannot be undone with the *Undo* command.

Common Uses for *Change Text, Change Field,* and *Move Field*

Correcting consistently misspelled words or names.

Use *Change Text* to search for the misspelled term and replace it with the correct spelling.

Updating author's names.

There may be variations of an author's name in your data. For example, "Joe Cool", "Joe A. Cool", "J. A. Cool.", etc. Since some styles prefer whole names and others abbreviated first and middle names, it is best to update names to full names and leave the work of abbreviating to the EndNote styles.

Marking the result of a search for easy retrieval.

If you have developed a complex search to locate a set of references, use *Change Fields* to add a unique keyword to those references, so that the next time you want to retrieve that set, you can just search for the keyword.

Cleaning up your keywords.

You can add a keyword to a group of references using *Change Fields*. Use *Change Text* to replace a term with a new one. If there is a keyword that you no longer want in your references, use *Change Text* to search for that text and replace it with nothing, thereby deleting it (you might also want to open your term list and delete it from there so that you do not use that term again).

Dating or labeling a set of imported references.

It can be useful to add the date or source of data to a batch of newly imported references. Only the imported references are "showing" in the Library window after importing. At this point, use *Change Fields* to add a word or phrase to any field in just those references.

Moving fields of information in a set of imported references.

Maybe your import filter or connection file consistently sent Note information to the Abstract field. Use *Move Fields* to cut all information from the Abstract field and move it into the Note field. (Don't forget to update your filter or connection file so it directs information to the correct field next time!)

Change Text

Use the *Change Text* command to find text in your references and replace it with other text. Changes can be restricted to a particular field in your references, and you can also apply "Match Case" and "Match Words" restrictions.

NOTE: The *Undo* command cannot be used to undo the results of the *Change Text* command. Make sure you have a backup before making changes.

To change any text in your references:

1. Decide which references you want EndNote to scan when it looks for text to change. Make sure only those references are showing in the Library window (use *Show All References, Hide Selected References, Show Selected References,* or *Search References* commands to control which references are showing).

2. From the *Edit* menu, choose *Change Text*.

3. From the *In Field* list, select the field to be searched.

4. In the "Search for:" box, type the text to be changed.

5. Change the "Match Case" or "Match Words" settings if necessary (see page 178 for details).

   By default, the "Match Words" option is always selected. If you change this setting, pay close attention to whether or not the term you are changing could appear as part of another word or in a different context depending on the capitalization. **This operation cannot be undone.**

6. In the "Change the text to:" box, type the text that should replace the original text.

7. Select the "Retain Capitalization" option to maintain the same capitalization as the text being replaced.

"Retain Capitalization" should be selected if replacing a term that might appear with different capitalizations. For example, any word may have its first letter capitalized if it is the first word in a title, but may also appear in all lowercase in other places. Do not choose "Retain Capitalization" if you are replacing an acronym with its unabbreviated version.

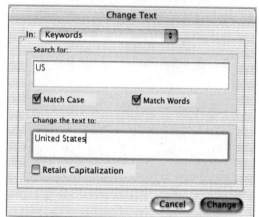

This set up changes all occurrences of "US" to "United States" in the Keywords field.

8. Click *Change* to search the showing references for the specified text and replace it with the new text. Before replacing any text, EndNote has you verify the change. The dialog EndNote presents provides information about 5 things:

   ♦ Which references were searched

   ♦ What text will be replaced

   ♦ Which fields were scanned for the text

   ♦ How many references were found to include the text in the specified field

   ♦ What text will replace it

9. Click *OK* if all of those items are correct. EndNote replaces the text and displays the number of references that were changed.

Important Points About the *Change Text* Command

◆ The *Change Text* command applies only to the references showing in the Library window.

◆ When using *Change Text*, the new text adopts the text style of the first character of the text being replaced. For example, if you replace an italicized word, the new text will also be italicized. If only the first term that you are replacing is italicized, as in "*Thecideid* genus" then all of the replacement text will be italicized: "*Thecideid Varigata genus.*"

◆ If you need to search for text and then *delete* it, simply leave the "Change the text to" box empty.

◆ When using the *Retain Capitalization* option, EndNote maintains ALL CAPITAL LETTERS and "Sentence style" capitalization. It will not recognize "Headline Style." If the first letter of the text to be replaced is lowercase, the replacement text will be capitalized exactly as it was entered in the dialog.

◆ To enter a carriage return in the text box, press OPTION-RETURN. To enter a Tab, press OPTION+TAB.

Change Fields

The *Change Fields* tab can change the contents of a field for the references that are "showing" in the Library window.

NOTE: This operation cannot be undone, so make sure you have backups before making changes.

To change the contents of a field:

1. Determine which references you want to modify. Make sure only those references are showing in the Library window.

2. From the *References* menu, choose *Change and Move Fields* to display the *Change Fields* tab.

3. From the *In Field* list, choose the field that you want to modify.

4. Select one of the following options:

   ◆ **Insert after field's text** appends text at the end of the chosen field. It does not modify the text already in the field.

   You may want to select the *Include a space before the new text* check box at the bottom of the dialog to insert a space between the existing text and the new text.

♦ **Insert before field's text:**
Inserts the text at the beginning of the chosen field. It does not modify text that is already in the field.

You may want to select the *Include a space after the new text* check box at the bottom of the dialog to insert a space between the new text and the existing text.

♦ **Replace whole field with:**
Replaces the entire contents of the field with the text entered in the text box.

♦ **Clear field:**
Deletes the entire contents of the chosen field. It is not necessary to put any text into the text box.

To enter a carriage return in the text box, press OPTION+RETURN. To enter a Tab, press OPTION+TAB.

5. In the text box, type the text that should be added to the field.

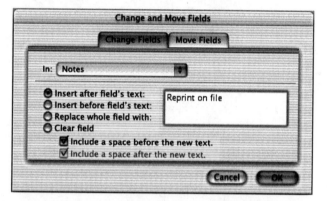

6. Click *Change*. EndNote will ask you to confirm the changes. The dialog EndNote presents provides information about 4 things:

♦ How many references will be changed

♦ The library in which the changes will be made

♦ The type of change that will be made

♦ The field that will be modified

7. Click *OK* to continue with the changes, or click *Cancel* to cancel this operation.

Move Fields

Use the *Move Fields* tab to move the entire contents of one field to another field within a reference. The command applies to all of the references that are "showing" in the Library window.

NOTE: This operation cannot be undone, so make sure you have a backup copy of your library before making changes.

To move the contents of one field to another:

1. Determine which references you want to modify. Make sure only those references are showing in the Library window.

2. From the *References* menu, choose *Change and Move Fields*.

3. Click the *Move Fields* tab.

4. In the dialog that appears, use the "Move from" list to select the field you want to move the data from.

5. Use the "Move to" list to select the field where you want that data to end up.

6. Click *Move* to move the data from one field to the other within each reference that is currently showing in the Library window.

You have the option of inserting the moved text before or after the data in the destination field, or replacing the entire contents of the destination field. In the latter case, you have the additional option of whether or not to move empty fields. If you uncheck the option "Don't move empty fields," then any reference with an empty originating field deletes the contents of the corresponding destination field (and thereby making it empty as well). If this option is turned on, the contents of the destination field will *not* be deleted if the originating field is empty.

The example below shows the *Move Field* options set up to move the contents of the Notes field into the Custom 1 field. If the Custom 1 field already has data in it, the contents of the Notes field will be added after the existing text.

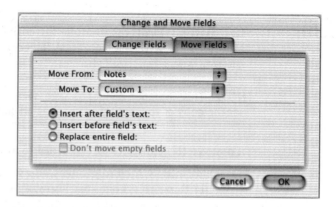

Sorting the Library

The *Sort References* command provides a way to arrange all references showing in the Library window for exporting, printing, copying, or just browsing.

EndNote libraries are typically sorted by the first author's last name, year, and record number. When you add a new reference, or modify an existing reference, EndNote automatically files it in this order. Use the *Sort References* command to change this order. The current sort order remains in effect until you change it again.

To change the sort order:

1. From the *References* menu, choose *Sort References*.

2. Select one or more field names from the lists in the dialog. Enter the field names in the order you want the references sorted. (You do not have to use all five options.)

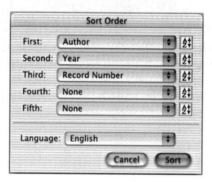

3. Click the button to the right of each field to indicate ascending or descending order.

4. With the field names entered as desired, click *Sort*.

The dialog shown above is set to sort the library by author names, in alphabetical order, and then references published by the same author are sorted by year (from oldest to newest).

Special Cases in Sorting

Except for title fields, quotation marks, parentheses and other punctuation marks are considered during a sort. In an alphabetic sort, punctuation comes first, then numbers, then letters A-Z.

Author Names

Author names are always sorted by last name first, then first name and middle initials. If a reference has more than one author, EndNote includes the additional authors in the sort before moving on to other fields.

If your EndNote library includes author names with connectives such as de, di, van, and von, you may want EndNote to skip these parts of the name in order to sort the references by the principal element of the surname. See "Sorting" on page 480.

Titles

When sorting by title fields, EndNote ignores the words *A*, *An*, and *The* as well as punctuation at the start of the titles. You may enter additional words that should be ignored for sorting purposes when they appear at the beginning of a title. To do so, see "Sorting" on page 480.

Sorting Diacritical Characters

EndNote sorts diacritical characters according to the rules of the language selected in the Sort References dialog. Characters with diacritics are sorted differently in English, Spanish, Swedish, and other systems.

Merging Libraries

There are two ways to merge libraries: import one library into another, or copy references from one library to another.

Any time you add references to a library, the newly added references are assigned new record numbers in the order that they are added to the library. This means that a reference that was #23 in a smaller library, could become #600 in a larger library. As a result, you cannot use the larger, merged library to format papers that have citations with the older record numbers.

NOTE: Before merging libraries, it is a good idea to make a backup copy of the library into which you are transferring references.

Importing EndNote Libraries

To import one EndNote library into another, use the *Import* command from the *File* menu. Choose the EndNote Library import option and be sure to pick the appropriate "Duplicates" setting (see page 150). The advantage of using the *Import* command over the other two methods mentioned here is its ability to filter out duplicate references. See Chapter 7 for details.

Importing from Open Libraries

You can import references from a library that is currently open in EndNote. When EndNote imports from a currently open library, it imports only those references "showing" in the Library window. For example, if the library says, "Showing 10 out of 200 references," EndNote imports only 10 references. If the library you are importing is locked or in "Read-Only" mode, *all* references are imported regardless of what is currently showing.

Using Drag and Drop

To copy specific references from one library to another, simply select them in one library (hold down the COMMAND key to select non-consecutive references; use the SHIFT key to select a range), click on any part of the selection and use the mouse to drag the selection to another library. The selected references are copied to the library where they were "dropped."

Copying References in Libraries

You can also use the *Copy* and *Paste* commands in the *Edit* menu to transfer references. Select the references that you want to copy and choose *Copy* from the *Edit* menu. Open the library to which you want to add the references and choose *Paste*.

NOTE: If you run out of memory during this process, copy the references in smaller batches.

Linking References to Files and Web Sites

With the *Link To* command in the *References* menu, you can link an EndNote reference to a file on your computer (such as a graphic, a word processing document, or a spreadsheet). The *Open Link* command can then be used to open that file at any time. *Open Link* can also be used with Web addresses (URLs).

Link a File to an EndNote Reference

To link a file to a reference in your EndNote library:

1. Select a reference in the Library window or open a reference.

2. From the *References* menu, choose *Link To*.

3. In the dialog that appears, select a file that you would like linked to the selected (or open) reference, and click *Open*.

This command simply enters the path to the chosen file into the URL field of the reference and hyperlinks it.

NOTE: The *Link To* option is only available when a single reference is selected in the Library window, or when you are editing a reference.

Using the Open Link Command

Once the path to a file has been hyperlinked in the URL field, the *Open Link* command can be used to open the linked file or Internet site.

To open a linked file or Internet site:

1. Select or open a reference in the Library window.

2. Choose *Open Link* (⌘+G).

The *Open Link* command opens the linked file with the appropriate program.

Note that when you type a Web address into the URL field, EndNote underlines it and changes the color of the URL to indicate that it will function as a clickable link to the Web site. Simply clicking the link works just like choosing the *Open Link* command.

You must have the necessary program installed on your computer in order for EndNote to open a file created by another program. Similarly, EndNote does not include a Web browser. So, if you do not already have a browser installed, you will need to install one before using this feature to open a link to a Web site. Use the *Online* settings in EndNote's preferences to select the Web browser that should open when the *Open Link* command is activated. See page 485 for details.

Using *Open Link* in Various Conditions

The *Open Link* command (⌘+G) on the *References* menu can be used to open a linked file or launch a URL entered into an EndNote reference under the following conditions:

◆ When just one reference is selected in the Library window, EndNote opens the file or URL that is listed in that reference's URL field.

◆ When multiple references are selected, EndNote checks the URL field in each of the selected references (in the order listed), and opens the first link it finds.

◆ If you choose *Open Link* when a Reference window is open and nothing is selected, EndNote only looks for a link in the URL field.

◆ When a Reference window is open and text in the reference is selected, EndNote sends the selected text to your Web browser and does not check the URL field for another link.

◆ If you need to enter multiple links into the URL field of one reference, enter them one per line. EndNote will open the first link in the field when you choose *Open Link*. If you have entered multiple URLs, you should be able to click on any one of them to activate the link.

What is a URL?

"URL" stands for "Uniform Resource Locator" and is a common term for the "address" used to identify the location of an item online. Most often, URLs refer to Web pages, such as this example of the EndNote Web page:

`http://www.endnote.com`

URLs can also be used to identify the location of FTP (File Transfer Protocol) sites, telnet addresses, and even files stored on your own hard drive.

Finding Related Online References

Highlight a reference and use the *OpenURL Link* command on the *References* menu to start your default web browser and display related record links in the browser window.

OpenURL Link connects to an OpenURL standard syntax server and uses EndNote's OpenURL preferences along with data in your EndNote record to find related online references.

NOTE: This command has no relation to the URL field found in EndNote references or to the *Open Link* command on the *References* menu.

To enable this feature, and find out what preferences are available, see "OpenURL" on page 492.

Chapter 9

Term Lists

Chapter 9   Term Lists

Introduction to Term Lists

EndNote's term lists are used to store terms such as keywords, author names, or journal names. You can use these stored terms when entering references to improve consistency and accuracy of information in your library. You can also use the Journals term list to store abbreviated journal names that EndNote can substitute for the full journal name in a bibliography.

Overview

To get a general sense of how the term lists work, here's a brief overview of how term lists can be built and used for someone with a new EndNote library. With the default term list settings in the preferences, all of the updating of terms, and auto-completion, happens automatically. If you do not like this behavior, you may turn off these settings (see page 487).

Term Lists are Automatically Maintained

When you create a new EndNote library, there are three empty term lists already set up and ready for you to use: Authors, Journals, and Keywords. As you enter new references into your library (whether by typing, importing, or pasting them) EndNote updates the term lists automatically so that the Authors, Journals, and Keywords lists include all of the author names, journal names, and keywords entered into your references.

Term Lists Help With Data Entry

When you use the *New Reference* command in the *References* menu to create new references, you will notice two other features associated with the term lists. As you begin entering an author name, EndNote attempts to complete the name for you by suggesting the closest matching name in the Authors term list. If you enter a new name that is not already in your Author list, the name appears in red text to indicate that it is a new addition to the term list. When you close or save the reference, that new term is added to the list.

When you are searching for references, you can also open a term list to pick the exact term or name for which to search.

Important Points About Term Lists

The following list includes useful information about term lists. These points are covered in more detail later in the chapter.

♦ Term lists are stored with the library and therefore are specific to only that library.

♦ A library must be open before you can edit its term lists.

♦ If you enter a lot of references manually, you may find it helpful to create new term lists for things like publisher and city names. Up to 31 term lists can be created for any library.

♦ There is no limit to the number of terms in a term list.

♦ One term can be up to 253 characters long.

♦ Terms can be copied from one list and pasted into another.

♦ Entire term lists can be exported and imported.

♦ By default, term lists are automatically updated from the terms entered in your references. New terms appear in red text in the Reference window. This functionality may be turned off using EndNote's Preferences.

♦ Term lists can be "linked" to specific fields so that EndNote associates the correct term list with the field you are editing.

♦ Terms lists can be used with the "Auto-entry" feature on or off. By default, this option is turned on so that EndNote will suggest the closest matching term as you type in a reference.

♦ The Journals term list stores various forms of journal names that can be used when creating bibliographies. EndNote provides 3 Journals lists (Humanities, Medical, and Chemistry) that can be imported for use with your EndNote libraries.

♦ Libraries with term lists can be used by earlier versions of EndNote. However, term lists are only accessible when using EndNote version 2 or later.

Adding Terms to a Term List

Terms can be added to the term lists using a variety of methods described in this section. Adding terms to a term list does not change any data that you have entered in your references.

Automatic Updating of Term Lists

By default, EndNote automatically updates the term lists in a library so they stay current with the data that has been entered into the references. If you enter a term into a reference, and that term is not in the associated term list already, the term appears in red text to alert you that you have entered a new term. This can help you to maintain a controlled vocabulary for keywords and other terms.

You can turn off automatic updating of term lists if you do not want to use the term lists at all (see page 209). You can also turn this option off and manually enter terms into your lists as described in the following sections. For example, you can manually enter all of the terms you plan to use into a term list before entering references into the library. This can be extremely helpful when you have someone else entering data for you and you want a specific vocabulary used for keywords or other terms. As references are entered into the EndNote library, the term lists can speed data entry, and if a red term appears, the person doing data entry knows that they have entered something that wasn't intended to be a valid term for that field.

Turning Off the Automatic Updating of Term Lists:

1. From the *EndNote* menu, choose *Preferences.*

2. Select the *Term Lists* panel.

3. Click the check boxes for "Update lists when importing or pasting references" and "Update lists during data entry" to remove the "X." The feature will be turned off.

Delimiters

EndNote has predefined term lists for authors, keywords, and journals. When you enter multiple terms into those fields and EndNote updates the term list, it needs to know when one term ends and the next term begins. We call the punctuation that separates the terms "delimiters."

For the Author fields, author names must always be entered one name per line. Carriage returns (end of line marks) are the only valid delimiter for this field. Journals normally have just one journal name per reference in this field, so delimiters are not important here. Keywords are the most complex of the three. By default, EndNote uses carriage returns (end of line marks), semicolons, and backslashes (\) as delimiters for the Keywords field. If you would like to use other delimiters, see "Delimiters used for Separating Terms" on page 213.

Using the "New Term" Command

To manually add a term to a term list:

1. From the *Tools* menu, choose *Open Term Lists* and select the term list that you want to modify.

2. On the *Terms* tab, click *New Term*.

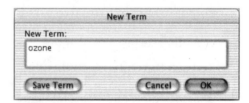

3. Enter the term and click *OK* to add it to the list and dismiss the "New Term" dialog.

Continue this way until you have added the last term, then click *OK* to dismiss the dialog.

If you are entering terms into the Journals term list, you will have options to enter different forms of the journal name. See page 222 for more information about using the Journal lists.

NOTE: The *Save Term* (or *Save Journal*) button is unavailable (dim) if the new term already exists in the term list.

Copying Terms Between Lists

You can copy terms from one list and paste them into another as a way to quickly transfer terms between lists. This is particularly useful because term lists are specific to an individual library.

To copy terms between lists:

1. From the *Tools* menu, choose *Open List* and select the list with terms you want to copy.

2. Select the term(s) to copy. (Hold down the ⌘ key to select multiple terms; use the SHIFT key to select a range of terms.)

3. From the *Edit* menu, choose *Copy* (⌘+C).

4. Open another list, and choose *Paste* (⌘+V) from the *Edit* menu.

Copying Terms From Other Sources

You can copy terms from any text, and paste them directly into a term list. If you are copying more than one term at a time, the terms must be separated by carriage returns (one term per line).

For example, to copy a word from a paper you are writing and paste that word into a term list, simply select the term in your word processor and copy it. Then switch to EndNote, open the desired term list, and choose *Paste* from the *Edit* menu. There is no need to use the *New Term* command—a new term is created automatically.

Manually Updating Term Lists

To create a term list automatically from words already in your library, use the *Update List* button on the *Terms List* dialog. This is useful if you have turned off the preference to automatically update your term lists, or if you have received a library from a colleague without a term list, or if you have deleted a term list and wish to recreate it.

The *Update List* command can apply to just the selected references or all references showing in the Library window. Use the *Search* command to show only those references from which you want to update the list. Or select references in the Library window and update the term list from just those references. Choose *Show All References* from the *References* menu before using the *Update List* command to be sure that you are updating the list from all of the references in your library.

Important points about the *Update List* command:

◆ *Update List* does not change the terms in your references; it only adds new terms from your references into the term list.

◆ *Update List* does not add duplicate terms to a list.

◆ *Update List* removes leading and trailing spaces, but does not change punctuation.

◆ *Update List* does not automatically link fields to a term list. For easy data entry, you can link a single term list to any number of fields. See "Linking Term Lists to Fields" on page 220.

To update a term list:

If you are updating the Journals list, see page 223.

1. Determine which references should be scanned for terms and make sure they are either "showing" or selected in the Library window.

2. From the *Tools* menu, choose *Define Term Lists* and select the term list that you would like to update.

3. Click *Update List*.

4. The currently linked fields are listed in the dialog as the fields from which EndNote gathers new terms. If necessary, remove a field from this list by selecting it and clicking *Remove Field*; or add a new field by selecting it from the *Add Field* list. Adding or removing field names from this list does not affect the links between fields and term lists.

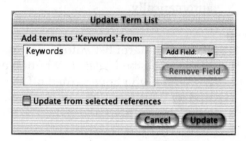

The Generic field names are used in this dialog. See the "Table of Predefined Reference Types" on page 354 to find the corresponding field names for the fields of various reference types.

5. To update a term list from only the currently selected references in your library, check the "Update From Selected References" option.

6. Click *Update* to begin the updating process. When finished, EndNote displays the number of terms added to the list. Click *OK* and the process is complete.

NOTE: Typing Esc or ⌘-. stops the update process, but all terms added up to that point are kept in the term list.

Delimiters used for Separating Terms

The text that is used to separate the terms in a particular field is determined by the "Delimiter" settings on the *Lists* tab of the Term Lists dialog (choose *Define Term Lists* from the *Tools* menu).

Select a term list and the delimiters used for it will be marked in the Delimiters section below.

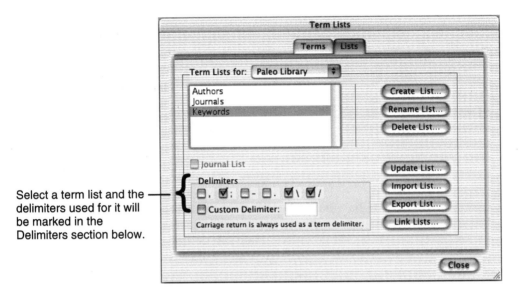

If your keywords are separated by a slash, such as:

`Antarctica/ozone/stratosphere`

you should type a slash (/) as the field's term delimiter. A carriage return is always interpreted as a delimiter, so it is not necessary to enter a delimiter for the Author fields, or any other field that has terms entered one-per-line. If different delimiters are used for the same field in your references, you will need to do more than one update process, updating from the references with different delimiters separately.

Cleaning Up After Updating

Click on the Terms tab, and scroll through the term list to make sure that the *Update List* command had the desired result. If it did not, you can highlight specific terms and remove them by clicking *Delete Term*.

After using the *Update List* command, you might find that due to errors or variations in spelling, you have multiple entries for the same term. Scan through the list and delete the unwanted terms.

If necessary, use the *Change Text* command to change all occurrences of a term in your library. For example, if both "geochronology" and "geo-chronology" are entered as keywords, you can delete the unwanted term "geochronology" from the term list, then click on the Library window, and choose *Change Text* (⌘+R) from the *Edit* menu to change "geochronology" to "geo-chronology" throughout the library.

Importing Terms Into Term Lists

EndNote provides three lists of journal names and abbreviations; there is a list for Chemistry, Medicine (Index Medicus), and the Humanities, all of which are stored in the Terms folder in the EndNote folder. If you are interested in using these abbreviated forms of the journal names in your bibliographies, you can import them into your term lists and adjust your styles to use the abbreviations (see "Creating Bibliographies With Journal Abbreviations" on page 224).

If you would like to look at the lists before importing them, you may open them in your word processor—but do not edit or save them. They must remain tab-delimited text files in order for EndNote to correctly import the terms.

Terms can be imported from any text file that lists the terms one per line. If you create a list of terms in a word processing document, be sure to save the list as plain text using the *Save As* command in your word processor so that you can import it.

To import a text file that contains terms:

1. From the *Tools* menu, choose *Define Term Lists* and highlight the term list to which you want to add terms. (Use *Create List* if you want to create a new list.)

2. Click *Import List*.

3. Select the text file to be imported and click *Open*. EndNote's Medical, Chemical, and Humanities lists are in the Terms folder in the EndNote folder.

The new terms are imported and sorted alphabetically into the existing term list. This import must be done for each library that you want to use these terms.

NOTE: EndNote provides lists of journal names for the humanities, medicine, and chemistry. See page 222 for more information about working with the Journals list and journal abbreviations.

Using Terms Lists for Data Entry and Searching

You can use term lists to enter terms directly into a reference or into the Search window.

Inserting Terms into References

Suggesting Terms As You Type (Auto-completion)

If you are entering text into a field that is linked to a term list, EndNote finds the first matching term in the list and suggests that as the term you want to enter.

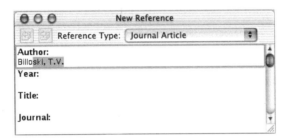

The suggested text appears highlighted after the cursor. Continue typing until EndNote suggests the correct term and then press ENTER, RETURN, or TAB to accept it. (RETURN will create another line in the field so that you can continue entering more author names, for example; TAB will move the cursor to the next field in the reference.)

When EndNote has suggested a term, you may also use the Up or Down arrows on your keyboard to have the suggested text change to the previous or next possible matching term in the term list.

If you enter a term that is not already in your term list, it appears in red to indicate that it is a new term. When you close or save the reference, that term is added to your term list and will no longer display in red.

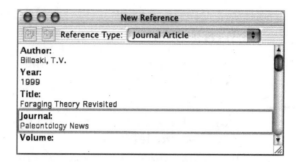

NOTE: These term list features may be turned off. To turn off the display of red text, you must turn off the preference to "Suggest Terms as You Type." See "Term Lists" on page 487.

Inserting Terms Without Using the "Suggestion" Feature

If you have turned off the option to suggest terms as you type, you can still insert terms into your references manually.

To insert a term from a Term List window:

1. Open a reference and position the insertion point where you want to add the term.

2. Press ⌘+1 to open the linked list (or choose *Open Term Lists* from the *Tools* menu and select the desired list).

3. Double-click a term to insert it directly into the reference.

Terms can also be selected by typing the first few letters of the term, by using the ARROW keys, or by clicking on the term with the mouse. Hold down the COMMAND (⌘) key to select multiple terms. Press RETURN to insert the selected term or click *Insert Term*. If multiple terms are selected and inserted, they are listed in the reference one per line in alphabetical order.

Selected terms can also be copied from the term list using the *Copy* (⌘+C) command in the *Edit* menu, and pasted into a reference using the *Paste* (⌘+V) command in the *Edit* menu.

NOTE: The insertion point must be in a field in a Reference window or Search window before you can insert a term.

Using Terms For Searches

To ensure that you are searching for the correct terms, you can use the term lists with EndNote's *Search* command. Terms can be entered into the Search window just as they are entered into references. For example:

1. From the *References* menu, choose *Search References* (⌘+F) and change the first search item to search the Keywords field.

2. From the *Tools* menu, choose *Open Term Lists* or simply press (⌘+1) to open the Keywords list (this key command opens the list that is linked to the field being searched).

3. Double-click a term to insert it into the Search window.

4. Click *Search* to search for your references.

Editing Terms and Term Lists

Any term in a term list may be modified or deleted without affecting any of the references in the library or any links between term lists and fields.

Modifying Terms

To edit a term in a term list:

1. From the *Tools* menu, choose *Define Term Lists* and select the list that contains the term to be modified. Then click on the Terms tab. (Term lists can be easily opened from within the field in a reference by pressing ⌘+1.)

2. Select a term and click *Edit Term*. If multiple terms are selected, only the first one opens.

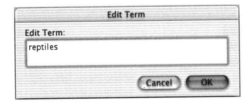

3. Change the term as necessary and click *OK* when finished. The modified term replaces the original term in the term list. (If the term already exists, the *OK* button is dim.)

NOTE: Editing a term in a term list does not change all occurrences of that term in your library. Use the *Change Text* command to find the old term in your references and replace it with the new one.

Deleting Terms

A term can be deleted by highlighting it in the list and clicking *Delete Term* or selecting *Clear* from the *Edit* menu. You can also use the *Cut* (⌘+X) command from the *Edit* menu to cut terms out of the list and *Paste* them elsewhere (such as into another term list). Deleting a term from a term list does not remove it from the references in the library.

Defining Term Lists

Use the *Define Term Lists* command in the *Tools* menu to create, rename or delete a term list. This command is also used to specify the punctuation that separates individual terms in a reference (delimiters).

Deleting and Renaming Term Lists

Term lists can be renamed without disturbing their links to reference fields or the terms within them. Deleting or renaming term lists does not change the data entered into your references.

To delete or rename a term list:

1. From the *Tools* menu, choose *Define Term Lists* (at least one library must be open to access this command).

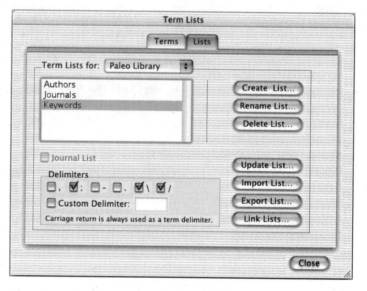

2. The drop-down menu at the top of the Lists tab lets you choose from a list of open libraries. Select the library for which you would like to modify the term lists.

- **To Rename a Term List:** Highlight a term list and then click *Rename List*. In the Rename List dialog, enter the new name for the list, and click *OK*.

- **To Delete a Term List:** Select a term list and then click *Delete List*.

3. Click *OK* to save your changes.

Configuring Term Separators (Delimiters)

EndNote uses the delimiters in the Define Lists dialog to determine what punctuation separates the individual terms in the same field in a reference.

For example, if you import data from a source that uses semicolons (;) to separate keywords:

```
Adult, Age Factors; Astigmatism; Follow-Up
Studies; Hospitals, University; Keratotomy,
Radial; Myopia; Refraction, Ocular
```

you would want to be sure that the semicolon was selected as a separator for your Keywords term list. You would also want to be sure that the comma was not chosen because the commas in this example are used within some of the terms.

By default, EndNote uses the semicolon (;) and backslash (\), and end of line markers as separators. Words or phrases entered on different lines in a field (by pressing RETURN) are always interpreted as separate terms, but the other separators can be changed depending on your needs.

To customize the delimiters for a term list:

1. Open a library.

2. From the *Tools* menu, choose *Define Term Lists*.

3. Verify that your library name is selected at the top of the dialog, then click on the name of the term list that you intend to modify.

4. Click the checkbox to the left of the desired separator to choose it (or to unselect it if it is already checked).

The last checkbox provides a place to enter a custom term delimiter, if necessary.

Creating Term Lists

Predefined Term Lists

Three empty term lists are available by default with every library: Authors, Journals, and Keywords. These lists are already linked to their corresponding fields: the Authors term list is linked to the Author, Secondary, Tertiary, and Subsidiary Author fields; the Journals term list is linked to the Secondary and Alternate Title fields; and the Keywords term list is linked to the Keywords field.

Creating a New Term List

To create a new term list:

1. From the *Tools* menu, choose *Define Term Lists*.

2. Click *Create List*, and enter the name for the new list. You cannot create a term list with the same name as an existing term list.

3. Click *OK*.

4. Check the "Journal List" box *only* if you want to create a term list for storing journal names and abbreviations. These different forms of the journal name can be used interchangeably when creating bibliographies (see "Journal Names" on page 386 for a description of this feature).

   The predefined Journals term list is already set up as a multi-column list. If you delete this list, you can create another one as described here. Do not create a 4-column journal list for non-Journal fields.

NOTE: New term lists must be linked to fields for the "Suggest terms as you type" and automatic updating features to work. Instructions for linking term lists to fields follow.

Linking Term Lists to Fields

Term lists are associated with fields using the *Link Term Lists* command from the *Tools* menu. When a term list is linked to a field, the list can be used to facilitate data entry. EndNote can also keep the term lists current by automatically adding new terms from linked fields. By linking term lists to particular fields, you can access the desired list immediately by choosing *Open Term Lists* (⌘+1) whenever you are entering data into the linked field. Each field can be linked to only one term list. However, you can link the same term list to different fields.

The three predefined term lists (Authors, Journals, and Keywords) are already linked to their corresponding fields. Any new term list that you create is not linked to a field until you set up the links. The links between term lists and fields are specific to each library.

To change these settings or to link a new term list to one or more fields:

1. Open a library.

2. From the *Tools* menu, choose *Link Term Lists*.

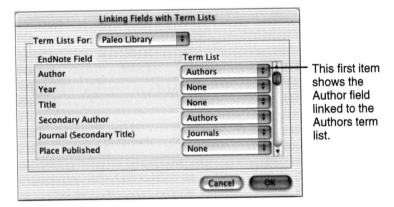

This first item shows the Author field linked to the Authors term list.

3. Choose a library from the list at the top of the dialog.

4. The names of the available term lists appear next to the field names with which they are linked. You may change the links here as necessary by choosing a different term list from the pop-up lists.

5. Click *OK* to save your changes and close the dialog.

These changes will not alter any data that is currently entered in either your references or your term lists. Term lists may be linked to multiple fields.

NOTE: After linking a term list to one or more fields, you should make sure the list is updated with the data from those fields. Go to the *Tools* menu, select *Define Term Lists*, select the list, and click *Update List.*

To unlink a term list from a field:

1. With the library open, choose *Link Term Lists* (⌘+3) from the *Tools* menu.

2. Scroll through the list of fields to find the field that you would like to be unlinked from a list. Choose *None* from the list next to the field name.

3. Save your changes by clicking *OK*.

Exporting and Printing Term Lists

Term lists can be exported and then imported into other term lists as a way to move complete lists from one library to another (see also "Copying Terms Between Lists" on page 210).

You can also open exported term lists in a word processor to print them.

To export a term list:

1. From the *Tools* menu, choose *Define Term Lists*.

2. Highlight the term list that you want to export.

3. Click *Export List*.

4. Name and save the text file that will be created during the export.

5. Click Save and the terms are exported to the text file and listed alphabetically, one term per line.

This file can now be imported into another EndNote term list or opened in a word processor to be printed. Term lists cannot be printed directly from EndNote.

Working with the Journals Term List

Important Points About Entering Journal Names

You do not have to use the abbreviation sections in a Journals term list, but if you do, keep these points in mind:

♦ Enter variations of the same journal name together in one term.

♦ Enter a consistent abbreviation format in each column. For example, all Index Medicus abbreviations could be entered under the Abbreviation 1, another format of abbreviated names in Abbreviation 2, and so on.

♦ Only the first term for each journal (the one in the Full Journal slot) is transferred when you insert a term.

♦ Use the *Journal Abbreviation* option in the styles to pick which form of the journal names should be used in the bibliography (see "Creating Bibliographies With Journal Abbreviations" on page 224).

♦ EndNote can remove periods from abbreviations during formatting. EndNote cannot add periods to an abbreviated journal name.

Updating a Journal List

For EndNote to accurately use the abbreviated journal names in your bibliographies, it is important to be consistent when entering different formats of a journal name. The first column should always list the full journal name, and subsequent columns should store consistent formats of abbreviated names. See page 222 for more information.

Journal lists are updated automatically unless you have turned off the preferences to update lists (see page 487). When journal lists are updated, the entry in the main Journal field goes into the first column of the list (Full Journal) and the journal entered into the Alternate Journal field goes into the second column (Abbreviation 1). Be consistent when entering data into these fields so that the Journals term list will be updated correctly. Note that if the name entered into the Journal field exists in any of the columns of the Journals term list, it is not added again. EndNote tries to avoid duplicate entries in the Journals list.

If you have turned off the preference to automatically update the term lists, you may manually update the lists as described here. When you are manually updating Journal lists, you can choose which columns in the list are used for which fields of data.

To update a journal term list:

1. Open a library and select the references from which you would like to update the Journals term list. Alternatively, use the *Search* command to find only those references that you would like to use.

2. From the *Tools* menu, choose *Define Term Lists*, and then *Journals*.

3. Click *Update List*.

4. Select the fields from which EndNote should extract the journal names. If importing from selected references, check the "Update from Selected References" option.

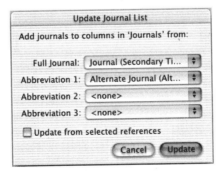

5. Click *Update*.

When the importing is complete, you will see a column of journal names listed in alphabetical order.

Loading Supplied Journal Abbreviations

You can load one of the supplied journal title lists to use for data entry. These lists also contain journal abbreviations for alternate output, and are used by certain output styles. The lists supplied in the EndNote\Term Lists folder are:

- Chemical.txt
- Humanitites.txt
- Medical.txt

To replace the existing Journals list with one of the supplied journal abbreviation lists:

1. From the *Tools* menu, select *Open Term Lists* and then *Journals Term List*.

2. Delete all existing terms from the list (you can click and drag to highlight all terms, and then click *Delete Term*).

3. Click on the Lists tab and highlight the Journals list.

4. Click *Import List*.

5. In the File dialog, navigate to the EndNote 7:Terms folder, select the list you want to use, and click *Open* to import the journal names and abbreviations from the file into the Journals term list.

Creating Bibliographies With Journal Abbreviations

When you insert a journal name from the Journals term list into a reference, only the first entry for the journal name is entered. However, you can create a bibliography that uses any abbreviation in the term list by editing the style used to format the paper:

To edit a style to use journal abbreviations:

1. From the *Edit* menu, choose *Output Styles* and select *Open Style Manager*.

2. Select the style that you would like to edit, and click *Edit*.

3. From the list of options at the left of the Style Editor window, click *Journal Names*.

4. Select one of the available options. (See Chapter 15 for more information about these settings.)

5. Close and save the style. Now when you format a paper or look in the preview pane of the Library window, all of the

journal names should be replaced with the appropriate abbreviation.

If a journal name in one of your references does not have the selected abbreviation entered in the Journals term list, the journal name appears in the bibliography exactly as it is entered in the Reference window.

Which Term List is Used for the Abbreviations?

Since it is possible (though not common) to have more than one multi-column journal list in a library, it is important to know how EndNote chooses which Journal list to use with the Journal Abbreviations feature. EndNote uses the multi-column list that is linked to the journal field used by the style. (For example, if the Alternate Journal field is specified by the style, EndNote uses the multi-column list linked to the Alternate Journal field.) If there is not a multi-column list that is linked to a journal field, EndNote uses the first multi-column list that it finds.

The predefined Journals term list that is added to every library is already set up as a multi-column list and it is linked to both the Journal and Alternate Journal fields. (These fields might also be called "Abbrev. Journal" and "Full Journal" if you have upgraded from the original EndNote program.)

Converting Old EndNote Journals Files

If you have previously used the Journal Abbreviations feature in an earlier version of EndNote (versions 1.0-1.3.2), you can import the journal names from your old Journal Abbreviations table into the Journals term list. The information in the old table is stored in the "EndNote Journals" file and it can be directly imported into the Journals term list using the *Import List* command (see page 214).

NOTE: In this version of EndNote, you can have a different set of journal abbreviations for each library, and you may want to update each library similarly.

Chapter 10

Using EndNote with Microsoft Word

Chapter 10   Using EndNote with Microsoft Word

Overview of the Cite While You Write Process

This chapter describes how to Cite While You Write™ (CWYW) with Microsoft® Word X to easily and quickly cite references, figures, and tables, and create a paper with properly formatted citations, a bibliography, figures, and tables. Cite While You Write gives you access to EndNote references and formatting commands with an *EndNote 7* submenu on Word's *Tools* menu.

You can start by basing your paper on a predefined Manuscript Template that is set up with publishing rules applied, as described on page 237. Then, create citations, a bibliography formatted according to any one of hundreds of styles, and cited figures and tables. Instant formatting technology can automatically update your citations and bibliography as you write.

A Traveling Library allows you to reformat references in your Word document even when your EndNote library is not available. If you are collaborating with other authors, you can rely on the Traveling Library to supply reference information. See "The Traveling Library" on page 283 for more information.

Word Processor Compatibility

To Cite While You Write, you must use Microsoft Word X. Cite While You Write can convert and use Word documents that previously used the EndNote Add-in or earlier versions of Cite While You Write, although we recommend that you first unformat those documents.

If you use a different word processor, or an older version of Word, please see Chapter 11.

To create a stand-alone bibliography that is not based on the citations in a paper, see "Independent Bibliographies" on page 309 in Chapter 12.

NOTE: Only one word processor at a time should be open when inserting citations and formatting documents.

Basic Instructions

The basic steps required to cite a reference and generate a bibliography with Microsoft Word X are summarized below. These procedures are described in more detail later in this chapter.

To Cite While You Write:

1. Open the EndNote library or libraries that contain the references you wish to cite.

2. Start Microsoft Word and open the paper you are writing. (We recommend using the template wizard to create your Word documents as described under "Using Predefined Manuscript Templates" on page 236.)

3. When you are ready to cite a source, position the cursor in the text where you would like to put the citation.

4. Go to the *Tools* menu in Word, then the *EndNote 7* submenu, and select *Find Citation(s)*. An EndNote Find Citations dialog appears, which shows the previous search results.

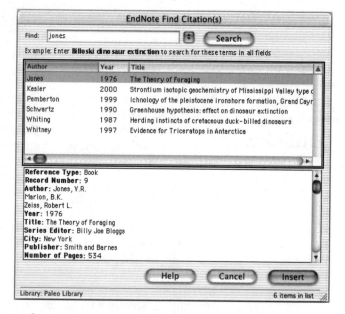

5. In the *Find* box, enter identifying text for EndNote to locate the appropriate reference. This could be an author's last name, a year, a keyword, or any other combination of terms found in the reference.

6. Click *Search* and EndNote compares the identifying text to your EndNote references and then lists the matching reference(s).

7. Identify, highlight, and *Insert* the appropriate reference(s).

8. Go back to step 4 to insert the next citation, and continue citing references this way.

NOTE: When Instant Formatting is turned on, each time you insert a citation it is formatted and a bibliography is updated at the end of your document. When you are done inserting citations, your document is done! Instant Formatting is turned on by default. To find out more about this setting, see "Instant Formatting" on page 263.

9. If your citations are not automatically formatted, and a bibliography is not updated each time you insert a citation, go to the *Tools* menu in Word, then the *EndNote 7* submenu, and select *Format Bibliography*.

   Even when Instant Formatting applies, you may want to *Format Bibliography* in order to change the style or layout of your citations and bibliography.

   A Format Bibliography dialog appears, where you can change, or simply verify, the style and layout of the bibliography.

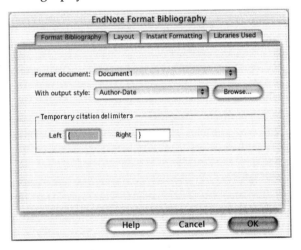

NOTE: The dialog lists the styles that are currently selected as your "favorites" in the Style Manager. If you need to choose a style that is not in the list, click *Browse* to locate it.

10. Click *OK*. EndNote scans your paper and, using the selected style, formats any temporary citations, reformats formatted citations, and appends a bibliography to the end of your paper.

Your paper is ready for publication!

If you need to make changes to the paper after formatting (such as adding or deleting citations), make the necessary changes, choose the *Format Bibliography* command again, and let EndNote do the rest.

If you want to insert figure or table citations, see "Inserting and Formatting Figures and Tables" on page 270.

Notes about Microsoft Word

Installing Cite While You Write Support in Word

EndNote's installation program installs Cite While You Write support for Microsoft Word X. If you install Word *after* installing EndNote, you must either reinstall EndNote or do a custom install of the word processor support. For more information, see "Manually Installing Support for Word X" on page 19.

EndNote commands appear on an *EndNote 7* submenu of the *Tools* menu in Word.

NOTE: If you limited your installation of Word with a Custom Installation, and attempting to use Cite While You Write results in a Visual Basic error, you need to reinstall Word using the Full Installation option.

The Cite While You Write Commands

When Cite While You Write is installed, several EndNote commands appear on an *EndNote 7* submenu of the *Tools* menu in Word:

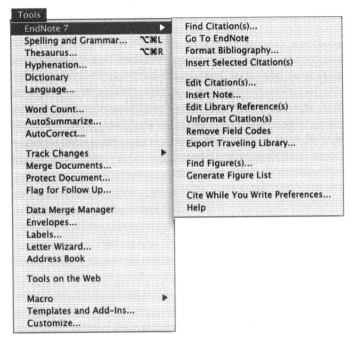

When you choose an EndNote command from the menu, the EndNote program starts (if not already running) and a *Cite While You Write* submenu appears on EndNote's *Tools* menu, displaying some of the same commands as the *Tools>EndNote 7* menu in Word.

These are brief descriptions of the Cite While You Write commands found on the *EndNote 7* submenu of Word's *Tools* menu:

♦ *Find Citation(s)* This command displays the EndNote Find Citations dialog, which allows you to search for EndNote references to select and insert as citations in your Word document. See page 242 for more information.

♦ *Go To EndNote* This command brings EndNote to the front of your screen. It launches EndNote if it is not already running.

♦ *Format Bibliography* This command formats (or reformats) your paper according to the rules of the selected style. The formatting process replaces the temporary citations in your paper with formatted citations, and builds a bibliography at the end of the document. See page 262 for more information.

NOTE: By default, Instant Formatting is turned on, so your citations and bibliography are automatically formatted as you work.

♦ *Insert Selected Citations* This command inserts citations for each reference currently selected in the open EndNote library. You can insert up to 50 citations within a single set of delimiters.

♦ *Edit Citations* This command displays the Edit Citation dialog, where you can edit existing individual or multiple citations. You can omit author and/or year from citations, or add prefix or suffix text (such as page numbers) to citations. See page 258 for more information.

♦ *Insert Note* Use the Insert Note dialog to add custom text citations to your Word document. See page 249 for more information.

♦ *Edit Library Reference(s)* Select citations in your Word document, then choose this command to directly edit the corresponding references in EndNote.

♦ *Unformat Citation(s)* Use this command to unformat a selected citation before editing it, or to unformat the whole document. This removes style formatting for the selected citations, and leaves temporary citations which usually consist of the author's last name, the year, and the record number surrounded by delimiters. See page 260 for more information.

♦ *Remove Field Codes* Use this item to save a copy of your document without formatted Cite While You Write field codes. Formatted citations and the bibliography are saved as text. This allows you to submit a copy of your paper to a publisher. See page 285 for more information.

♦ *Export Traveling Library* Use this command to create an EndNote library from the references used in a paper. See page 283 for more information.

♦ *Find Figure(s)* This command displays the EndNote Find Figures dialog. Search for an EndNote reference that contains an image, and insert a figure or table citation in your Word document. The citation is numbered, and the figure or table is automatically added to the document. See page 271 for more information.

- *Generate Figure List* This command updates your figure and table citations plus the formatted figures and tables found within the body of the document or in a list at the end of the document. See page 262 for more information.

- *Cite While You Write Preferences* Use the Preferences dialog to change general Cite While You Write preferences and the EndNote keyboard shortcuts available in Word. See page 494 for more information.

- *Help* Display help specific to inserting citations and generating bibliographies in Word.

You may prefer to execute these commands from the keyboard. Note the keyboard shortcuts defined under *Cite While You Write Preferences*.

You can also use the corresponding EndNote 7 toolbar for easy access.

Field Codes

Cite While You Write places field codes around and inside your formatted citations in Word. These hidden codes allow EndNote to format, unformat, and reformat citations within Word.

For example, this formatted citation:

(Schwartz and Billoski 1990)

appears with these field codes:

```
{ ADDIN EN.CITE
<EndNote><Cite><Author>Schwartz</Author><Year>1990</Ye
ar><RecNum>5</RecNum><MDL><REFERENCE_TYPE>7</
REFERENCE_TYPE><AUTHORS><AUTHOR>Schwartz,
M.T.</AUTHOR><AUTHOR>Billoski,
T.V.</AUTHOR></AUTHORS><YEAR>1990</YEAR><TITLE
>Greenhouse hypothesis: effect on dinosaur
extinction</TITLE><SECONDARY_AUTHORS><SECONDAR
Y_AUTHOR>B.T.
Jones</SECONDARY_AUTHOR><SECONDARY_AUTHOR>S
mith,
N.V.</SECONDARY_AUTHOR></SECONDARY_AUTHORS>
<SECONDARY_TITLE>Extinction</SECONDARY_TITLE><P
LACE_PUBLISHED>New
York</PLACE_PUBLISHED><PUBLISHER>Barnes and
Ellis</PUBLISHER><PAGES>175-
189</PAGES><KEYWORDS><KEYWORD>dinosaurs</KEYW
ORD><KEYWORD>extinction</KEYWORD></KEYWORDS>
</MDL></Cite></EndNote>}
```

NOTE: We recommend that you *not* view field codes in Word. If you choose to view field codes, please do not modify them. Always keep backups of your papers!

Field codes for formatted citations include a Traveling Library of the EndNote references cited. The reference data saved with each citation includes all fields except Notes, Abstract, Image, and Caption. This allows you to use the document on a computer that doesn't contain a copy of your EndNote library.

Word's Cite While You Write field codes are supported by Word X. Once you start using Cite While You Write, you must take precautions before opening those files in other word processors or another version of Word. If a formatted document is opened and saved with an incompatible word processor, the formatted EndNote citations and bibliography lose their field codes. When this happens, EndNote cannot reformat the document.

Before you open a paper in a different word processor or give a publisher an electronic copy of your final formatted document, please see "Sharing Your Word Documents" on page 282 for instructions.

Using Predefined Manuscript Templates

Many predefined Microsoft Word manuscript templates are supplied with EndNote to ease electronic submissions to publishers. We provide them as guides to make your writing process easier, but they are not required in order to use Cite While You Write. Plus, you can use a manuscript template even when you don't plan to use Cite While You Write on that particular document.

When you use one of these templates to start your paper, many formatting issues are already set up for your target publication, such as proper margins, headings, pagination, line spacing, title page, abstract page, graphics placement, and font type and size. As with bibliographic formats, there are hundreds of variations between publishers.

Creating a Word Document Based on a Template

You can start a new Microsoft Word document based on predefined templates either from within EndNote or directly from Word. You can also copy and edit one of the predefined manuscript templates.

To create a document based on one of the predefined manuscript templates:

1. Start EndNote.

2. From the *Tools* menu, select *Manuscript Templates*.

3. In the File dialog, browse to the Templates folder found in the EndNote folder. (EndNote should automatically select this location.)

4. Select and open the template named for a particular editorial style guide or the publisher to which you intend to submit your manuscript.

   This opens a new document in Microsoft Word that is based on the template file, and starts a manuscript template wizard to help you set up your paper.

NOTE: The first time you launch the manuscript template wizard, you may receive a notice about macros. Accept macros to continue with the wizard.

---

5. Enter the information requested by the template wizard. (See the next section, "Supplying Information to the Template Wizard" on page 239 for more information.)

   As you enter information, the wizard places it in all of the appropriate places in the document. The windows that appear, and the information requested, varies depending upon the publisher.

6. To complete the wizard:

   ◆ Click *Next* to continue providing information. If you do not know how to respond to an information request, simply click *Next* to continue with the wizard. You can later enter the appropriate information in the designated, bracketed fields in Word.

♦ On the final template wizard window, click *Finish* to close the wizard and start writing!

NOTE: You can click *Finish* at any time to bypass the wizard and start working in the document. You will need to manually enter information that would have been inserted by the wizard. Clicking *Cancel* will stop the creation of a new document.

The resulting Word document already contains the information you provided to the wizard. To start entering text into the document, look for indicators to guide you. See "Writing Your Paper" on page 240 for tips about writing in the new document.

The manuscript templates are also available from within Word:

1. Start Microsoft Word.

2. From Word's *File* menu, select *Project Gallery*.

3. Select the EndNote item to display the supplied templates.

4. Select the template you wish to use, and click *OK*.

5. The EndNote manuscript template wizard will start, as described earlier, and will lead you through the process of setting up your paper.

When you complete the wizard, you are ready to start writing!

To edit a manuscript template:

1. Start Microsoft Word.

2. From Word's *File* menu, select *Open*.

3. Navigate to EndNote's Templates folder.

4. Select and *Open* the manuscript template you wish to modify.

5. Make changes to the template, and then save a copy of the file with a new name.

NOTE: Changes to a manuscript template may disable the manuscript wizard for that template.

Supplying Information to the Template Wizard

The EndNote document template wizard asks you to supply information, required by the publisher, which the wizard then places in your document. If the same information is required in more than one place, you enter it once and the wizard copies it as needed to the appropriate places and in the appropriate format.

Each publisher maintains its own guidelines, and those guidelines vary greatly. As you follow the wizard, you may be asked for:

Title

Depending on the publisher, you may be asked to provide the full title as well as a short title or running header.

Author Contact Information and Affiliation

Publishers typically require author information on title pages, but they may also require it in acknowledgements or in headers throughout the document. You should provide information about each contributing author.

Click *Add Author* to type information about each contributing author. You also have the option to click *Import vCard* to link to an existing address book and easily insert existing author information.

Once you add an author name with contact information, it is retained in an Authors on File list to use later. For subsequent papers, you can simply select names from the list.

Select the check box next to the corresponding author (the contact person).

Keywords

Almost every publisher requires that you provide keywords for indexing the manuscript. You can either provide your own keywords, or the publisher may require MeSH terms (the National Library of Medicine's Medical Subject Headings).

Sections

The manuscript sections required by the publisher are listed, such as Abstract, Introduction, Acknowledgements, Reference List, Tables, and Figures. These requirements vary significantly between publishers. The wizard lists the required sections, but you can select or remove sections as needed.

Writing Your Paper

You selected the Word template appropriate for your publisher. Then, you followed the template wizard to provide basic information, so your new Word document already contains that information. Now, you are ready to write your paper.

Tag Line Indicators

To start entering text into the document, look for tag line indicators to guide you. For example, you may see a tag that says:

```
[Insert Introduction text here (no subheadings)]
```

You can select this tag and overwrite it as you type the introduction. Next, you may see:

```
[Insert Acknowledgements here]
```

Again, select the tag and overwrite it as you type your acknowledgements.

Most of the sections of the paper are tagged in this way. These tags may tell you of character limits, indicate whether you should include subheadings, and contain font and style formatting. They organize your manuscript and help you follow the rules of the publisher.

Cite While You Write Markers

There are several instances where a section tag acts as a marker for Cite While You Write:

Figure Lists: When you insert a figure citation into your document, and the current output style is set to create a figure list at the end of the document, the figure list is created at a [Figures] tag. To change the position of the figures in your document, or to move the figure list to a separate file, see "Placing Figures and Tables" on page 275.

Table Lists: When you insert a figure citation where the image comes from EndNote's Chart or Table reference type, and the current output style is set to create a table list at the end of the document, the table list is created at a [Tables] tag. To change the position of the tables in your document, or to move the table list to a separate file, see "Placing Figures and Tables" on page 275.

Bibliographies: When you insert an in-text reference citation in the body of your document, the bibliography is created at the [References] tag.

The manuscript template applies a corresponding output style to the bibliography. For example, the Nature manuscript template would use the Nature output style to format the bibliography, although you can apply a different output style if you wish.

Citing Sources As You Write

You can enter EndNote temporary citations into a paper at any time, but most writers prefer entering citations as they write the paper rather than waiting to insert them after the text is written.

Forms of Citations

A "citation" is the brief bibliographic information in the body of a paper that refers the reader to a complete reference in the bibliography. A citation typically consists of a bibliography number or the author and year in parentheses:

```
... of the species at hand¹.
```

```
... of the species at hand (Argus, 1991).
```

Citations can appear as either unformatted or formatted in your Word document.

Unformatted (Temporary) Citations

An unformatted citation is a temporary placeholder, and does not reflect final output. It may appear after you *Find Citation(s)* and *Insert, Insert Selected Citation(s)*, drag-and-drop or copy and paste citations from EndNote to Word, *Unformat Citation(s)*, or manually enter unformatted citations. It contains information to find a unique, corresponding EndNote reference in the currently open library.

NOTE: If you have Instant Formatting turned on, you may never see an unformatted citation. Instant Formatting is turned on by default.

An unformatted citation typically consists of the first author's last name, year, and the EndNote record number, with citation delimiters at each end to identify the text:

```
{Author, Year #Record Number}.
```

For example:

```
{Alvarez, 1994 #8}
```

The unformatted citation makes it easy to identify the record cited. Even if your final goal is numeric citations, you can see meaningful information while you are working on your document.

EndNote relies on these temporary citations to determine which references to include in the bibliography.

Formatted Citations

The *Format Bibliography* command uses an output style to convert all unformatted citations into formatted citations, and reflects final output.

NOTE: When Instant Formatting is turned on, formatting is done as you insert citations–but you can still use *Format Bibliography* to change the style or layout of your citations and bibliography.

Formatted citations include hidden Word field codes in case you want to *Format Bibliography* again later, either after adding more citations or because you want to format in a different style.

Citations formatted in an Author-Date style might look like this:

```
(Alvarez 1994; Turnhouse 1987)
```

This is the same citation formatted in the Numbered style:

```
[1,2]
```

You can easily revert from formatted citations back to unformatted citations at any time. See "Unformatting Citations" on page 260.

Finding and Inserting Citations

You can search for EndNote references and insert them without ever leaving Word.

This is the easiest way to find and insert a citation into a Word document:

1. Open the EndNote libraries that contain the references you wish to cite.

2. Open the Word document and position the cursor at the location where you would like the citation.

3. From Word's *Tools* menu, select the *EndNote 7* submenu and *Find Citation(s)* to display the EndNote Find Citations dialog.

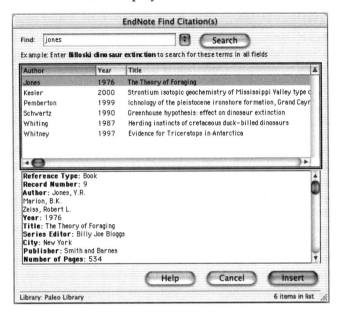

4. In the *Find* text box, enter text to identify the reference you wish to cite. EndNote assumes an "and" between each word, and will search all fields in your records.

5. Click *Search*, and EndNote compares the text to text in your EndNote references and lists the matching reference(s).

6. Identify, highlight, and *Insert* the appropriate reference(s).

   If no references match your text, you need to modify your search text and click *Search* again.

Citations are inserted directly into your paper in the same font as the surrounding text. Once a citation is inserted, it contains complete reference information in hidden codes.

You can insert citations in an existing manuscript or as you write. Remember to *Save* your document as you work.

To format your citations and generate a bibliography, see "Generating Bibliographies" on page 262. In most cases, Instant Formatting applies as you insert citations.

Finding and Inserting from Highlighted Text

To find and insert a citation from highlighted text:

1. As you are typing, enter text to identify the reference you wish to cite, and highlight that text.

2. From Word's *Tools* menu, select the *EndNote 7* submenu and *Find Citation(s)* to display the EndNote Find Citations dialog.

EndNote inserts your highlighted text into the Find box. Use the Find Citation(s) dialog as described above under "Finding and Inserting Citations."

Inserting Selected Citations

To insert references selected in EndNote:

1. Open the Word document and position the cursor at the location where you would like the citation.

2. From the *Tools* menu in Word, go to the *EndNote 7* submenu and then *Go to EndNote*.

3. Highlight the desired reference(s) in your EndNote library.

4. From the *Tools* menu in EndNote, select the *Cite While You Write* submenu and choose *Insert Selected Citation(s)*.

Using Drag-and-Drop or Copy and Paste

You can drag selected citations from your EndNote library and drop them into your paper at the desired location for the citation.

You can also copy citations from the EndNote Library window and paste them into the document (using *Copy* from EndNote's *Edit* menu and *Paste* from Word's *Edit* menu).

Manually Inserting Citations

You can manually type temporary citations if you prefer. See "Typing Citations into Your Paper" on page 252 to learn what types of citations EndNote recognizes.

Inserting Multiple Citations

There are several ways to insert multiple references in one in-text citation. When formatted, they appear as one multiple citation, sorted as your bibliographic style requires:

Unformatted: `{Hall, 1988 #77; Baker, 1988 #16}`

Formatted: `(Baker, 1988; Hall, 1988)`

EndNote can insert up to 50 citations within a single set of delimiters.

NOTE: If one of the citations in a multiple citation is not matched during formatting, the entire citation remains unformatted. Notes cannot be inserted as part of a multiple citation.

To insert multiple citations from Word:

1. From the *Tools* menu in Word, go to the *EndNote 7* submenu and select *Find Citation(s)*.

2. Enter a generic search term that will find the references you want, and click *Search*.

3. Hold down the COMMAND key while clicking on the desired references in the list (or hold down the SHIFT key to select a continuous range of references) in order to highlight the references.

4. Click *Insert*.

To insert multiple selected citations from EndNote:

1. In EndNote, hold down the COMMAND key while clicking on the desired references in your library (or hold down the SHIFT key to select a continuous range of references).

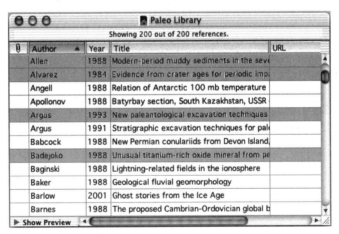

2. From EndNote's *Tools* menu, go to the *Cite While You Write* submenu and choose *Insert Selected Citation(s)*.

To insert multiple citations individually:

Another option is to insert citations individually, but immediately next to each other. Cite While You Write merges adjacent citations during formatting. Citations do not merge if *any* character separates them—including a space or punctuation mark.

Unformatted: {Hall,1988 #77}{Baker, 1988 #16}

Merged when Formatted: (Baker, 1988; Hall, 1988)

NOTE: You can add citations to an existing in-text citation, or change the order of citations within the delimiters with the Edit Citations dialog.

To insert, remove, or edit citations within an existing in-text citation:

1. Click on the formatted citation.

2. From Word's *Tools* menu, go to the *EndNote 7* submenu and *Edit Citation(s)* to display the EndNote Edit Citation dialog.

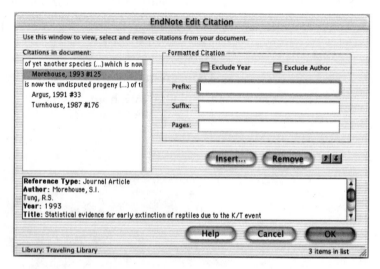

All of the cited references in the document are listed in the left column of the dialog. An ellipses shows where a citation appears within text. The line below shows the cited reference(s).

3. Highlight a citation, and then:

 ◆ Click *Remove* to delete it.

 ◆ Click *Insert* to insert another citation within the same set of delimiters.

 ◆ Use the arrow buttons to change the order of the citation in a multiple citation. (If a Citation Sort Order is applied by the current output style, changing the order of citations in a multiple citation has no effect.)

You can use the other features on this dialog as described on page 247.

Inserting From Multiple Libraries

You can cite references from multiple libraries. Simply open the selected libraries before you begin inserting citations.

If possible, though, we recommend that you use a single library when writing a paper. Keeping all of your references in one library simplifies the writing process because you know exactly where to find each reference, there is little likelihood of duplicate references, and you only need to have one library open when inserting citations.

NOTE: If you plan to insert citations from more than one library into a paper, read about the "Merge Duplicates in Bibliography" preference in the "Preferences" chapter on page 482.

Customizing Individual Citations

There may be cases where you want individual citations to differ from the standard format. You may want to remove the year or author from a citation if either was mentioned in the context of the sentence. Or, you might want to add a page reference or comment before or after the citation.

For example, assume a formatted citation looks like this:

    Hall's discovery (Hall, 1988)

You can omit the author's name from the citation:

    Hall's discovery (1988)

You can omit the date from the citation:

    the 1988 discovery (Hall)

You can add a suffix with page number to the citation:

    the discovery (Hall, 1988 p.4)

You can add a prefix to the citation:

    the discovery (see Hall, 1988)

To customize a formatted citation:

1. Insert and format the citation.

2. Click on the formatted citation.

3. From Word's *Tools* menu, go to the *EndNote 7* submenu and *Edit Citation(s)* to display the EndNote Edit Citation dialog.

EndNote Edit Citation

Use this window to view, select and remove citations from your document.

Citations in document:

of yet another species (...) which is now
  Morehouse, 1993 #125
is now the undisputed progeny (...) of t
  Argus, 1991 #33
  Turnhouse, 1987 #176

Formatted Citation

☐ Exclude Year   ☐ Exclude Author

Prefix: [   ]

Suffix: [   ]

Pages: [   ]

(Insert...) (Remove) [↑][↓]

Reference Type: Journal Article
Author: Morehouse, S.I.
Tung, R.S.
Year: 1993
Title: Statistical evidence for early extinction of reptiles due to the K/T event

(Help) (Cancel) (OK)

Library: Traveling Library   3 items in list

All of the cited references in the document are listed in the left column of the dialog. An ellipses shows where a citation appears within text. The line below shows the cited reference(s).

4. Highlight the citation you want to customize.

5. Customize as needed:

   ◆ **Exclude Author:** Select this to omit the author name from the formatted citation.

   ◆ **Exclude Year:** Select this to omit the date from the formatted citation.

   ◆ **Prefix:** Enter text here to print immediately before the citation text (spaces are significant).

   ◆ **Suffix:** Enter text here to print after the citation text (spaces are significant). You can enter page numbers here if you always want them to print *after* the citation.

   ◆ **Pages:** Page numbers entered here are considered entered into a "Cited Pages" field, so they can be manipulated on output just like any other EndNote field. In order to print, the Cited Pages field must be listed in the citation template and/or footnote template of your output style. This is typically used to print the page numbers within a full footnote citation. Most EndNote styles that require a special format for citations in footnotes are already configured this way. For information about how to modify your output style to include Cited Pages, see Chapter 15.

6. Click *OK* to implement the change(s) to the citation.

Including Notes in the List of References

Some journal styles (such as Science) require that you include notes along with the list of works cited at the end of the document. In such a system, notes are numbered just like citations, and are included in the reference list in order of appearance, along with bibliographic references.

Including notes in this way makes sense only when you are formatting your paper with a numbered style (not an author-date style).

To insert text as a numbered note in the reference list:

1. Position the cursor at the location in your text where you would like the number indicating the note.

2. From the *Tools* menu, go to the *EndNote 7* submenu and select *Insert Note* to display the EndNote Insert Note dialog.

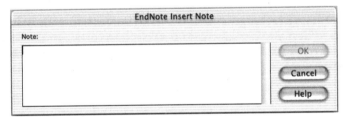

3. Type your note text into the text box. There is no limit on the amount of text you can enter.

4. Click *OK* to insert a numbered note.

When your paper is formatted by EndNote using a numbered style, the note text is assigned a number and listed along with the references at the end of the paper.

The way that notes are displayed when unformatted can be changed in the Temporary Citations preferences (see page 477).

To manually type text as a numbered note in the reference list:

1. Type the text into the body of your document where you would want the number for the note to appear.

2. Be sure to surround the entire section of text with your Temporary Citation Delimiters (curly braces by default), and begin it with "NOTE:". For example:

```
{NOTE: The authors would like to
acknowledge the support of...}
```

Restrictions on the Use of the "NOTE" Feature:

♦ This feature requires that a numbered style be used for formatting; otherwise, the note appears as text in the body of your paper.

♦ Enter text only. Do not enter graphics, equations, or symbols.

♦ Do not use the temporary citation delimiters as part of the text of the note. Other markers, such as the record number marker, the prefix marker, and the multiple citation separator may be used.

♦ Notes cannot be combined with regular bibliographic citations within the same set of delimiters (such as parentheses or brackets). They must be cited separately—each in its own set of delimiters.

Inserting Citations into a Formatted Paper

If you need to add one or more citations to a paper that has already been formatted, simply insert the new citations into the text (as described earlier in this chapter) and choose *Format Bibliography* when you are ready to update the bibliography and citations.

To add a new reference to an existing citation, insert the new reference *next to* (not within) the existing citation, like this:

```
(Hockney and Ellis, 1996){Argus, 1984 #1}
```

Adjacent citations are merged during formatting, and the formatted citations are sorted according to the style:

```
(Argus, 1984; Hockney and Ellis, 1996)
```

NOTE: Do not insert a citation into the middle of a formatted citation. Insert it immediately before or after the existing citation, with no space between them.

Citing References in Footnotes and Endnotes

Once you have created a footnote or endnote in Word, you can cite references in that footnote or endnote just like you cite them in the body of the document.

To cite a reference in a footnote or endnote:

1. Use the appropriate command in Word to create the footnote or endnote. (EndNote does not create the footnote or endnote in the document, but is used to insert and format citations in the note.)

2. Position the cursor in the footnote or endnote where you would like the citation(s) to appear.

3. Insert the citation as you normally would.

The EndNote style that is selected when you choose *Format Bibliography* determines how citations in footnotes and endnotes are formatted. EndNote can format these citations as brief in-text citations or like complete references in the bibliography. It can also create a special format specific to footnotes or endnotes, including options like "Ibid." and other variations of shortened references when a citation appears more than once in the footnotes or endnotes. See Chapter 15 for more information, and "Bibliography and Footnote Templates" on page 373.

If you are citing full references in footnotes, you can include specific page numbers to be formatted like a regular EndNote field. See "Customizing Individual Citations" on page 247. Or, if you are manually typing citations, see "Citing Specific Page Numbers in Footnotes" on page 256.

Typing Citations into Your Paper

There are many ways to insert citations in your paper, as discussed previously in this chapter. The most flexible way is to manually type temporary citations directly into your paper. Your hands never have to leave the keyboard.

The rules described in this section govern how EndNote recognizes and interprets temporary (unformatted) citations. Use these rules when typing temporary citations directly into your document.

Notes About Temporary Citations

♦ Each citation must match only one reference in the library.

♦ When Instant Formatting is turned off, a temporary citation is enclosed in citation delimiters and typically includes the first author's last name, the year of publication, and the record number for that reference: {Schwartz, 1990 #5}.

♦ Within one set of citation delimiters you can have several citations separated by semicolons: {Schwartz, 1990 #5; Billoski, 1992 #28}.

♦ Curly braces ("{" and "}") are the default temporary citation delimiters, although they can be changed (see page 477). EndNote looks for these markers to find citations in your word processing documents.

♦ In addition to the citation delimiters, these are other possible components to a temporary citation: Author, Year, Record Number, Prefix Text, Suffix Text, and any other text found in the record.

♦ Any part of a temporary citation can be omitted, as long as enough information remains to match just one reference in the library. If you omit an author or year from a temporary citation, those components are omitted from the formatted citation as well—although you can change this preference. (See "Omitting Authors or Years from Citations" on page 254.)

Components of a Temporary Citation

The typical EndNote temporary (unformatted) citation consists of an author's last name, a year, and a record number, all enclosed in citation delimiters. However, temporary citations can take on various other formats.

Temporary citations must begin and end with the opening and closing citation delimiters, but the other components of a temporary citation can vary.

You can type any string of text found in the reference, as in:

`{dinosaur extinction}`

Or, you can type any of these items in this order (comma placement is significant):

`{Prefix \Author, Year #Record Number Suffix}`

`{Prefix \Author, Year, Any Text, Suffix}`

Each component is briefly described below; more detailed information follows.

♦ **Author's Last Name:** Only the last name of one author is listed in a temporary citation. It can be any author associated with the reference, and not just the first author. Include a comma after the author's name to limit the search only to author fields:

> `{Schwartz, 1990}`

♦ **Year:** The year should appear exactly as it does in the reference, and it should be preceded by a comma. Even if you leave out the author name, include a comma before the year to limit the search to the Year field:

> `{, 2001}`

♦ **Record Number:** The record number is EndNote's unique number for a reference. It is the only part of a temporary citation that you can count on to *always* identify just one reference in your library. The record number must be preceded by a number sign:

> `{Jones, 1987 #84}`

♦ **Any Text:** Any text that appears in the reference can be used to help EndNote locate the reference in the library. In order for this to be helpful, choose words that are unique to that reference. Enter the specific text only, or enter the text in place of the record number part of the temporary citation and after a second comma:

> `{greenhouse}`
>
> `{Schwartz, 1990, greenhouse}`
>
> `{Schwartz, , greenhouse}`

In the third example, where the date is omitted, you must insert a space between the two commas or EndNote will not recognize any citation matches.

♦ **Prefix Text:** To add text to print before the formatted citation, type the text immediately after the opening brace and then a backslash "\" to separate prefix text from the search text:

```
{see \Jones, 1987 #84}
```

♦ **Suffix Text:** To add text to print after a formatted citation, enter the suffix text immediately after the record number or enter a *third* comma after the search text and then type the suffix text:

```
{Smith, 1995 #98 p.293}

{Smith, 1995, dinosaur, p.293}
```

NOTE: For an easy way to modify individual Cite While You Write citations once they are formatted, see "Customizing Individual Citations" on page 247.

Omitting Authors or Years from Citations

While your style may normally include the author's name and date in each in-text citation, you may want to omit the author and/or year from a particular citation. This is useful if you have mentioned the author or year in the context of the sentence and do not want to repeat the information in the citation.

To remove the author's name or date from a citation, simply leave that information out of the unformatted citation.

To omit the author's name, enter:

```
...Wyatt's recent discovery {, 1993 #38}.
```

which will format as:

```
...Wyatt's recent discovery (1993).
```

To omit the date, enter:

```
...about his 1993 discovery {Wyatt, #38}.
```

which will format as:

```
...about his 1993 discovery (Wyatt).
```

NOTE: *Numbered* citations do not print the author name or year in any case, so these settings would be ignored.

If you want a reference to appear in your bibliography, but not as a citation in your paper, you can exclude both the author and year, leaving only the record number. When you format your paper with a style that formats authors and years in the citations, this particular citation will not display in text, but will be included in the bibliography.

However, if you would rather have the author and year appear in the formatted citation regardless of whether or not they are in the temporary citation, choose *Preferences* from EndNote's *EndNote* menu, select the *Formatting* option, and uncheck the setting to "Omit Author and/or Year from formatted citation if removed from temporary citation." With this setting turned off, you may enter just the record number "{#34}" as a temporary citation, and still format the paper accurately with a style that requires authors and years in the in-text citations.

NOTE: For an easy way to modify individual Cite While You Write citations once they are inserted, see "Customizing Individual Citations" on page 247.

Citation Prefixes

You can type a prefix in front of any *unformatted* in-text citation, using a backslash to separate the prefix text from the reference. For example, an in-text citation such as:

```
{see also \Hall, 1988 #77}
```

formatted in the APA style would be:

```
(see also Hall, 1988)
```

When there is only one prefix in a multiple citation and it is at the beginning of the citation, it will stay there regardless of how the citations are sorted. For example, this citation:

```
{e.g. \Hall,1988 #77; Argus, 1991 #11}
```

after being formatted in the APA style will appear as:

```
(e.g. Argus, 1991; Hall, 1988)
```

If the prefix is not at the beginning of the multiple citation, or if there is more than one prefix in a multiple citation, the prefix text remains with the reference it precedes. For example, this citation:

```
{Argus, 1984 #11; especially \Hall, 1988 #77}
```

formatted in the Author-Date style will be:

```
(Argus, 1984; especially Hall, 1988)
```

Changing the Citation Prefix Marker

You can change the prefix marker from a backslash to another character by choosing *Preferences* from EndNote's *EndNote* menu, selecting the *Temporary Citations* option, and changing the character in the "Citation Prefix Marker" box. Use a character that is not otherwise used in the citations. Letters, numbers, semicolons, "@" and commas cannot be prefix markers. See "Temporary Citations" on page 477 for more information.

Citation Suffixes

Text typed after the record number or search text in an unformatted citation appears immediately after the citation when it is formatted. For example, these citations:

```
{Hall, 1988 #77, p. 5}

{Smith, 1995, dinosaur,, p.293}
```

after being formatted in the APA style will appear as:

```
(Hall, 1988, p. 5)

(Smith, 1995, p.293)
```

In multiple citations, the suffix text remains with the citation that it follows, even if the citations are sorted differently during the formatting process. For example, this citation:

```
{Hall, 1988 #77 p. 5; Argus, 1991 #11}
```

formatted in the Author-Date style will be:

```
(Argus, 1991; Hall, 1988 p. 5)
```

Including Semicolons & Other Citation Delimiters in a Citation

In order to print an actual semicolon or the prefix marker (\) as part of a citation, type an accent grave (`) before the character. The accent grave tells EndNote to treat the following character as regular text, and not as a significant character for parsing the citation. For example, to create a citation that is formatted as "(see Figure 1; Jackson, 1994)" the unformatted citation must look like this: {see Figure 1`; \Jackson, 1994 #28}. The ` character before the semicolon tells EndNote not to treat the semicolon as a separator between citations.

Citing Specific Page Numbers in Footnotes

When citing full references in footnotes, you might want to include specific page numbers. EndNote provides a way to do this where the page numbers that you type into a temporary citation can be manipulated by the EndNote style just like a field in your EndNote reference. You can add specific pages to the temporary citation, and have the EndNote style include them wherever they need to be in the formatted citation. The style can also apply special pages formatting, like deciding whether to add "p." or "pp." before the page numbers, and how to list the range of pages.

The easiest way to add cited pages is to use the Edit Citation dialog. See "Customizing Individual Citations" on page 247.

To manually include specific page numbers to a reference in an unformatted footnote citation, simply enter the page number preceded by "@" at the end of the temporary citation:

```
{Smith, 1999 #24 @145-6}
```

All text that follows the @ symbol (up to the next space) is considered the "Cited Pages." You must also configure the EndNote style used to format the paper to use "Cited Pages" in the footnote template. Most EndNote styles that require a special format for citations in footnotes are already configured this way.

When EndNote formats the citation, the cited pages ("145-6" in the example above) are inserted in the correct location and formatted as appropriate for the style. See Chapter 15 for more information about EndNote's styles.

NOTE: If you enter page numbers at the end of the temporary citation without the "@" character, they will still appear in a formatted *in-text* citation, but EndNote will not be able to manipulate them by changing the page format or by moving them to a different position in the formatted citation. They will simply appear, as entered, at the end of the formatted in-text citation. This is a perfectly acceptable way to enter page numbers for in-text citations (or for footnotes formatted just like your in-text citations). See "Citation Suffixes" on page 256 to see how this works. This method will not work for citations in footnotes that are formatted as full bibliographic references or with a special footnote format. For those cases, you must use the @ symbol to identify the cited pages in the temporary citation.

Examples of Modified Citations

The following examples demonstrate how different modifications to a temporary citation affect its formatted citation in either an author/year or numbered style. In the first column is an example of a modified temporary citation before formatting, and to the right are two examples of that citation formatted in different styles.

Examples of Modified Citations

Unformatted Citation	Formatted with Author-Date	Formatted with Numbered	Comments
{Hall, #77}	(Hall)	[1]	To remove the year from the formatted citation, simply delete it from the unformatted citation.
{, 1988 #77}	(1998)	[1]	To remove the author from the formatted citation, delete just the author's name from the unformatted citation. Note that the comma remains in the temporary citation to indicate the omission of the author.
{#77}	No citation appears	[1]	This temporary citation removes the author and the year from the formatted citation. When formatted with an author-date style, the in-text citation is eliminated, but the reference still appears in the bibliography. Numbered citations appear as usual.
{Hall,1988 #77 p.4}	(Hall 1988 p.4)	[1 p.4]	To add text after the formatted citation, add it after the record number in the unformatted citation. With this temporary citation, the text after the record number, including spaces and punctuation, is added to the formatted citation.
{see \Hall, 1988 #77}	(see Hall 1988)	[see 1]	To add text before the formatted citation, type the text immediately after the opening curly brace, and type a backslash "\" to separate the text from the author's name. (See "Citation Prefixes" on page 255.)
{Hall, #77, p.4}	(Hall, p.4)	[1, p.4]	This temporary citation eliminates the year from the formatted citation, but adds the additional text ", p.4". Type additional text after the record number or after a third comma when using additional search text.

Changing Existing Citations

You can change citations at any time. After making changes, choose *Format Bibliography* to (re)format the new or modified citations and regenerate the bibliography.

Editing Citations

Once you have inserted and formatted a citation, you should not edit it directly (although you *can* do so, if you feel you must). Direct edits are lost the next time EndNote formats the bibliography.

You can almost always get EndNote to format your citations exactly to your specifications by editing the style, the EndNote reference, or the citation (as described here).

To safely edit a formatted citation:

1. Click on the citation you wish to change.

2. From Word's *Tools* menu, go to the *EndNote 7* submenu and *Edit Citation(s)* to display the EndNote Edit Citation dialog.

All of the cited references in the document are listed in the left column of the dialog. An ellipses shows where a citation appears within text. The line below shows the cited reference(s).

3. Select the appropriate citation from the list at the left of the dialog (you can scroll through all citations in the document) and make any of the following changes to the highlighted citation:

- ♦ **Exclude Author:** Select this to omit the author name from the formatted citation.

- ♦ **Exclude Year:** Select this to omit the date from the formatted citation.

- ♦ **Prefix:** Enter text here to print immediately before the citation text (spaces are significant).

- ♦ **Suffix:** Enter text here to print after the citation text (spaces are significant).

- ♦ **Pages:** Enter page numbers here to print as Cited Pages. To print, the Cited Pages field must be listed in the citation template or footnote template of the output style.

4. You can add or remove citations from a multiple citation, or change the order of citations.

- ♦ **Insert:** Use this to add another citation within the same set of delimiters.

◆ **Remove**: Highlight a citation and click *Remove* to delete it from the in-text citation.

◆ **Up and Down Arrows:** Highlight a reference and use the arrows to change the order of display. (If a Citation Sort Order is applied by the current output style, using this dialog to change the order of citations in a multiple citation has no effect.)

5. Click *OK* to implement your change(s).

Unformatting Citations

Unformatting reverts formatted citations to temporary citations, removes the bibliography, and turns off instant formatting.

If your citations are formatted in a numbered style, you can unformat your paper to easily identify citations as you work. You can Format Bibliography again later.

NOTE: Unlike formatted citations, *un*formatted citations require that you have the corresponding EndNote library open in order to format the paper again. Unformatting removes the Traveling Library.

To unformat citations:

1. Determine which citations you want to unformat:

◆ To unformat a particular citation, highlight only that citation.

◆ If the citation you want to unformat is part of a multiple citation, highlight the multiple citation. All citations within the delimiters will be unformatted.

◆ To unformat a section of the document, highlight that section.

◆ To unformat the entire document, either select nothing or highlight the entire document.

2. From Word's *Tools* menu, go to the *EndNote 7* submenu and *Unformat Citation(s)*. If you are unformatting the entire document, this unformats all of the in-text citations and removes the current bibliography.

You can tell when a paper is unformatted because the citations appear in the temporary citation format (such as "{Smith, 1999 #25}").

Unformatted citations are temporary placeholders that do not reflect final output. If you want to send your final formatted document to a publisher, see "Removing Field Codes" on page 285.

NOTE: When you unformat citations, Instant Formatting is disabled. To format your paper, go to the *Tools* menu, then the *EndNote 7* submenu, and choose *Format Bibliography*. From the Format Bibliography dialog, you can enable Instant Formatting again on the Instant Formatting tab.

Moving or Copying Citations

You can highlight any text that includes citations, then use the *Edit* menu commands to *Cut* or *Copy* and then *Paste* it elsewhere in the document. You can do this with formatted or temporary (unformatted) citations.

To move or copy only the citation itself, make sure you highlight the entire citation (including surrounding delimiters). Then *Cut* or *Copy* and *Paste* it elsewhere in the document.

Deleting Citations

To delete an unformatted citation, simply highlight the entire citation (including delimiters), and press the backspace or delete key.

While it is possible to highlight a formatted citation and simply press the delete key on your keyboard, we do not recommend you do that. If you do not completely delete the citation and all associated codes, you could corrupt your document.

To safely delete a formatted citation:

1. Highlight the citation you want to delete.

2. From the *Tools* menu in Word, go to the *EndNote 7* submenu and select *Edit Citation(s)* to display the EndNote Edit Citation dialog.

   All of the cited references in the document are listed in the left column of the dialog. An ellipses shows where a citation appears within text. The line below shows the cited reference(s). The citation you highlighted in the document should be highlighted in the list.

3. In the left column, make sure the highlighted citation is the one you want to delete.

   If the citation is part of a multiple citation, make sure you select just the citation you want to delete.

4. Click *Remove*.

5. Click *OK*.

Generating Bibliographies

Formatting a bibliography serves two functions:

♦ It formats each in-text citation according to a bibliographic style.

♦ It adds a complete bibliography to the document (unless you override this with a setting in the output style).

The format used for citations and references is determined by the output style selected.

Basic Instructions

When you have finished writing your paper in Word, and all of your EndNote citations have been inserted into the text, you are ready for EndNote to format the paper and generate a bibliography. This can be done in one of two ways:

♦ *Instant Formatting* actually works as you insert citations, and is enabled when you first start using Cite While You Write. EndNote uses the currently selected style to format citations and update the bibliography each time a citation is inserted. However, if you want to change the style or layout of references, you must use the *Format Bibliography* command.

♦ *Format Bibliography*, selected from the *EndNote 7* submenu on the *Tools* menu, allows you to modify style and layout settings before formatting your document. This is also where you enable or disable Instant Formatting.

These are the basic formatting instructions:

1. From the *Tools* menu in Word, go to the *EndNote 7* submenu and select *Format Bibliography*.

2. On the Format Bibliography tab, use the *With output style* option to select an output style to format references. It is okay to experiment with different styles because you can simply reformat again.

3. Click *OK* to format all citations and build the bibliography.

Instant Formatting

Instant Formatting works while you work. As you insert citations, EndNote uses the currently selected style to format citations and update the bibliography. By default, Instant Formatting is enabled.

To change the style or layout of references, or to change Instant Formatting settings, you can use the *Format Bibliography* command, which is described in the next section.

In some cases, Instant Formatting is disabled, such as when you unformat your paper.

NOTE: To turn Instant Formatting on or off for *new* Word documents, see "General Preferences" on page 494.

To enable or disable Instant Formatting in the current document:

1. From the *Tools* menu in Word, go to the *EndNote 7* submenu and select *Format Bibliography*.

2. Click the Instant Formatting tab.

3. Click *Enable* or *Disable* to toggle Instant Formatting.

   When enabled, you can click the *Settings* button to change these Instant Formatting controls:

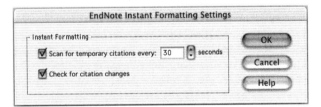

   ◆ **Scan for temporary citations** turns on scanning of temporary citations. This finds and formats all citations, including those you may have entered manually. You can select how often EndNote scans your document.

   ◆ **Check for citation changes** turns on background scanning that looks for citation changes.

   Click *OK* to save changes to the Instant Formatting settings.

4. Click *OK* to format all citations and build the bibliography.

NOTE: When Instant Formatting is enabled, leaving the Format Bibliography dialog--whether you click *OK* or *Cancel*-will always trigger formatting in your document.

Formatting the Bibliography and/or Changing Bibliography Settings

You may be halfway through inserting citations, or you may have finished writing your paper. You may have instant formatting enabled, or you may have manually inserted citations with formatting disabled. It doesn't matter. As long as you have citations entered in your document, you can format your paper at any time. You can reformat after adding more citations or to change the style or layout settings.

NOTE: The first time a citation is formatted, the corresponding EndNote library must be open. After that, EndNote can use the Traveling Library for reference information. See "The Traveling Library" on page 283 for more information.

To format citations and generate a bibliography:

1. From the *Tools* menu in Word, go to the *EndNote 7* submenu and select *Format Bibliography*.

2. On the Format Bibliography tab, change or verify these settings:

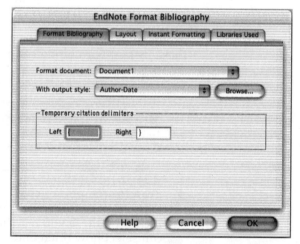

Format document: Make sure the appropriate Word document is selected from the list of open Word documents.

With output style: Select the appropriate output style to format references. You can experiment by reformatting with various output styles. To add more output styles to the list, see "Adding Styles to the Output Styles List" on page 266.

Temporary citation delimiters: These are the opening and closing delimiters for temporary citations. Make sure they are unique delimiters, and not characters you would normally use in your paper. The defaults are curly braces.

3. On the Layout tab, change or verify these settings:

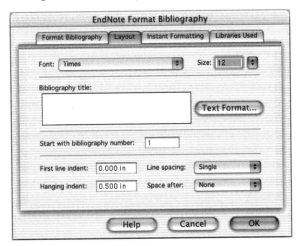

Font and Size: These are the text font and size used for the bibliography.

Bibliography title: To print a title at the top of your bibliography, type the title in this text box.

Text Format: The Text Format button displays a dialog where you can change the format of the reference list title.

Start with bibliography number: Enter a starting reference number if you want to number your bibliography.

First line indent and **Hanging indent**: Use these settings to set a paragraph indent, a hanging indent, or no indent at all. The hanging indent applies to the second and subsequent lines of a reference in the bibliography. Type measurements as centimeters (cm), inches (in), lines (li), or points (pt).

Line spacing and **Space after**: Set the Line spacing for within a reference and the Space after for spacing between references.

4. On the Instant Formatting tab, you can *Enable* or *Disable* Instant Formatting. See the Instant Formatting section above for more information.

5. Click the Libraries Used tab to see which libraries are referenced in the document.

6. Click *OK* to save changes and format your citations and bibliography.

NOTE: You do not have to verify each tab every time you format. If all you want to do is change the output style, choose *Format Bibliography*, select the output style on the Format Bibliography tab, and click *OK*.

Adding Styles to the Output Styles List

The bibliographic style selected on the *Format Bibliography* dialog determines how EndNote formats the citations in your paper and the references in the bibliography. The style takes care of text styles, punctuation, and sorting required for the citations and bibliography, as well as which fields are included in the bibliography.

You can use Format Bibliography to select a different style and reformat your document at any point.

If you do not see the style that you want to use listed in the *Output Style* list:

1. In EndNote, go to the *Edit* menu, choose *Output Styles*, and then select *Open Style Manager*.

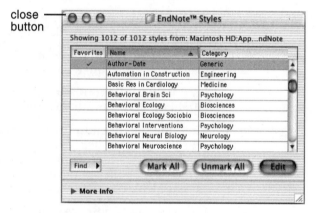

close button

2. Find the style that you need.

♦ You can quickly select a style by typing its name, or scroll through the list to find what you need.

♦ Click on the column headings to sort the styles by either name or category. Click a second time to reverse the sort order.

♦ Use the *Find* button in the Style Manager window to find entire categories of styles or to search for a style by a word in its name. For example, click the *Find* button and choose *Chemistry* to display all of the styles in the category "Chemistry."

The *Style Info* item in the information panel can be changed from *Style Info* to *Style Preview* to display a preview of how the selected style formats EndNote's sample references.

3. Click in the column box to the left of the style's name to choose it as one of your favorites. Or, to mark all of the styles that are displayed, perhaps a whole category, click *Mark All*.

All styles marked as "favorites" appear on the *Output Styles* menu.

Use the *Find* option to quickly locate categories of styles or individual styles.

The Less Info/More Info option shows or hides the information pane.

Choose between showing the style information or preview

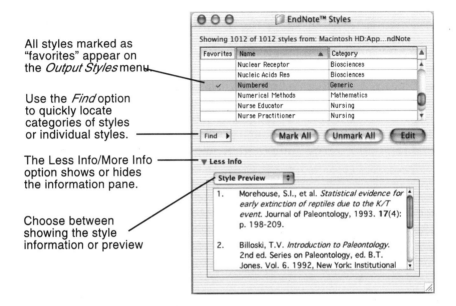

4. Close the Style Manager by clicking the close button or choosing *Close Style Manager* from the *File* menu.

Styles marked as favorites appear in the *Output Styles* list of EndNote's *Edit* menu as well as the styles list in Word when you *Format Bibliography*.

All styles can be modified to meet your specifications. You can also create completely new styles if necessary. See Chapter 15 for instructions about creating and modifying styles.

Reformatting Papers

Adding New Citations to Formatted Papers

If you add more citations to your paper after the formatting process, you can update the citations and the bibliography by simply choosing the *Format Bibliography* command again.

NOTE: You do not need to unformat your citations in order to reformat them.

Reformatting with Different Styles

Similarly, if you would like to reformat your paper in a different style, go to the *Tools* menu, then the *EndNote 7* submenu, and choose *Format Bibliography* again. Select a new style from the Format Bibliography dialog and click *OK*. Your citations and bibliography are updated for the new bibliographic style. (See "Adding Styles to the Output Styles List" on page 266 for information about expanding the list of available styles.)

Creating a Bibliography from Multiple Documents

You can use Word's Master Document feature to generate a single bibliography from multiple documents. This allows you to create a cumulative bibliography from any number of book chapters.

To generate a single bibliography:

1. In each of your documents, or chapters, insert your citations to link them to references in an EndNote library.

2. *Close* all of your documents.

3. Create a *New* document

4. Designate the new document as a master document, then insert and display each of your chapters as subdocuments. (Check Word's documentation if you need step-by-step instructions.)

5. From the *Tools* menu, go to the *EndNote 7* submenu and select *Format Bibliography*.

6. Verify the formatting options and click *OK*.

EndNote creates the bibliography, using citations from the master document and all displayed subdocuments, and places it at the end of the master document. You can move the bibliography anywhere within the master or subdocuments, and it will remain in that location even when you reformat.

NOTE: If you choose Word's *Insert> File* command and select the "Link" option to insert a document into the text, EndNote will *not* format the linked document when you format the main document. The text from the linked document will be skipped.

Directly Editing Bibliographies

It is always best to make changes to your final bibliography by correcting the data in the EndNote library, editing the output style you are using, or adding or deleting citations from your paper. Then, after making the necessary changes, choose *Format Bibliography* and the corrections are automatically made to the bibliography.

It is not always possible for EndNote to format the bibliography exactly as needed, so you might have to manually edit the formatted bibliography. If you must do this, remember that if you reformat a paper *after* editing the bibliography, EndNote will *not* preserve your edits. When EndNote reformats a bibliography, it deletes the existing one and puts a new one in its place.

You can edit the bibliography as you would any text. The bibliography may be shaded, but you can still edit it. If you later reformat the paper, your edits will be gone.

You can add text *after* the bibliography, but make sure to put it after the end of the formatted bibliography—outside of the bibliography field.

NOTE: See the Styles chapter (Chapter 15) for instructions about editing styles. If necessary, contact technical support for assistance.

Moving Bibliographies

Cite While You Write always creates the initial bibliography at the end of the Word document that it has formatted. If you move the bibliography to a different location in the document (you can drag-and-drop or Cut and Paste), EndNote keeps it there even if you reformat the paper.

NOTE: When using Instant Formatting, use drag-and-drop to move a bibliography. If you try to use *Cut* and *Paste*, Instant Formatting will create a new bibliography at the end of the document before you have a chance to Paste.

Deleting Bibliographies

To delete a bibliography, simply select the bibliography and delete it.

Make sure you drag the cursor across the very beginning of the bibliography to select the entire bibliography field. Press the BACKSPACE or DELETE key. You can also choose *Cut* from the *Edit* menu if you want to paste the bibliography somewhere else.

Inserting and Formatting Figures and Tables

Once images are organized in an EndNote library, they are available for inserting into a manuscript with Cite While You Write commands. The finishing touch is the automatic creation of a figure list and/or a table list that presents a sequential list of all graphics inserted in a manuscript.

A figure citation is a brief numbered citation in the body of a paper that refers the reader to a figure at the end of the paragraph or to a figure in a complete list of figures at the end of the paper.

In-text figure citations are sequentially numbered and formatted like this:

> *Marrella splendens* is a small "arthropod" somewhat reminiscent of a trilobite. This illustration also shows the dark "blob" produced by body contents which were squeezed out of the animal after burial. (Figure 1)

It includes the word "Figure" (or "Table"), the sequential number, and surrounding parentheses. The field may be shaded by Word to help you see citations, but shading does not print. You can turn field shading off in Word.

The current output style determines the placement of formatted figures and tables. They appear either within the body of the paper, directly after the paragraph where they are cited, or in a list at the end of the document, after the bibliography.

Notes About Formatting Figures and Tables

♦ Do not use Microsoft Word Captioning in conjunction with EndNote figure captioning or in-text citations.

♦ Images found in the *Chart or Table* reference type are inserted into word as tables, which are labeled and numbered separately from figures. (You still use the generic *Find Figure(s)* and *Generate Figure List* commands.)

♦ If you open an existing document that already has figure citations in the body (that were not inserted with EndNote's *Find Figure(s)* command), those figures will not be included in the figure list. You will need to add the existing figures to references in EndNote, and then use the *Find Figure(s)* command to insert them into the document.

♦ You can format figures either directly after the paragraph in which they are cited, or in a list at the end of the document. See "Placing Figures and Tables" on page 275.

♦ The Instant Formatting that applies to bibliographies does not apply to figures. In-text figure citations are always formatted as you insert them, but if you move or delete a figure citation in your paper, you must manually select *Generate Figure List* from the *Tools* menu to update the document.

♦ Figure and table captions are added from the Caption field in the EndNote reference.

♦ If more than one in-text figure citation references the same figure with the same caption, those citations are assigned the same figure number, and the figure appears only once in a figure list.

♦ You can manually insert a page break between figures if you prefer each figure on a separate page. These page breaks will be remembered if you choose *Generate Figure List* again.

Finding and Inserting Figures and Tables

You can search EndNote references and insert a graphic or file from the Image field of a reference into your Word document. The Image field in your references may be titled Image or have a custom name assigned by you.

NOTE: The file types accepted are dependent on your version of Word and other software installed on your computer. For example, some versions of Word will not accept PDF files.

To insert a graphic or file that is stored in an EndNote reference:

1. Open the EndNote library that contains the figure you wish to insert.

2. In the Word document, position the cursor at the location where you would like the figure citation to appear.

3. From Word's *Tools* menu, select the *EndNote 7* submenu and *Find Figure(s)* to display the EndNote Insert Figures dialog.

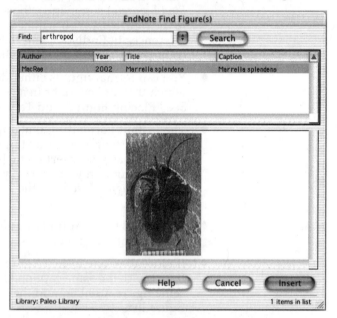

4. In the *Find* text box, enter text to identify the reference that contains the image. EndNote assumes an "and" between each word, and will search all fields in your records, including the Caption field.

5. Click *Search*, and EndNote compares the text to text in your EndNote references and lists each matching reference that contains an image.

   Endnote displays the Author, Year, Title, and Caption field from each matching reference. Drag the vertical bars between the column titles to display more or less of a field. The Caption field should contain a description of the image.

6. Identify, highlight, and *Insert* the appropriate figure.

   If no references match your text, you need to modify your search text and click *Search* again.

EndNote places an in-text figure citation at the cursor location and inserts and labels the figure itself. For example:

Marella splendens is a small "arthropod" somewhat reminiscent of a trilobite. This illustration also shows the dark "blob" produced by body contents which were squeezed out of the animal after burial. (Figure 1)

Figure 1. Marrella splendens

NOTE: Images found in the *Chart or Table* reference type are inserted into word as tables, which are labeled and numbered separately from figures.

The figure or table number represents the order of the image in the document.

EndNote inserts the image itself, along with the caption, immediately after the paragraph that cites it. You can modify the output style to place figures and tables in lists at the end of the document, after the bibliography. See "Figures and Tables" on page 408 for more information.

You can insert figures and tables in an existing manuscript or as you write. Remember to *Save* your document as you work.

NOTE: The Instant Formatting that applies to bibliographies does not apply to figures.In-text figure citations are always formatted as you insert them, but if you move or delete a figure citation in your paper, you must manually select *Generate Figure List* from the *Tools* menu to update the document as described next.

Updating Figures and Tables

In-text figure citations are always formatted as you insert them. By default, they appear directly after the paragraph in which they are cited. However, you can direct the output style to format tables and figures in lists at the end of the document.

If you move or delete a figure citation in your paper, you must manually generate the figure list to update the figure citation numbering and placement.

From Word's *Tools* menu, select the *EndNote 7* submenu and choose *Generate Figure List*. Or, click the *Generate Figure List* button on the CWYW toolbar.

EndNote will number each figure and table citation sequentially in the Word document, as shown in this example:

> This family tree is not a chronological progression. Rather, it illustrates how evolution incorporates traits that evolved for unrelated reasons into a novel structure. (Table 1)
>
> *Marella splendens* is a small "arthropod" somewhat reminiscent of a trilobite. This illustration also shows the dark "blob" produced by body contents which were squeezed out of the animal after burial. (Figure 1)
>
> As researchers look at evidence, even the crest on the modern Cockatiel provides insight into the evolution of feathers. (Figure 2)

EndNote also inserts and displays the actual figures (graphics, figures, tables, charts, equations, or files) and labels them with figure or table numbers (to match each in-text reference) and Caption text (up to 245 characters from the Caption field in the EndNote reference).

If your figures are listed at the end of the document:

♦ In a figure or table list, if more than one citation references the same figure with the same caption, those citations are assigned the same figure number, and the figure appears only once in the list.

♦ You can continue to add figure citations to the Word document. If you change the position of figure citations in your document (with the *Copy* and *Paste* commands), choose *Generate Figure List* again to update figure numbers and the corresponding figures.

♦ You can manually insert a page break between figures if you prefer each figure on a separate page. These page breaks will be remembered if you choose *Generate Figure List* again. Or, direct the output style to always insert page breaks between figures.

A figure list at the end of the document:

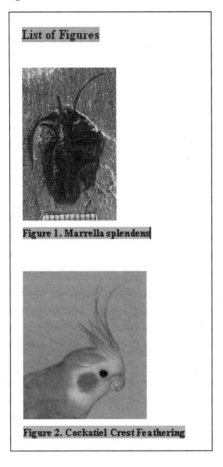

List of Figures

Figure 1. Marrella splendens

Figure 2. Cockatiel Crest Feathering

Placing Figures and Tables

Figures and tables are formatted either after the paragraph where cited or in a list at the end of the manuscript. This placement is determined by the current output style.

NOTE: Images from any reference type other than Chart or Table are inserted and formatted as Figures. Images from the Chart or Table reference type are inserted and formatted as Tables. Both are inserted with the *Find Figures* command and formatted with *Generate Figure List*.

Automatic Placement by the Output Style

The selected output style determines where figures and tables are initially placed in a document and when you *Generate Figure List*.

By default, output styles are set up to place figures and tables immediately after the paragraph in which they are cited. You can edit individual output styles to place figures and tables either after the paragraph in which they are cited or in a list at the end of the document.

For information about editing your output style for figure placement, see "Figures and Tables" on page 408. The Figures panel determines the placement of figures and their captions, the Tables panel determines the placement of tables (images from the Chart or Table reference type) and their captions, and the Separation and Punctuation panel determines image separation and punctuation of labels and captions.

Selecting a Different Output Style

To apply a different output style in Word, go to *Tools>EndNote 7>Format Bibliography*. Select an output style on the Format Bibliography tab and click *OK*. You can use *Format Bibliography* to select an output style even if you have no bibliographic citations in your paper. If you *do* have bibliographic citations, remember that your output style choice affects both bibliographic citations *and* figure and table citations.

Cite While You Write Override of the Output Style

As you work in your document, you may adjust the placement of actual figures and tables by cutting the pictures and pasting them elsewhere in the document. Normally, when you Generate Figure List again, the output style puts them back in their initial location! You can override the output style, and tell EndNote to leave existing figures and tables where they are currently placed. See "Figures and Tables in Word" on page 496 for information about Cite While You Write preferences that affect Figures and Tables.

Moving Figures and Tables

Moving In-text Figure and Table Citations

To move or copy a figure or table citation:

1. Highlight the entire citation, including the surrounding parentheses. For example:

```
(Figure 1)
```

2. Use *Copy* or *Cut* from the *Edit* menu to copy or move the citation to the Clipboard. (You could also use drag-and-drop to move a figure citation.)

3 Move the cursor to the new location.

4. From the *Edit* menu, *Paste* the Clipboard contents at the new location.

5. From the *Tools>EndNote 7* menu, select *Generate Figure List* to renumber the in-text citations and update figures and tables.

The selected output style determines whether figures and tables appear directly after the paragraph where cited or in a list at the end of the document. To modify this section of your output style, see "Figures and Tables" on page 408.

Moving Individual Figures and Tables

To move an individual figure or table within the text of the manuscript:

1. *Cut* the figure (or table), including the label and caption, and *Paste* it in the appropriate position in your manuscript.

2. In Word, go to the *Tools* menu and select *EndNote 7>Cite While You Write Preferences*.

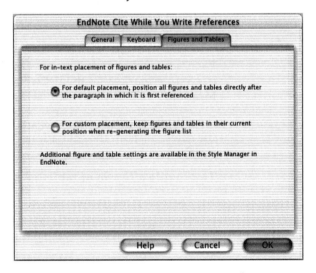

3. On the Figures and Tables tab, select the bottom button for custom placement of figures and tables and click *OK*.

4. From the *Tools* menu, select *EndNote 7>Generate Figure List*.

EndNote will update figure and table numbering, but will not change the position of existing figures and tables.

NOTE: This custom placement is honored only when the current output style is set up to print figures and tables within the text of the manuscript. When the output style is set up to list figures and tables in lists at the end of the document, using *Generate Figure List* will always move figures and tables to the appropriate list at the end of the document.

Moving Figure and Table Lists

When an output style is modified to print figures and tables in a list at the end of a document, the lists appear after the bibliography. However, you may want the list to appear elsewhere in your document. Some publishers even require that figures be provided in a separate file.

To move a figure or table list elsewhere in your document, such as *before* the bibliography:

1. Highlight the entire list, especially the very beginning of the list which contains a hidden marker.

2. From the *Edit* menu, *Cut* the list to move it to the Clipboard.

3. Move the cursor to the new location.

4. From the *Edit* menu, *Paste* the Clipboard contents at the new location.

Each time you choose *Generate Figure List*, EndNote looks for the beginning marker, so the list will be updated in its current location.

If multiple in-text figure citations reference the same figure with the same caption, those citations are assigned the same figure number, and the figure appears only once in a figure list.

To provide a figure or table list in a separate file:

1. Finalize your manuscript and figure list.

2. Highlight the entire list, and then use the *Copy* and *Paste* commands to paste the list into another Word document.

3. Delete the figure or table list from the manuscript file.

NOTE: Do not choose *Generate Figure List* again within either document.

Deleting a Figure Citation or Figure List

To delete a figure or table citation:

1. Highlight the entire citation, including the surrounding parentheses.

2. Press delete.

3. From the *Tools>EndNote 7* menu, select *Generate Figure List* to renumber the remaining in-text figure and table citations and update the formatted figures and tables.

To delete a figure or table list:

To remove a single figure or table from the list, delete the corresponding in-text figure citation. Then, use *Generate Figure List* to generate an updated list at the end of the document.

If you want to completely remove the figure or table list, first delete all in-text figure citations and update the list with *Generate Figure List*. Then, to completely remove any mention of a figure or table list, highlight the List of Figures marker or List of Tables marker and pressDelete.

NOTE: Do not delete the figure (picture) itself from the document. Remove the in-text figure citation and then *Generate Figure List*. If you do not remove the in-text citation, *Generate Figure List* will use that information to display the picture again!

Figure and Table Preferences

For information about output style settings that affect the placement of figures and tables, see "Figures and Tables" on page 408.

For information about Cite While You Write preferences that override output style settings for figures and tables, see "Figures and Tables in Word" on page 496.

Setting Cite While You Write Preferences

You can access and set Cite While You Write preferences from either EndNote or Word. The same dialog appears, and changes are saved in the same place:

◆ From Word's *Tools* menu, go to the *EndNote* submenu and select *CWYW Preferences*.

◆ From EndNote's *Tools* menu, go to the *Cite While You Write* submenu and select *CWYW Preferences*.

Cite While You Write preferences include general preferences, the ability to assign keyboard shortcuts to menu commands, and the ability to control placement of figures. See "Cite While You Write Preferences" on page 494 for detailed information about these preferences.

For information about other EndNote preferences that directly affect Cite While You Write, see "Temporary Citations" on page 477 and "Formatting" on page 482.

Making Changes to the EndNote Library

Once you have inserted and formatted citations in Word, changes to the corresponding EndNote library could affect reformatting.

Finding Cited References in a Library

You can quickly jump from a bibliographic in-text citation (not a figure citation) to the corresponding EndNote reference.

To find an EndNote reference:

1. Make sure both your Word document and your EndNote library are open.

2. Highlight the citation(s) in your Word document.

3. From the *Tools* menu in Word, go to the *EndNote 7* submenu and select *Edit Library Reference(s)*.

EndNote opens the corresponding reference for editing.

Editing a Reference in the Library

You may insert a citation in a Word document, and then later edit the corresponding reference in EndNote. Are those changes reflected in your Word document?

Your citations and bibliography will reflect the edits the next time you reformat the paper with the EndNote library open. Open your document, open your EndNote library, and choose *Format Bibliography* from the *EndNote 7* submenu on the *Tools* menu in Word.

EndNote will not be able to make the update if the library is not open during formatting. Instead, it will take the original reference information from Word's field codes.

NOTE: The author's last name and the publication year are both used to identify a reference, so changes to these items in an EndNote reference are *not* reflected in the in-text citation. Cite While You Write will no longer identify a match between the citation and the reference, and will use reference information from Word's field codes (the traveling library).

If you make changes to an image in an EndNote reference, you must manually replace the figure in your Word document.

Deleting a Reference From the Library

The first time a citation is formatted, EndNote uses information from the unformatted citation to look in the open library and find the corresponding reference. If you later reformat, EndNote again looks in the library for that reference. If the reference has been deleted from the library, EndNote takes the reference information from hidden field codes in Word (the Traveling Library).

So, if you deleted a cited reference from the library, the required information is still available in the hidden field codes surrounding each *formatted* citation–even though the reference is no longer in the library.

However, an *unformatted* citation is simply a temporary placeholder. If a citation is unformatted, and you have deleted the corresponding reference from the EndNote library, EndNote will not be able to find the reference information for formatting.

If you add the reference to the library again, it will be assigned a different record number. You would need to re-insert the citation in Word.

Record Numbers

EndNote assigns a unique record number to each reference as it is added to your library. These record numbers appear in temporary citations to ensure that the correct reference is used when the paper is formatted:

    {Argus, 1991 #11}

The record number for a reference is also visible in the title bar of the Reference window.Keep the following points about record numbers in mind:

- EndNote automatically assigns a record number sequentially to each reference as it is added to a library.

- If the same reference appears in two different libraries, the record numbers will most likely be different.

- Record numbers are never reused or reassigned within a library. When you delete a reference, the corresponding record number is never used again in that library.

- You cannot modify or reassign record numbers.

- We recommend that you *not* rely on EndNote's record numbers as a means of filing or numbering your office reprints, because *you have no control over this number.* Instead, enter your own unique number into the Label field, or any Custom field, and use that number for your reprints.

If you add the reference to the library again, it will be assigned a new, different record number, so EndNote still will not be able to find it when formatting your paper. You will need to reinsert the citation into the paper using the new reference in your library.

Sharing Your Word Documents

You can directly share your Word X files with colleagues. Each formatted citation is surrounded by field codes which contain full reference information (also referred to as the Traveling Library).

If you want to convert your document for use with a previous version of Word or a different word processor, you should Unformat Citations before saving in the different file format. Then, you may be able to reformat. The corresponding EndNote library (or libraries) must be available in order to format.

To send a final, formatted document to a publisher, you should Remove Field Codes to save the formatted citations and bibliography as text.

Of course, if you just want to print a copy of the paper for someone, you do not need to do anything to your document other than print it!

NOTE: Cite While You Write codes are directly compatible between Word 98, Word 2001, and Word X. Figure citations from a Word X document are ignored when the file is saved in an older version file format.

The Traveling Library

Each formatted citation in your Word document is saved with field codes that embed reference data in the document. The paper contains a "Traveling Library" of references cited.

The first time a citation is formatted, EndNote looks in the open library and finds the corresponding reference. If you later reformat, EndNote again looks in the open library for that reference. However, if the library is not available or not open, EndNote uses the Traveling Library for reference information.

Because reference data is kept with each formatted citation, you can collaborate with other authors on a paper without each author having the same EndNote library.

The reference data saved with each citation includes all fields except Notes, Abstract, and Image.

NOTE: Do not unformat your document if you do not have the original references in your libraries. Unlike formatted citations, *un*formatted citations require that you have the corresponding EndNote libraries open in order to format references.

Exporting Word's Traveling Library to an EndNote Library

There may be occasions where you want to copy all of the references used in a Microsoft Word document to an EndNote library. Perhaps you received only the formatted Word document from a colleague, and would like to create EndNote references to use later. Or, you may have a large EndNote library, but want to create a smaller EndNote library with only the subset of references used in your paper.

NOTE: The traveling library does not contain Notes, Abstracts, Images, or Captions.

To export references from a Word document to an EndNote library:

1. Open the document in Word.

2. From the *Tools* menu, go to the *EndNote 7* submenu and choose *Export Traveling Library*.

3. On the Export Traveling Library dialog, select either:

   ◆ An existing EndNote library:
   Select a library from the drop-down list of available libraries, or click *Browse* to locate a library.

◆   A new EndNote library:
    You will be prompted to name and *Save* the new library.

NOTE: We recommend that you export to a *new* EndNote library, so you can review the records before adding them to an existing library.

There is an alternate way to copy references from your Word document to an EndNote library. Open both your Word document and the EndNote library. Then, in EndNote, go to the *Tools* menu, then the *Cite While You Write* submenu, and choose *Import Traveling Library*.

Working on Different Computers

If you are working on a single paper and moving between different computers, it is best to keep a copy of your reference library with your paper. That way you will always access the same library when inserting citations. If you separately add references to a copy of the library at home and to a different version at work, record numbers may not match up correctly and EndNote may have to rely on the Traveling Library for reference information. That isn't necessarily bad, but you want to make sure that any library edits are reflected in your Word document.

If you are inserting citations on only one machine, it is fine to move the document itself to other machines—as long as you will be accessing the document with the same version of Word.

NOTE: If you are collaborating with other authors, you will want to rely on the traveling library.

Saving Files for Other Versions of Word and Other Word Processors

Formatted citations are Word "fields" specific to the version of Word that created them. If you open your document with a different version of Word, or use the *Save As* command to save a formatted copy of your paper in another format, you may lose the ability to format citations in that document.

If you plan to use your document with a different word processor, a different version of Microsoft Word, or on a different platform (such as DOS or Windows), you should either *Unformat Citations* or *Remove Field Codes* from the Word file before converting the document to the other file format.

◆   **Unformatting Citations:** Unformatted citations are regular text; however, they are temporary placeholders that do not reflect final output. (See "Unformatting Citations" on page 260.) You may be able to unformat citations, save to another file format, and use a different method to format citations from these placeholders (such as using the EndNote Add-in commands in WordPerfect).

♦ **Removing Field Codes:** When you remove field codes, you save a copy of the document and convert formatted fields to regular formatted text. Graphics are no longer linked, but are saved as though you had used the Copy and Paste commands. The copy reflects final, formatted output, but you cannot reformat later. See "Removing Field Codes" on page 285 for more information.

NOTE: Cite While You Write codes are directly compatible between Word 98, Word 2001, and Word X. Because reference data is kept with each formatted citation, you can collaborate with other authors on a paper without each author having the same EndNote library.Figure citations from a Word X document are ignored when the file is opened or saved in an older version file format.

Submitting the Final Paper to a Publisher

Many publishers ask that you submit an electronic copy of your paper in addition to a printed copy. Because the field codes in your document may be incompatible with the publishing software, you should submit a copy of your paper without field codes, as described next.

Removing Field Codes

You may need to remove Cite While You Write field codes in order to share your document with a publisher or colleague.

♦ Most publishers require that field codes be removed.

♦ If your colleague is using the same version of Word that you are, you can share your formatted document as is; the document includes a "Traveling Library," which includes all required information for the formatted citations and bibliography. See "The Traveling Library" on page 283 to learn more about the Traveling Library.

♦ If your colleague is using a different word processor or an incompatible version of Word, you could remove field codes to share your final document. However, removing field codes saves the formatted citations and bibliography as text, and does not allow reformatting.

♦ Removing field codes means deleting Word's Cite While You Write field codes and saving the formatted citations and bibliography as text. This removes only Cite While You Write field codes, and not all other Word field codes.

♦ When field codes are removed, in-text figure citations are no longer linked to an EndNote reference or to the figure list. In-text figure citations become plain text. Pictures in the figure list become GIF files as though they were copied and pasted into the document.

♦ Because EndNote and Cite While You Write cannot reformat or unformat your paper once field codes are removed, the *Remove Field Codes* command makes a *copy* of your document without codes.

NOTE: If you are working with master and subdocuments in Word, the *Remove Field Codes* command warns that it will strip codes from the original documents. You should first manually save copies of the master and subdocuments, and then remove codes from the copies.

To remove field codes and save the formatted citations and bibliography as text:

1. Open your formatted Word document.

   If you are working with Master and Subdocuments, work with *copies* of your documents.

2. From the *Tools* menu, go to the *EndNote 7* submenu and select *Remove Field Codes*. A copy of the document, without field codes, appears in a new document window.

3. From the *File* menu, *Save* the document.

   Single document: In Word's Save As dialog, type a new name for this copy of your document and click *OK*.

   Master and Subdocuments: You may be advised to save a copy of the master and each subdocument.

Word saves your document without embedded formatting codes, so you can submit your paper to a publisher or share your final paper with a colleague using a different word processor (including a different version of Word).

NOTE: The copy does not contain Cite While You Write field codes, so you cannot reformat with Cite While You Write. To reformat, start with the original document, which retains field codes.

Chapter 11

Scanning and Formatting RTF Files

Chapter 11   Scanning and Formatting RTF Files

Scanning and Formatting RTF Files

This chapter describes how to create formatted citations and bibliographies for your papers *without* using Cite While You Write™ for Microsoft® Word.

Word Processor Compatibility

This chapter describes how to cite references and create bibliographies for documents that can be saved as RTF, including documents created with:

♦ Microsoft® Word
♦ WordPerfect®
♦ OpenOffice
♦ Nisus Writer
♦ AppleWorks (ClarisWorks)
♦ Adobe® FrameMaker®
♦ Almost any application that can save as RTF (Rich Text Format)

To format references and create a bibliography (Cite While You Write) with Microsoft Word X, see Chapter 10. While you *can* use the RTF Document Scan described in this chapter to format Word files, it is much easier and more efficient to use Cite While You Write.

To create a stand-alone bibliography that is not based on the citations in a paper, see "Creating an Independent Bibliography" in Chapter 12.

For up-to-date compatibility information, see our Web site at www.endnote.com.

Basic Instructions

The basic steps required to cite references in a paper and "format" that paper using EndNote are covered here. More details about how to switch between programs and various tips for citing references are described in the sections following these basic instructions.

Citing references is a straight-forward process of copying temporary citations from EndNote and pasting them into your word processing document. While writing a paper in your word processor, you can have EndNote running in the background so that it's easy to switch between the two programs when you need to cite a source. Although you can enter the EndNote temporary citations into a paper at any time, most writers find it convenient to enter the citations as they are writing the paper instead of waiting to insert them after the text is written.

NOTE: The RTF Document Scan command works on RTF documents. You create your paper and insert citations with your word processor. When you are ready to scan and format citations, you must first save a copy of your paper as RTF, and then scan that copy of the paper.

To practice using the RTF Document Scan feature, you can follow this procedure using one of the example Paleo documents found in the EndNote 7:Examples folder. We recommend experimenting with the Paleo.RTF file along with the Paleo library.

To cite a reference in a paper:

1. Start your word processor and open the paper you are writing.

    As an example, you can locate and open Paleo.RTF found in the EndNote 7:Examples folder.

2. When you are ready to cite a source, position the cursor in the text where you would like to put the citation.

    `...a commonly documented phenomena `|`.`

3. Start EndNote and open your library (if it is not already open). See "Switching Between EndNote and a Word Processor" on page 296 if you need help with this step.

4. Select the reference(s) in your EndNote library that you want to cite. Press the COMMAND key (⌘) while clicking on the references to select multiple references; press the SHIFT key to select a range of references.

5. Choose *Copy* (⌘+C) from the *Edit* menu, then return to your word processor and *Paste* (⌘+V) the temporary citation into the text of your document.

    OR

    Drag-and-drop the selected citations into your paper.

    The pasted citation appears in EndNote's temporary format: first author's last name, year of publication, and record number, all enclosed in curly braces:

    `{Morehouse, 1993 #125}`

If multiple references were selected, their citations appear together within one set of delimiters in the order in which you selected them in the Library window.

```
{Hall, 1999 #90; Baker, 1988 #38}
```

This citation is *not* the final citation, but rather a temporary citation that will be formatted later. The number in the temporary citation is not a *bibliography number* but a unique *record number*. When you format this paper, EndNote builds a bibliography based on the temporary citations that it finds in the paper, and reformats them according to the selected style.

Continue following steps 2-5 to insert citations as you write your paper.

To save your document:

6. When you have finished adding citations, choose *Save* from your word processor's *File* menu to save all changes to your document.

7. If the file you created is not an RTF document, save a copy of the file as RTF. From the *File* menu, choose *Save As*. In the file dialog, set the type of file as RTF. RTF retains most styles and formatting.

8. Close your document by choosing *Close* from the *File* menu. You can leave your word processor running.

To generate the bibliography:

9. Return to EndNote.

10. From the *Tools* menu, go to the *RTF Document Scan* submenu and then *RTF Document Scan*.

11. Navigate the file dialog to locate and select the RTF document you just saved.

    The next time you choose *RTF Document Scan* you will see your recently used files listed for easy access.

12. Check the Citations window to make sure that EndNote was able to find matching references for all of the citations.

    During the scanning process, EndNote locates temporary citations in the paper, and searches the library to find references that match each of the citations. When scanning is complete, EndNote displays the Citations window. The Citations window lists the citations found in the paper together with the number of matching references in the open libraries.

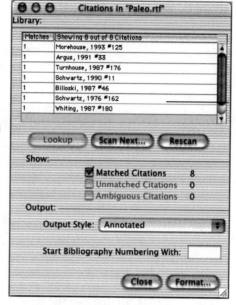

Numbers in the Matches column show how many references in your library match each citation. Each citation should have a single match.

These citations were taken directly from a paper EndNote scanned.

The citations in the Citations window appear in the order they are cited in the paper. If a reference is cited more than once in a paper, it is listed more than once in this window; however the reference will appear only once in the bibliography.

Every citation listed in the Citations window should have a "1" next to it in the Matches column, meaning that EndNote found exactly one reference in the library to match the citation in the paper. When all of the citations in the window have a "1" next to them, you are ready to go on to the next step of formatting a paper. If a "0" or a number greater than one appears in the Matches column, see "Correcting Mismatched Citations" on page 528.

13. Select a style from the *Output Styles* list on the Citation window. Enter a starting bibliography number if you wish.

The individual styles listed are the styles that are currently selected as your "favorites" in the Style Manager. If you need to choose a style that is not in the list, choose *Select Another Style* to open the Style Manager. Mark your favorite styles there, and start this step again. See "Adding Styles to the Output Styles List" on page 266 for details.

14. Click *Format* to have EndNote create a copy of your paper complete with formatted citations and a bibliography.

15. You are then prompted to name and save the formatted copy of the paper.

EndNote automatically adds the name of the output style to your existing filename. You can change the name of the formatted document if necessary by typing a new name in the text box. You can also use the Folder menu at the top of the window to change the location where EndNote saves the file. By default EndNote saves the formatted file in the same location as the unformatted file.

IMPORTANT: *Never* save the formatted paper with the same name as the original unformatted document. You must have the unformatted document if you ever want to format the paper again.

While EndNote is formatting, the cursor changes to a wait cursor. When the formatting has finished, the cursor returns to an arrow and the Citations window remains open. Now that EndNote has generated a formatted copy of the paper, you can open that paper in your word processor.

16. Switch to your word processor.

17. Choose *Open* from the word processor's *File* menu and select and open the formatted version of the paper. Remember that you want to open the file that has the name of the style appended to the file name.

In the formatted paper, EndNote has replaced the temporary citations with formatted citations and inserted a bibliography. The paper is ready to be printed and submitted!

Making Changes to the Paper

If you need to make changes to the paper (such as change a citation, add more text, or change the bibliographic style), you should edit the *original* unformatted document, and then format it again. EndNote will generate a new formatted copy of the paper. See "Reformatting a Paper" on page 302.

Using Macintosh Services

EndNote supports Macintosh OS X Services by making RTF Document Scan commands available within other applications, so you can run RTF Document Scan either from EndNote or from within your word processor.

NOTE: EndNote supports Macintosh OS X Services for any application that includes the Services feature. In an application, look under the menu named after the application for a *Services>EndNote* submenu. (If an application does not support Macintosh OS X Services, the EndNote commands will be dimmed and not available.)

Three EndNote RTF Document Scan commands are available in most word processors on the *Application Name>Services>EndNote* menu. Use the *Find Citation(s)* and *Insert Citation* commands to insert temporary citations in your word processor document. Then, highlight the text you wish to scan (typically the entire document), and use *RTF Document Scan* to scan the file, format citations and a bibliography, and save the text to an RTF file.

Find Citation(s)

This command is available when an EndNote library is open and text is selected in the document. Use it to locate and insert temporary citations:

1. In your document, put the cursor where you want to cite a reference.

2. Type in the text you want to use to locate the reference in EndNote, and then highlight the text.

3. From the *Application Name>Services>EndNote* menu, choose *Find Citation(s)*.

   EndNote uses the highlighted text to search for matching references in the open library, and displays the matching references in a list.

4. Select the reference (or multiple references) you want to cite, and click *Insert*.

   The EndNote reference is inserted into the document as a temporary citation, replacing the highlighted search text.

Insert Citation

This command is available when an EndNote library is open. Use it to insert references that are selected in EndNote as temporary citations:

1. Highlight a reference (or multiple references) in your EndNote library.

2. Switch to your document and put the cursor where you want to insert the citation.

3. From the *Application Name>Services>EndNote* menu, choose *Insert Citation.*

   The EndNote reference is inserted into the document as a temporary citation. If any text was selected in your document, the insertion will replace that text.

RTF Document Scan

This command is available when an EndNote library is open and text is selected in the document.

You should first use the *Find Citation(s)* and/or the *Insert Citation* commands to insert temporary citations. Then, use this command to run EndNote's RTF Document Scan on the selected text:

1. Highlight the text you wish to scan. In most cases, you will *Select All* to select the entire document (the full text of your paper that contains temporary citations that you wish to format and use to create a bibliography).

2. From the *Application Name>Services>EndNote* menu, choose *RTF Document Scan.*

   EndNote scans the highlighted text for temporary citation delimiters and displays a Citation Matches window listing the matching EndNote references plus any unmatched or ambiguous citations.

3. (optional) If there are any unmatched or ambiguous citations, you can make changes to your document and then click *Rescan* on the Citation Matches window.

4. On the Citation Matches window, select an output style and click *Format.*

5. On the file dialog, name and save the new RTF document that contains citations and a bibliography formatted according to the selected output style.

Tips on Citing Sources

Temporary vs. Formatted Citations

A "citation" is the bibliographic information in the body of a paper that refers the reader to a complete reference in the bibliography. Normally a citation consists of a bibliography number or the author and year in parentheses:

`... of the species at hand`[1].

`... of the species at hand (Argus, 1991).`

When you first copy an EndNote citation and paste it into your paper, it appears in EndNote's **temporary citation** format. This format consists of the first author's last name, year, and the EndNote record number, with citation delimiters at each end.

`{Author, Year #Record Number}`

When EndNote formats this paper it replaces the temporary citations with **formatted citations**.

Temporary Citation: {Argus, 1991 #11}

Formatted Citation (in APA): `(Argus & Matthews, 1991)`

EndNote relies on the temporary citations to determine which references to include in the bibliography. During formatting, EndNote scans your word processing document for temporary citations, finds their matching references in the EndNote library, and creates a duplicate of your document complete with "formatted" in-text citations and a bibliography at the end. This new document is called your "formatted" paper.

NOTE: By default, citation delimiters are curly braces. If you have other text within curly braces, you may want to change your citation delimiters. See page 531.

Switching Between EndNote and a Word Processor

With your EndNote library and word processing document both open, you can switch between the two files without closing either program.

If an EndNote icon and your word processor icon appear on the Dock along the edge of the screen, simply click on the appropriate icon to start or switch to that program.

To start EndNote and open your EndNote library while working in your word processor:

1. Switch from your word processor to the Finder.

Finder icon

   ◆ If the icon of your hard drive is visible on the right side of the screen, simply click once on your hard drive to return to the Macintosh Finder.

   ◆ Or, click on the Finder icon found on the dock along the edge of the screen.

2. Now that you are back in the Finder, locate your EndNote library and double-click it to open it in the EndNote program. Your EndNote library is probably in your EndNote folder, although it can be anywhere that you chose to put it.

At this point, you should have both your library and your word processing document open. You are now ready to copy and paste references from your EndNote library into your word processing document.

To switch between your word processor and EndNote when both are running:

EndNote and TextEdit icons on the Dock

◆ Once both programs are running, an EndNote icon and your word processor icon appear on the Dock along the edge of the screen. Click on the appropriate icon to switch to that program.

◆ Or, simply click on the document which should be visible in the background:

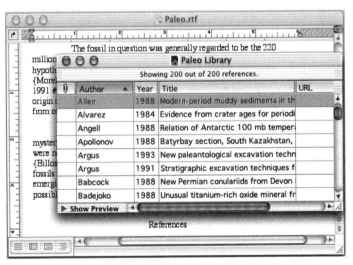

Every time you click on your word processing document to paste a temporary citation, the EndNote library moves to the background behind your paper. You can rearrange or resize the windows for the EndNote library and the word processing document so that the EndNote library is not completely obscured by the word processing document every time you switch back to your word processor. With the windows set up this way, you can click on part of the EndNote Library window to bring it forward on the screen, and then click on the word processing document when you want to return to it.

Multiple References in One Citation

If you need multiple references in one in-text citation, you can accomplish this in one of two ways. One option is to insert all of the citations together:

To insert multiple citations:

1. Hold down the COMMAND key while clicking on the desired references in your library (or hold down the SHIFT key to select a continuous range of references).

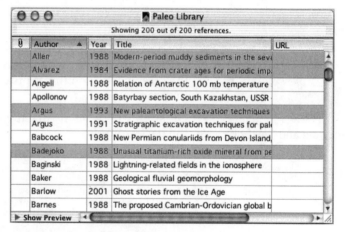

2. From the *Edit* menu, choose *Copy.*

3. Position the cursor in your word processing document where you want the citations, and choose *Paste* from the *Edit* menu.

The citations are inserted together in one set of delimiters. Once formatted, they appear in one multiple citation, sorted as your bibliographic style requires:

Unformatted: {Hall, 1999 #90; Baker, 1988 #38}

Formatted: (Baker, 1988; Hall, 1999)

The other option is to add the citations to the paper individually. EndNote merges *adjacent* citations automatically during the formatting process. Citations do not merge, however, if any character, including spaces or punctuation, separates them.

Unformatted: {Hall, 1999 #90}{Baker, 1988 #38}

Merged when Formatted: (Baker, 1988; Hall, 1999)

NOTE: If one of the citations in a multiple citation cannot be matched during formatting, the entire citation will remain unformatted.

Citing References in Footnotes

Once you have created a footnote or an endnote in your word processing document, you can cite references in the footnotes or endnotes just like you cite them in the body of the text.

To cite references in footnotes:

1. In your EndNote library, select the reference(s) that you would like to cite and choose *Copy* from the *Edit* menu.

2. Create the footnote or endnote using the appropriate command in your word processor. (EndNote does not actually create the footnote or endnote in the document, but it is used to insert and format the citations in the notes.)

3. Position the cursor in the footnote or endnote in your paper where you would like the citation(s) to appear and choose *Paste* from the *Edit* menu.

The EndNote style that is selected when you choose *Format Bibliography* determines how the citations in the footnotes or endnotes will be formatted. EndNote can format these citations as brief in-text citations or like the complete references in the bibliography. It can also create a special format specific to footnotes or endnotes, including options like "Ibid." and other variations of shortened references when a citation appears more than once in the footnotes or endnotes. See Chapter 15 for more information.

Important Note for AppleWorks (ClarisWorks) users

If you have cited references in the footnotes of your document, the formatted paper that EndNote creates may display the footnote regions incorrectly (for example, by displaying superimposed text).

To correct this, open the formatted document and immediately choose *Page Setup* from the *File* menu. On the Page Setup dialog, simply click *OK*. This makes the footnote regions reformat themselves properly, so footnote regions will display correctly.

Limitations for Nisus Users

EndNote cannot scan citations in the footnotes of Nisus documents—citations in footnotes are ignored.

To cite full references in the footnotes of Nisus documents, you can use the *Copy Formatted* command (or hold down the OPTION key when using drag-and-drop) to insert a complete reference (as opposed to an in-text citation) in a footnote.

1. With your document open, create a footnote using the appropriate Nisus command.

2. Switch to EndNote and select the desired reference(s).

3. Pick a style from the *Output Styles* submenu of the *Edit* menu and then choose *Copy Formatted* (⌘+K) from the *Edit* menu.

4. Return to your word processor, put the cursor in the footnote, and choose *Paste* (⌘+V) from the Nisus *Edit* menu. This pastes the formatted reference into the footnote.

Related Sections

The following is a list of related sections in this manual that provide tips for working with the citations in your paper. Some of these sections are in Chapter 10, which describes how to Cite While You Write with Microsoft Word. These sections also apply to citing references in other word processors. Just remember to return to this chapter for specific instructions about how to format and cite references in RTF documents.

Inserting Citations and Writing Your Papers with EndNote

♦ You may type your temporary citations by hand, as well as add text to or omit text from them, provided you follow the rules outlined under "Typing Citations into Your Paper" on page 252.

♦ "Omitting Authors or Years from Citations" on page 254 describes how to modify your temporary citations when you need to remove the author or the year from specific citations.

♦ If you commonly use curly braces in your writing, they might not be a good choice for the markers that are used to surround the EndNote temporary citations. In this case, you might want to consider using a different character for your citation delimiters. See "Changing the Citation Delimiters" on page 531.

♦ If you run into any problems with citations in your paper not being correctly matched to references in your library (that is, citations appearing with numbers other than 1 in the Matches column of the Citations window), see "Understanding Mismatched Citations in RTF Files" on page 526.

Formatting Citations and Creating Bibliographies

Bibliographic Styles

The bibliographic style determines how EndNote formats the citations in your paper and the references in the bibliography. The style takes care of all text styles, punctuation, and sorting required for the citations and bibliography, as well as which fields are included in the bibliography.

Choose a style on the Citation Matches window after choosing *RTF Document Scan*. You can always run RTF Document Scan to select a different style and reformat your unformatted (original) RTF document at any point.

The EndNote Styles collection includes more than 1000 styles, all of which can be modified to meet your specifications. You can also create completely new styles if necessary. Related sections in this manual:

♦ See "Adding Styles to the Output Styles List" on page 266 to learn more about the Styles Manager and how to get the styles you need to appear in EndNote's *Output Styles* list.

♦ To learn about how the styles work, and how you can modify them, see Chapter 15.

Reformatting a Paper

Since EndNote creates a *copy* of the paper during the formatting process, you can always reformat the original document, if necessary, to create a new document with the changes that you need.

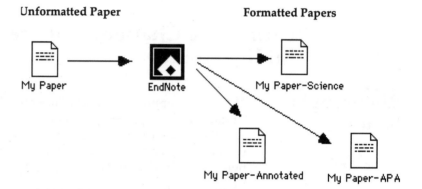

Reformatting with Different Styles

The appearance of both the in-text citations and the bibliography in the formatted paper is determined by the selected style. If you need to create a copy of your paper in a different style than what you did originally:

1. From the *Tools* menu in EndNote, choose *RTF Document Scan>RTF Document Scan*. Open the *original* unformatted copy of your paper (the one with the EndNote citations surrounded by curly braces or brackets).

2. On the Citations window, select a new output style from the Output Style drop-down list. You can select one of the "favorite" styles currently in the list, or choose *Select Another Style* to pick a style from the 1000+ styles shipped with EndNote.

3. If the Citations window shows that all the citations in the paper are correctly matched, click the *Format* button.

4. EndNote will prompt you to name and save the new formatted copy of the paper. Notice that the style name is included as part of the new paper's name. That will help you distinguish between various copies of one paper (perhaps formatted to be submitted to different journals).

When you open the new formatted copy of your paper, you should see that your citations and bibliography use the new bibliographic format.

IMPORTANT: When you need to make changes in your paper, remember to work only with the *unformatted* copy of the paper (the one with the bracketed temporary citations), rather than the formatted copy that EndNote created.

Adding New Citations to Formatted Papers

If you have already formatted your paper, and you see that it needs to be edited by either adding or removing citations, you must return to the original, unformatted copy of the document (the one with EndNote's "temporary citations"). Open that document in your word processor. Add, modify or delete citations as necessary, and then save the paper as RTF. You may now format the paper (as described above) to create an updated copy of it.

Creating One Bibliography From Several Papers

EndNote can format a series of separate word processing documents and put a cumulative bibliography at the end of the last one. This is useful if you are collaborating with other EndNote users and you have each written a separate part of the paper, or if you have separated a lengthy paper into different chapters.

To create one bibliography from several papers:

1. From the *Tools* menu, choose *RTF Document Scan>RTF Document Scan* to open and scan the first paper.

2. A *Scan Next* button appears on the Citations window. (The *RTF Document Scan* command on the menu changes to *Scan Next*). Click *Scan Next* in the window, or select it from the menu, to open each of the subsequent papers in the correct order. Each paper's citations will be added to the list of citations in the Citations window.

3. When the last paper has been scanned, select an output style on the Citations window and click *Format*.

During the formatting process, EndNote makes a formatted copy of each paper and puts a cumulative bibliography at the end of the last paper. Only the last paper in the series will include the bibliography. By default, each formatted paper retains its original name with the style name appended to it, however you have the option to change the names.

Specifying the Starting Number of a Bibliography

When you choose *RTF Document Scan* to display a Citations window, EndNote includes an output style list to confirm or change the style that should be used to format the paper. It also gives you the option to change the starting number for your citations and bibliography.

If you would like EndNote's numbering to start with a number other than "1" for the document that you are formatting, enter that number here. This setting is ignored if you are formatting the paper with a style that does not create numbered references in the bibliography.

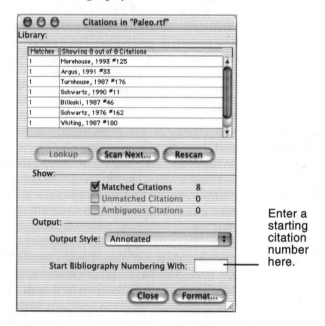

Enter a starting citation number here.

Copying Formatted References

There may be times when you want to insert a fully formatted reference into the body or footnotes of your paper without having to format an entire document.

To insert a fully formatted reference:

1. Select a style from the list of styles on the Toolbar.

2. Select the reference(s) in the Library window.

3. Choose *Copy Formatted* from EndNote's *Edit* menu.

4. Switch to your word processing document, position the cursor in the text, and select *Paste* from the *Edit* menu.

If your word processor supports drag-and-drop, you may also drag the references and drop them on your paper with the OPTION key pressed. This produces the same results as using the *Copy Formatted* command.

Multiple references are sorted according to the rules of the selected style. Fonts and character styles are transferred if you are pasting into a program that interprets styled text or Rich Text Format (RTF) information on the Clipboard.

Rescanning the Paper

If there is a problem with your citation matches after choosing *RTF Document Scan*, leave the Citations window open and switch to your word processor to make the necessary changes. After saving your changes, close your document and switch back to EndNote. On the Citations window, click *Rescan Paper*.

EndNote then updates the information in the Citations window to reflect the recent changes made to the paper. If the paper was modified and saved since it was last scanned, EndNote prompts you to rescan the paper before formatting.

For more information about fixing mismatched citations, see "Understanding Mismatched Citations in RTF Files" on page 526.

Modifying References in Your Library

If you add or change a reference in your library while the Citations window is open, make sure you click *Rescan* to have those changes reflected in the Citations window and in the formatted paper.

For example, if you typed the citation {Geoffery, 1988} into your paper but forgot to enter the reference in the library, EndNote would list a "0" in the Matches column for that citation on the Citations window. You can leave the Citations window open and enter the Geoffery reference into your library. Bring the Citations window forward and use the *Rescan* button to recheck the library for matching references. This should change the "0" match to a "1."

For more information about troubleshooting mismatched citations, see "Understanding Mismatched Citations in RTF Files" on page 526.

Finding EndNote References for Editing

In the Citations window, you can select any number of matching references and then click *Lookup* to search and display those references in EndNote's Library window. You can open each record for viewing or editing. If you edit a reference, make sure you *Rescan* your paper to reflect the changes.

Chapter 12

Creating an Independent Bibliography

Chapter 12   Creating an Independent Bibliography

Independent Bibliographies

There may be times when you want to create a bibliography without an associated paper. We call this an "independent bibliography" because EndNote does not generate the bibliography based on citations found in a paper—instead, the bibliography is generated independently of a paper.

Any one of the procedures described in this chapter can be used to create an independent bibliography. Each has its own advantages, so look for the option that best suits your needs:

♦ Use drag-and-drop to instantly transfer a bibliography to a word processing document

♦ Copy formatted references from a library and paste them into a word processing document

♦ Export references from a library

♦ Print references from EndNote

Styles Determine the Look of the Bibliography

The appearance of your independent bibliography depends entirely on which EndNote style is selected in the *Output Styles* submenu of the *Edit* menu (or the drop-down style list on the toolbar). The styles determine what information is included in the bibliography, how it is arranged, and what punctuation and text styles are used.

Select a style that meets your needs before exporting, printing or formatting references. If you do not see the style that you need in the *Output Styles* submenu of the *Edit* menu, choose *Open Style Manager* from the *Output Styles* submenu, and mark the styles that you need. Once the styles are marked as "favorites" in the Style Manager, they will show up in your styles menus. For more information, see "Adding Styles to the Output Styles List" on page 266. For information about modifying styles, see Chapter 15.

Using Drag-and-Drop to Create an Instant Bibliography

"Drag-and-drop" is a way of moving or copying selected text (or other items) by clicking on the text and dragging it to a new location. Simply release the mouse button when the cursor is over the destination, and the text will either be moved or copied to the new destination.

If your word processor supports drag-and-drop, you can drag a bibliography from an EndNote Library window directly into your paper.

To drag your bibliography:

1. Open your library and select the desired references.

2. Select the necessary style from the *Output Style* submenu of EndNote's *Edit* menu.

3. Hold down the OPTION key as you drag the references from the library and drop them directly onto a word processing document in the background.

This creates a fully formatted bibliography with the references formatted and sorted according to the selected style. The font used for the bibliography in this case is the "General Display Font." You can change this font by choosing *Preferences* from the *EndNote* menu, selecting *Display Fonts*, and choosing a new font and size under the General Display Font heading. All text style information (such as bold and italic) is retained if you "drop" the bibliography into a program that recognizes RTF (Rich Text Format) or styled text.

If your word processor does not support drag-and-drop, read about the *Copy Formatted* command below.

NOTE: Dragging with the OPTION key pressed transfers the formatted references to the word processing document. If you do not hold down the OPTION key, only the temporary citation is transferred. Use this latter method to cite references in your paper.

Copy Formatted

Use the *Copy Formatted* command to quickly create and copy a bibliography that you can paste into a word processing document, or anywhere else. The references are sorted and formatted according to the rules of the selected style.

The font used for the *Copy Formatted* command is the "General Display Font" which can be changed by choosing *Preferences* from the *EndNote* menu, selecting *Display Fonts*, and choosing a new font and size under the General Display Font heading. All text style information (such as bold and italic) is retained if you paste into a program that recognizes RTF (Rich Text Format) or styled text.

To copy formatted references from EndNote and paste them into a word processing document:

1. From EndNote's *Edit* menu, go to the *Output Style* submenu and select the necessary style.

2. Open your EndNote library and select the desired references in the Library window.

3. From the *Edit* menu, choose *Copy Formatted* (⌘+K) to copy the references to the Clipboard.

4. Open a document in your word processor, put the cursor where you would like the references to appear, and choose *Paste* (⌘+V) from the word processor's *Edit* menu.

NOTE: If EndNote runs out of memory during this procedure, and you are trying to format 50 or more references, select fewer references to copy at one time, or use the drag-and-drop or *Export* methods described in this chapter.

Exporting References

Exporting bibliographies from EndNote is easy and flexible. When you export from a library, EndNote creates a file of references formatted according to the chosen style.

Only showing references are included:

If any references in the Library window are selected, the EndNote export dialog gives you the option of exporting just those selected references. If you don't choose the option to "Export Selected References," then all of the references that are *showing* in the Library window will be exported.

♦ To export all of the references in the Library, choose *Show All References* from the *References* menu. If any references are selected, be sure to uncheck the "Export Selected References" checkbox in the export dialog.

♦ To export a subset of references, use the *Search References*, *Hide Selected References*, or *Show Selected References* commands to show the subset of references you want to include.

Supported Formats

Use the *Export* command to create a free-standing bibliography in any of the following formats:

♦ **RTF (Rich Text Format)**
The RTF export is an ideal way to create a free-standing bibliography that can be edited or printed using a word processor. This format can be opened by all popular word processors and preserves font and text style information.

♦ **Text Only**
The *Text Only* export option is suitable for draft purposes or exporting references to be imported into another database.

♦ **HTML**
Documents exported in HTML (HyperText Markup Language), provide an easy way to post reference lists on the World Wide Web.

♦ **XML**
The XML option exports in a proprietary EndNote XML format.

NOTE: The *Export* command exports only text; images are not included. However, if you import the references back into an EndNote library, you can restore images by copying the image files from the original library's DATA folder into a DATA image folder for the new library.

Using the *Export* Command

To export a bibliography from EndNote:

1. Open the library from which you will export, and show the references you want to export. See "Only showing references are included:" on page 311.

2. Sort the references if necessary, using the *Sort References* command.

   References are exported in the order in which they are listed in the Library window. The sort order specified by the bibliographic style is not used. (Selected references are unselected during the sort. If you had previously selected specific references to export, use the *Show Selected* command from the *References* menu before sorting.)

3. From EndNote's *Edit* menu, go to the *Output Styles* submenu and choose a style (or use the style menu in the toolbar).

4. From EndNote's *File* menu, choose *Export*.

5. From the "Save File as Type" list at the bottom of the dialog, select the type of file to be exported.

6. Enter a name for the exported file and use the Folder list to specify where it should be saved.

folder list —

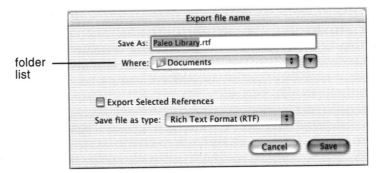

NOTE: The Export feature creates a new file; it does not append to an existing file. If you enter the name of a file that already exists, that file will be overwritten.

7. Select the "Export Selected References" option if desired, and click *Save*.

8. Open the exported file in a word processor to edit or print it. At this point, the file is just like any other text document. You can change the font, margins, line spacing, or other page layout features if necessary.

   If you exported the references in HTML format, your exported reference list is ready to be posted directly to your Web site.

NOTE: The *Export* command exports only text; images are not included.

Printing References

Use the *Print* command (⌘+P) from the *File* menu to print references directly from EndNote. This command is intended for use as a quick way to put your references on paper—no special page layout options are provided. Typical uses might include printing a list of references to take to the library with you, printing your notes, or generating a complete printout of the references in an EndNote library.

Important Points

The currently active (topmost) window affects which references are printed with the *Print* command:

♦ If a library window is displayed, you can print either the selected (highlighted) references or all references showing in the list.

♦ If an individual reference is open for viewing, EndNote prints only that specific reference–as displayed on the screen with field labels. No output style is applied.

In addition to the selected style, the appearance of the printed references is determined by the following items:

♦ Each printed page has 1-inch margins, left-justified text, and a header that displays the library name in the upper left corner and the page number in the upper right corner. There are no options to customize the margins, headers or footers of the printouts. Use one of the other options for creating an independent bibliography if you need to modify these aspects of your printout.

♦ The font and size of the printed references are determined by the General Display Font. Choose *Preferences* from the *EndNote* menu, and click the *Display Fonts* option to change the font and size if necessary.

♦ Choose *Page Setup* from the *File* menu to specify other printing options including the paper size and page orientation. Page setup options vary depending on the printer used.

Printing Instructions

To print a list of references directly from EndNote:

1. Make sure that all of the references you want to print are either selected (highlighted) or showing in the Library window.

2. From EndNote's *Edit* menu, go to the *Output Styles* submenu and choose a style (or use the style menu in the toolbar).

3. From the *References* menu, use the *Sort References* command to sort the Library if necessary.

   References are printed in the order in which they are listed in the Library window. When printing only selected references, the references are printed in the order in which they were selected. The *Sort References* command unselects any selected references so use the *Show Selected References* command if necessary before sorting to retain the subset of references you selected.

4. From the *File* menu, choose *Print* (⌘+P).

   In the print dialog, specify the number of copies and the range of pages to print. By default, EndNote prints only the selected references. To print all the references showing in the Library window, turn the "Print Selected References" option off. Depending on your printer software, you might need to choose *EndNote 7* from the popup list in the dialog in order to see the "Print Selected References" option. If no references are selected, this option is not available.

5. Click *Print* to print the references.

Including Notes, Abstracts, and Other Information in a Reference List

Most of the styles included with EndNote produce standard bibliographies without including additional information such as notes or abstracts. Two of EndNotes standard styles are the Annotated style and the Show All style. The Annotated style includes the Abstract field after each reference, and the Show All style lists all of the field names and the information found in those fields for each reference.

See Chapter 15 for detailed information about editing and creating styles. What follows here are two examples of common ways you might want to edit styles for your printouts or for stand-alone bibliographies.

Creating Annotated Bibliographies

To create a bibliography that includes abstracts, you can use the Annotated style included with EndNote. The Annotated style is based on the Author-Date style, and creates an alphabetical listing of the references (by author), with the abstract appended to each reference. You can modify any other style to include the Notes or Abstract field as well.

For this example, we modify the Numbered style to include the Abstract field.

1. From the *Edit* menu, choose *Output Styles* and select *Open Style Manager*.

2. Choose a style from the list in the Style Manager window, and click the *Edit* button. The Style window opens.

3. Choose *Layout* from the options under the *Bibliography* heading and click in the text box under the "End each reference with" heading. Text or fields inserted into this section appear at the end of each reference in the bibliography.

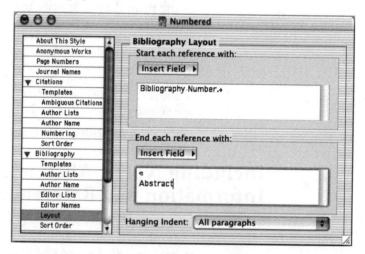

4. To insert the abstracts on a new line after each reference: choose ¶ *End of Paragraph* from the *Insert Field* list, and then choose *Abstract* from the same list.

5. From the *File* menu, choose *Save As* and give the style a new name.

This annotated version of the style will appear in the *Output Styles* submenu of the *Edit* menu (and in the styles menu in the Main toolbar). If you format a paper, print, or export references using this style, the abstracts are included in the bibliography.

Printing Only the Notes

To print only the notes for each reference, create a new style that includes only the Notes field.

To create a style that prints only notes:

1. From the *Edit* menu choose *Output Styles* and select *New Style*.

2. Click on the *Templates* panel under the *Bibliography* heading.

3. Click in the "Generic" template and choose *Notes* from the *Insert Field* list. Press the RETURN key to add a blank line after the notes for each reference.

4. From the *File* menu, choose *Save As*. Name and save the style. You should now see this new style in the *Output Styles* submenu of the *Edit* menu.

5. Close the style by clicking the close button.

Select this style whenever you want to print or export only the Notes from your references. This style is also useful to preview just the notes in the preview pane of the Library window.

Chapter 13

Creating Subject Bibliographies and Subject Lists

Chapter 13   Creating Subject Bibliographies and Subject Lists

Overview

This chapter explains how to create subject bibliographies and subject lists.

Subject List	Subject Bibliography
Archaeology Astronomy Biology Geochemistry Geology Hydrology	**Archaeology** Parker, F. and B. J. Parker (1997). Educational Philanthropist George Peabody (1795-1869) and First U.S. Paleontology Professor Othniel Charles Marsh (1831-99) at Yale University. U.S., Tennessee. **Astronomy** Lowman, P. D., Jr. (2001). Evidence from Apollo. <u>Science Teacher</u>. 68: 22-25.

A general bibliography is a continuous listing of citations in a particular order. A subject bibliography is made up of smaller listings, each appearing under a distinct heading. Despite the name, a subject bibliography (or a subject list) can be based on any EndNote field or combination of fields.

Subject bibliographies have diverse uses, including: generating lists of journal abstracts; current awareness lists; subject indexes; or lists of holdings by category. Typical subject bibliography headings are by Keyword, Author, Journal Title, or Call Number.

You can print entire bibliographic citations, information from one or more fields, record IDs, or nothing at all under each heading.

Printing a Subject Bibliography

Basic Procedure

This section walks through the basic steps to create a subject bibliography. If you would like to practice with a hands-on tour, see "Part IV: Creating a Subject Bibliography" on page 60 in the Guided Tour.

To print a subject bibliography:

1. In the current Library window, highlight the references you wish to include in a subject bibliography.

    ◆ You can use *Search References* to find a subset of references, then *Select All* to highlight that subset for your subject bibliography.

    ◆ If you select individual references, use the *Show Selected References* command to view a list containing only those references that will be used to create the subject bibliography.

    ◆ If no references are selected, all references in the library are used for the subject bibliography.

2. From the *Tools* menu, select *Subject Bibliography* to display a list of the EndNote fields by default field name.

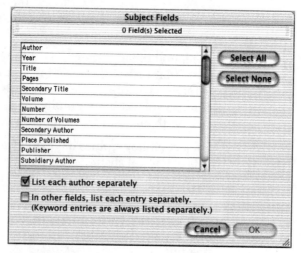

3. Highlight the field(s) whose contents you wish to use as subject headings.

    ◆ The most common selection is the single Keywords field to create a subject bibliography.

    ◆ You can include any number of fields. If you build the list of headings from more than one field, the subject headings generated from these fields are combined into a single list.

    ◆ If you mix date fields with other fields, dates will sort before alphabetic subject headings.

    ◆ To quickly select all fields or clear all fields, use the buttons on the right side of the dialog. You can click on individual fields to select or deselect them.

4. Select the check boxes as needed to determine whether an entire field is used as a heading, or whether a field should be split into multiple headings.

◆ *List each author separately*, when checked, will list each author name as a separate heading. If not checked, all authors from a single field will appear as a single heading.

◆ *In other fields, list each entry that is separated by slash, carriage return, or line feed*, when checked, separates any non-author field into multiple subject headings.

◆ Terms in the Keywords field are always listed as separate headings.

5. Click *OK* to display the terms found in the fields you selected.

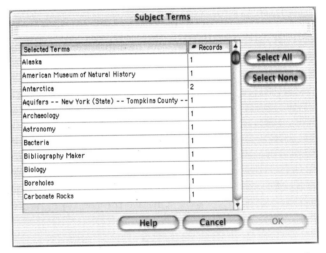

6. Select those terms you wish to include as subject headings.

◆ To quickly select all terms or clear all terms, use the buttons to the right of the dialog.

◆ You may want to select all terms and then click to deselect the few terms you do not want included.

7. Click *OK* to format the subject bibliography on the screen.

If you want to modify the term selections you just set, to either add or remove terms from the selected field(s), click on the *Terms* button.

NOTE: Subject headings print as they appear in your records. No special formatting of author names and no journal title substitution is applied.

---

8. Click on the *Layout* button to modify the layout and style of your subject bibliography. Verify the settings on the References, Terms, Page Layout, and Bibliography Layout tabs (all four tabs are discussed later in this chapter under "Subject Bibliography Settings"), particularly these items on the References tab:

◆ Output Style, which determines the bibliographic style used to format each reference.

◆ Reference List Title, which prints at the top of the bibliography

◆ Reference List Order, which determines the order of references under each subject heading

Use the Terms tab to set options specifically for subject headings. For a subject bibliography, it is important to select the *Subject Terms and Reference List* item.

Click *OK* to save changes to all of the Layout tabs.

9. Once your subject bibliography is set up the way you want it, you can do one of these:

◆ Display a formatted page view by clicking *Print Preview*. (Macintosh OS version 10.1.5 requires that you first click *Print* to display the Print dialog, and then click *Preview*.)

◆ Print to your printer by clicking the *Print* button. A Print dialog will appear. Verify settings and click *OK* or *Print*.

◆ Print to a disk file (Text, RTF, or HTML) by clicking the *Save* button. A dialog appears for you to name the file. Choose the file type, name and place the file, and click *Save*.

10. *Close* the Subject Bibliography window when you are done viewing it.

Printing a Subject List

A subject list is a sorted list of unique terms (words or phrases) that occur in particular fields of the records you choose. You can base a subject list on any EndNote field or combination of fields.

To print a subject list:

1. Determine which references you want EndNote to use when building the subject list, and highlight only those references in the Library window.

   ♦ You can use *Search References* to find a subset of references, then *Select All* to highlight that subset for your subject list.

   ♦ If you select individual references, use the *Show Selected References* command to view a list containing only those references that will be used to create the subject list.

   ♦ If no references are selected, all references in the library are used for the subject list.

2. From the *Tools* menu, choose *Subject Bibliography*. A Subject Fields dialog appears, listing the EndNote fields by default field name.

3. Highlight the field(s) whose contents you wish to use as subject headings.

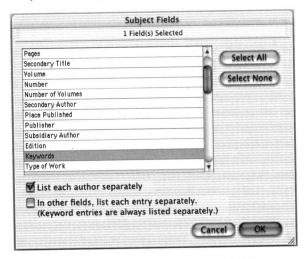

   ♦ You can include any number of fields.

   ♦ If you build the list from more than one field, the terms generated from the fields are combined into a single list.

◆ To quickly select all fields or clear all fields, use the buttons to the right of the dialog.

◆ Click on individual fields to select or deselect them.

4. Select the check boxes as needed to determine whether an entire field is used as a term, or whether a field should be split into multiple terms.

◆ *List each author separately,* when checked, will list each author name as a separate entry. If not checked, all authors from a single field will appear as a single entry.

◆ *In other fields, list each entry that is separated by slash, carriage return, or line feed,* when checked, separates any non-author field into multiple entries.

◆ Terms in the Keywords field are always listed as separate entries.

5. Click OK to display the terms found in the field(s) you selected.

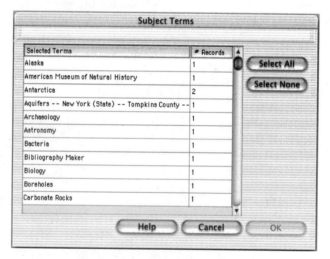

6. Select the terms you want in the subject list.

◆ To quickly select all terms or clear all terms, use the buttons on the right side of the dialog.

◆ You may want to select all terms and then click to deselect the few terms you do not want included.

7. Click OK to display your subject list. If the window does not display a simple list of terms, you must modify settings on the Configure Subject Bibliography dialog as described next.

8. Click the *Layout* button to display the Configure Subject Bibliography dialog.

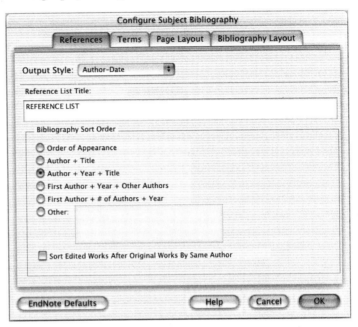

9. On the References tab, enter a Reference List Title, which will print at the top of the list.

   When you print a subject list, the other settings on the Reference List tab are simply ignored. The output style is ignored because you are not printing formatted references, and the sort order set here applies only to formatted references. The sort order of terms is set on the Terms tab.

10. On the Terms tab:

   ◆ *Reference List* must be set to Subject Terms Only.

   ◆ *Include* may include Subject Term Counts and/or a List of Record IDs if you wish.

   ◆ *Subject Term Layout* can be set to print terms in Alphabetical or Term Count order and in Ascending or Descending order.

   ◆ Do not include a *Prefix*, and include a caret-p (^p) as a *Suffix* so each term prints as a new paragraph on a new line.

◆ Apply *Styles* as you wish. However, if you print to a text file all styles are stripped.

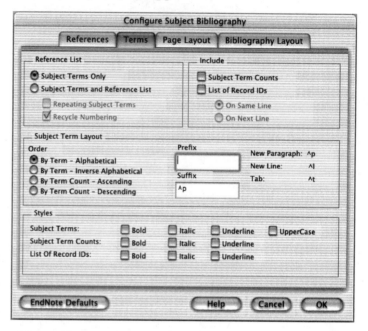

11. Click on the Page Layout tab if you wish to change the font, size, or page margins.

NOTE: The Bibliography Layout tab applies to subject bibliographies only, and does not affect a simple subject list.

---

12. Click *OK* to save changes to the dialog and update the list in the Subject Bibliography window.

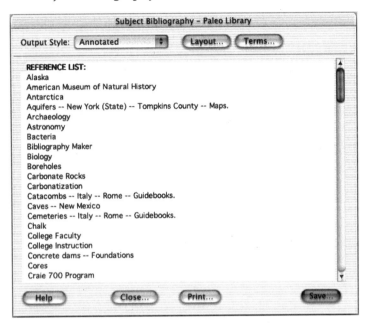

If the window still doesn't show the list you need, you can click on the *Terms* button to select or deselect terms from the selected field(s) or click *Layout* again to make more changes to the Configure Subject Bibliography dialog.

13. View, print or dismiss the list:

♦ Click *Print Preview* to see a page layout view of the bibliography. (Macintosh OS version 10.1.5 requires that you first click *Print* to display the Print dialog, and then click *Preview*.)

♦ Click *Print* to print to a printer. The Print dialog appears. Verify settings and click *OK* or *Print*.

♦ Click *Save* to print to a disk file. A file dialog appears for you to name the file. Choose the file type (text, RTF, or HTML), name the file, and click *Save*.

♦ Click *Close* to dismiss the Subject Bibliography window and return to your record list.

NOTE: Terms are printed as they appear in your records. No special formatting of author names and no journal abbreviations are applied.

Subject Bibliography Settings

To access subject bibliography settings, first generate a subject bibliography from the *Tools* menu. Once the subject bibliography or subject list is displayed, a *Layout* button becomes available.

NOTE: Some subject bibliography settings are updated from the current output style, so changes you make are not saved for future subject bibliographies. If you have special settings that you want to always use for subject bibliographies, it may be easier to copy and modify an output style specifically for generating subject bibliographies.

The References Tab

When you select *Subject Bibliography* from the *Tools* menu to format a subject bibliography or subject list, a *Layout* button is available to display a Configure Subject Bibliography dialog and change settings. This section describes the References tab available on that dialog.

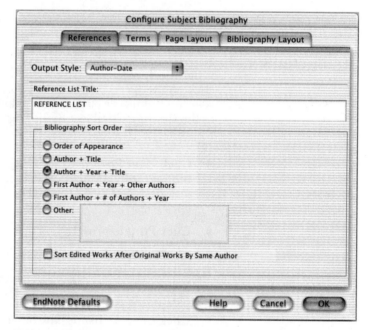

Output Style: Use the drop-down list to select an output style from the list or to *Select Another Style* that doesn't currently appear in the list.

If you opt to *Select Another Style*, EndNote will display the Choose a Style window, where you can choose from over 1,000 output styles. Use the *Find* button to narrow the list of output styles by discipline. Then, select a style in the list and click *Choose*.

The output style is used to format the references in a subject bibliography. This setting is ignored for a subject list.

Reference List Title: Type a title in the text box to print at the top of your subject list or subject bibliography.

Bibliography Sort Order: Click on a button to select the sort order you wish to use for the formatted references printed under each subject heading in a subject bibliography. This setting is ignored for a subject list.

The Terms Tab

When you select *Subject Bibliography* from the *Tools* menu to format a subject bibliography or subject list, a *Layout* button is available to display a Configure Subject Bibliography dialog and change settings. This section describes the Terms tab available on that dialog.

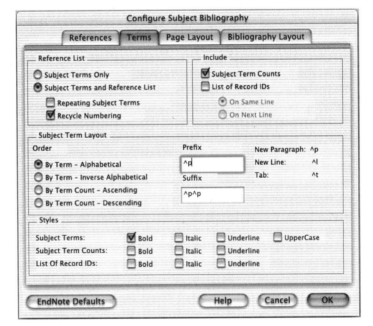

Selecting a Subject List or Subject Bibliography

In the Reference List area of the Terms tab, select one of the two radio buttons:

♦ **Subject Terms Only** prints each unique subject term. It does NOT print formatted references below each term.

♦ **Subject Terms and Reference List** prints each subject term with related references listed below it.

NOTE: The options on this tab are saved for this subject bibliography session and for future sessions, until you change them again. So, if you generate a list of Subject Terms Only, the next time you choose Subject Bibliography, you will produce a simple subject list again. To include formatted references, click the *Layout* button and the Terms tab to select Subject Terms and Reference List.

When printing subject terms with reference lists, EndNote typically prints each unique subject heading only once with the related references listed below. You can select the *Repeating Subject Terms* box to print a subject term before each formatted reference. For example:

American Museum of Natural History

1. *Personalities in Paleontology.* 2002, American Museum of Natural History.

Antarctica

2. Quilty, P.G., *Cycleryon glaessner (crustacea, decapoda) from the jurassic of Ellsworth Land, Antarctica.* Journal of Paleontology, 2000. 62(4): p. 619.

Antarctica

3. Whitney, J.R., T.V. Billoski, and V.R. Jones, *Evidence for Triceratops in Antarctica, in New Directions in Paleontology*, T.V. Billoski, Editor. 1997, Academic Press: New York. P. 24-27.

Select the *Recycling Reference Numbers* box to restart reference numbering for each subject heading. For example:

Recycling Reference Numbers	Continuous Reference Numbers
Heading Number One	*Heading Number One*
1. First formatted reference	1. First formatted reference
2. Second formatted reference	2. Second formatted reference
Heading Number Two	*Heading Number Two*
1. First formatted reference	3. First formatted reference
2. Second formatted reference	4. Second formatted reference

Including Subject Term Counts or Record IDs

In the Include area of the Terms tab you can check a box to include, for the records selected for output:

♦ **Subject Term Counts** prints a number next to the subject term to indicate how many records contain the term. For example:

```
Evolution (1)
Excavation (4)
Extinction (12)
```

Subject Term Counts always print on the same line as the subject term, surrounded by parentheses, and separated from the term by three spaces.

♦ **List of Record IDs** prints the record IDs of the records that contain the term. You can print the list of record IDs on the same line as the subject term (set apart by three spaces) or on the next line. For example:

```
Excavation  34, 33, 6, 48
Extinction  34, 46, 6, 48, 96, 98, 10, 125, 132, 148, 162, 11
```

or

```
Excavation
    34, 33, 6, 48
Extinction
    34, 46, 6, 48, 96, 98, 10, 125, 132, 148, 162, 11
```

When you print these items on the same line as the term, they are always separated by three spaces. That way, you can save to a word processor file, replace the three spaces by a tab character, and convert the text to a table, using the tab as a separator. You can print both term counts and record IDs:

```
Excavation (4)
    34, 33, 6, 48
Extinction (12)
    34, 46, 6, 48, 96, 98, 10, 125, 132, 148, 162, 11
```

Sorting the Subject Terms

You have four options for ordering your subject terms:

♦ **By Term - Alphabetical** sorts subject terms by Date for date fields, and then alphanumeric order (1-9, A-Z) for all other fields.

♦ **By Term - Inverse Alphabetical** simply reverses the By Term - Alphabetical order (Z-A, 9-1, Dates).

♦ **By Term Count - Ascending** lists terms based on how often they appear in records. For example, a term that appears in only one reference would display at the top of the list, whereas a term used in 20 references would appear further down in the list.

♦ **By Term Count - Descending** reverses the By Term Count - Ascending order, so the most-used terms are listed first.

NOTE: This sort order setting affects subject headings only. If you want to change the order of the references printed below each heading, do so on the References tab of the Configure Subject Bibliography dialog.

Inserting Space or Text Around Subject Terms

Use the Prefix and Suffix text boxes to print text or punctuation before or after each subject term.

Each term may include a subject term count and/or a list of record IDs. The order of output is:

Text Before | Subject Term | Subject Term Count | List of Record IDs | Text After | Reference List

You can use these special formatting codes in the text boxes:

New Paragraph:	^P
New Line:	^L
Tab:	^T
Bold:	⌘+B
Italics:	⌘+I
Underlining:	⌘+U

By default, the Prefix box contains "^p" and the Suffix box contains "^p^p" in order to leave blank lines between each subject heading and the first citation listed below it.

When you print Subject Terms Only, you will probably want to print only a single "^p" after each term, so each subject term begins on a new line with no blank lines between them.

Applying Styles

In the Styles area of the Terms tab, check the appropriate boxes to separately apply styles to Subject Terms, Subject Term Counts, and the List of Record IDs. You can combine styles in any way, such as:

<u>Antarctica</u> *(2)* **144, 12**

1. Quilty, P.G., *Cycleryon glaessner (crustacea, decapoda) from the jurassic of Ellsworth Land, Antarctica.* Journal of Paleontology, 2000. 62(4): p. 619.

2. Whitney, J.R., T.V. Billoski, and V.R. Jones, *Evidence for Triceratops in Antarctica, in New Directions in Paleontology,* T.V. Billoski, Editor. 1997, Academic Press: New York. P. 24-27.

Apply styles to bibliographic references by modifying the output style.

If you save your list to a text file, all styles will be stripped.

The Page Layout Tab

When you select *Subject Bibliography* from the *Tools* menu to format a subject bibliography or subject list, a *Layout* button is available to display a Configure Subject Bibliography dialog and change settings. This section describes the Page Layout tab available on that dialog.

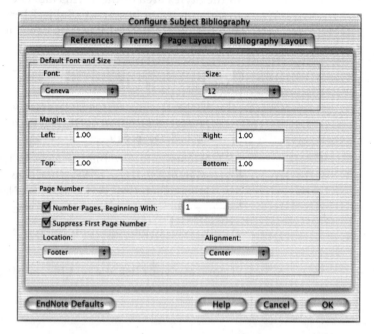

Select the Default Font and Size: Use the drop-down lists to select a default font and size for your subject headings or subject terms. Font and size for bibliographic references are set in the output style.

Set Margins: Enter your page margins in inches.

Position Page Numbers: Use the check boxes to determine whether your pages are numbered and whether to suppress the first page number. Use the drop-down lists to determine location and alignment of page numbers.

The Bibliography Layout Tab

When you select *Subject Bibliography* from the *Tools* menu to format a subject bibliography or subject list, a *Layout* button is available to display a Configure Subject Bibliography dialog and change settings. This section describes the Bibliography Layout tab available on that dialog.

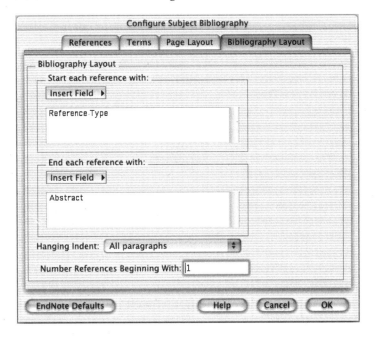

The options available on the Bibliography Layout tab affect only the bibliographic references printed in a subject bibliography. These settings are not used when you print a simple subject list.

NOTE: When you select an output style, the settings on this tab change to reflect the settings found in the output style. You can override those settings for this session, but changes to this tab are not saved after you close the subject bibliography window. If you want to make the changes permanent, edit the output style. You can make a copy of the output style to edit specifically for subject bibliographies.

Starting and Ending Each Reference with a Special Character or Text

Use the *Start each reference with* and the *End each reference with* text boxes to enter fields, text, or punctuation to print before and after every formatted reference.

Simply click in one of the text boxes and type text. You can use the *Insert Field* button to enter control characters or fields of information as described below.

◆ Use one of the *Insert Field* buttons to insert these control characters in a text box:

End of Paragraph inserts a paragraph marker, which moves the following text to the next line.

Tab inserts a tab character. The spacing for tabs is determined by the ruler settings in your word processor.

Forced Separation inserts a vertical bar. Use vertical bars to attach punctuation to a specific field, so that if the field is empty the punctuation will not print.

For example, to include the text "Note: " before the note field, first insert a vertical bar, type the text "Note: ", insert the Notes field, then insert another vertical bar. Your "Notes: " text will print only when a Notes field contains information, and not when it is empty.

Link Adjacent Text keeps text together so that it will not be broken between lines or pages.

Singular/Plural changes between the singular and plural version of a word, such as editor versus editors.

◆ Enter these fields of information in the *Start each reference with* box by clicking the *Insert Field* button and selecting the field name:

Reference Type prints the Reference Type (such as Journal Article or Book) of each reference.

Label prints the label field from each reference.

Citation prints the in-text citation form of each reference.

Bibliography Number prints the sequential number assigned to the reference in the sorted list below each heading.

Record Number prints the unique EndNote record number from each reference.

- Enter these fields of information in the *End each reference with* box by clicking the *Insert Field* button and selecting the field name:

  Label prints the Label field from each reference.

  Keywords prints the entire Keywords field for each reference.

  Abstract prints the Abstract field from each reference.

  Notes prints the Notes field from each reference.

  Record Number prints the unique EndNote record number from each reference.

Setting a Hanging Indent

Use the drop-down list to apply a hanging indent to paragraphs in each formatted reference.

Numbering References

Enter a starting reference number for bibliographic references printing below each heading. This setting is ignored if reference numbering is not applied from the current output style.

Examples of Subject Bibliographies

Using Author Names as Subject Headings

This example uses author names as subject headings. The *List each author separately* box was checked on the Subject Fields dialog, so that single author names are used for headings rather than entire author fields. Uppercasing was applied to the Subject Terms.

BAKER, V.R.

1. V. R. Baker, *Geological Society of America Bulletin,* 100, 1157 (1988).

BARLOW, CONNIE

2. C. Barlow, *Natural History* 110, 62 (Sept., 2001).

BARNES, C.R.

3. C. R. Barnes, *Geological Magazine* 125, 381 (1988).

Using Keywords as Subject Headings

This example uses keywords as subject headings, and restarts reference numbering after each subject heading. You would select *Recycle Numbering* in the Configure Subject Bibliography dialog on the Terms tab. The starting reference number is set on the Bibliography Layout tab.

Geochemistry

1. J. A. Izbicki, *Dissertation Abstracts International*, 61, 2957 (2000).

2. C. Megnien, *Bulletin d'Information des Geologues du Bassin de Paris*, 37, 142 (June, 2000).

Geology

1. S. A. Lebedev, Ph.D., Princeton University (2000).

NOTE: Whether references are numbered or not is determined by the output style selected.

Using Call Numbers as Subject Headings

You can create a two-column output with Call Numbers, such as:

DL312	Forbes, C. S. (1860). Iceland: <u>Its volcanoes, geysers, and glaciers</u>. London, J. Murray.

To create a two-column output:

1. In the Subject Fields dialog, select the Call Number field.

2. Select an output style that does not number citations.

3. On the Layout/Terms tab:

    ♦ Select Subject Terms and Reference List with Repeating Subject Terms.

    ♦ Do not include Subject Term Counts or a list of Record IDs.

    ♦ Insert a tab between each subject heading and reference with the Suffix box (insert ^t).

4. Save the subject bibliography to a word processor file.

5. With your word processor, convert the output to a two-column table, sort by the first column, adjust the column widths, and reformat the paragraph style.

Chapter 14

Customizing Reference Types

Chapter 14 Customizing Reference Types

Introduction

What is a Reference Type?

Your EndNote library can contain references from a variety of different sources, such as books, journal articles, and newspaper articles. We call these different sources **reference types**. EndNote provides built-in forms for these and other common reference types.

In addition to an all-encompassing "Generic" reference type, EndNote has three unused and 25 pre-defined reference types: Journal Article, Book, Book Section, Manuscript, Edited Book, Magazine Article, Newspaper Article, Conference Proceedings, Thesis, Report, Personal Communication, Computer Program, Electronic Source, Audiovisual Material, Film or Broadcast, Artwork, Map, Patent, Hearing, Bill, Statute, Case, Figure, Chart or Table, and Equation.

Important Points About Reference Types

♦ You can assign a particular reference type to each reference entered into your library.

♦ The Reference Types table, accessible through EndNote's Preferences, determines which fields are available for each of the different reference types.

♦ The Reference Types table allows up to 29 different types of references, each capable of supporting up to 40 fields.

♦ Of the 29 reference types, all but the Generic type can be modified.

♦ Use the Reference Types table to add, delete, or rename fields. You can also add or remove complete reference types.

♦ The layout of the Generic reference type should be used as a guide when modifying or creating reference types. *Rows reserved for Authors should be used only for names.*

♦ Changes made to the Reference Types table are stored for each user in an EndNote Prefs file which is located in the folder Users: [Your Folder]: Library: Preferences: EndNote ƒ. They apply to all libraries opened under the current user account.

♦ If you move your library to a different computer, your references will follow the layout of the Reference Types table for the current user account on that computer, unless you also transfer a copy of your EndNote Prefs file to the other user's Preferences: EndNote ƒ folder.

◆ *Do not enter reference data into the Reference Types table.* This table is designed to store just the names of the reference fields.

Reference Types and Data Entry

The chosen reference type specifies which fields appear in the Reference window. For instance, an EndNote journal article reference includes the fields "Journal," "Volume," and "Issue," while a book reference includes fields such as "Publisher" and "City." The Reference window only displays the fields that are relevant to the chosen reference type.

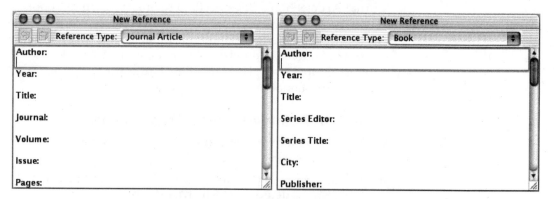

It is best to select the reference type before entering the bibliographic information in a reference. However, you can change the reference type of a reference at any time using the *Reference Type* list at the top of the Reference window.

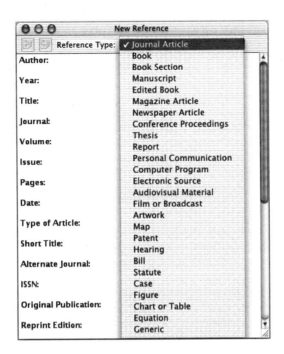

Relationship Between Reference Types and Styles, Filters, and Connections

Styles, filters, and connection files can include templates for all of the different reference types. This enables various types of references to be formatted differently in a bibliography or imported differently, as necessary.

The reference types and fields available to you when editing a style, filter, or connection file depend on how the reference types are configured in the Reference Types table. These files update automatically to reflect changes made in the Reference Types table (such as changing the name of a field).

The Reference Types Table

The Reference Types table displays all available reference types and the fields that each reference type contains. Use the Reference Types table to add, remove, or rename fields—or to add a completely new reference type.

To access the Reference Types table:

1. From the *EndNote* menu, choose *Preferences*.

2. Click the *Reference Types* option in the list of preferences.

3. Click the *Modify Reference Types* button and the Reference Types table will open.

NOTE: The *Modify Reference Types* command is enabled only when all Style, Filter, Connection, and Reference windows are closed.

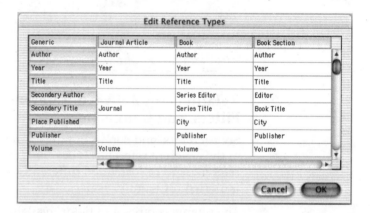

Each column in the table represents a different type of reference. The rows correspond to the 40 possible fields that each reference type can contain.

The first column of the Reference Types table is reserved for the **Generic** reference type which lists all of the available fields. The remaining columns in the Reference Types table represent the 28 other reference types. Each cell in a column represents a field that appears in the reference. The name of the fields should correspond to their Generic field names at the start of the row.

The Generic column is the complete set of fields that can be included in any type of reference—no fields can be added to this list, nor can the names of the Generic fields be changed. As described below, the Generic reference type serves as a model for constructing all other reference types.

Navigating in the Reference Types Dialog

♦ Use the horizontal scroll bar to view additional columns of reference types; use the vertical scroll bar to see the other fields available for each reference type.

♦ The UP or DOWN ARROW keys select the previous or next field, respectively, within the same reference type.

♦ The TAB key can be used to select the cell to the right of the current selection; SHIFT+TAB moves to the left.

♦ Pressing RETURN closes the dialog. Press the ESC key or click *Cancel* to exit from the Reference Types table without saving any changes.

The Generic Type

When entering references into your library, use the Generic type only for references that do not fit any of the other reference types. The more important function of the Generic reference type is to set up a guide for the other reference types to follow.

The Generic field names are used throughout the EndNote program (for example, in the Sort References and Search dialogs) to refer to a similar category of fields that can be found in the different reference types. When you choose a Generic field name in any of these dialogs, it refers to all fields in that row of the Reference Types table. For example, if you use the *Search* command to search the Author field, EndNote searches all fields that appear in the Generic "Author" row of the Reference Types table, including fields such as "Artist," "Reporter," and "Cartographer."

As a result, when editing the Reference Types table it is important that you keep similar fields across the reference types in the same row, as defined by the Generic field names at the start of the row. Each reference type can call these fields by a different name; however, the content of the fields should be similar.

Using the Generic Type in Styles

Although the Generic reference type is rarely used for data entry, it plays an important role in formatting bibliographies. In addition to formatting Generic references, the Generic template in a style is used to format any reference types that are not specifically defined in the style. Consequently, every bibliographic style should contain a Generic template so that all references get formatted when EndNote creates a bibliography.

Special Fields

Each of the 40 different EndNote fields is capable of storing up to about eight pages of text (32,000 characters) with a total limit on any one record of 64,000 characters. Few restrictions are placed on the type of text that can be entered. However, there are a few fields that are reserved for specific functions.

Author Fields

The Author, Secondary Author, Tertiary Author, and Subsidiary Author rows in the Reference Types table are specially configured to handle author names, and should not be used for any data other than names.

When EndNote creates a bibliography, the information in these fields is formatted according to the specifications of the selected style's *Author List* and *Editor List* settings. (The *Author List* is used for the Author field; *Editor List* is used for Secondary Author, Tertiary Author, and Subsidiary Author fields.) If you put text other than personal names in any of these fields, EndNote will still try to interpret it and format it as a person's name.

The Library window displays the last name of the first author that it finds in the Author field. That name is also used in the temporary citations inserted into word processing documents.

NOTE: If you have a corporate author name in an Author field, put a comma after the name so that EndNote does not interpret it as a first and last name. For example, Acme Corporation should be entered as "Acme Corporation,".

Title Fields

The three fields that the Generic type uses for titles—Title, Secondary Title, and Tertiary Title—are usually found under different names in other reference types. For example, a section of a book which is part of a series will use all three title fields: the chapter title would belong in the main Title field, the book title corresponds to the Secondary Title field, and the series title corresponds to the Tertiary Title field.

The Generic Secondary Title and Alternate Title fields map to the Journal and Alternate Journal fields, respectively. These two fields in the Journal Article reference type are the only ones that can be used with the Journals term list to modify the journal names in formatted bibliographies (see page 222).

Pages Field

The fields in the row reserved for page numbers are the only ones that work with the *Page Numbers* option in the styles. This feature lets you specify how EndNote should format the page numbers in the bibliography (first page only or a full or abbreviated range of pages). Similarly, any field in the Pages row of the Reference Types table can take advantage of a special formatting character in the styles: the caret (^). This character allows you to pick a singular and plural form of a term to precede or follow the pages in a bibliography, for example "p. 25" and "pp. 32-45". If you enter page numbers in any other part of the reference, they cannot be used with these features.

URL Field

When a reference is selected and *Open Link* is chosen, EndNote checks the URL field for a URL. No other fields are checked. See "Linking References to Files and Web Sites" on page 201.

Image Field

The Image field stores a graphic or file attachment. This field is included in all reference types. See "Inserting Images" on page 117 for information about adding images to a reference.

To add or remove the Image field from a reference type, use the Preferences dialog to edit reference types, as described in the next section.

Use the text field immediately following the Image field, the Caption field, to enter relevant information pertaining to the image or file.

Customizing the Reference Types

All of the reference types, except for Generic, can be modified using the Reference Types table. Whenever you make a change to a reference type, you should also edit your styles to make sure that they correctly format the new or modified reference types.

Do not try to use the Reference Types table to rearrange information within your references. For example, if you delete the "Journal" field and retype "Journal" elsewhere in the column for Journal Articles, you are simply telling EndNote to close the original "Journal" field and display a new field called "Journal" in another location—this does not move your data from the original "Journal" field to the new one. Any references that had data in the original "Journal" field will still show that information, but the field will have its "Generic" name of "Secondary Title." The new "Journal" field will remain empty.

Adding, Deleting, and Renaming Fields

There are different ways you can customize the various reference types. If an existing reference type does not contain all of the fields that you need, you can define a new field or rename an existing field. Similarly, if there is a field that you know you will never use, you can delete it from the reference type so that it no longer appears in your references.

NOTE: Be sure to read the previous section about "Special Fields" on page 348 before changing any fields.

To rename a field:

1. From the *EndNote* menu, choose *Preferences*, select the *Reference Type* option in the list of preferences, and click *Modify Reference Types* to open the Reference Types table.

2. Using the horizontal scroll bar, browse the column headings to find the reference type that you want to change.

3. Within the column for that reference type, find the field name that you want to change, click on it, and type a new name for the field to replace the current name.

4. Click *OK* to return to the main Preferences window for Reference Types.

5. Click *Save* to save your changes.

Styles, filters, and connection files update automatically to use the new name.

To add a field to a reference type:

1. From the *EndNote* menu, choose *Preferences*, select the *Reference Type* option in the list of preferences, and click *Modify Reference Types* to open the Reference Types table.

2. Find the column for the reference type you want to modify.

3. Look at the field names listed in the Generic column and find the one with the most similar meaning to the field that you want to add. Make sure that the corresponding cell is blank for the reference type that you are modifying. If it is not blank, then you should use another field.

4. Click in the blank cell and type the name for the new field.

5. Click *OK* to return to the main Preferences window for Reference Types.

6. Click *Save* to save your changes.

To delete a field from a reference type:

1. From the *EndNote* menu, choose *Preferences*, select the *Reference Type* option in the list of preferences, and click *Modify Reference Types* to open the Reference Types table.

2. Find the column for the reference type where the field appears. Find the name of the field you want to delete and select it.

3. Press the DELETE or BACKSPACE key to clear that field name.

4. Click *OK* to return to the main Preferences window for Reference Types.

5. Click *Save* to save your changes.

The deleted field no longer appears in any references using that reference type. However, if there was any information in the deleted field, it still appears in the reference, but the field is displayed with its Generic name. For example, suppose you remove the Editor field from the Book reference type. Thereafter, when you add new book references to your library, there will be no available field for entering an editor. However, if you edit an old book reference, one in which you had entered an editor's name, the name will be displayed in the field titled Secondary Author. It is the same Editor field that was used originally, however it is now displayed with its Generic name.

Data in a field is not deleted by deleting a field from a reference type format. To remove all text from a field, use the "Clear Field" option in the *Change Field* command. You can also move data from one field to another using the *Move Field* command on the *References* menu.

Adding and Deleting Reference Types

There are three Unused columns in the Reference Types table where a new type of reference can be added. If these columns are filled, you can overwrite other reference types that you do not need in order to create new reference types. For example, if your subject area never involves art, you will probably have no use for the Artwork reference type; you could replace it with another, more useful reference type.

To add a new reference type:

1. From the *EndNote* menu, choose *Preferences*, select the *Reference Type* option in the list of preferences, and click *Modify Reference Types* to open the Reference Types table.

2. Scroll across to the far right of the Reference Types table and select one of the "Unused" column headings. If all of the "Unused" columns have been taken, click on the column heading for a reference type that you are willing to overwrite.

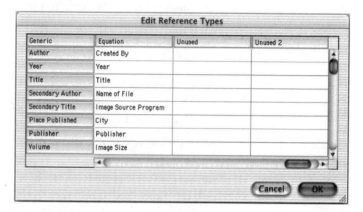

3. Type a name for that new reference type into the column heading.

4. Continue down the column for that reference type, adding new fields as necessary. (Delete or rename unwanted fields if you are overwriting another reference type.) Remember to match the meaning of the fields you add with the Generic row headings. It is often helpful to use the other reference types as guides.

5. Click *OK* after you have added all of the necessary fields, and you will return to the main Preferences window for Reference Types.

6. Click *Save* to save your changes.

You can now use this new reference type when entering references. You should also edit your styles so that they correctly reflect the type of format required for this new reference type. If you overwrite an existing reference type, any references that used the old reference type will change to use the new reference type.

NOTE: If you ever plan to use journal articles in your library, do not overwrite the Journal Article reference type. That first reference type column is the only one for which the Journal Abbreviation replacements can be made with the Journals Term List.

To hide an unwanted reference type:

1. From the *EndNote* menu, choose *Preferences*, select the *Reference Type* option in the list of preferences, and click *Modify Reference Types* to open the Reference Types table.

2. Add a period before a reference type's name (the column heading) to have EndNote remove that option from the *Reference Type* list in the Reference windows and elsewhere. The format, however, remains in the table if you later wish to restore it by removing the period.

   For example, if you were hiding the Map reference type, the column heading would be ".Map".

3. Click *OK* to return to the main Preferences window for Reference Types.

4. Click *Save* to save your changes.

Where Are These Changes Saved?

Your reference type settings are stored in a file called "EndNote Prefs," which is found in the folder Users: [Your Folder]: Library: Preferences: EndNote ƒ.

If you modify your reference types and later move your library to another computer, you should also modify the reference types on the other computer, or copy your EndNote Prefs file into the other computer's Preferences Folder. (Be careful not to overwrite someone else's preferences with yours. See the note below.)

The EndNote Prefs file also stores information about other EndNote preferences. These preferences might need to be reset if you ever replace your preferences file.

NOTE: Replacing another user's EndNote Prefs file overwrites all changes to their Reference Types table and other preferences. Instead of replacing the preferences file with yours, you can rename theirs and then copy your EndNote Prefs file into their Preferences Folder. Only the file called "EndNote Prefs" will be used by EndNote. To restore their original preferences, remove or rename the newer preferences file and change the name of their old preferences file back to "EndNote Prefs."

Table of Predefined Reference Types

The table presented on the following pages shows which fields are used in each of the different reference types and what the fields are called.

Fields with special functions are shaded. Descriptions of the unique qualities of these fields are provided on page 348.

Generic	Journal Article	Book	Book Section	Manuscript
Author	Author	Author	Author	Author
Year	Year	Year	Year	Year
Title	Title	Title	Title	Title
Secondary Author		Series Editor	Editor	
Secondary Title	Journal	Series Title	Book Title	Collection Title
Place Published		City	City	City
Publisher		Publisher	Publisher	
Volume	Volume	Volume	Volume	
Number of Volumes		Number of Volumes	Number of Volumes	
Number	Issue			Number
Pages	Pages	Number of Pages	Pages	Pages
Section				
Tertiary Author			Series Editor	
Tertiary Title			Series Title	
Edition		Edition	Edition	
Date	Date			Date
Type of Work	Type of Article			Type of Work
Subsidiary Author		Translator	Translator	
Short Title	Short Title	Short Title	Short Title	Short Title
Alternate Title	Alternate Journal	Alternate Title	Alternate Title	Alternate Title
ISBN/ISSN	ISSN	ISBN	ISBN	
Original Publication	Original Publication	Original Publication	Original Publication	
Reprint Edition	Reprint Edition	Reprint Edition	Reprint Edition	
Reviewed Item	Reviewed Item		Reviewed Item	
Custom 1				
Custom 2				
Custom 3				
Custom 4				
Custom 5				
Custom 6				
Accession Number	Accession Number	Accession Number	Accession Number	Accession Number
Call Number	Call Number	Call Number	Call Number	Call Number
Label	Label	Label	Label	Label
Keywords	Keywords	Keywords	Keywords	Keywords
Abstract	Abstract	Abstract	Abstract	Abstract
Notes	Notes	Notes	Notes	Notes
URL	URL	URL	URL	URL
Author Address	Author Address	Author Address	Author Address	Author Address
Image	Image	Image	Image	Image
Caption	Caption	Caption	Caption	Caption

Special functions of shaded fields are described on page 348.

Edited Book	Magazine Article	Newspaper Article	Conference Proceedings	Thesis
Editor	Author	Reporter	Author	Author
Year	Year	Year	Year of Conference	Year
Title	Title	Title	Title	Title
Series Editor			Editor	
Series Title	Magazine	Newspaper	Conference Name	Academic Department
City		City	Conference Location	City
Publisher			Publisher	University
Volume	Volume		Volume	
Number of Volumes			Number of Volumes	
	Issue Number			
Number of Pages	Pages	Pages	Pages	Number of Pages
		Section		
			Series Editor	Advisor
			Series Title	
Edition		Edition	Edition	
	Date	Issue Date	Date	
	Type of Article	Type of Article		Thesis Type
Translator			Sponsor	
Short Title	Short Title	Short Title	Short Title	Short Title
Alternate Title	Alternate Magazine			
ISBN	ISSN	ISSN	ISBN	
Original Publication	Original Publication	Original Publication		
Reprint Edition	Reprint Edition	Reprint Edition		
	Reviewed Item	Reviewed Item		
Accession Number	Accession Number	Accession Number	Accession Number	Accession Number
Call Number	Call Number	Call Number	Call Number	Call Number
Label	Label	Label	Label	Label
Keywords	Keywords	Keywords	Keywords	Keywords
Abstract	Abstract	Abstract	Abstract	Abstract
Notes	Notes	Notes	Notes	Notes
URL	URL	URL	URL	URL
Author Address	Author Address	Author Address	Author Address	Author Address
Image	Image	Image	Image	Image
Caption	Caption	Caption	Caption	Caption

Special functions of shaded fields are described on page 348.

Generic	Report	Personal Communication	Computer Program	Electronic Source
Author	Author	Author	Programmer	Author
Year	Year	Year	Year	Year
Title	Title	Title	Title	Title
Secondary Author	Series Editor	Recipient	Series Editor	Series Editor
Secondary Title	Series Title		Series Title	Series Title
Place Published	City	City	City	City
Publisher	Institution	Publisher	Publisher	Publisher
Volume				Access Year
Number of Volumes				
Number				Access Date
Pages	Pages	Description	Description	Description
Section				
Tertiary Author				
Tertiary Title				
Edition			Version	Edition
Date	Date	Date		Last Update Date
Type of Work	Type	Type	Type	Type of Medium
Subsidiary Author				
Short Title	Short Title	Short Title	Short Title	Short Title
Alternate Title	Alternate Title		Alternate Title	Alternate Title
ISBN/ISSN	Report Number		ISBN	ISBN
Original Publication	Contents		Contents	Contents
Reprint Edition				
Reviewed Item				
Custom 1			Computer	
Custom 2				
Custom 3				
Custom 4				
Custom 5				
Custom 6				
Accession Number	Accession Number	Accession Number	Accession Number	Accession Number
Call Number	Call Number	Call Number	Call Number	
Label	Label	Label	Label	Label
Keywords	Keywords	Keywords	Keywords	Keywords
Abstract	Abstract	Abstract	Abstract	Abstract
Notes	Notes	Notes	Notes	Notes
URL	URL	URL	URL	URL
Author Address	Author Address	Author Address	Author Address	Author Address
Image	Image	Image	Image	Image
Caption	Caption	Caption	Caption	Caption

Special functions of shaded fields are described on page 348.

Chapter 14: Customizing Reference Types 357

Audiovisual Material	Film or Broadcast	Artwork	Map	Patent
Author	Director	Artist	Cartographer	Inventor
Year	Year	Year	Year	Year
Title	Title	Title	Title	Title
Series Editor			Series Editor	
Series Title	Series Title		Series Title	
City	Country	City	City	Country
Publisher	Distributor	Publisher	Publisher	Assignee
Extent of Work				
Number				Application Number
	Running Time	Description	Description	Pages
	Producer			
Edition	Edition		Edition	
Date	Date Released	Date	Date	Date
Type	Medium	Type of Work	Type	
Short Title	Short Title	Short Title	Short Title	Short Title
Alternate Title	Alternate Title	Alternate Title	Alternate Title	
ISBN	ISBN		ISBN	Patent Number
Contents				Priority Numbers
Cast	Cast		Scale	
Credits	Credits			Issue Date
	Genre			Attorney/Agent
Format	Format			References
				Legal Status
Accession Number	Accession Number	Accession Number	Accession Number	Accession Number
Call Number	Call Number	Call Number	Call Number	Call Number
Label	Label	Label	Label	Label
Keywords	Keywords	Keywords	Keywords	Keywords
Abstract	Synopsis	Abstract	Abstract	Abstract
Notes	Notes	Notes	Notes	Notes
URL	URL	URL	URL	URL
Author Address	Author Address	Author Address	Author Address	Inventor Address
Image	Image	Image	Image	Image
Caption	Caption	Caption	Caption	Caption

Special functions of shaded fields are described on page 348.

Generic	Hearing	Bill	Statute	Case
Author				
Year	Year	Year	Year	Year
Title	Title	Title	Name of Act	Case Name
Secondary Author				
Secondary Title	Committee	Code	Code	Reporter
Place Published	City			
Publisher	Publisher			Court
Volume		Code Volume	Code Number	Reporter Volume
Number of Volumes	Number of Volumes			
Number	Document Number	Bill Number	Public Law Number	
Pages	**Pages**	**Code Pages**	**Pages**	**First Page**
Section		Code Section	Sections	
Tertiary Author				
Tertiary Title	Legislative Body	Legislative Body		
Edition	Session	Session	Session	
Date	Date	Date	Date Enacted	Date Decided
Type of Work				
Subsidiary Author		**Sponsor**		**Counsel**
Short Title	Short Title	Short Title	Short Title	Abbreviated Case Name
Alternate Title				
ISBN/ISSN				
Original Publication	History	History	History	History
Reprint Edition				
Reviewed Item				
Custom 1				
Custom 2				
Custom 3				
Custom 4				
Custom 5				
Custom 6				
Accession Number	Accession Number	Accession Number	Accession Number	Accession Number
Call Number	Call Number	Call Number	Call Number	Call Number
Label	Label	Label	Label	Label
Keywords	Keywords	Keywords	Keywords	Keywords
Abstract	Abstract	Abstract	Abstract	Abstract
Notes	Notes	Notes	Notes	Notes
URL	**URL**	**URL**	**URL**	**URL**
Author Address	Author Address	Author Address	Author Address	Author Address
Image	**Image**	**Image**	**Image**	**Image**
Caption	Caption	Caption	Caption	Caption

Special functions of shaded fields are described on page 348.

Generic	Figure	Chart or Table	Equation	UNUSED1/2/3
Author	Created By	Created By	Created By	
Year	Year	Year	Year	
Title	Title	Title	Title	
Secondary Author	Name of File	Name of File	Name of File	
Secondary Title	Image Source Program	Image Source Program	Image Source Program	
Place Published	City	City	City	
Publisher	Publisher	Publisher	Publisher	
Volume	Image Size	Image Size	Image Size	
Number of Volumes				
Number	Number	Number	Number	
Pages	Description	Description	Description	
Section				
Tertiary Author				
Tertiary Title				
Edition	Version	Version	Version	
Date	Date	Date	Date	
Type of Work	Type of Image	Type of Image	Type of Image	
Subsidiary Author				
Short Title				
Alternate Title				
ISBN/ISSN				
Original Publication				
Reprint Edition				
Reviewed Item				
Custom 1				
Custom 2				
Custom 3				
Custom 4				
Custom 5				
Custom 6				
Accession Number	Accession Number	Accession Number	Accession Number	
Call Number	Call Number	Call Number	Call Number	
Label	Label	Label	Label	
Keywords	Keywords	Keywords	Keywords	
Abstract	Abstract	Abstract	Abstract	
Notes	Notes	Notes	Notes	
URL	URL	URL	URL	
Author Address	Author Address	Author Address	Author Address	
Image	Image	Image	Image	
Caption	Caption	Caption	Caption	

Special functions of shaded fields are described on page 348.

Chapter 15

Bibliographic Styles

Chapter 15   Bibliographic Styles

Introduction

What is an Output Style?

The term **output style** (or just "style") is used to describe a particular method of documenting your work. Each style is designed as a complete solution for formatting in-text citations, footnote citations, and bibliographies for all types of references.

You can think of styles as templates that show EndNote how to arrange the information in each of your EndNote references for citations and bibliographies. For example, this reference:

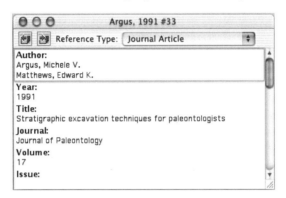

could be formatted in the Chicago style like this:

```
Argus, Michele V., and Edward K. Matthews. 1991.
Stratigraphic excavation techniques for paleontologists.
Journal of Paleontology 17:119-127.
```

Or it could be formatted in the Nature style like this:

```
1.    Argus, M. V. & Matthews, E. K. Stratigraphic excava-
      tion techniques for paleontologists. Journal of Pa-
      leontology 17, 119-127 (1991).
```

The Output Styles Menu

The style selected in the *Output Styles* submenu of the *Edit* menu (or the style menu in the Main toolbar) determines how references are formatted for the preview in the Library window as well as for the *Format Bibliography*, *Format*, *Print*, *Export*, and *Copy Formatted* commands.

By default, EndNote's four standard bibliographic styles are installed in your *Output Styles* menu:

♦ **Annotated:** generates an Author-Date style bibliography with abstracts.

♦ **Author-Date:** generates bibliography alphabetized by author name, and in-text citations with Author and Year.

- **Numbered:** generates a numbered bibliography with corresponding numbered in-text citations.

- **Show All:** generates a list of the references as entered, including all fields and the names of the fields.

Mark individual styles as your favorites in the Style Manager to have them appear in the *Output Styles* menu, the style menu in the Main toolbar, and the confirm formatting dialog.

The Style Manager

EndNote includes more than 1000 individual bibliographic styles. Each one of these styles is stored as an individual file in the Styles folder in your EndNote folder.

The name of the style refers to the journal or publisher that has defined the bibliographic format. The Nature style, for example, is based on the format required by the journal *Nature*, and the Chicago style is named after the *Chicago Manual of Style*. Styles in the Export category, such as "RIS" are not bibliographic styles, but rather export styles designed to aid in transferring EndNote data into other databases.

To see if your journal's style is included in EndNote, peruse the list of styles in the Style Manager or consult the EndNote Help file. If your style is not available, any style can be modified to suit your needs and you can create new styles.

To see the available styles in EndNote's Styles folder, choose *Output Styles* from the *Edit* menu, and select *Open Style Manager*.

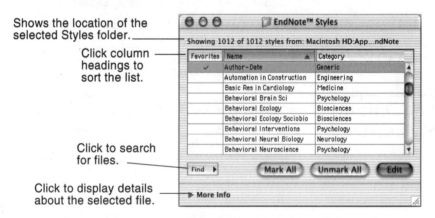

Shows the location of the selected Styles folder.

Click column headings to sort the list.

Click to search for files.

Click to display details about the selected file.

The Style Manager lists the names of all of the styles available in the Styles folder and gives you the options to edit them or select them as "favorites" for quick access from the style menu in the Main toolbar, the *Output Styles* menu on the *Edit* menu, or the confirm formatting dialog.

Marking Your Favorite Styles

When you have found a style that you will want to use in the future, click in the Favorites column next to it to mark it as a favorite. All styles that are marked as favorites appear in the *Output Styles* submenu of the *Edit* menu, and the styles menu of the Main toolbar. This gives you easy access to the styles you use most often.

Use the *Mark All* button as a quick way to select a whole category of styles. For example, click the *Find* button and choose a category from the available list. EndNote displays only the styles in that category. Click *Mark All* to mark all of them as favorites and they will appear in your *Output Styles* menu. Choose *Show All* from the *Edit* menu to bring all of the styles back into view. The *Unmark All* button may be used to unmark all of the output styles that are showing in the list.

Navigating in the Style Manager

Use the following features to locate the output style that you want to use:

◆ If you know the name of the style that you want to use, you may start typing it and the first file that matches what you type will be selected.

◆ Click the *Find* button and choose category (such as Medicine or Humanities) to find only the bibliographic styles for a specific discipline.

◆ Click the *Find* button, and choose *by Name* to search for the file by the name of the style. You can enter a partial name or the full name. EndNote will display all matching results.

◆ Click the *Find* button and choose *All Styles* to return all of the styles to the displayed list.

◆ Click the column headings to sort the styles by name or by category. Clicking the same column heading a second time will change the sort order from ascending to descending. Click again to set it back to ascending order.

◆ Click the *More Info* button at the bottom of the dialog to display additional information about the selected style (such as modification and creation dates, and any comments or limitations). *More Info* toggles with *Less Info*. You also have the option of displaying a preview of the style in the "More Info" panel.

Previewing Styles and Showing Information

Click *Less Info* in the Style Manager to hide the information panel. (When you choose *Less Info*, the button changes to *More Info*, which will display the panel.) The information panel is used to display more detail about the selected style.

♦ **Style Information:** When the pop-up list is set to *Style Info*, details about the style are displayed in the Information panel. These include the creation and modification dates, category, which style guide the style is based on, and any limitations or comments about using the style.

♦ **Style Preview:** Click *Style Info* to change it to *Style Preview*. In the preview section, EndNote shows how a journal, book, and book section would be formatted with the selected style.

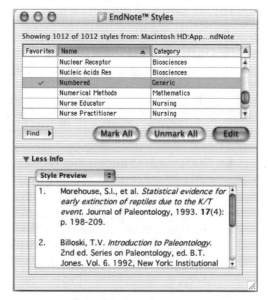

Previewing Styles Using Your Own References

EndNote uses built-in examples for the previews in the Style Manager window. If you want to preview a style using your own references:

1. In the Style Manager, mark the style as a favorite by clicking in the Favorites column next to its name. This adds the style to the *Output Styles* menu.

2. From the *Edit* menu, choose *Output Styles*, and select the style to preview.

3. Open a library, and click the *Show Preview* button at the bottom of the Library window.

4. Select any reference in your library to have it displayed in the Library window's preview panel.

The preview pane displays only one reference at a time. If you would like to preview a group of references, use the *Copy Formatted* command and the Clipboard:

1. From the *Edit* menu, choose *Output Styles* and select a style.

2. Select one or more references in your library and choose *Copy Formatted* (⌘+K) from the *Edit* menu.

3. *Paste* from the Clipboard into a word processor document to see the formatted references as they would appear in a bibliography.

Copying Styles

Because each style is a separate file on your hard drive, you can copy them as you would copy any file on your hard drive using the Macintosh Finder.

To copy a style to a removable disk, select the style on your hard drive and drag it onto a disk.We recommend that you use this method to make backup copies of your styles after you modify them (see Appendix A).

To make a copy of a style from within EndNote:

1. From the *Edit* menu, choose *Output Styles* and select *Open Style Manager*.

2. Select the style you want to copy and click *Edit*.

3. Without making any changes to the file, choose *Save As* from the *File* menu.

4. Give this copy of the file a new name, and save it in your Styles folder if you would like access to it from within EndNote. If you save the style outside of the Styles folder (such as on a CD to take a copy to a different computer, or to backup the file), it will not be available within EndNote.

The new style will remain open. The original style will be left untouched.

Saving Styles

To save a new style that you have just created, or to save changes to a style you have just modified, choose *Save* from the *File* menu. Alternatively, choose *Save As* from the *File* menu when you want to save a modified style with a new name.

If you close a Style window before saving a style, EndNote prompts you to save or discard the changes you have made, or choose *Cancel* to return to the style. If you quit from EndNote while a Style window is open, the same dialog appears.

EndNote automatically saves new styles to your designated style folder. (The Style Manager within EndNote only provides access to the styles that are in the designated styles folder). Your Styles folder, by default, is the folder called "Styles" in your EndNote folder. You may also specify a different folder if necessary. For instructions see "Folder Locations" on page 486.

Deleting Styles

To delete a style from within EndNote:

1. From the *Edit* menu, choose *Output Styles* and select *Open Style Manager*.

2. Select the style to be deleted.

3. Choose *Clear* from the *Edit* menu, or CONTROL-click on the style and choose *Delete* from the shortcut menu.

You can also delete an unwanted style by switching back to the Macintosh Finder, and opening the Styles folder in the EndNote folder. Then, drag the style from the Styles folder to the Trash.

Renaming Styles

Rename styles using the *Save As* command in EndNote's *File* menu. This allows you to make a copy of any style that you want to modify, so you can keep several variations of the same style. You can also rename styles by switching to the Finder, locating the style file in the Styles folder, clicking on the file name, and typing a new name.

Reverting Changes to a Style

If at any time you need to revert your changes back to the last saved copy of the style, choose *Revert Style* from the *File* menu. Once you close the Style window the changes are permanent until changed again.

Closing a Style

To close a Style window, click the close button in the upper left corner of the window, or choose *Close Style* from the *File* menu. If you have not saved your changes to the style, EndNote prompts you and gives you the option to save or discard any changes that you have made.

What Should I Do if My Style Is Not Included?

EndNote supplies over 1000 journal styles for your convenience; however, because there are thousands of journals published, the style you need may not be included. This should not be a problem because you can design a style of your own or modify any of EndNote's preconfigured styles.

If a style that you need is not included with EndNote, we recommend modifying a style that is similar to what you need.

To find and modify a similar style:

1. From the *Edit* menu, choose *Output Styles* and select *Open Style Manager*.

2. In the Style Manager, change the setting in the information panel from *Style Info* to *Style Preview*. The preview of the selected style should now be displayed.

3. Scroll through the list of available styles to see if you can find one that is similar to what you need.

4. Once you have found a similar style, select it, and click the *Edit* button. The Style window opens.

5. Choose *Save As* from the *File* menu, give this copy of the style a new name that corresponds to the name of the journal you want to use it for, and click *Save*. This will also keep the original style unchanged, in the event that you need to use it later.

6. The new Style window remains open for you to edit it as you need. For more details about editing parts of a style, read "Basic Components of a Style" and "Modifying Style Templates" starting on page 370.

Once the new copy of the style has been saved, it will be added to your style menus.

NOTE: You can download the latest output styles available from ISI ResearchSoft. Visit the EndNote Web site (www.endnote.com) for available styles.

Accessing Styles in Other Places

The *Style Manager* displays only the styles in the chosen styles folder. Only styles from one folder can be displayed in the *Styles* menu at any given time; styles in subfolders within the selected folder are ignored.

By default, the Style Manager displays the styles that are in the "Styles" folder in the EndNote folder. You may copy files into this folder to have them displayed in the Style Manager, or you may change this to use a different folder, if necessary. To do so, choose *Preferences* from the *EndNote* menu, select the *Folder Locations* panel, and click the *Select Folder* button in the Styles section of that panel. See "Folder Locations" on page 486 for details.

Basic Components of a Style

The best way to understand how a style works is to open one up and look at it.

◆ To create a new style: From the *Edit* menu, choose *Output Styles* and select *New Style*. If you are interested in creating a new style, also read "Creating a New Style" on page 410.

◆ To edit a style: From the *Edit* menu, choose *Output Styles* and then *Open Style Manager*. Select the file to edit and click *Edit*. The most recently used style can also be opened by selecting *Output Styles* from the *Edit* menu, and choosing *Edit <style>*.

The Style Window

After choosing the option to edit an existing style or create a new one, EndNote opens the Style window.

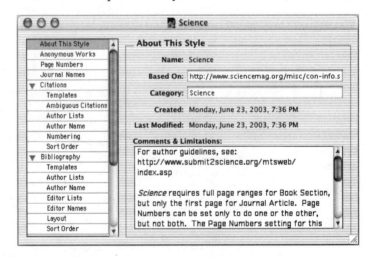

All of the different options for editing a style are listed on the left side of the Style window. The first four items (*About This Style*, *Anonymous Works*, *Page Numbers*, and *Journal Names*) apply to citations, bibliographies, and citations in footnotes. The rest of the options in the Style window are grouped under one of four headings:

Citations: Panels listed under the *Citations* heading apply only to citations in the body of the text.

Bibliographies: The items listed under the *Bibliography* heading apply to the bibliography that EndNote creates when you format a paper. These settings are also used with the *Export, Print, Copy Formatted,* and *Preview* options.

Footnotes: The items under the *Footnote* heading apply to citations that have been inserted into the footnotes or endnotes in a word processing document. (You must first create the footnotes in your word processor, and then insert EndNote citations into them.)

Figures and Tables: The items under *Figures and Tables* apply to EndNote figures and tables that have been inserted into a Microsoft Word document.

Click on the triangle next to one of the headings to expand or collapse the view to show or hide the related options. Click on an item under the headings to view the associated panel. You may switch between panels as needed while editing the file. No changes are saved in any of the panels, however, until you choose *Save* or *Save As* from the *File* menu.

Style Templates

The *Citation, Bibliography,* and *Footnote* sections of the style all have a *Template* panel and other options for fine tuning the style.

The *Templates* panels are the major component of the styles. They include the field names and punctuation organized in the way EndNote should format the references for that particular style. The templates look like citations or bibliography entries, except that field names are used in place of the actual data. During the formatting process, EndNote replaces the field names with the corresponding information from the references.

For details about working with style templates see page 372.

Other Style Options

Under each heading in the Style window (*Citations, Bibliography,* and *Footnotes*) there are a series of options for how to fine-tune the formatted references in citations, bibliographies, or footnotes. Many of these options are repeated for the three sections (such as the settings that determine how author names are treated), because each of these three areas of the document might require a slightly different format. The *Figures and Tables* section applies specifically to EndNote figures and tables inserted into a Word document. These options are described starting on page 385.

Modifying Style Templates

If you are creating a bibliography that requires a style not included with EndNote, then you can modify a style to suit your needs. (See "What Should I Do if My Style Is Not Included?" on page 369.) Editing a style requires a general understanding of how styles work and the components of a style. Read "Basic Components of a Style" on page 370 to become familiar with the terms used in this section.

Citation Template

Click on *Templates* under the *Citation* heading to view the Citation panel. This template tells EndNote how to format the in-text citations in the body of your paper. For example, the Numbered style uses a bracketed bibliography number for the in-text citation. (The bibliography number corresponds to a numbered reference in a bibliography.) An author-year type of style would probably display something such as "(Author, Year)" in the citation template.

You may change the template by deleting unwanted field names or punctuation, retyping the punctuation you want, and inserting new fields with the *Insert Field* button. More information about editing templates is provided later in this section.

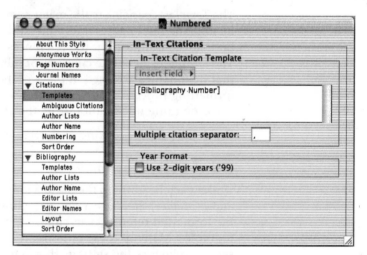

Multiple Citation Separators

Use the "Multiple Citation Separators" section of this dialog to specify the punctuation to separate multiple citations in your papers. A multiple citation is an in-text citation that includes more than one reference within a single set of delimiters, such as:

(Argus, 1993; Billoski, 1993; Hall, 1988). This example uses a semicolon and a space as the separator between citations.

The separator can be changed by typing other text in the "Multiple citation separator" box. Remember to include a space in the separator section when necessary.

Year Format

If you would like EndNote to use 2-digit years (such as '99) in the in-text citations, check the "Use 2-digit years" option. Years from all centuries will be abbreviated to display just the last two digits. This applies only to the years in the in-text citations.

Bibliography and Footnote Templates

Click *Templates* under the *Bibliography* or *Footnotes* heading to see the templates for how those references are formatted.

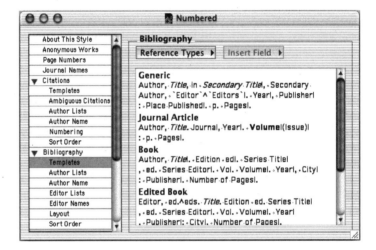

For footnote and bibliography templates, each has a "Generic" template, and other reference-type-specific templates to format the various reference types in a bibliography.

The following examples show how journal articles, books, and book sections, respectively, would be formatted with the Numbered style. Notice that each reference type is formatted differently, which is why different templates are required:

1. Emiliani, C., *Competitive evolution.* Journal of Theoretical Biology, 1982. **97**: p. 13-33.

2. Jones, V.R., *The Theory of Foraging*, B.J. Bloggs, Editor. 1976, Smith and Barnes: New York.

3. Whitney, J.R., T.V. Billoski, and V.R. Jones, *Evidence for Triceratops in Antarctica, in New Directions* in *Paleontology,*

T.V. Billoski, Editor. 1987, Academic Press: New York. p.24-27.

Generic Template

The Generic template is used to format references that use the Generic reference type or do not have their own template in the style. For example, if a Book template had not been included in the style, book references would be formatted using the Generic template.

Other Reference Type Templates

The rest of the templates in the style tell EndNote how to format specific reference types, such as journals, books, and book sections.

Footnote Template Options

Styles have varying requirements for how citations in footnotes should be formatted. The options at the top of the Footnote *Templates* panel allow for the different conditions.

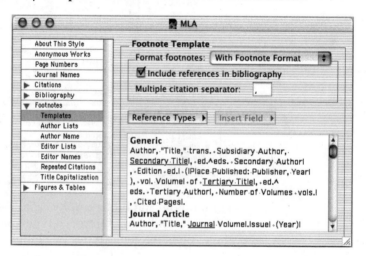

For some styles, citations in footnotes are formatted just like in-text citations (in the body of the paper). In that case, there is no need to create a special template for footnotes, simply choose the *Same As In-text* option from the Footnote Format options.

Similarly, some formats request that citations in footnotes are formatted as full bibliographic references, exactly like the bibliography. For those styles, you can set the footnote format option to *Same as Bibliography*.

However, if you need the footnotes to use their own special format (most styles for the humanities require this), you would choose the option to format citations in footnotes with a unique footnote format. For this option, you need to define the templates for how citations in footnotes should be formatted.

Changing the Punctuation in a Formatted Reference

Punctuation that appears in your formatted references can be changed by editing the style you are using. When you edit a style, you can delete unwanted punctuation, replace it with other punctuation, or add additional punctuation where necessary.

For example, if the Numbered style creates a perfect bibliography for your document *except* that it puts a comma after the authors' names where you need a period, you can edit the Numbered style to make this change.

To edit the Numbered style:

1. Choose the Numbered style in the *Output Styles* menu.

2. Choose *Edit Numbered* from the *Output Styles* menu to open the Numbered Style window.

3. Click the *Templates* option under the *Bibliography* heading.

4. For each reference type (such as Generic, Journal Article, and Book), delete the comma that follows the field name "Author" and type a period.

   The style's bibliographic templates should now look like the example below. Notice that the punctuation after the Author field in each template has been changed to a period.

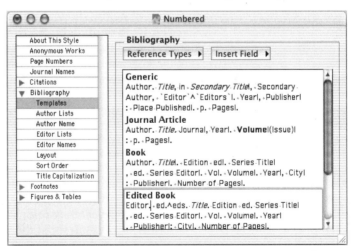

5. From the *File* menu, choose *Save As*. In the dialog that appears, enter a new name for this modified Numbered style and click *Save*.

Or, if you prefer to just update the original Numbered style, choose *Save* instead of *Save As*.

Now you can use the new style to create a formatted bibliography that puts a period between the author names and the titles.

For information about making punctuation or spaces appear only under certain circumstances see "Special Formatting Characters" on page 381. That section also explains the use of the non-breaking spaces (·), vertical bars (|), accent grave (`), and the carets (^) that you see in the style templates.

NOTE: If you save a new style into a folder other than the current styles folder, it will not be available in the Style Manager. You should save new styles to your Styles folder, or see "Accessing Styles in Other Places" on page 369 if necessary.

Adding and Removing Fields in a Formatted Reference

The field names (such as Author, Year, and Title) that you see when editing a style template, indicate what information is included in your formatted reference. If you want to include a field, such as notes, along with your references, you should add the Notes field to the style that you use. Similarly, to exclude unwanted information that is appearing in a bibliography, you must delete the field name that contains that information from the style's bibliography template.

The examples below show two common scenarios in which fields are added to or removed from the formatted bibliography. Whenever you change the fields in a style template be sure to check the surrounding punctuation to make sure that it is still accurate.

Adding a Field to a Style Template

To insert a new field into a style template:

1. From the *Edit* menu, choose *Output Styles* and select *Open Style Manager*.

2. Select the style that you want to edit, and click *Edit*.

3. Click on the *Templates* option under the *Bibliography* heading, and position the cursor at the location in the template where you want to add a field.

4. Click the *Insert Field* button and choose the field to be added.

5. After the field is inserted, add any punctuation or spacing that is necessary to correctly incorporate the new field into the style.

NOTE: As a short-cut, you can use the options in the *Layout* panel to add text or punctuation before or after *every* reference in a bibliography. See "Adding Text Before Each Reference" on page 398 and "Adding Text After Each Reference" on page 399.

Deleting a Field from a Style Template

If EndNote includes information in your bibliography that you do not want to be there, you can edit the style and delete the unwanted field's name and any associated punctuation.

For example, if a style includes the issue number in your journal references, and you do not want the issue to appear:

1. In the Style Manager, select the style and click the *Edit* button.

2. Under the *Bibliography* heading, click the *Templates* option.

3. Select the text to be deleted (which includes ".Issue|" in this example), and press the DELETE or BACKSPACE key.

Journal Article
Author. "Title." Journal·Volumel·Issue·(Year)l:·Pagesl.

Along with the Issue field, also remove the period that precedes it and the vertical bar, a special formatting character, that follows the Issue field. (See "Special Formatting Characters" on page 381 for more information about the vertical bar.)

Adding New Reference Types

When a style does not include a template for a specific reference type, such as Report, EndNote uses the style's Generic template to format that reference type. Although there are times when the Generic format suffices, often it is not sufficient because the other reference types need to be formatted differently. Therefore, you should make specific templates for the different reference types that you will be including in your bibliographies.

To add a new reference type template to a style:

1. From the *Edit* menu, choose *Output Styles>Open Style Manager* and select the style that you want to modify.

2. With the style selected, click the *Edit* button.

3. In the Style window, click the *Templates* panel under the *Bibliography* heading.

4. Choose the name of the desired reference type from the *Reference Types* popup list. (Reference Types that are already defined appear in the list with check marks next to their name.)

A new template for that reference type is added at the bottom of the Style window (scroll to the bottom of the Style window if you do not see it).

Defining the Format for the New Reference Type Template

Defining the format for a new template is a process of inserting the necessary fields and punctuation in the correct order. For this example, we want a report to look like this (Author, Title, Report Number, Year, Institution, and City):

```
Trift, M, Aspects of the tethyan rifting, 88-101.
1998, Institute for Tethyan Rifting: Austin, TX.
```

We can insert the fields and type the punctuation to create a template for the Report reference type. Use the *Insert Field* button at the top of the Style window to insert the fields in the correct order. After inserting a field name, type the punctuation and spacing that should follow it. Apply text styles, such as italics for the Title, by selecting the text to change and using the *Style* commands in the *Edit* menu.

The final template for the Report reference type looks like this:

```
Report
Author, Title, Report Number. Year, Institution: City.
```

Fonts and Text Styles

By default, text entered into a Style window appears in EndNote's *Plain Font*, *Plain Size*, and *Plain Style* settings, which allow the bibliography that EndNote creates to adopt the font settings in your paper. For example, if you type your paper in 10 point Courier font, EndNote uses that font for the paper's bibliography.

EndNote's *Edit* menu commands let you apply any font, size, or text style to your Style templates.

All text attributes entered into a style template carry over into the bibliography that EndNote creates. You can use this feature, for example, to italicize titles or make the volume numbers bold. Any font or text style changes entered in an EndNote Reference window carry through the bibliography as well. For example, any italicized terms in your references will still appear italicized in your bibliography, regardless of the text attributes that the EndNote bibliographic style applies.

Rules for Working with Style Templates

There are four basic rules of *dependence* that govern how text, spaces, and field names influence each other when they are used in a style template. If necessary, these rules can be circumvented in specific situations using the special formatting characters described in the next section of this chapter.

Rule #1: Basic dependence

Any text or punctuation that is not separated from a field name by an ordinary space is *dependent* on the adjacent field.

In this context, "dependent" means that the text or punctuation adjacent to a field *only* appears in your bibliography if the adjacent field contains data. For example, in this excerpt:

```
Volume (Issue)
```

the parentheses around "Issue" only appear in a formatted reference if there is an issue number for the reference.

Rule #2: The preceding field takes precedence over the following field.

When punctuation appears between two fields with no intervening spaces, it is dependent on the preceding field.

In this example,

```
Volume:Issue
```

the colon is dependent on the Volume field. This means, if there is no volume in the reference, the colon will not appear. If there is a volume, the colon will appear

---

NOTE: This example shows a case where the rules of dependence might not do what you want. For example, you might want to have the colon only show when there is an issue. This can be done using the special formatting characters described in the next section.

Rule #3: The first space after a field is dependent on that field. Additional spaces are independent.

The first ordinary space following a field is always dependent on that field. Any consecutive spaces after that are independent and will always appear in the formatted references.

For example, if EndNote formats an anonymous book using a template that has the Author field followed by a space and the Title field:

```
Author. Title
```

the title will *not* be preceded by a space in the final formatted reference because the space, just like the period, is dependent on the Author field. However, if the style includes two spaces between the Author and the Title:

```
Author.  Title
```

the title will be preceded by one space for all anonymous references. The first space, being dependent on the Author field, disappears when there is no author, however the second space is *independent,* so it remains in the formatted reference.

Independent spaces can be forced to be dependent on an adjacent field using the special formatting characters discussed later.

Rule #4: Independent text always appears in the bibliography.

Any text or punctuation that is not dependent on a field name always appears in the formatted references. For example, if:

`Edition ed.`

is entered into a style's Book template using only an ordinary space to separate the text "ed." and the field "Edition", the text "ed." will appear in all Book references—regardless of whether or not there is an edition for that reference.

NOTE: The non-breaking space can be used in place of a regular space to link independent text to a field. See "Link Adjacent Text (Using the Non-breaking Space)" below.

EndNote Cleans Up

Too confused about all these rules? Well, even if you don't get everything quite right according to the rules, EndNote will do its best to clean up the formatted reference. Obvious problems (such as a leftover parenthesis or a comma followed by a period) are fixed automatically.

Special Formatting Characters

EndNote has special formatting characters that add flexibility and precision to the grouping of punctuation and fields in the style templates.

Link Adjacent Text (Using the Non-breaking Space)

If you type `Edition ed.` into a style template and use an ordinary space to separate the field name "Edition" from the abbreviation "ed.", then "ed." will appear regardless of whether or not the reference has an edition (see Rule #4).

To avoid this problem, make "ed." *dependent* on the Edition field by linking "ed." to the Edition field with a non-breaking space. Think of a non-breaking space as bibliographic formatting glue. It joins two or more items together so they act as a single unit. Thus, any text or punctuation "glued" to a field will drop out of the bibliography if that field is empty.

You can insert a non-breaking space by selecting *Link Adjacent Text* from the *Insert Field* list in the *Templates* panels. You can also enter it by typing OPTION+SPACE.

It appears on the screen as a small diamond. Look at the example below to understand the correct locations for a non-breaking space.

```
Journal Article
Author. Title. Journal Volume|: ·Pages|, ·Year|.
```

The non-breaking space is converted to a normal space in the formatting process. Common uses of the non-breaking space include (where "·" is used as a non-breaking space):

```
p^pp·Pages

Edition·ed.

vol·Volume

Editor·Ed.^Eds.
```

The non-breaking space is also used in conjunction with the vertical bar (see next section) to change the dependency of a punctuation mark from one field to another.

```
Volume|:·Issue|.
```

In this case, the colon (:) is linked to the Issue field with a non-breaking space, so it does not print in the bibliography if the Issue field is empty.

Forced Separation—Using the Vertical Bar

If you do not want text or punctuation to be dependent on the preceding or following field, use the vertical bar character (|), to force a separation of the text from a field. The vertical bar can be found on the same key as the backslash (\ ). It can also be inserted from the *Insert Field* list in the *Templates* panels.

Think of a vertical bar as *breaking* dependence, or forcing separation between two dependent items. (The vertical bar works in exactly the opposite way as the non-breaking space.)

For example, the Journal Article templates in some styles require a period between the volume and issue. A template for such a style might look like this:

```
Journal Article
Author. "Title." Journal Volume.Issue (Year): Pages.
```

However, when this style formats a journal article that does not include an issue number, the bibliography entry will be incorrect, as in the following example:

```
Clark, H. and Carlson, T. "Hearers and Speech
Acts." Language 58.(1982): 332-373.
```

Notice that the period used to separate the volume from the issue appears here in the absence of an issue because it is dependent upon the Volume (Rule #2). And the space separating the volume and the year is lost because that space is dependent upon the Issue field (Rule #3).

EndNote has a way of avoiding these problems. The vertical bar character (|) can be used to break the automatic grouping of spaces and punctuation with adjacent fields.

If you insert the vertical bar before the period in our example, the period's dependency switches from the Volume field to the Issue field. Add another vertical bar before the space that follows the Issue field, and the space will no longer be dependent on the Issue field. Use the vertical bar character in conjunction with the non-breaking space. With these changes the style looks like this:

Journal Article
Author. "Title." Journal Volume|.Issue| (Year): Pages.

And the formatted reference without an issue is correct:

```
Clark, H. and Carlson, T. "Hearers and Speech
Acts." Language 58 (1982): 332-373.
```

Other common examples for using the vertical bar include:

```
Publisher|: City
```

```
Pages|.   (to make the final period independent)
```

Field Names in Bibliographies

Sometimes you may need to use text in a template that is also an EndNote field name for that reference type. For example, you may want to use the word "Editor" after the editor's name:

```
Jones, V.R., B.K. Marion, and R.L. Zeiss, The
Theory of Foraging, in A History of Foraging
Behavior, B.J. Bloggs, Editor. 1976, Smith and
Barnes: New York.
```

Normally, EndNote interprets the word "Editor" as a field name when it appears in a book's style template. This is even true of field names that appear as part of a word, such as "Editors" or "Issued." Field names need not be capitalized to be recognized.

To force EndNote to interpret a word as just text and not as a field name in a template, put an accent grave character before and after the word: `` `Editor` ``. The accent grave is found in the upper left corner of most keyboards on the same key as the tilde (~). Remember to also use the non-breaking space to link the text, `` `Editor` ``, to the Editor field.

Book Section

Author, *Title*. in Book Title, Editor, `Editor`|. Year, Publisher|: City|, p. Pages.

Singular/Plural Term Separator (Caret ^)

You can specify both singular and plural forms of labels for editors or pages in a formatted reference by using a caret (^) to separate the terms. For example, some styles put "Ed." after a single editor and "Eds." follows several editors' names. Or, similarly, "p." might precede a single page, while "pp." precedes multiple pages. This feature can be applied to any field that corresponds to the Generic field for Author, Secondary Author, Tertiary Author, Subsidiary Author, Pages, and Cited Pages.

In the style template, enter both the singular and plural forms of the label separated by a caret (insert it from the *Insert Field* list or type SHIFT+6). Any text before the caret, back to but not including the preceding space, is used for the singular form; text after the caret, up to the next space, is used for the plural form. These terms must also be linked to the relevant field using a non-breaking space. For example, a style template might look like this:

Edited Book

Editor, ed.^eds. *Title* . Number of Volumes vols
|. Vol. Volume|, *Series Title* |. City|: Publisher|, Year|.

Or like this:

Journal Article

Author. "Title." <u>Journal</u> Volume|. Issue| (Year)|: p.^pp. Pages|.

Additional Style Formatting Options

The templates determine the general layout of the formatted references and citations. The remainder of the panels in the Style window can be used to fine-tune certain aspects of a style.

Anonymous Works

Anonymous works are defined by EndNote as references where the Author field is blank (not "Anonymous"). The settings in the *Anonymous Works* panel apply to all sections of a style (*Citations*, *Bibliography*, and *Footnotes*).

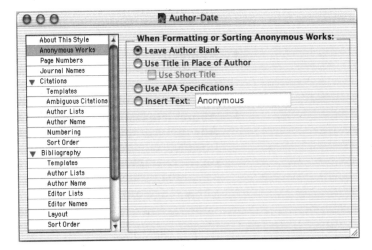

- ◆ **Leave Author Blank**: The author section of the formatted reference is left empty. If the references are to be sorted by author names, the anonymous works would be sorted at the top of the list because they have no author.

- ◆ **Use Title in Place of Author**: Where the author would have appeared, the title is used instead. If the references are sorted by author, the anonymous references will be sorted as though the title were the author. If you would prefer that EndNote use the contents of the "Short Title" field in place of the full title (where available), click the "Use Short Title" checkbox. If EndNote encounters a reference that does not have anything entered into the Short Title field, it uses the contents of the regular Title field instead.

- ◆ **Use APA Specifications**: The American Psychological Association format (used by many journals) requires a special variation of the "Use Title in Place of Author" option.

- ◆ **Insert Text**: The text that you enter here appears in the author's place in the formatted reference, and it is used for sorting purposes if the references are to be sorted by author names. Commonly this text would be something like the word "Anonymous" or "Anon."

Page Numbers

The *Page Numbers* panel allows you to specify how the page numbers should be formatted for your references:

♦ **Don't change page numbers**
The contents of the Pages field are used directly in the formatted reference. No changes are made.

♦ **Show only first page**
Only the first characters in the Pages field up to, but not including, the first dash or comma are included in the bibliography. **Example:** "123-125" in the Pages field becomes "123" in the formatted reference.

♦ **Abbreviate last page**
Any digits of the last page number that are the same as the first page number are eliminated. **Example:** "123-125"in the Pages field becomes "123-5" in the formatted reference.

♦ **Abbreviate last page, keeping two digits**
Any digits of the last page number that are the same as the first page number are eliminated, down to a minimum of two digits. **Example:** "123-125"in the Pages field becomes "123-25" in the formatted reference.

♦ **Show range of pages**
Leading digits are added to the last page number, if necessary, so the full page range is used. **Example:** "123-5" in the Pages field becomes "123-125"in the formatted reference.

♦ **Show only first page for Journals and full range for others**
Journal articles are formatted differently from other types of references.

NOTE: The section "Special Formatting Characters" on page 381 describes how to instruct EndNote to add text such as "p." vs. "pp.", or "page" vs. "pages" to the formatted references using the caret (^).

Journal Names

Different journals have different standards for abbreviating journal names. For example, some styles may require "Proceedings of the National Academy of Science" to be abbreviated as "Proc. Nat. Acad. Sci.," "P.N.A.S." or "PNAS." EndNote's Journals term list provides a way for you store up to four variations of journal names (the full name and three forms of abbreviations) to be used in your bibliographies.

The Journals term list that is created for every library is automatically linked to the Journal and Alternate Journal fields, and therefore it is ready to be used with the Journal Names options. You simply need to be sure that the necessary information is in the Journals term list, and that your style is set up to use the correct form of the journal name.

If your Journals term list includes the name of the journal as it is entered in your EndNote references, and the form of the journal name that you would like to appear in your bibliographies, you may simply set your preference in a style to have EndNote substitute a form of the name in the Journals term list for what was entered into your references.

EndNote provides a journal abbreviation list for each of three different disciplines (medicine, chemistry, and humanities). If you are interested in using one of these lists, you may import it into your Journals term list (see page 214) and set up a bibliographic style to use one of the abbreviations for the formatted bibliography. If EndNote does not provide a journal term list that applies to your area of research, you may also enter the journal abbreviations yourself. See "Working with the Journals Term List" on page 222.

To modify a style to use the abbreviations in a Journals term list:

1. From the *Edit* menu, select *Output Styles* and choose *Open Style Manager*.

2. Select the style that you would like to modify and click *Edit*.

3. Select the *Journal Names* panel from the list at the left of the Style window to see the available options:

♦ **Full Journal Name**
When creating a bibliography, EndNote replaces the Journal name in the reference with the form of that name in the first column of the Journals term list. This first column is normally used for full names.

♦ **Abbreviation 1**
Abbreviation 2
Abbreviation 3
In the bibliography, the journal name for each reference is replaced with the form of that name in the second, third, or fourth column of the Journals term list, respectively.

♦ **Don't Replace**
In the bibliography, EndNote uses the journal name exactly as it appears in the reference in the EndNote library. No changes are made.

- ♦ **Abbreviate in Journal Articles Only**
  The substitutions made with the Journal Names option can apply to all Secondary Title fields, or to the Secondary Title field for only the Journal Article reference type. If you uncheck this option to apply this feature to all reference types, EndNote also abbreviates fields such as Conference Name, and the names of magazines and newspapers.

- ♦ **Remove Periods**
  Choose this option to have EndNote eliminate the periods from all journal names in the bibliography that it is creating, regardless of the abbreviation being used. This option does not require that the journal names be in the Journals term list. For example, if the journal names are entered into your references using periods, and you do not have a Journals term list that includes the names without periods, you can still just check this option and the periods will be stripped out of the journal names when EndNote formats a bibliography.

If a journal name is not found in the specified column of the Journals term list, the style uses the journal name as it appears in the Reference window. No replacement is made for that journal.

If nothing is entered in the Journals term list or if there is no special Journals term list, the *Journal Names* option always defaults to *Don't Replace*, and EndNote uses the journal name exactly as it appears in the original reference.

NOTE: None of these changes actually takes place in the EndNote library. These options only determine what information goes into the bibliography that is generated using the *Copy Formatted, Print, Export,* and *Format Bibliography* commands.

Ambiguous Citations

With in-text citations like (Smith, 1995) or (Smith 246-9), references can have identical in-text citations if they are by the same author or the authors have the same last name. This leads to ambiguity in the citations that would make it impossible for the reader of your paper to know which reference to Smith you are referring. EndNote provides various ways to avoid this sort of ambiguity in your citations.

Any combination of the following options may be used. Click in the checkbox next to all options that apply. Note that these settings assume the author is used in the in-text citation. They are not relevant for styles that use bibliography numbers for the in-text citations as it is not possible to have ambiguous citations when they are uniquely numbered.

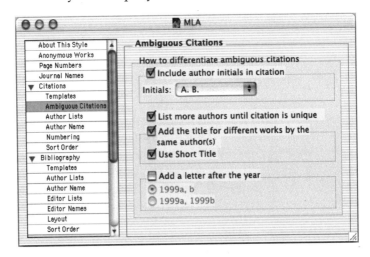

♦ **Include author initials in citation**
Check this option to have EndNote include initials with author names to distinguish between citations by different authors that happen to have the same surname. Choose how the initials should appear from the *Initials* option in the section. For example, the MLA style uses just author names and page numbers in citations. Initials are added to clarify which Smith wrote the cited reference:

```
(S. Smith 241-5)    and    (L. Smith 12-20)
```

♦ **List more authors until citation is unique**
Some styles request that only a fixed number of authors be listed in the in-text citation, and then "et al." or "and others" is inserted to indicate that the author list was abbreviated. Choose this option if you would like EndNote to list additional authors to make the citation unique. For example, if the in-text citations were set to list only 3 authors, and you have two references in which the first three authors are the same, EndNote would add a fourth author to the citations, and continue in that manner until the list of authors was different between the two citations.

♦ **Add the title for different works by the same author(s)**
If you have two works by the same author, it won't help to add initials or list more authors to differentiate the two. In this case, some styles request that the title of the reference (or a shortened form of the title) be added to the in-text citation. If you choose this option and check the "Use Short Title" option, EndNote includes the contents of the Short Title field when available. Otherwise, it uses the full title. The format of

the title is taken directly from the bibliography. This is an example in the MLA style, which normally includes only the author and page number in a citation:

(Smith, *History of Our Times* 35)

(Smith, *Looking Forward* 77)

♦ **Add a letter after the year**
For citations in an (Author, Year) format, EndNote can add a letter to the year to make citations from the same author published in the same year distinguishable from each other. The letter appended to the year will appear in both the in-text citations and references in the bibliography.

(Smith 1995a)
(Smith 1995b)

Numbering Citations

The settings in the citation *Numbering* panel apply only when "Bibliography Number" is used in the citation template (see page 372). This creates uniquely numbered citations in the text of the paper; the numbers correspond to entries in the bibliography. For papers formatted with a numbered style, these options are relevant to multiple citations grouped within one set of citation delimiters. When unformatted, a multiple citation looks like this:

{Keys, 1998 #93; Jen, 1996 #88; Yagi, 1998 #199}

♦ **Use number ranges for consecutive citations**
When this option is checked, consecutive bibliography numbers appearing in a multiple citation are joined by a single dash, for example:

…as shown by the Berkeley studies conducted in 1987[3-6] and 1989[1,7].

♦ **Grouped References**
The "Grouped Reference" option allows you to cite with one number any references that always appear together in the paper as multiple citations. The citations are not given their own numbers, but rather one number is used both in the text and the bibliography to identify the whole group of citations. With this setting, you also have the option to specify how the grouped references in the bibliography should be separated.

This option shows a semicolon and a space as a separator:

1. McCormick, MP, *Geophysical Research Letters* (1999) **15**, 907; Pemberton, SG, Jones, B, *Journal of Paleontology* (1999) **62**, 495; Postma, G, *Sedimentary Geology* (1999) **58**, 47.

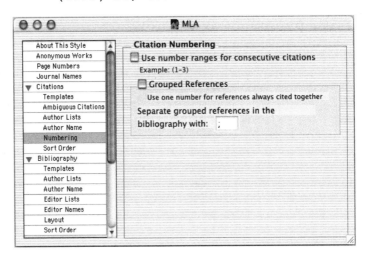

Citation Author Lists

If the style you are using lists the author names in the Citation template of the Style window, you can use the *Author List* options (as well as the *Author Names* panel) to control how the authors appear in your in-text citations. If your citations do not include the author names, ignore the *Author List* panel.

Separators Between Author Names

In the "Separators" box, enter any punctuation and spaces that separate the individual author names in a citation. In references with multiple authors, it is standard to separate the names with a comma and a space. Use the "Separator between authors" box to enter a comma and a space, or any other required punctuation. In the "Separator before last author" box, enter the separator that appears before the *last* author in a reference. Sometimes this is something other than a comma and a space, such as ", and " or an ampersand (&) followed by a space.

Normally only the first row in the Separators box is used (with the range of authors set at "1 to 100") so that the separators in that row apply to all of the authors cited in a reference. However, there are styles in which two authors are listed as "Smith and Jones" (without a comma), and more than two are listed as

"Smith, Jones, and Johnson" (with a comma before the word "and"). In this case, make " and " the "Separator before last author" when there are only two authors; and enter ", and " when there are 3 or more authors (as shown in the example below).

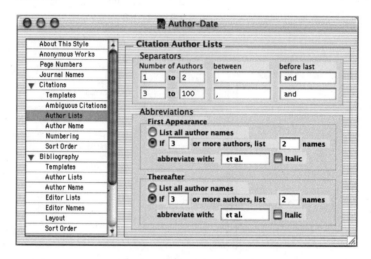

NOTE: Include spaces after commas as well as before and after the word "and". The spaces are not visible in this dialog.

Abbreviating Author Names (et al.)

Some journals require that you abbreviate the list of authors, using "et al." or an equivalent, after a certain number of authors. The "Abbreviation" section of the Author List panel allows you to specify the number of authors needed to trigger this abbreviation, how many authors to include in the formatted reference, and what the abbreviation should be.

◆ **List all author names**
Choose this option if you do not want to abbreviate the author lists.

◆ **If ___ or more authors, list ___ names...**
Select this option and fill in the blanks with the appropriate numbers if you would like the list of authors abbreviated.

The example shown above abbreviates author lists of three or more names to show only the first two authors followed by " et al." You can italicize the abbreviation by selecting the "Italics" checkbox in the dialog.

First Appearance vs. Thereafter

In some bibliographic styles, if a reference is cited more than once in your paper the first appearance of it in an in-text citation is formatted differently from subsequent citations. For example, the first citation might list all authors, while subsequent citations list only the first author followed by "et al."

Use the "First Appearance" author list settings to specify the way the authors appear the first time the reference is cited. Use the "Thereafter" options to format authors in all other appearances of the citation.

Citation Author Names

Name Format

The Name Format section allows you to specify how the author names should look—whether the first or last name should come first, and whether there should be a comma after the last name.

- ◆ **First Author/Other Authors:** Using the list for "First Author" and "Other Authors", you can have the first author appear differently from the other authors in a reference. From these lists, choose the example that shows the name in the order that you would like it to be in the citation. If the in-text citations use only the last name, this setting is not important.

- ◆ **Capitalization:** Specify how you would like the author names to appear.
  - As Is (as entered in the reference)
  - Normal (first letter of each name is capitalized)
  - ALL UPPERCASE
  - SMALL CAPS (not supported by Cite While You Write)

- ◆ **Initials:** Choose from the available options in the list to specify how the initials should look in the citations. Choose *Last Only* if you only need the last name of the authors to appear in the citations.

  "Use initials only for primary authors with the same name"
  This option allows for initials to be used only when there are primary authors with the same last name included in the bibliography. Regardless of whether or not the resulting citations are ambiguous (that is, they could be from different years), EndNote will add the initials to those citations to clarify that they are from different authors who happen to have the same surname.

Consecutive Citations by the Same Author

If a multiple citation includes works by the same author, some styles request that you not repeat the author name. Check the setting to "Show author name only once" and EndNote will omit the author name from the citation after it first appears. In order for this setting to be used, the citations must all be grouped together in a multiple citation, and the citations by the same author must appear one right after the other.

For example, a reference such as this:

(Smith, 1993; Smith, 1999; Wyatt, 2000)

would be changed to look like this:

(Smith, 1993, 1999; Wyatt, 2000)

You have the additional option in this case to choose the separator to use between these citations. Notice in the example above, the style normally uses a semicolon to separate multiple citations. But when there are a series of citations by the same author, the repeated author names are dropped and the years are separated by commas. In this case, a comma and a space should be entered as the punctuation with which to separate the consecutive citations by the same author.

If you have entered citations with suffixes and you would like those citations excluded from this formatting, check "Don't change citations with suffixes." For example, if two references by the same author included page numbers:

(Smith, 1993 p 24; Smith, 1999 p 5; Wyatt, 2000)

some styles request that you do leave the author name in the second citation for clarity.

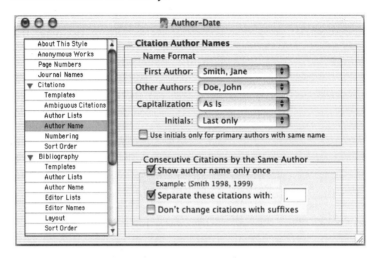

Author List (Bibliography and Footnotes)

The *Author List* panels under the *Bibliography* and *Footnotes* headings let you specify exactly how the authors are to appear in the formatted bibliographic references or in your footnotes. You can format author names different in the footnotes and bibliography, so be sure that you check the *Author List* settings under both the *Bibliography* and the *Footnotes* headings to adjust settings. The settings in these panels apply to all reference types formatted with the current style.

These panels are identical to those provided for the *Author List* panel under the *Citations* heading, except that there is no option for "First Appearance" and "Thereafter". See "Citation Author Lists" on page 391 for details about the settings in these panels.

Author Names (Bibliography and Footnotes)

Name Format

There is an *Author Names* panel for bibliographies and footnotes, as well as for citations. Some styles request that author names are formatted differently in all three cases. Be sure that you choose the *Author Names* panel from under the appropriate heading. The author names format for citations is described on page 393. This section describes the options that are available for both the footnote and bibliography *Author Names* panel.

These settings are for choosing how author names should look—for example, whether the first or last name should come first, whether there should be a comma after the last name, and how the names should be capitalized.

♦ **First Author/Other Authors:** Using the list for "First Author" and "Other Authors", you can have the first author appear differently from the other authors in a reference. From these lists, choose the example that shows the name in the order that you want in the reference.

♦ **Capitalization:** Specify how author names should appear.
  • As Is   (as entered in the reference)
  • Normal   (first letter of each name is capitalized)
  • ALL UPPERCASE
  • SMALL CAPS (not supported by Cite While You Write)

♦ **Initials:** Choose from the available options in the list to specify how the initials should appear in the formatted references. Click the "Initials" list to choose how the authors' first and middle names should be formatted. If you have not entered the full first names and you choose the *Full Names* option, EndNote uses the names as you have entered them into the reference. Choose *Last Only* to show just the last name, with no first or middle initials.

NOTE: Initials entered into an EndNote reference must be separated by a period or a space (such as M.J. Stein or M J Stein). Two letters together (such as MJ Stein) will *not* be interpreted as two initials, but instead as a two-letter first name.

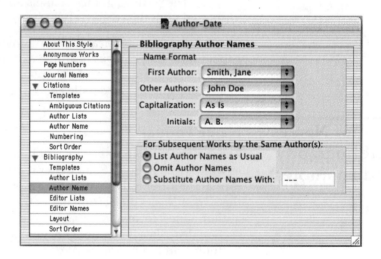

For Subsequent Works by the Same Author

When listing multiple works by the same author or authors, some styles request that the author names are omitted from all but the first reference. This can help the readability of a bibliography that is sorted by author name because you can more easily scan the left margin of the bibliography to identify the names of the authors. The options you have for listing works by the same author include:

♦ **List Author Names As Usual:** All authors are listed according to the settings in the *Author List* panel.

♦ **Omit Author Names:** When references by the same author (or set of authors) are listed in succession, the author names are omitted from all references except the first by that author (or group of authors).

♦ **Substitute Author Names With:** Enter text here that should be used in place of the author names. Often this is a series of dashes. For example:

```
Billoski, T. V. (1992). Introduction to Paleontology. New
     York, Institutional Press.

--- (1993). "Debate II." Science 77: 5-6.

--- (1997). "Debate over nemesis theory grows." Science
     77: 5-6.
```

Editor List and Editor Names

To specify how the editors' names are to be formatted, select *Editor List* or *Editor Names* from under the *Bibliography* or *Footnote* heading. In those panels you will find some of the same settings that have been described for formatting author names.

The *Editor List* settings apply to the generic Secondary Author, Tertiary Author, and Subsidiary Author fields. These fields includes "Editor" in the Book Section and Conference Proceedings reference types, and "Series Editor" in the Book and Edited Book reference types.

The instructions for the Editor List panel are identical to those described for the *Author List* panel (see page 395). Similarly, the Name Format options in the *Editor Names* panel are the same as those for *Author Names* described on page 395.

"Editors" Are Considered Primary Authors for Edited Book Reference Types

The *Author List* and *Author Names* settings apply to the primary author field of each reference type. Therefore, *Author List* and *Author Names* apply to the editor's name in an Edited Book. And the *Editor List* and *Editor Names* settings apply to the Series Editor's name in an Edited Book reference type.

Bibliography Layout

Under the *Bibliography* heading there is a *Layout* option that provides options for inserting text before and after each reference in a bibliography, as well as applying hanging indents to your references.

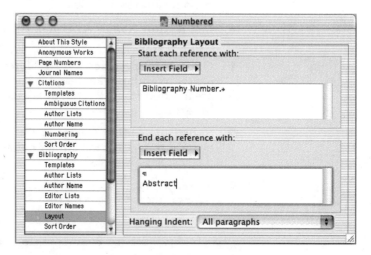

Adding Text Before Each Reference

In the "Start each reference with:" section, you can specify what information, if any, should appear before each reference in your bibliography. (For information on how to add a prefix before a *citation*, see "Citation Prefix Marker" on page 478.)

A common reference prefix is the bibliography number, which is used by all numbered styles to number the references in a bibliography.

To add a bibliography number before each reference:

1. Open the Style Manager by choosing *Output Styles* from the *Edit* menu and selecting *Open Style Manager*.

2. Select the style that you would like to edit, and click *Edit*.

3. After the Style window opens, choose *Layout* from under the *Bibliography* heading.

4. Click in the text box below the "Start each reference with" section, and select *Bibliography Number* from the *Insert Field* list.

5. Type the necessary punctuation after the bibliography number (such as a period and a space) or insert a tab from the *Insert Field* list.

With a style configured in this way, EndNote creates a bibliography with numbered references, such as:

```
1. Argus, M.V. "New paleontological excavation
   techniques" Nature 19, 234-237 (1993).
```

NOTE: To create a hanging indent, where the second and subsequent lines of a reference are indented, see page 400.

Other Reference Prefix Fields

Other commonly used reference prefixes appear in the *Insert Field* list.

Some bibliographic styles use a *Label* in the citation and the bibliography to refer to each entry with a short mnemonic code, often the author's name and the last two digits of the year. When you enter references into your library, you can type the mnemonic code directly into the Label field. When EndNote builds a bibliography, it can put that code before each reference.

Choosing *Citation* as a reference prefix allows you to label the references in the bibliography with the in-text citation.

Reference Type will insert the reference type (such as Journal Article or Book) before each reference.

Record Number will insert the record number before each reference. The record number is the number that EndNote assigns to each reference in the library, and it is also used in the in-text citations. Add *Record Number* as a reference prefix in any style in order to print all the references in your library with their unique EndNote record numbers.

Adding Text After Each Reference

Use the "End each reference with" section of the *Layout* panel to specify what information, if any, should follow each reference in your bibliography. (For information on how to add text after an in-text citation in your document, see "Citation Suffixes" on page 256.)

This command can be used to add the content of the Label, Keywords, Abstract, or Notes field, or the Record Number. Any other text or punctuation can also be entered as a reference suffix and it will appear at the end of each reference in the formatted bibliography. Two common uses for the *Reference Suffix* command are shown below.

Example: Adding Notes to the Bibliography

If you have notes that you want to print together with your references, you should add the Notes field as a reference suffix in the style that you are using to print or format the references.

1. Open the Style Manager by choosing *Output Styles* from the *Edit* menu and selecting *Open Style Manager*.

2. Select the style that you would like to edit, and click *Edit*.

3. After the Style window opens, choose *Layout* from under the *Bibliography* heading.

4. Click in the text box below the "End each reference with" section, and select *Notes* from the *Insert Field* list. This will append the Notes field to every reference in the bibliography when you format a paper with the style.

If you want the notes to begin on a new line after the reference, insert a paragraph mark from the *Insert Field* list before "Notes." If you want the notes to be indented, like the start of a new paragraph, insert a Tab before the word "Notes."

Adding or Removing Blank Lines Between References

Another common use for the *Layout* options is to add a blank line between references. To do this, edit the style as described above, and insert a paragraph mark (using the *Insert Field* list) into the "End each reference with" section.

To tighten up the bibliography and get rid of the blank line after each reference, edit the style, click on the *Layout* panel, and select and delete the paragraph mark (¶) to get rid of the blank line.

Hanging Indents

Many numbered bibliographic styles require a hanging indent, as shown in this example:

1. Postma, G., Nemec, W. & Kleinspehn, K.L. *Sedimentary Geology* **58**, 47 (1988).

2. Nyamweru, C. *Journal of African Earth Sciences And The Middle East* **8**, 40-42 (1988).

EndNote provides a few hanging indent options. Normally, each reference is one paragraph, so some of these options wouldn't apply. But if you have a reference that includes more than one paragraph, EndNote gives you options for which paragraph within a reference the hanging indents should apply. Examples of multi-paragraph references include annotated bibliographies where the abstracts follow each reference, or a style such as those common in anthropology journals where the authors are on a line of their own

Hanging indent options include: *None, All Paragraphs, First Paragraph Only, Second Paragraph Only,* and *All Paragraphs but the First.* The following is an example of when you would use *Second Paragraph Only.* The style requires that authors begin on the left margin, and then the year (and the rest of the reference) starts on a new line and is indented. The style applies a hanging indent to the second paragraph only, and inserts a tab before and after the year. In the word processing document, the spacing for the hanging indent should be aligned with the second tab stop.

```
Curtis, S.A., and N.F. Ness
    2000    Remanent magnetism at Mars. Geophysical
            Research Letters 15(8):737.
```

The spacing used for tabs and indents is determined by the ruler settings in your word processor.

NOTE: If you are creating a numbered bibliography, as shown in the previous example, insert a tab after the bibliography number to have the references line up correctly.

Tabs

Tabs may be inserted from the *Insert Field* list. A tab entered into a style will appear as a tab in the formatted bibliography. The tab appears as an arrow on the screen. The width of the tab as it appears in the bibliography is determined by the tab settings in your word processor.

Tabs are often entered after the bibliography number as part of the *Layout* settings. This helps to align the start of each reference after the number, which is especially important if the bibliography entries use a hanging indent.

Sort Order: Bibliographies and Multiple Citations

Each style has instructions for sorting references in the bibliography, and how to sort formatted multiple citations in the text of your paper. Select *Sort Order* from under either the *Citations* or *Bibliographies* headings.

Multiple Citation Sort

The *Sort* panel under the *Citation* heading allows you to set the order that the style uses to sort multiple in-text citations. For example, an unformatted multiple citation looks like this:

`{Lee, 1990 #5; Jacob, 1994 #22; Zoler, 1983 #19}`

Formatted with the Author-Date style, the citations are sorted chronologically and the formatted citation looks like this:

`(Zoler 1983; Lee 1990; Jacob 1994)`

Options for sorting multiple citations include:

♦ **Same as Bibliography**
  Sorts multiple citations in the same order as the Bibliography Sort Order (see page 403).

♦ **Author + Title**
  Sorts multiple citations first by authors and then by title.

♦ **Author + Year + Title**
  Sorts multiple citations first by authors, then by year, and then by title.

♦ **Year + Author**
  Sorts multiple citations chronologically. Then citations from the same year are sorted based on author names.

♦ **Don't Sort**
  Multiple citations remain in the same order as they appear in the unformatted temporary citations.

♦ **Other**
  A custom sort order is applied to multiple citations. See "When sorting by Author field, EndNote sorts based on all information in the Author field, including all author names (not just the first author) and initials. To see about omitting parts of author names or the initial words of a title when sorting, read "Sorting" on page 480." on page 404.

Bibliography Sort Order

The "Bibliography Sort Order" section determines how the bibliography should be sorted. Common options are listed, and you may also configure a custom sort order.

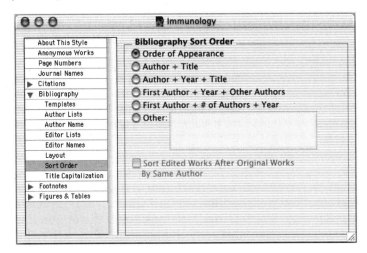

♦ **Order of Appearance**
References are listed in the order in which they are cited in the paper.

♦ **Author + Title**
References are sorted by the Author field. References with identical authors are sorted by title.

♦ **Author + Year + Title**
References are sorted by the Author field, then references with identical authors are sorted by year. References with identical authors and years are then sorted by title.

♦ **First Author + Year + Other Authors**
References are sorted by just the first author, then references with identical primary authors are sorted by year. References with identical primary authors and years are then sorted based on the other authors in the reference.

♦ **First Author + # of Authors + Year**
References are sorted by just the first author, then by the number of authors in the reference. For references with the same primary author and the same number of authors, they are then sorted chronologically based on the Year field.

♦ **Other**
A custom sort order is applied to the references in the bibliography. See "When sorting by Author field, EndNote sorts based on all information in the Author field, including all author names (not just the first author) and initials. To see

about omitting parts of author names or the initial words of a title when sorting, read "Sorting" on page 480." below.

♦ **Sort Edited Works After Original Works By Same Author:** Some styles request that if the same person is the author for a book and the editor for an edited book, the original works by that author are sorted first, and then the edited works follow. This is an exception to the sorting rules that can be applied to the other sort options provided.

NOTE: When sorting by Author field, EndNote sorts based on all information in the Author field, including all author names (not just the first author) and initials. To see about omitting parts of author names or the initial words of a title when sorting, read "Sorting" on page 480.

Custom Sorting

To sort references or multiple citations differently from the options in the "Citation Sort Order" or "Bibliography Sort Order" sections, select the option for *Other* and choose from the lists any combination of up to five fields in ascending or descending order.

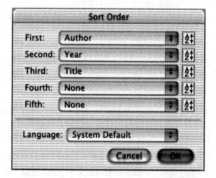

This window is identical to the one that appears when you choose *Sort References* from the *References* menu. You do not need to use all five options. The button at the right of each box controls the direction of the sort, either ascending or descending order. Clicking these boxes toggles the sort order between ascending and descending order.

Once you have set up your sorting strategy, click *OK* to return to the main Sort Order panel for the style. The *Other* button will now display your custom sorting instructions.

Title Capitalization

Both the *Footnotes* and *Bibliography* sections have a *Title Capitalization* panel. This lets you enter one style of capitalization for the titles in your bibliographic references, and another format for when the references appear in footnotes.

Options for title capitalization include:

- **Leave Titles As Entered:**
  No changes are made.

- **Headline Style Capitalization:**
  The first letter of every significant word is capitalized. Articles and prepositions are not capitalized.

- **Sentence Style Capitalization:**
  Only the first letter of every title is capitalized.

NOTE: See "Change Case" on page 481 to enter words or acronyms that should not be adjusted when EndNote changes the capitalization of titles.

Repeated Citations (in Footnotes)

Most of the complex formatting in footnotes is relevant only to styles in the humanities. There is a wide variety of formats required for citing references in the footnotes of a paper. These options are provided in the *Repeated Citations* panel under the *Footnote* heading.

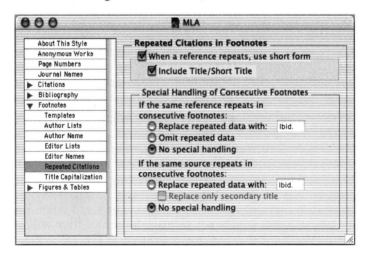

When a reference repeats, use short form

One common setting for citing references in footnotes is to list a shortened form of a reference after the first time it is cited in a footnote. So, for example, the first time the reference is cited, the full references appear (as specified in the *Templates* panel). The second time that reference appears in a footnote, only a shortened form of it (the Author name, and cited pages if there are any) is listed. Check the option to "Include Title/Short Title" if you would like both the author and the title to appear in the shortened form of the footnote references. The contents of the Short Title field will be used, if available; otherwise, the regular title will be added to the citation. The format of the title (such as italic, underlined, or in quotations) is determined by the format of the title in the footnote *Templates* panel.

Here is an example of the first occurrence of a citation in a footnote, a consecutive citation to the same reference, and a third instance of that source being cited, but the volume and cited pages are different:

```
1 George Harding, California Wildlife, 2 vols.
(New York: Nature Press, 1989), 1: 207.
```

[This is the first, and therefore complete, reference to the work].

```
2 Ibid.
```

[With no intervening reference, a second reference to the same volume and page of Harding's work requires only Ibid.]

```
3 Ibid., Vol. 2, p.51.
```

[Here another volume and page number of the reference are used.]

Special Handling of Consecutive Footnotes

Some styles take the shortening of references in footnotes even farther when the repeated references appear in consecutive footnotes (or in the same footnote). EndNote provides additional options for the special handling of these cases:

♦ **If the same reference repeats in consecutive footnotes:**
   When the same reference repeats in consecutive footnotes, you have the option of replacing the repeated data with text of your choice. This is normally "Ibid" (or a variation of the term). The next option allows you to simply omit the repeated data, and replace it with nothing. Or you may apply no special handling and when references repeat in consecutive footnotes they will be handled just like other repeated references in footnotes.

♦ **If the same source repeats in consecutive footnotes:**
   This setting does not apply to the identical *reference* that repeats in consecutive footnotes, but rather if any of the source data repeats in two consecutive footnotes. For

example, if two different references happen to be from the same journal, these settings would apply to the journal name, volume, and issue (or whatever portion of that source information is identical). You may choose "No special handling" for these cases, so that these references are not abbreviated. Or you may choose to replace the repeated data with "Ibid" (or the text of your choice). If you choose this option, you may limit the replacement to only the Secondary Title field (this includes the journal, magazine, or newspaper name, or the title of a book for a book section).

NOTE: We realize that many of these detailed settings for the style can be confusing. We have done our best to configure the styles for you so that you will not need to edit them and work through these details on your own. However, if you find that you need to modify these parts of your styles, please consult your style guide for more detailed descriptions and examples of handling repeated citations in footnotes.

Figure and Table Placement and Captions

The Figures and Tables settings apply to images inserted into a Word document from EndNote. You can place images where they are cited in a document or at the end of the document, and you have control over the placement and punctuation of labels and captions.

While style guidelines tend to be very specific in regard to formatted citations and bibliographies, they are often vague about figure and table placement. They may require different placement for different document types (theses, term papers, journal articles, etc.), or they may not offer instructions at all.

EndNote's default figure and table placement settings are the same for all output styles. Please check your own style documentation (or check with your editor or teacher) for specific guidelines about image placement for the type of document you are creating.

NOTE: Additional Figures and Tables settings are available under Cite While You Write Preferences, and can override output style settings. See "Figures and Tables in Word" on page 496.

Figures and Tables

Under the Figures and Tables heading in the left column of the output style editor, select either Figures or Tables. Tables are images inserted from the Image field in the Chart or Table reference type. Figures are images inserted from the Image field of any other EndNote reference type. The same options are available under each, which allows you to place figures differently than tables.

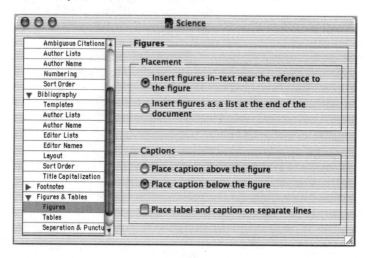

Placement

Under Placement, select a button to either place the images within the text of the document, near the reference to the figure, or to place images in a list at the end of the document.

If your images are placed in-text, you can use Cite While You Write preferences to override this automatic placement when your document is reformatted. This is helpful if you have moved your images around in the document and want to retain their placement. See "Figures and Tables in Word" on page 496.

Caption

Next, under Caption, select a button to place the label and caption either above or below the image. You can also select the check box to place the label and caption on separate lines.

NOTE: The label inserted by EndNote is "Figure #" for images found in the Figure and Equation reference types as well as for most other reference types. The label is "Table #" for images found in the Chart or Table reference type. The Caption is the text typed into the Caption field of a reference.

Separation and Punctuation

Under Image Separation, you can enter separators for images inserted within the text of a document and for images that are listed at the end of a document.

NOTE: The settings on this panel affect both figures and tables.

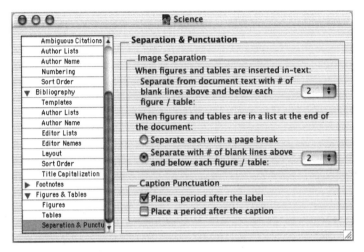

Image Separation

When images are inserted in-text, you can specify the number of lines to insert before and after the image to separate it from text. This setting affects both figures and tables that are placed in-text. If your images are placed in a list at the end of the document, this setting is ignored.

When images are placed in a list at the end of the document, you can separate each figure or table with a page break or a specified number of blank lines before and after each image. If your images are placed in-text, this setting is ignored.

Caption Punctuation

For each figure or table inserted into Word from an EndNote reference, EndNote generates a label and then inserts the caption from the Caption field of the EndNote reference. For example:

```
Table 1. Bird Evolution
```

You can select the check boxes to insert a period after the label and/or after the caption. This affects the labels and captions for both figures and tables.

EndNote will attempt to remove double punctuation in case you inadvertently include a period within the record as well as selecting one here.

Creating a New Style

It is often easier to modify an existing bibliographic style that closely resembles a style that you need than it is to create a new style from scratch. (See "Modifying Style Templates" on page 372.) If you do wish to create a new style, this section gives you a general overview of the process.

Creating a bibliographic style involves building templates for the in-text citations and the bibliographic references to mimic how you want them to appear in your paper. Then adjust the various options to be sure that authors, titles, pages, and other fields are being formatted according to your requirements. The following example guides you through the creation of a fictitious author-date type of style.

Example: Creating an Author Date Style

Part I: Creating the Templates

A new style need only contain a Citation template and a Generic Bibliography template for it to produce citations and bibliographies for any paper. The Citation template applies to all in-text citations, and the Generic bibliography template applies to all reference types that do not have templates of their own in the style. The Generic template should be considered a default template, and you should add additional templates for the standard reference types which you use. If you define a specific template for any reference types, they are formatted according to that template, and not the Generic format.

To create style templates:

1. To create a bibliographic style, go to the *Edit* menu to select *Output Style* and then *New Style*, and a new Untitled Style window appears.

2. Click the *Templates* panel under the *Citations* heading to specify the format of the in-text citations.

    Our style uses the author name and the year in the citation. They are surrounded by parentheses and separated by a comma.

3. With the cursor in the Citation Template, type an open parenthesis, click the *Insert Field* button and choose *Author* from the list of available fields, type a comma, choose *Year*

from the *Insert Field* list and then type the closing parenthesis.

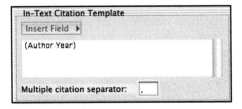

Next, define the Generic format which serves as the default template for reference types that do not have their own template. We know that books should be formatted like this, so we can set up the Generic template to accommodate that format:

```
Jones, VR, BK Marion, et al. (1976). The
Theory of Foraging. New York, Smith and
Barnes.
```

4. Click the *Templates* option under the *Bibliography* heading, then click in the "Generic" section of that *Templates* panel.

5. Choose *Author* from the *Insert Field* list to add the Author field to the style template. (You can also type "Author" but it is safer to select the field name from the list.) Type a period and a space. And continue inserting fields and punctuation until you have created a template that mimics the format of the reference:

```
Author. (Year). Title. Place Published,
Publisher.
```

6. In this style, the title must be italicized, so double-click the word Title to select it, then from the *Edit* menu, choose *Style* and *Italic*. 7.Save the new style by choosing *Save* from the *File* menu. In the dialog that appears, type "Practice Style" as the name of this style and click *Save*. This will save the style and add it as an option in the *Output Styles* submenu of the *Edit* menu.

Test the Style

Open your library and choose *Show Preview* from the bottom of the Library window. Select different references in your library to see how they format. You will probably see that the books look good, but journal articles do not display enough information. You will need to return to the style and create a template to format journal articles. To do so:

Create a New Template for Journals

In the *Templates* panel under the *Bibliography* heading, choose *Journal Article* from the *Reference Type* list. This will create a new section for a Journal Article template. Insert the fields and punctuation to create a template as shown below:

```
Author (Year). "Title." Journal Volume: Pages.
```

Once again, save the style by choosing *Save* from the *File* menu. Return to the Library window, and check the preview to see how journal article references are formatted.

Finishing the Style

Continue testing how other reference types format, and include additional reference type templates as necessary. See "Modifying Style Templates" on page 372 for specifics about creating and modifying style templates.

Look at how the author names are formatted, and change the necessary settings. You should also take a close look at pages, title capitalization, the sort order of the references, and various other options provided in the Style window. These are described in the "Additional Style Formatting Options" section starting on page 385.

Chapter 16

Filters

Chapter 16   Filters

Introduction to Filters

The *Import* command on EndNote's *File* menu provides a way to import text files of reference data into EndNote libraries. EndNote has a number of built in import options as well as a large collection of configurable import "filters." Filters are designed to import references downloaded from specific online or CD-ROM bibliographic databases.

This chapter describes how to edit and create these import filters. The process of importing references using the *Import* command is described in Chapter 7.

NOTE: You can download the latest filters available from ISI ResearchSoft. Visit our website at www.endnote.com.

What is a Filter?

The import **filters** provide a wide range of import options. A filter is selected during the import process to show EndNote exactly how to interpret the information in your **data file** (the records downloaded or saved from an online or CD-ROM database). A filter does this by mapping the information in each downloaded reference to the corresponding fields in EndNote.

Because each database offered by the various information providers has its own way to organize reference data, there needs to be a different filter for each database. Each filter provided with EndNote has been configured to import data files from a specific database offered by a single information provider. You can easily modify any of the supplied filters or create a new filter to import from other databases.

A Comment About Difficult Data Files

Although EndNote's filters are very powerful and flexible import tools, there are still some data files that cannot be conquered. Whereas some databases provide very clean tagged data, others are almost impossible to discern. Lack of consistency in the source data and the omission of reference type tags often make it difficult for a person to understand the information; the task of creating a perfect filter to handle these files is futile. When fine tuning our filters, we have done our best to always capture the necessary data—even if that means dropping it all into the Notes field. If you find filters that can be further improved, please let us know. It may also help to contact your information provider to let them know that the inconsistencies in the data entry for the database are keeping you from most efficiently making use of it.

The Filter Manager

EndNote provides hundreds of import filters for a variety of sources. To peruse the list of available filters in EndNote's Filters folder, choose *Import Filters* from the *Edit* menu, and select *Open Filter Manager*.

Shows the location of the selected Filters folder

Click column headings to sort the list

Click to search for files

Click to display details about the selected file

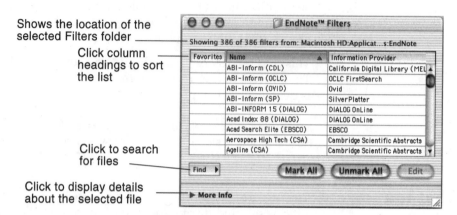

The **Filter Manager** lists the names of all of the import filters available in the Filters folder and gives you the option to edit them or select them as "favorites" for quick access when you use the *Import* command.

Use these features to locate the import filter you want to use:

♦ If you know the name of the filter that you want to use, you may start typing it and the first file that matches what you type will be selected.

♦ Click the *Find* button and choose an information provider's name (such as Ovid or SilverPlatter) to find only the import filters for a specific information provider.

♦ Click the *Find* button, and choose *by Name* to search for the file by the name of the database from which you are downloading references (such as Medline). You can enter a partial name or the full name. EndNote will display all matching results.

♦ Click the *Find* button and choose *All Filters* to return all of the import filters to the displayed list.

♦ Click a column heading to sort the import filters by name or by information provider. Clicking the same column heading a second time will change the sort order from ascending to descending. Click again to set it back to ascending order.

♦ Click the *More Info* button at the bottom of the dialog to display additional information about the selected filter.

Marking Your Favorite Import Filters

When you have found a filter that you will want to use in the future, click in the Favorites column next to it to mark it as a favorite. All filters that are marked as favorites appear in the *Import Options* list in the Import dialog. You can get to the Import dialog by choosing *Import* from the *File* menu. This gives you easy access to those files you use most often.

To mark all of the filters for a specific information provider, click *Find* and, from that list, choose the name of the information provider. Now, with just that subset of filters listed in the Filter Manager window, click *Mark All*. The *Unmark All* button may be used to unmark all of the filters that are showing in the list.

Editing Import Filters

If you would like to modify a filter, select it in the list and click *Edit*. The remainder of this chapter goes into detail about how to work with the filters. Read the section that applies to the aspects of the filter that you would like to modify.

Copying Filters

There are two ways to copy filters. Since each filter is a separate file on your hard drive, you can copy them as you would copy any file on your hard drive using the Macintosh Finder.

To make a copy of a filter from within EndNote:

1. From the *Edit* menu, choose *Import Filters* and select *Open Filter Manager*.

2. Select the filter you want to copy and click *Edit*.

3. Without making any changes to the file, choose *Save As* from the *File* menu.

4. Give this copy of the file a new name, and save it in your Filters folder if you would like access to it from within EndNote. If you save the filter outside of the Filter folder (such as on a CD to take a copy to a different computer, or to backup the file), it will not be available within EndNote.

After clicking *Save* to save the new copy of the file, the new filter remains open. The original filter will be left untouched.

Saving Filters

To save a new or modified filter, choose *Save* from the *File* menu. Or, to save changes to a filter that you have just opened or modified while leaving the original filter unchanged, choose *Save As* from the *File* menu (see "Copying Filters" on page 417).

When saving a new filter, or saving a filter under a different name, EndNote automatically saves the filter to your designated filter folder. (The Filter Manager within EndNote only provides access to the filters that are in the designated filter folder). Your Filter folder by default is the folder called Filters in your EndNote folder. You may also specify a different folder if necessary. For instructions see "Folder Locations" on page 486.

Deleting Filters

To delete a filter from within EndNote:

1. From the *Edit* menu, choose *Import Filters>Open Filter Manager*.

2. Select the filter to be deleted.

3. Choose *Clear* from the *Edit* menu, or CONTROL-click on the filter and choose *Delete* from the shortcut menu.

You can also delete an unwanted filter by switching back to the Macintosh Finder, and opening the Filter folder in the EndNote folder. Then, drag the filter from the Filter folder to the Trash.

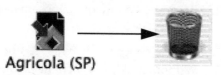

Agricola (SP)

The Basic Components of a Filter

The basic components of an import filter are described in this section. This information is useful if you want to customize or create a filter.

♦ **To create a new import filter:** From the *Edit* menu, choose *Import Filters* and select *New Filter*. If you are interested in creating a new filter, also read "Creating a New Filter" on page 449.

♦ **To edit a filter:** From the *Edit* menu, choose *Import Filters* and select *Open Filter Manager*. Select the file to edit and click *Edit*. The most recently used filter can also be easily edited by selecting *Import Filters* from the *Edit* menu, and choosing *Edit <filter>*.

The Filter Editor window

After choosing the option to edit an existing filter or create a new one, EndNote opens the Filter window.

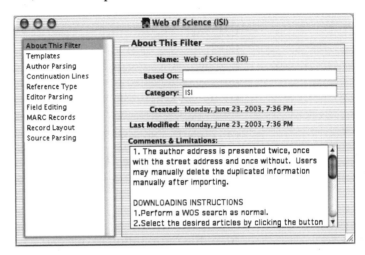

All of the different options for editing a filter are listed on the left side of the Filter window. Click on an item to view the associated settings. You may switch between panels as needed while editing the file. No changes are saved in any of the panels until you choose *Save* or *Save As* from the *File* menu.

If at any time you need to revert your changes back to the last saved copy of the filter, choose *Revert Filter* from the *File* menu.

To close a Filter window, click the button in the upper left corner of the window, or choose *Close Filter* from the *File* menu. If you have not saved your changes to the filter, EndNote prompts you and gives you the option to save or discard any changes that you have made.

"About this Filter" Panel

The Filter window opens to display the *About this Filter* panel (see the picture in the preceding section). This panel contains descriptive information about the file. None of the information used in this panel has any impact on establishing the connection.

Name: Displays the name of the file as it appears in the Filters folder in the EndNote folder. The name of the file cannot be changed here; you would need to close this window and switch back to the Macintosh Finder to rename the file.

Based On: Enter any information about what documentation was used to create the file. Commonly the server documentation is available on the Web, so you could enter a URL here as well to make it easy to later retrieve that information.

Category: The category is typically the information provider (such as Ovid or SilverPlatter), but you may enter anything that will help you categorize and organize your filters. The category information is also listed in the Filter Manager window in the column next to the name of the file. In that window, you may sort filters by category and also search for them by category.

Created: The date the file was installed or created.

Last Modified: The date the file was last modified.

Comments and Limitations: Enter any helpful information such as how to download the references in the format that works with this filter.

All of the information in this panel is visible in the Filter Manager if you click the *More Info* option at the bottom of the Filter Manager window. This is helpful because you do not need to edit a filter to view the comments or other descriptive information. You may simply scroll through the available filters in the Filter Manager window and view the information there.

Templates

The most important part of the filter is the *Templates* section. The templates define how the various lines of tagged data in your data file should be imported and filtered into the different EndNote fields (such as Author, Year, and Title). Different sets of templates are required for the different reference types that may be in your data file. All of the details about filter templates are covered in "Working with Filter Templates" on page 421.

Options

The rest of the options in the Filter window involve refining the data that is imported using the filter templates. For example, these options include instructions for how EndNote should interpret author names and initials, change the capitalization of fields, or even omit certain characters or terms that you do not want to be imported. Each of the various options is explained in its own section. See "The Filter Options" on page 429.

Working with Filter Templates

The *Templates* panel consists of individual Reference Type templates which correspond to the way the reference data is presented in the data file.

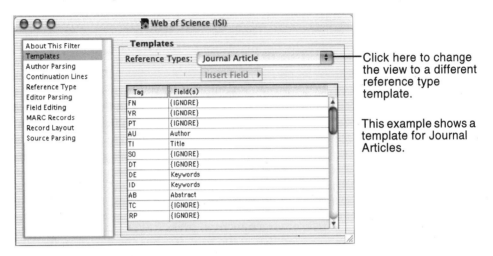

Click here to change the view to a different reference type template.

This example shows a template for Journal Articles.

Navigating in the Templates Panel

The *Templates* panel is divided into a Tag column and a Field(s) column. The tag and its corresponding field(s) are two separate cells in a row. To move from one cell to the next, simply press the TAB key or click the mouse in the desired cell. To move back to the previous cell, hold down the SHIFT key while pressing the TAB key.

To change the width of the Tag column in the Filter window, position the cursor over the vertical line dividing the Tag and Field(s) columns. The cursor changes to indicate that you are in the correct place. Click and drag to the right or left to resize the column widths.

Click the Reference Type list to change the view to a different reference type (such as from Journal Article to Book).

Templates for Different Reference Types

The *Templates* panel includes templates for all of the various reference types (Journal Article, Book, etc.).

♦ Click the Reference Type list to change the view to a different reference type (such as from Journal Article to Book).

The only reference types templates that need to be filled in are the ones that correspond to the reference types in your data file. For example, if the database from which you are downloading contains only journal articles, you would only need to fill in the templates for the Journal Article section in that particular filter.

Within each reference type template there is a list of tags and their corresponding EndNote field names. These templates should exactly match the way the information is organized in the data file. Any text or punctuation that you see that is not part of a field name (such as "vol." before the Volume) is included to make the template exactly match the data file.

Adding and Deleting Rows in the Filter Template

When adding and deleting rows, the order of the tags does not have to match the order of the tags in the data file. There is one case in which the order of the tags is important: if you are entering multiple variations of one tagged line, you should enter the repeated lines for that tag in order from the most complex to the simplest. This is because EndNote looks for matches starting from the top of the window working down the list of tags. It stops at the first template that matches the tagged data.

♦ To enter a new row, press RETURN or ENTER. The new row is added below the row that has the cursor in it.

Cutting, Copying and Pasting Rows

You may use the *Cut, Copy,* and *Paste* commands to move or duplicate a cell or a row of cells. To do so:

1. Select a row by dragging the mouse across both columns. (Dragging the mouse vertically across more than one row selects a range of rows.)

Tag	Field(s)
TI: Title	Title
AU: Author	Author
AF: Author Affiliation	Author Address
CF: Conference	Notes

2. To duplicate the selected row(s) elsewhere in a filter, choose *Copy* (⌘+C) from the *Edit* menu. If you want to delete the selected row and move it to another location, choose *Cut* (⌘+X).

3. Click where you would like the cut or copied row to appear, and choose *Paste* (⌘+V) from the *Edit* menu. The pasted row will be inserted above the row where the cursor is.

Copying and Pasting Between Reference Type Templates

By choosing *Select All* (⌘-A) from the *Edit* menu, you can select all the rows in a given Reference Type template. This is useful for copying an entire template to a new reference type or filter. After copying the entire set of templates for a reference type, you may choose a different reference type from the Reference Type list at the top of the window, click in the Tag cell for the new reference type, and choose *Paste*.

When you copy information from one reference type (such as Journal Article), and paste the rows into another reference type (such as Newspaper), the field names automatically change to reflect the names used by the new reference type. If there is not a corresponding field name in the new reference type, the original field name in the template is replaced with {IGNORE}, indicating that the data for that tag will be ignored.

Literal Text vs. EndNote Fields

When you look at a filter, you will notice that some of the templates contain information other than EndNote field names. For EndNote to identify which data should go into a particular EndNote field, you must include punctuation and any literal text or spaces that appear in your data file. Punctuation and literal text act as delimiters allowing EndNote to parse the data into multiple EndNote fields. None of these "delimiters" actually gets imported into an EndNote library, they merely serve as guides for EndNote to correctly import the data.

Here is an example of a data file's source line (SO:) where, in addition to punctuation, there is literal text such as "v", "n" and "p" preceding the data:

```
SO:   Youth Theatre Journal. v6 n4 p3-6
```

The "v", "n" and "p" are considered literal text because they are not EndNote field names; they represent the literal text from the data file that precedes the data that you want to import. In this particular source line, there are four different pieces of information: the journal name, volume, issue, and pages. To help EndNote determine when one field ends and the next one begins, you must insert the literal text, punctuation, and spaces found in the data file next to the appropriate field name.

As a result, the above SO: tag line should be represented in a filter like this:

```
SO:  Journal. vVolume nIssue pPages
```

In some databases, you may find lines of data that include a word that is also an EndNote field name. The following source line contains the word "pages" before the page numbers:

```
SO:    Town-planning-review. vol. 62, no. 4,
       pages 461-469.
```

If entered into the filter, EndNote would normally interpret the word "pages" as a field name. (This is true whether you type it in the filter or insert it using the *Insert Field* list.) To force EndNote to read a field's name as literal text, surround the name with accent grave characters, as in `pages`. The accent grave character is found in the upper left corner, under the tilde (~) key of the keyboard. To match the SO: line shown above, the source line in the filter should appear as:

```
SO:  Journal. vol. Volume, no. Issue, `pages` Pages.
```

The {IGNORE} Field

There may be pieces of information in a line of data that you do *not* want imported into your EndNote library. To force EndNote to ignore pieces of information, use the *Insert Field* list to insert "{IGNORE}" in the appropriate place. For example, suppose you want EndNote to ignore bracketed text that sometimes follows the title of an article:

```
TI:    Research funds are dwindling. [letter]
```

You should add a new TI tag and template to your filter (above the existing "TI: Title" line) that looks like this:

```
TI:  Title. [{IGNORE}]
```

The Source Line

The source line is typically the most complex line of data in a record because it contains all of the information about the source of publication. For a journal article, the source line may contain the journal name, the volume number, the issue number, page numbers, and the year of publication. For a book, the source line may contain the publisher, the city, and the number of pages.

The source line in your filter must match exactly the source line in the data file in order for EndNote to distinguish one piece of information from another. You will often find more than one variation of a source line for a given reference type in a single data file, in which case you will need to create a separate source line for each variant, starting with the most complex source. The three source lines displayed below come from a single database:

```
SO: Semin-Oncol. 76(3):465-71 1998

SO: Semin-Oncol. 127:5-24 1999

SO: Eur-J-Cancer. 118/6 (654-657) 1998
```

In the first SO: tag line, parentheses enclose the issue number "(3)". In the second SO: tag line, there is no issue, so a colon separates the volume number and the page numbers "127:5-24". In the third SO: tag line, a slash separates the volume number and the issue number "118/6", and parentheses enclose the page numbers "(654-657)".

Each variant in the data file's source lines must be defined in your filter. Since EndNote tries to match the source line in the data file with the first defined source line in your filter, you should place the most detailed source line first, followed by progressively less detailed source lines.

The filter for the above source lines should look like this:

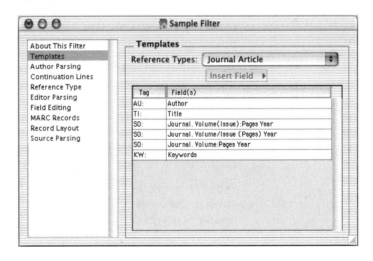

NOTE: If the filter fails to match a variation of the source line for a journal article, it is possible to have EndNote interpret the data on its own. See "Source Parsing" on page 441.

The Reference Type Tag

A reference type tag identifies the kind of work or publication being referenced in a particular record in your data file. In the Filter window, a reference type tag is only defined by the characteristic of having literal text, and no fields, entered into the field column. This literal text is not imported into EndNote, but it is used only to identify a record's reference type.

Although a reference type tag can be any tag at all, two common reference type tags are "DT" and "PT" (which stand for Document Type and Publication Type).

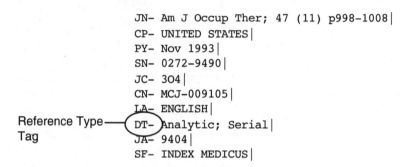

```
              JN- Am J Occup Ther; 47 (11) p998-1008|
              CP- UNITED STATES|
              PY- Nov 1993|
              SN- 0272-9490|
              JC- 304|
              CN- MCJ-009105|
              LA- ENGLISH|
Reference Type    DT- Analytic; Serial|
Tag               JA- 9404|
              SF- INDEX MEDICUS|
```

To ensure that EndNote imports the data into the correct reference type, you must type the Reference Type tag in the Tag column, and the reference type name (or other identifying text) exactly as it appears in the data file in the Field(s) column. (The matching is case-sensitive.) The Reference Type tag can be placed anywhere in the appropriate Reference Type template.

When EndNote imports a record, it first scans the data file, looking for a reference type tag in your filter. Then it looks for a match in the record it's importing. The first reference type tag match encountered determines which of the Reference Type templates EndNote will use to parse the record. This match also determines which reference type EndNote assigns the record in the EndNote library.

When entering the Reference Type tag in your filter, the text you enter in the Field cell must be interpreted by EndNote as literal text. A problem can arise when you have text that contains an EndNote field name. For example, the following Reference Type tag contains the field name "Journal":

```
DT- Journal Article
```

Because the field name "Journal" appears in the template, EndNote will not interpret this DT- tag line as the Reference Type tag. Instead, the filter would import the word "Journal" (from the data file's DT: line) into the Journal field.

To force EndNote to interpret the word Journal (or any other field name) as literal text, put an accent grave character at the start and end of the word. (The accent grave character is found in the upper left corner of the keyboard, under the tilde (~) key.) The above Reference Type tag should appear in a filter as:

```
DT-  `Journal` Article
```

If the database you use does not specify a Reference Type tag, all reference types in your data file will import as the default reference type (see page 435).

Fields with Special Characteristics

Certain EndNote fields contain special restrictions on what sort of data can be imported. These settings cannot be modified and apply to all import filters.

Author Fields
The words "And Others" get converted to "et al" and the word "and" is omitted. Years as well as parenthetical or bracketed text are removed by default. See also "Author Parsing" on page 429.

Year
Only 4-digit numbers (1### or 200#) are imported.

Title
The following punctuation is removed from the end of a title: Period, comma, semicolon, colon, forward slash, back slash, opening parenthesis, dash, and caret.

Pages
A "P" or "p" before the number is automatically removed.

Volume
A "V" or "v" before the number is automatically removed, as is a number that appears to be a year.

Issue
An "N", "No" or "No." before the number is automatically removed (this is not case sensitive).

When Punctuation Repeats Within a Field

A special formatting character called a "vertical bar" (|) can be placed in a filter to indicate a repeating separator within a field. For example, you may have a data file where a period followed by a space separates a journal name from the volume. However, in some cases, this separator is part of the journal name itself, with the result that a period and a space cannot be reliably used to distinguish a journal name from the volume. For example:

```
SO:   Science. 10 (3): p. 80-90
```

The above source line would be defined in a filter as:

SO:	Journal. Volume (Issue): p. Pages

Another source line in the same data file might look like this:

```
SO:   Proc. Nat. Acad. Sci. 13 (2): p. 34-45
```

The problem arises in the second source line where the separator between the journal and volume (period and a space) is found repeatedly within the journal. The SO: line in the filter instructs EndNote to import the data up to the period and space into the Journal field. Consequently, EndNote would parse "`Proc.`" as the journal name, and everything after the period up to the open parenthesis as the volume, so the volume would be "`Nat. Acad. Sci. 13`".

There is a way to indicate a repeating separator within a field in the filter. If you place a vertical bar (|) before the separator, this instructs EndNote to read up to the last occurrence of this separator. In the example above, if we place a vertical bar before the repeating Journal field separator (period and space), the SO: line in the filter would look like this:

SO:	Journal|. Volume (Issue): p. Pages

This SO: line in the filter instructs EndNote to import all the data with the period followed by a space separator as a journal. Here, EndNote would import "Proc. Nat. Acad. Sci." as the Journal, and "13" as the Volume.

The Filter Options

The remainder of the options listed in the Filter window below *Templates* provide the tools for fine tuning your filter. These options include, among other things, how author names should be interpreted, how text is indented in your data file, and which characters should be omitted when you import records into an EndNote library.

EndNote's "Smart" Settings

When possible, EndNote provides a "Smart" option for your choices in configuring the filters. Wherever you choose a "Smart" option, it means that EndNote will do it's best to interpret the data. If you don't know exactly how the reference is configured in the data file, or if there is a lot of variability among the format of the references, then the Smart options are probably going to be the most reliable settings. In cases where the "Smart" option doesn't work for your data file, you may try the other options provided for that particular setting.

Author Parsing

Use the *Author Parsing* panel to specify how author names are arranged in your data file. These settings apply only to authors in EndNote's main (Generic) Author field. The *Editor Parsing* panel applies to editors, translators, and other authors that are in EndNote's Generic Secondary Author, Tertiary Author, and Subsidiary Author fields.

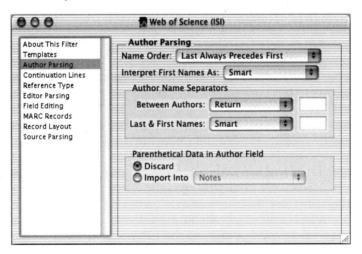

Name Order

Use the "Name Order" settings to specify the order in which first and last names are arranged in the data file. Examples appropriate to each setting are shown below:

Last Always Precedes First

```
AU: Smith, J.; Caton, K.; Jordan, L.
```

First Always Precedes Last

```
AU: J. Smith, K. Caton, L. Jordan
```

Name Order is Inconsistent

```
AU: Smith, J., K. Caton, L. Jordan
```

Interpreting First Names

The "Interpret First Names as" option allows you to specify exactly how EndNote should interpret the part of the author name that it has identified as the first name or initials.

The default is set to *Smart*, which uses the following rule: If there are three or fewer contiguous uppercase letters, these letters are imported as initials. Otherwise, the letters are imported as a whole name. For example, if the author's name appears in the data file as:

```
AU:   Childs, Jackie D
```

Smart parsing will interpret "Jackie" as the first name, and "D" as the middle initial. This author name would import as:

```
Author:
Childs, Jackie D.
```

If the author's name appears in the data file as

```
AU:   von Braun, ED
```

Smart parsing will interpret ED as initials; thus the author name would import into EndNote as:

```
Author:
von Braun, E. D.
```

EndNote would only import ED as a first name "Ed" if you selected the *Whole Names* option.

The *Whole Names* and *Initials Only* options should only be used in special cases. The *Whole Names* option should be used in the case where the authors in your data file are all uppercase, and full names are used. This option prevents EndNote from converting names consisting of two or three uppercase letters, as in "SUE" or "AL" to initials. For example, if the author's name appears in the data file as:

```
AU:   TOBIES, SUE
```

the *Whole Names* option would correctly import the author's first name as "Sue." By contrast, EndNote's *Smart Parsing* would interpret the whole name SUE as three initials, as "S.U.E." Likewise, if you select *Initials Only*, EndNote imports all first names as initials only. You would only choose this latter option if the all the first names in your data file are initials.

Author Name Separators

The Author Name Separators tell EndNote how to extract the individual authors from a line containing several authors.

Between Authors

The "Between Authors" option refers to the punctuation that is used to separate individual author names. It is extremely important that this setting is correct so that the author names import correctly into EndNote. Author names in an EndNote references are listed one name per line.

The default for the *Between Authors* option is set to *Smart*. With this option selected, EndNote looks for a common separator, either a semicolon (;), a carat (^) or a vertical bar (|), and use this delimiter to identify where one name ends and the next name begins.

In this example, multiple authors are separated by a semicolon:

```
AU:   Buning ME; Hanzlik JR
```

EndNote's *Smart* parsing recognizes the semicolon separating the two author names and correctly imports them into an EndNote library as:

```
Author:
Bunting, M. E.
Hanzlik, J. R.
```

Therefore, in this example, you do not need to change the setting. However, if your data file has a delimiter other than a semicolon (;), a caret (^), or a vertical bar (|) separating multiple authors, you must select another option from the adjacent list. To type any punctuation such as a dash or a slash, choose *Other* and type the character there. A space and a return (where the authors are listed one per line) can be selected directly from the list.

If you choose *Import As Is* from the list, EndNote will not try to separate the names that follow the author tag. Everything that follows that tag in the data file will be imported exactly as it appears in the file.

Last and First Names Separator

Once EndNote knows how to identify an individual author name in a list of authors, it looks at that name and tries to determine what the first name is and what the last name is. The Last and First Names separator is used to do this, along with the Name Order settings (page 430).

The default *Last & First Names* setting is *Smart*. With this option selected, EndNote attempts to interpret an author's name based on the following separators: a space, a comma, or a period. In your data file, if the separator used between the last name and the first name is something other than a space, a comma, or a period, you can select a separator from the adjacent list.

Parenthetical Data in Author Field

It is not uncommon for information providers to include additional information about the authors (such as date of birth or institutional affiliation).

```
AU: Takahashi, J (1944-); Izumi, R (1969-)
```

When this information is mixed in with the list of authors on the tagged author line, EndNote provides two options for what to do with it.

- ◆ **Discard:** All parenthetical information is discarded during the import.

- ◆ **Import Into:** All parenthetical data mixed in with the author names is imported into the field that you choose. We suggest that you import it into the Notes field, Author Address, or another custom field that is appropriate.

NOTE: It is not appropriate for EndNote to import that data into the Author field because it would produce an incorrectly formatted bibliography to have the parenthetical data included with the author names.

Continuation Lines

In general, EndNote ignores lines of text which do not begin with a tag *unless* the lines of text are continuations of a previous tagged item. We call these continuation lines. Here is an abstract from a data file illustrating the concept of continuation lines (all but the first are considered continuation lines):

```
AB- A single-subject research design that used
    multiple baselines across behaviors compared
    traditional adaptations to computers.
```

Because EndNote only imports tagged lines and continuation lines, it can avoid importing extraneous text that might interrupt a reference, such as your logging on or logging off text. Examples of extraneous lines are:

```
-->>Press any Key to continue

<Record 5 of 42>
```

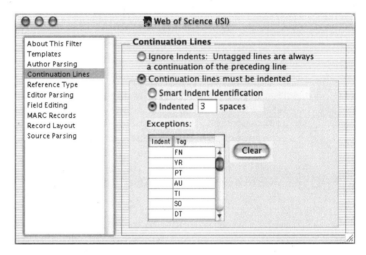

EndNote provides two general options for dealing with continuation lines:

Ignore Indents: Untagged lines are always a continuation of the preceding line

With this option set, every line of text in the data file will import according to the tags that are defined in the *Templates* panel. Do not choose this option if there is any text in your data file that is not tagged. If you use this option and do not want to import certain tagged lines, you must use the "{IGNORE}" option (see page 424).

Continuation lines must be indented

This option allows you to specify the exact number of spaces on the left margin for the continuation lines.

The following example is an abstract where the first line of data is indented four spaces from the left margin, and the continuation lines are properly indented four spaces. EndNote's default *Smart Indent Identification* would import this abstract correctly. (Spaces are shown as periods for clarity.)

```
AB-.Two experiments compared the performance of 23 12 yr
....old dyslexics with that of 8 age-matched controls on a
....battery of tests of motor balance. A dual-task paradigm
....was used: Ss performed each test as a.single task and as
....a task concurrent with a secondary task. In all single-
....task conditions there was no difference between groups.
```

However, you may find data files where the continuation lines are not aligned with the first line of data. In the following example, the continuation lines are indented two spaces from the left margin, whereas the first line is indented four spaces:

```
AB-.Beyond the inevitability of countertransference feelings
..is the question of countertransference enactments. From a
..two-person, participant-observer or observing-participant
..perspective,enactments are inevitable. The analyst becomes
..influenced by the patient (and influences the patient as
..well) and enmeshed in the patient's internalized
..interpersonal configurations.
```

For EndNote to treat the subsequent lines as continuation lines in the preceding example, the filter must specify the exact number of spaces indented on the left margin. In the example just given, you would enter "2" in the "Indent _ spaces" option.

If most of the lines in a data file import a fixed number of spaces (like two spaces in the example above), but one tagged field is indented differently (perhaps keywords are indented four spaces), you can enter exceptions in the table provided. Simply enter the number of spaces in the left column next to the tag. You only need to enter a number for the tagged field with the inconsistent import. All other lines that are left blank will use the general indent setting.

NOTE: For a quick and reliable way to count how many spaces are inserted on the left margin, turn on the setting in your word processor to display formatting characters.

Reference Type

Default Reference Type

The default reference type tells EndNote which reference type to use if it cannot identify the reference type of a record. For example, suppose that in one filter, you specify Journal Article as your default reference type, and create a template for it. If you import a data file containing conference proceedings records for which you have not defined a Reference Type template, any conference proceedings records will import as Journal Articles. Also, if the database that you use does not specify a Reference Type tag, all reference types in your data file will import as your default reference type. (See page 426 for information about defining the reference types tag in a template.)

NOTE: The default reference type is always indicated with an asterisk (*) in the *Reference Types* list on the *Templates* panel.

Identifiers

Some information providers, such as Ovid Technologies, Inc., provide a button on their Web site to allow EndNote users to send search results right from the Web page to the EndNote library. In this case, there is no need for you to go through the extra steps of saving the information from the Web site to a text file, and then using EndNote's *Import* command to pick a filter and import the text file. All of that happens behind the scenes.

These identifiers are also used to import data files that contain references from multiple databases. EndNote can import multi-source files like that as long as each record in the data file has a vendor and a database tag at the start of the reference. The identifiers must also be entered into the appropriate filters in the Filters folder. When you are ready to import a file that has data from multiple sources in it, be sure to choose the *Multi-Filter* import option in the Import dialog.

The way that EndNote is able to know which filter to use is by these Identifier tags entered into the filter. Both identifiers must be used. The first identifier should be the tag that includes the name of the information provider. For this example it is "VN." The exact text that follows that tag for each record should be entered into the corresponding box in the Identifiers section. The next tag is used to identify the database, such as Medline or BIOSIS. Enter the tag used for the database name, and then enter the database name exactly as it appears in each reference.

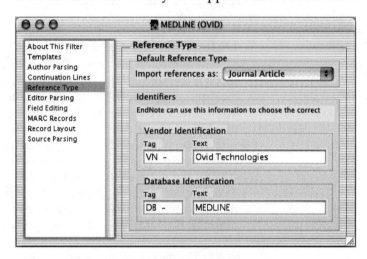

EndNote would know to use the filter shown above if the data file that it was trying to import contained those two tags and lines of text:

```
<1>
VN      Ovid Technologies, Inc.
DB      MEDLINE
AU      Jacobson, R; Campbell, S.
PY      1999
etc.
```

Field Editing

Converting Text from Uppercase to Lowercase

If the text in your data file appears entirely in uppercase letters, EndNote can convert the text to either *Sentence, Headline* or *Lowercase* format, depending on which option you specify in the *Field Editing* panel.

To control the lowercasing of a field, select the appropriate field from the "Field Editing for:" list at the top of the window. The EndNote fields are listed here by their Generic names. (For a list of reference type fields and their corresponding Generic field names, see "Table of Predefined Reference Types" on page 354.) Then pick a capitalization option from the "Change UPPERCASE text to:" list.

For example, a title that appears in a data file as "COMPOST AS A HUMAN NUTRIENT AND HORMONE CARRIER" would import in *Headline* capitalization as:

`Compost as a Human Nutrient and Hormone Carrier`

or in *Sentence* capitalization as:

`Compost as a human nutrient and hormone carrier`

To keep a field's text entirely in uppercase characters, choose the *Do NOT Lowercase* option.

You can apply lowercasing on any field as long as *all* the text in the field is uppercase. If any of the text in the field is in mixed case, EndNote will import it in mixed case.

The Author, Editor, and Translator fields are treated differently from all other EndNote fields. Upon importing author fields into an EndNote library, these fields are automatically converted from uppercase to headline. Due to the special characteristics of these particular fields, the option to change the case is not available in the *Field Editing* panel.

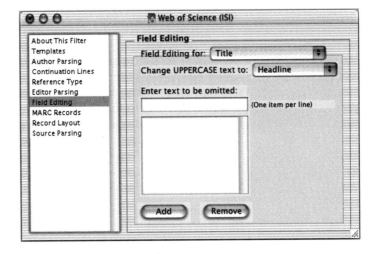

Omitting Unwanted Characters

Some lines of data have superfluous characters, such as an asterisk (*) or a dash (-), that you may not want to import. For example, in the following lines of data there are dashes in the journal name, and there is an asterisk before each keyword:

```
SO-   American-journal-of-preventive-medicine;
      12(9)

DE-   *COMPUTER SYSTEMS DESIGN; *DISPLAY
      DEVICES; *INTERFACES
```

To prevent unwanted characters from being imported into your EndNote library, use the *Field Editing* panel to specify the characters that you want to omit:

1. From the "Field Editing for:" list, select the EndNote field that contains unwanted characters. You will find that the EndNote fields are listed by their Generic names. For a list of reference type fields and their corresponding Generic field names, see "Table of Predefined Reference Types" on page 354.

2. Type the unwanted text in the "Enter text to be omitted (one item per line)" box, and then click *Add* to add it to the omission list.

When you prevent characters from being imported into an EndNote field, you are omitting the characters from the corresponding Generic field, so the omission applies to every reference type field that corresponds to the particular Generic field. For example, the Secondary Title field corresponds to both the Journal field in a Journal Article reference type and the Series Title in a Book reference type. Therefore, if you omit a dash (-) from the journal name, any dashes found in a Series Title for a Book reference type will also be omitted.

Each item that you want to omit should be entered on a separate line. For example, let's say that you wanted to omit both underscores (_) and forward slashes (/) from your records' keywords. First add the underscore, and then add the forward slash. Entering both items on the same line would cause EndNote to omit only instances of "_/", while all other instances of underscores and forward slashes would end up in your keywords. You can omit up to 254 characters per EndNote field.

To remove an item from the list, simply select the item and click *Remove*. You may select more than one item by holding down the SHIFT or COMMAND key while clicking on multiple items.

NOTE: The more items added to the list, the longer it takes EndNote to import records into EndNote. To avoid slowing down the importing process, you may want to start by importing the data into an EndNote library without specifying any omissions. Then use the *Change Text* command in EndNote to delete the unwanted words and other text.

Record Layout

Use the options in the *Record Layout* panel to modify how EndNote interprets the end of a reference in a data file.

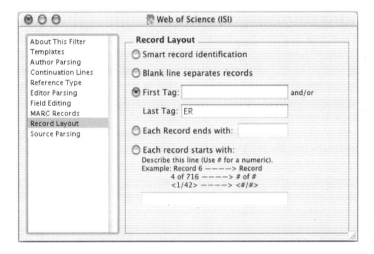

Smart Record Identification

Smart Record Identification, EndNote's default setting for Record Termination, creates a new record in EndNote each time a tag in the data file repeats out of sequence *and is preceded by a blank or extraneous line.* EndNote will not create a new record if the same tag appears in succession, provided that they are not separated by a blank line.

For example, some databases list authors one per tagged line, with the AU tag appearing two or more times in succession, as in the following example:

```
AU- D'Orazio, MG
AU- Tamura, TS
```

When EndNote sees consecutive tags, it does not start a new reference unless it finds the same tag preceded by a blank or extraneous line.

More Specific Record Layout Options

A more precise way of identifying a new record is to specify in your filter exactly how the records are terminated in your data file. The remaining options in the Record Layout panel allow you to do this.

To determine how records are terminated, open your data file in either a word processor or text editor. Check for the pattern consistently separating one record from another. Once you have determined the correct record termination, click the appropriate button under in the *Record Layout* panel to select the best option for your data file. You may choose only one option as a record terminator.

Blank line separates records

Choose this option if the only blank lines in a data file are the ones in between references.

Using "First Tag" and "Last Tag" Options

This option lets you specify a first tag that starts the record and/ or a final tag that ends each record. Only one tag is required.

♦ Before choosing this option as your record terminator, verify that the first or last tag is consistently present in each record. This option will function correctly only if the chosen tag appears in every record.

♦ You do not need to enter both a first and last tag; either tag will suffice to distinguish one record from the next.

♦ Enter the tag exactly as it appears in the data file, including the delimiter (colon, dash, etc.) that follows the tag. EndNote treats these delimiters as part of their respective tags.

♦ You do not need to include these tags in the templates of your filter, unless you wish to import the associated data.

Each record ends with:

Choose this option if your references consistently end with a specific set of unique characters. Note that whatever you enter into this option needs to be unique enough that it doesn't appear elsewhere in your references. One common set of characters that is used to terminate each record is " | | ".

Each record starts with:

Choose this option if your references consistently start with text that is not a tag. For example, it is common for some information providers to begin each reference with a counter such as:

<1>

or

Record 1 of 53

In these cases, enter the text exactly as it appears in the data file, but substitute a number sign (#) for the actual number. For the examples above, you would enter "<#>" and "Record # of #".

Example

The following example illustrates a data file that contains neither a blank line, nor text terminating each record. However, there is a consistent first tag, "ND:" starting each record. So for this example you would want to specify "ND:" as the record termination by clicking the "First Tag" button, and type "ND:" in the box.

```
First Tag ——— ( ND:)43052953|
             BASE:BA83|
             AU:HILDEN O^PAHTAMAA T|
             TI:DEVELOPMENT OF THE RAZORBILL POPULATION OF THE QUARK
             IN 1957-1990|
             SO:ORNIS FENNICA^69 (1). 1992. 34-38.^1992|
             LA:English|
             SH:CHORDATE TAXONOMY-AVES^BEHAVIOR BIOLOGY-ANIMAL
             BEHAVIOR^ECOLOGY-ANIMAL^
             01:1.00/000002 DIMDI: -BIOSIS PREV AB /COPYRIGHT BIOSIS|
First Tag ——— ( ND:)93110787|
             BASE:BA83|
             AU:NAKAZAWA Y^FURUSAWA M^HOHNO H^SHIDA T|
             TI:MANUFACTURE AND PROTEOLYTIC PROPERTIES OF YOGURT FROM
                 MILK CONCENTRATED BY ULTRAFILTRATION|
             SO:LEBENSMITTEL-WISSENSCHAFT & TECHNOLOGIE^24 (6). 1991.
                 491-494.^1991|
             LA:English|
```

Source Parsing

The **source line** refers to the line in the data file that represents the source information for the journal (typically journal, volume, issue, pages, and sometimes the year). It is most often the most complex and inconsistent line of data in your data file—and it is also the most important. As a result, the EndNote filters provide a sort of safety net to catch inconsistently entered source data.

The tags and templates defined in the *Templates* panel are used first to import source data. If a source line in a data file does not match any of the options in the templates, then EndNote provides you with additional options for how to handle that. The first thing you need to do is to make sure that EndNote has correctly identified the journal article source tag.

Identifying the Source Tag

If the source tag for the Journal Article reference type in the *Templates* section of a filter is SO or JN, EndNote automatically identifies this tag as the source tag. However, if the source tag defined in your filter is something other than a "SO" or "JN", you must choose the appropriate tag from the *Journal Article Source Tag* list. (All of the tags that have been defined in the Journal Article template will appear in the "Source Tag" list.)

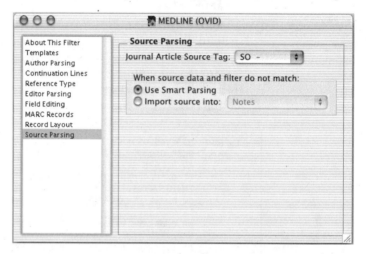

When source data and filter templates do not match

If a journal article's source line in your data file does not match a source line in your filter, you can choose how EndNote should treat the unmatched source line. The default option is *Use Smart Parsing*. EndNote's *Smart Parsing* does its best to distinguish the journal name, the volume number, the issue number, the page numbers, and the year, and import each into the corresponding EndNote field. Any information that is not identified as a journal, volume, issue, pages, or year is imported into the Notes field, along with the comment "Using Smart Source Parsing." (After importing, if you suspect that some references may not have matched the defined source template, it is helpful to use EndNote's *Search* command to search for the text "Using Smart Source Parsing" in the Notes field of the imported references. You may then check those specifically to see if EndNote correctly interpreted the data.)

If you choose the other option to import the source data into a separate field, EndNote does not attempt to parse the source information, and instead imports the entire unmatched source line into whatever field you have specified.

For any reference type other than a Journal Article, unmatched source lines are automatically imported into the Notes field. Therefore, if you have not defined an exact match for a source line found in a book record in your data file, EndNote imports the entire source line into the Notes field.

Importing MARC Records

What Are MARC Records?

"MARC" stands for <u>Ma</u>chine <u>R</u>eadable <u>C</u>ataloging format. It is a standardized format developed by the Library of Congress for producing machine-readable bibliographic records. It is much more difficult to read than regular tagged data formats, but it can still be imported in much the same way using EndNote's filters.

The MARC Format and Connection Files

Many connection files use the MARC format because it is specified as part of the Z39.50 standard. When creating a new connection file, the *Templates* and *MARC Records* portions of the connection file are automatically set up to import standard USMARC (MARC21) data. If you need to customize these parts of the connection file, the instructions in this section would apply.

Unique Aspects of MARC Records

MARC records differ from other bibliographic records in two important ways:

Numeric Tags

The primary way in which MARC records differ from non-MARC bibliographic records is in their reliance on numeric tags. Numeric tags typically consist of three digits followed by two spaces and two more digits. For example:

```
245 10   $a When you realize you have too many
         kids: $b a guide / $c Hugh B Dunn.

245 14   $a The angel with a dirty mouth /$c Nick
         Steel ; illustrated by Melissa Fips.
```

Subfields

The second way in which MARC tags differ from other bibliographic records is the use of subfields.

Each numerically tagged line in a MARC record may contain any number of subfields. A subfield typically consists of two consecutive characters, the first of which is the subfield delimiter which denotes the start of a new subfield. Examples of subfields are "$a" and "$x." The subfields do not have to be consecutive, as in the second record in the example above.

If you were creating a conventional filter for importing bibliographic records from a MARC database, you would have to anticipate a vast number of possible combinations, both of tags and of subfields.

Because it is difficult to anticipate every possible combination of tags and subfields in MARC records, EndNote provides you with a simplified way of creating filters for MARC records. The two sections that follow tell you how to create a filter specifically for MARC records, and then alert you to the different rules that EndNote uses when importing MARC records into an EndNote library.

Creating a Filter for MARC Records

Once you have created a new filter, or you have opened an existing filter, select the *MARC Records* panel in the Filter window.

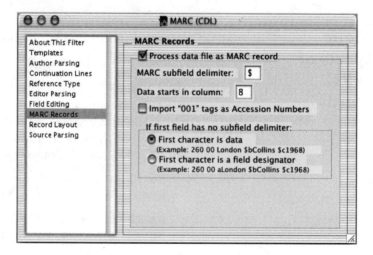

Click the "Process data file as MARC record" checkbox. The dollar sign ($) will appear in the "MARC Subfield Delimiter" box, since this is the subfield delimiter in most cases. If the subfield delimiter is something other than a dollar sign, delete the dollar sign and type in the appropriate delimiter.

Data Start Column

The reference data in a MARC reference normally starts in column 8 (that is, the sixth character from the left margin). If the MARC records in your data file start the actual reference data (as opposed to tags and subfield delimiters) in some other position, enter that number in the text box for *Data starts in column*.

Accession Numbers

The Accession Number is a unique number assigned to each record in a database. (The information provider's database; not the EndNote database.) Also referred to as "unique identifiers," these numbers sometimes appear immediately after the numeric tag, and without the two-digit subfield codes seen in other MARC fields. Since a common type of accession number often appears after the 001 tag, EndNote includes an *Import "001"tags as Accession Numbers* check box which lets you import this number into EndNote's Accession Number field. Accession numbers which appear in lines other than 001 often begin with a subfield, so you can set up the filter to import the number into the Accession Number field.

If first field has no subfield delimiter:

Normally the first character that precedes the record data is the subfield delimiter (commonly a dollar sign $). If this subfield delimiter is not present for the first field of each tagged line, you will need to tell EndNote how to interpret the first character by checking the appropriate option under the MARC records dialog. Is it part of the real data of a reference or is it a field designator (such as "a" or "b") that just happens to be missing the subfield delimiter?

Rules for MARC Import Filters

The *Templates* panel for a filter created for MARC records looks something like this:

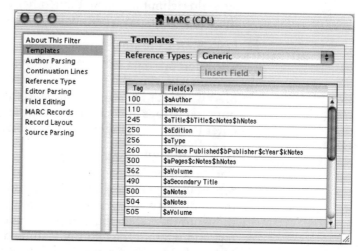

EndNote observes these rules when importing MARC records:

♦ EndNote allows you to specify only the first three digits of the tag when designing a filter for MARC records. You can disregard spaces and digits appearing immediately after the first three digits. The tag for both of the following examples would be 245.

```
245 10   $a When you realize you have too many
         kids: $b a guide / $c Hugh B Dunn.

245 14   $a The angel with a dirty mouth /$c Nick
         Steel ; illustrated by Melissa Fips.
```

♦ You do not have to define all the subfields in a tagged line. There may be some subfields that contain information you do not want to import into your EndNote library. EndNote will ignore any subfields that are not defined in your filter.

♦ Source lines cannot take advantage of the "Smart Source Parsing" option. You may, however, enter multiple variations of the subfields in a source line. Be sure to enter all subfields *after the same tag* (do not repeat the tag for each), and list the most complex subfield formats first. For example:

```
773 $gVolume(Issue), p. Pages$gVolume, p.Pages
```

♦ With the exception of the reference type tag, EndNote allows you to define a tag only once; therefore you should include all of the subfields that contain data you want to be imported. For example, the following line in a filter for MARC records would successfully import any or all of the three lines that follow:

245	$a Title $b Title $c Notes

```
245 14  $a The hollow horn : $b Bob Dylan's
        reception in the United States and
        Germany / $c by Dennis Anderson.

245 10  $a Bob Dylan, spellbinding songwriter /
        $c Nathan Aaseng.

245 00  $a Down in the groove.
```

Example: Modifying an Existing Filter

Modifying an existing filter is useful if you want to create a new filter for a different database by the same provider. Although some information providers offer radically different formats for their different databases, there are others who provide fairly consistent tags and organized data across their databases.

Common reasons for editing a filter include adding a tag to import additional information; removing a tag or using {IGNORE} to omit unwanted data; or fine-tuning the current settings for importing authors or journal source data. The specifics about how to work with templates and options are described earlier in this chapter. This example is intended to provide a general overview of the process of editing a filter.

Adding a Tag and Field to a Filter

Let's say that you want to modify a filter to import the language of the publication into EndNote's Notes field. In this particular database, the language is preceded by the tag "LA-".

```
          TI- Zum Beginn des mathematischen Frauenstudiums in Preussen.|
          TI- <Translated> The beginnings of mathematical studies for
              women in Prussia|
          AU- Tobies. Renate
          JN- NTM Schr. Geschichte Natur. Tech. Medizin|
          SO- <JN> NTM Schriftenreihe fur Geschichte der Naturwissenschaften
              Technik und Medizin|
          SO- <PY> 1991|
          SO- <VO> 28|
          SO- <NO> no. 2,|
          SO- <PG> 151-172.|
Language —(LA-)German|
Tag       DT- Journal|
```

To add the LA tag and direct its contents to the Notes field:

1. From the *Edit* menu, choose *Import Filters* and select *Open Filter Manager*. (The most recently used filter also appears as an option in the *Import Filters* submenu. You may choose *Edit <filter name>* to directly edit that filter as well.)

2. In the Filter Manager, select the filter that you want to edit and click *Edit*.

3. Click the mouse in any cell of the Journal Article template, and press RETURN or ENTER to create to a new row.

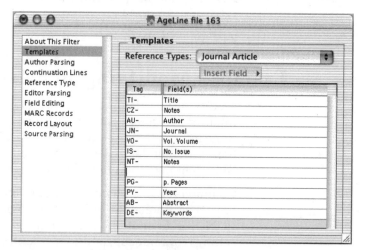

4. Type LA– in the Tag cell, then press a TAB to move to the Field cell. Insert the Notes field from the *Insert Field* list. Doing so tells EndNote to import the language information into EndNote's Notes field.

5. You can add the LA– tag to the remaining Reference Type templates in the filter. Use the *Reference Type* list to switch to each reference type template in your filter and repeat the process described above. (Reference types with check marks next to them in the list are the ones that have templates defined for them.

6. To keep the original filter unmodified, choose *Save As* from the *File* menu, give the modified version of the filter a new name, and click *Save*. Or, to save the changes to the original filter, simply choose *Save* from the *File* menu.

Creating a New Filter

This section provides a general overview of how to create a new filter. It includes an example of a data file, and the templates portion of a filter to match it. Specific instructions for configuring templates and filter options can be found in the earlier sections in this chapter.

Overview

The basic steps to create a new filter are:

1. From the *Edit* menu, choose *Import Filters* and select *New Filter*.

2. If you'd like, you may enter a category for the filter (usually the information provider is used for the category), and any other comments about what the filter is based on or what data it is used to import.

3. Click on the *Templates* option.

4. From the *Reference Types* list choose the first reference type that you would like to define, and enter the necessary tags and the corresponding fields into the reference type template. (See "Working with Filter Templates" on page 421.)

5. Define additional reference types, as necessary, by selecting them from the *Reference Types* list and entering the tags and fields for them as well.

6. Click on the *Reference Type* option in the list of panel names, and choose the default reference type for the filter.

At this point, you may have entered enough information to use the filter successfully. Try it out by choosing it as the import option to import your data file into a new, empty library. Review the imported references to be sure that they imported correctly. Fine tune the filter as necessary (see "The Filter Options" on page 429).

NOTE: If you need a reference type that does not appear in the *Reference Type* list, see"Adding and Deleting Reference Types" on page 351.

Tips for Entering Tags and Fields

Not every tag in your data file needs to be in your filter.

There is no need to define every tag that appears in your data file, provided that the contents of the corresponding field start on the same line as the tag itself; and the records' continuation lines are not flush left. If you need to define every tag that appears in a record, but only want to import the information associated with certain tags, insert the {IGNORE} field from the *Insert Field* list where appropriate.

NOTE: You do not need to specify all data fields, *unless* each tag appears on a line by itself, with the data starting below it on the next line. You may also want to specify all tags if the continuation lines in your records are flush left, in which case an undefined tag appearing immediately after a continuation line will be read in as text.

You might need to enter multiple variations of a source line.

You will often find more than one variation of a source line for a given reference type in a database, in which case you will need to define a separate source line in your template for each such variant. The most complex source line should appear first, followed by source lines of decreasing complexity. In the case of Journal Articles, be sure to specify the appropriate *Source Parsing* option (refer to "Source Parsing" on page 441).

MARC formats are an exception. See page 446.

A colon, dash, space or other character that appears along with a tag is treated as part of the tag.

When defining tags in a filter, these characters need to be included in the tag column of the filter for EndNote to find an exact match. If spaces are inserted within a tag, as in "SO-<VO>," they need to be defined as part of the tag as well.

Example Data File and Templates

Below is a sample of a record in a data file and the filter *Templates* panel configured to import the data. See "Working with Filter Templates" on page 421 for details about configuring templates.

Sample Record from a Data File

```
FN- DIALOG MEDLINE file 155
AN- 08791562|
AN- <NLM> 94106562|
TI- Adaptive computer use for the visually
    impaired
AU- Buning ME; Hanzlik JR|
CS- School of Occupational and Educational
    Studies, Fort Collins, Colorado.|
JN- Am J Occup Ther; 47 (11) p998-1008|
CP- UNITED STATES|
PY- Nov 1993|
SN- 0272-9490|
JC- 304|
CN- MCJ-009105|
LA- ENGLISH|
DT- ANALYTIC; SERIAL|
JA- 9404|
SF- INDEX MEDICUS|
AB- A single-subject research design that used
    baselines across behaviors compared
    adaptations (e.g., the use of readers) to
    computer technologies for typical reading |
GS- Case Report; Human; Male; Support, U.S.
    Gov't, Non-P.H.S.; Support, U.S. Gov't,
    P.H.S.|
DE- *Microcomputers; *Vision,
    Subnormal--Rehabilitation--RH; Activities |
ID- EC 4.1.1.1   (Pyruvate Decarboxylase)||
```

NOTE: The trailing vertical bars at the end of each line will be stripped out by EndNote. *Do not include them in the filter.*

To create a template for the Journal Article reference type:

1. Type TI- in the tag cell, then press TAB to move to the Field column. Insert the Title field using the *Insert Field* button.

2. Press RETURN to move to the next line.

3. Type the next tag to import and insert the corresponding field. Continue entering the rest of the tags and fields until all of the necessary information is covered by the filter. Skip any tags for data that you are not interested in importing.

Here's what the resulting *Templates* panel of the filter looks like:

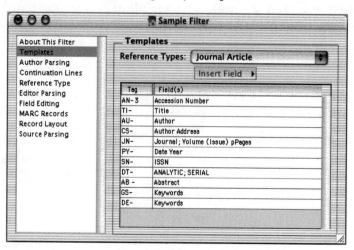

NOTE: It is important to remember that the source line in a filter must exactly match the source line in the data file for EndNote to distinguish one field from another. You will often find more than one variation of a source line for a given reference type in a database, in which case you will need to create a separate source line for each variant in your download, starting with the most complex source line and ending with the least complex source line. As a backup, select the appropriate *Source Parsing* option, as outlined in "Source Parsing" on page 441.

Chapter 17

Connection Files

Chapter 17   Connection Files

Introduction to Connection Files

The *Connect* command in EndNote's *Tools* menu connects you to online databases and library catalogs so that you can search them from within the EndNote program and retrieve references directly into EndNote. EndNote is able to make these connections using the information stored in the hundreds of individual "connection files."

This chapter describes how to edit and create these connection files. The process of using the *Connect* command is described in Chapter 6.

NOTE: You can download the latest connection files available from ISI ResearchSoft. Visit our website at www.endnote.com.

What is a Connection File?

A connection file contains all the information necessary to connect to, search, and import references from a remote database or online library catalog. Each connection file represents a different online database (such as the Library of Congress or PubMed from the National Library of Medicine).

The connection files are located in the Connections folder in your EndNote folder. You can view all of the available connections by choosing *Connection Files* from the *Edit* menu and selecting *Open Connection Manager*.

The Connection Manager

EndNote provides hundreds of connection files for a variety of sources. To peruse the list of available connection files in EndNote's Connections folder, choose *Connection Files* from the *Edit* menu, and select *Open Connection Manager*.

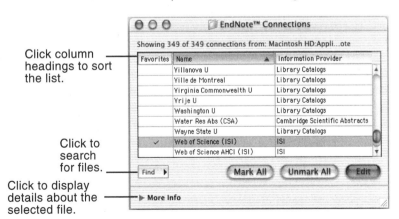

Click column headings to sort the list.

Click to search for files.

Click to display details about the selected file.

The Connection Manager lists the names of all of the connection files available in the Connections folder and gives you the options to edit them or select them as "favorites" for quick access when you use the *Connect* command.

Use these features to locate the connection file you want to use:

♦ If you know the name of the connection file that you want to use, start typing it to select the first file that matches what you type.

♦ Click the *Find* button and choose an information provider's name (such as Ovid or SilverPlatter) to find only the connection files for a specific information provider.

♦ Click the *Find* button, and choose *by Name* to search for the file by the name of the database. You can enter a partial name or the full name. EndNote displays all matching results.

♦ Click the *Find* button and choose *All Connections* to return all of the connection files to the displayed list.

♦ Click the column headings to sort the connection files by name or by information provider. Clicking the same column heading a second time will change the sort order from ascending to descending. Click again to set it back to ascending order.

♦ Click the *More Info* triangle button at the bottom of the dialog to display additional information about the selected connection file. Or, click *Less Info* to hide the additional information.

Marking Your Favorite Connection Files

When you have found a connection file that you will want to use in the future, click in the Favorites column next to it to mark it as a favorite. All connection files that are marked as favorites appear in a submenu when you choose *Connect* from the *Tools* menu. This gives you easy access to the files you use most often.

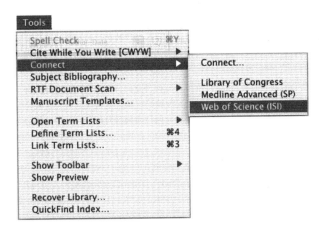

An easy way to mark a whole category of connection files (such as all of the connections for Ovid databases) is to click the *Find* button, choose a category from the list, and then when all of the files for that category are showing, click the *Mark All* button.

Editing Connection Files

If you would like to modify a connection file, select it in the list and click *Edit*. The remainder of this chapter goes into detail about how to work with connection files.

Copying Connection Files

There are two ways to copy connection files. Since each connection file is a separate file on your hard drive, you can copy them as you would copy any file on your hard drive using the Macintosh Finder.

To make a copy of a connection file from within EndNote:

1. From the *Edit* menu, choose *Connection Files>Open Connection Manager* to open the Connection Manager.

2. Select the connection file you want to copy and click *Edit*.

3. Without making any changes to the file, choose *Save As* from the *File* menu.

4. Give this copy of the file a new name, and save it in your Connections folder if you would like access to it from within EndNote. If you save the connection file outside of the Connections folder (such as on a CD to take a copy to a different computer, or to backup the file), it will not be available within EndNote.

After clicking *Save* to save the new copy of the file, the new connection file will remain open. The original connection file will be left untouched.

Saving Connection Files

To save a new or modified connection file, choose *Save* from the *File* menu when the Connection File window is open. Or, to save changes to a connection file while leaving the original connection file unchanged, choose *Save As* from the *File* menu (see "Copying Connection Files" on page 457).

When saving a new connection file, or saving a connection file under a different name, EndNote will automatically save the connection file to your designated Connections folder. (The Connections Manager within EndNote only provides access to the connection files that are in the designated connections folder.) Your Connections folder by default is the folder called Connections in your EndNote folder. You may also specify a different folder if necessary. For instructions see "Folder Locations" on page 486.

Deleting Connection Files

To delete a connection file from within EndNote:

1. From the *Edit* menu, choose *Connection Files>Open Connection Manager*.

2. Select the connection file to be deleted.

3. Choose *Clear* from the *Edit* menu, or CONTROL-click on the connection file and choose *Delete* from the shortcut menu.

You can also delete an unwanted connection file by switching back to the Macintosh Finder, and opening the Connections folder in the EndNote folder. Then, drag the connection file from the Connections folder to the Trash.

Basic Components of a Connection File

The basic components of a connection file are described in this section. This information is useful if you want to modify or create a connection file. To create a new connection file see "Creating Connection Files" on page 466.

Editing a Connection File

If you are editing a connection file and would like to keep the original file unchanged, choose *Save As* from the *File* menu immediately after opening the connection file for editing. Name the new copy of the connection file and save it in the Connections folder. Your original connection file will remain untouched, and keep its original name. The newly named copy of that connection file will now be open for you to modify as you wish.

To edit a connection file:

1. From the *Edit* menu, choose *Connection Files* and select *Open Connection Manager*.

2. Select the file to edit and click *Edit*.

The most recently used connection file can also be easily edited by selecting *Connection Files* from the *Edit* menu, and choosing *Edit <connection file>*.

The Connection File Window

After choosing the option to edit an existing connection file or create a new one, EndNote opens the Connection File window.

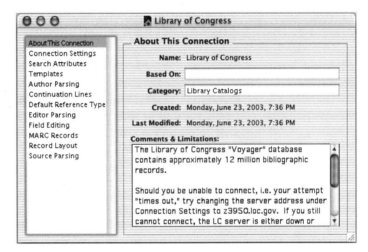

All of the different areas of the connection file are listed on the left side of the Connection File window. Click on an item to view the associated settings. You may switch between panels as needed while editing the file. No changes are saved in any of the panels until you choose *Save* or *Save As* from the *File* menu.

If at any time you need to revert your changes back to the last saved copy of the connection file, choose *Revert Connection* from the *File* menu.

To close the Connection Editor window, choose *Close Connection* from the *File* menu, or click the close button in the top left corner of the window.

"About this Connection" Panel

When the Connection Editor window opens, it displays the *About this Connection* information (shown in the preceding section). This panel contains descriptive information about the file, and has no impact on establishing the connection.

Name: Displays the name of the file as it appears in the Connections folder in the EndNote folder. The name of the file cannot be changed here; you would need to close this window and switch back to the Macintosh Finder to rename the file.

Based On: Enter any information about what documentation was used to create the file. Commonly the server documentation is available on the Web, so you could enter a URL here to make it easy to later retrieve that information. If this connection file is a modified copy of another connection file, it may be helpful to enter the name of the original file in this field for future reference.

Category: The category is typically the information provider (such as Ovid or SilverPlatter), but you may enter anything that will help you categorize and organize your connection files. The category information is also listed in the Connection Manager window in the column next to the name of the file. In that window, you may sort connection files by category and also search for them by category.

Created: The date the file was installed or created.

Last Modified: The date the file was last modified.

Comments and Limitations: Enter any useful comments here that would help you remember how to search the remote database. Limitations to preconfigured connection files may be documented here as well.

All of the information in this panel is visible in the Connection Manager if you click the *More* information option at the bottom of the Connection Manager window. This is helpful because you do not need to edit a connection file to view the comments or other descriptive information. You may simply scroll through the available connection files in the Connection Manager window and view the information there.

The Connection Settings

Click on *Connection Settings* to view the panel where all the data is stored to establish a connection. The Connection Settings information is *required* for EndNote to be able to connect to the remote database. These terms and descriptions are part of the Z39.50 standard.

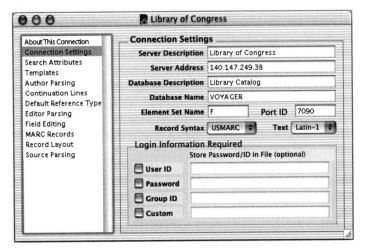

Server Description: The name of the information provider or institution. EndNote displays this name in the title of the Retrieved References window, and it is also listed in the Connection Manager window. This information is not used to establish the connection.

Server Address: The server address for the remote database. This can be either a numerical IP address or a domain name.

Database Description: The name of the remote database. This name is displayed in the Title bar of the Retrieved References window to help you identify the database to which you are connected. It is not used to establish the connection.

Database Name: The command used to select the database on the remote server. This is often a four character code.

Element Set Name: This is normally F for "Full" or B for "Brief." The Element Set Name determines the amount of information that is provided by the server for each retrieved reference. Not all servers support both options, and the fields returned for each option also vary.

Port ID: The TCP/IP port at the server that is used for a Z39.50 connection. For most Z39.50 connections this is port 210.

Record Syntax: USMARC (United States Machine Readable Cataloging), **UNIMARC** (Universal Machine Readable Cataloging), **SUTRS** (Simple Unstructured Text Record Syntax), and **OPAC** (Online Public Access Catalog) formats are supported by EndNote. The USMARC format is a standard format commonly used by Z39.50 servers. When you create a new connection file in EndNote, the filter and record syntax are automatically set up to work with USMARC data. Consequently, the filter section for connection files using SUTRS, UNIMARC, and OPAC must be constructed manually. UNIMARC and OPAC use variations of the MARC format (OPAC commonly adds holdings data). The SUTRS format, because it is "unstructured," does not have a standard format among different databases. The SUTRS format often uses tags (such as "AU" or "Author") to identify the reference data.

Text: The *Text* option is used to specify how EndNote should interpret the incoming text. Choose from ANSEL and Latin-1. Choose ANSEL if the Record Syntax for the connection file is set to a MARC format (USMARC, UNIMARC, OPAC). Choose Latin-1 if the Record Syntax is set to SUTRS. It is uncommon, but some servers do use Latin-1 text encoding in their MARC format. If records retrieved using a MARC-based format appear with asterisks in place of common western diacritical characters, change the Text option to Latin-1.

Required Login Information: This section is divided into four separate options: Password, User ID, Group ID, and Custom ID Authentication String. Select the options required to login to the remote database in order to have EndNote prompt you for that information when you connect. You can also store your password and/or IDs in the connection file so that you don't have to enter them each time you connect. Simply type the password or ID into the box provided.

NOTE: Passwords and IDs may be saved in the connection file for convenience, but do so at your own risk: passwords are not protected or encrypted. If someone else copies or uses your connection file, they will be able to use your stored password.

Custom ID Authentication String

Sometimes a database server requires a custom format for presenting the password and IDs. For these situations, you may skip the regular password or ID option, check the "Custom ID Authentication String" option, and enter the text specified by your server's Z39.50 documentation. You may either enter your actual password and ID along with the text, or use one of the following placeholders to have EndNote prompt you for the necessary items: ?PASSWORD, ?USERID, ?GROUPID.

For example, the California Digital Library's MELVYL system requires that passwords be presented by Z39.50 clients in the following manner:

```
pass=?PASSWORD/dla_ui=yes
```

If you wanted to store your password ("abc123" for this example) it would look like this:

```
pass=abc123/dla_ui=yes
```

Search Attributes

The Search Attributes section of a connection file contains a table that defines the various search options for a particular database.

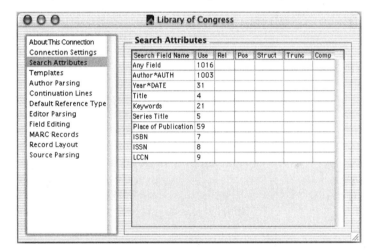

◆ **Search Field Name:** The first column identifies the name of a search. This is the word or phrase that appears in the menus in the Search dialog.

Use EndNote's Generic field names as the search field names whenever possible. Doing so makes it easier to have a search apply to various remote sources and local EndNote libraries.

EndNote's preconfigured connection files often use parenthetical text after the search field name to help describe the search, if necessary. This parenthetical text is not considered part of the search field name when you change the focus of the search and EndNote looks for a matching search field name. (See "Changing the Focus of the Search" on page 138. Generic field names are listed on page 354.)

♦ **Attributes**: The rest of the items in a particular row are the various search attributes that control what index is being used for the search, and how the search term is interpreted.

What is an "attribute"?

A Z39.50 **search attribute** is a value used to define the characteristics of a search term. For example, if your search term is "ebola virus," the various attributes would be sent to the server along with that term to tell the server where to look for "ebola virus" and what qualifies as a matching reference.

Available attributes, as defined by the Z39.50 standard, are:

1. Use	The index to be searched (such as Keywords)
2. Relation	The relation of the search term to the index (such as equal, greater than, or less than)
3. Position	The position of the search term in the MARC record field (first, last, anywhere, etc.)
4. Structure	The structure of the term, such as a word or phrase
5. Truncation	Available truncation options used to interpret the search term (for example: right truncation, wildcards, no truncation)
6. Completeness	Indicates whether or not the search term should be the complete subfield in the MARC record corresponding to the field searched

The "Use" attribute is the most important here, indicating which index will be searched to find the search term. The other attributes will all have varying default values for each remote database. These options are most often left blank to use the server's defaults, but the default attribute values can be overridden by entering another value for the attribute.

Each database has its own supported subset of Use attributes and associated combinations of the other attributes. Consult the configuration information for the remote database to determine which values for these attributes are supported. ISI ResearchSoft does not provide this information. You will need to obtain it from the organization (or "information provider") that maintains the server. Much of this information is also available at the EndNote Web site (http://www.endnote.com/home/z3950.htm). Our Z39.50 resources page will link you to the server's original documentation whenever possible.

Tip for Editing Search Attributes

When modifying the search attributes in a connection file, it is useful to first test the search with the new attribute combination before actually changing the connection file. You can do this by entering the new attribute values using the command-line search method (see page 468). This lets you test new attribute combinations without having to edit and save the connection file, and reconnect to the server every time you want to test a modification.

Filter Information

The Filter section of the connection file contains the information used to import each reference and get the reference data into the correct EndNote fields.

For most connection files, the filter is set up to interpret references in the MARC format. When you create a new connection file, the Filter section will be set up to interpret references in a standard USMARC format.

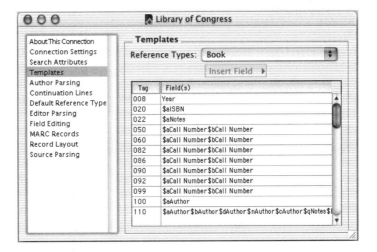

This part of the connection file is identical to the regular Filter window. For more information about editing a filter consult Chapter 16.

If the retrieved references aren't importing the way you would like, you should compare the filter settings of the connection file to the original text that EndNote receives from the remote database. To do so, choose *Show Connection Status* from the *Window* menu when retrieving references. Set the view in the Status window to show *Record Data* and compare the record data to what is in the filter. This record data is also stored in the log file, Connect.log, which is located by default in the EndNote folder. This file is simply a text file and may be opened in any word processor to view it.

To change the location of the Connect.log file, see "Online Preferences" on page 485.

Creating Connection Files

Before you begin actually creating or modifying a connection file, you must obtain the Z39.50 client configuration instructions for the database you want to access. Contact your librarian or information provider for this information.

If the database is not available on a Z39.50 server, you will not be able to use EndNote's *Connect* feature to access it directly. Follow the instructions in Chapter 7 instead to import references that have been downloaded to text files.

Steps to Create a New Connection File

Once you have the Z39.50 client configuration information in hand, follow these steps to create a new connection file:

Create the File and Enter the Basic Information

1. From the *Edit* menu choose *Connection Files* and select *New Connection File*.

2. The new Connection File window opens to display the *About this Connection* information panel. Enter any comments or descriptions here for your own use. (These comments do not affect how the connection functions.)

3. Click on the *Connection Settings* option and enter the connection information (see "The Connection Settings" on page 461).

4. Click on the *Search Attributes* option to modify the default search attributes if necessary (see "Search Attributes" on page 463).

5. Choose *Save As* from the *File* menu. Name the new connection file and save it in your Connections folder.

Test the Connection and Searching

6. From the *Tools* menu, choose *Connect* and select your new connection file. If the connection cannot be established, check the settings in the *Connection Settings* panel of the connection file, save your changes, and try again.

7. If the connection was established, the Search window should open automatically. Enter a simple search to see if the search

attributes were correctly configured. If the Search doesn't work correctly or it returns an error, check the *Search Attributes* settings in the connection file. (If you modify the connection file at this point, you must save the connection file, then close the Retrieved References window and reconnect in order for your changes to take effect.)

Test the Filtering of Reference Data

8. Once you are able to connect and search, retrieve a dozen or so references to test how accurately they are filtered into the EndNote Reference windows. Double-click a retrieved reference to open it to verify that the data are in the correct fields.

    Note that if you are paying for the references you retrieve, these may not come through correctly, so it is best to retrieve only a few. All references retrieved are saved to a connection log file, so they are not lost. This log file is replaced the next time you run EndNote. See "The Log File" on page 143.

9. If the reference data is not being correctly filtered into the appropriate fields in the EndNote Reference window, you'll need to compare the downloaded data to the filter templates in your connection file.

    Close the Retrieved References window and open the Connect.log file in a word processor to view the original format of the retrieved references. (See "The Log File" on page 143 for information about the Connect.log file.)

    From the *Edit* menu, choose *Connection Files* and select *Edit <Connection File>* to edit the newly created connection file. Look at the *Templates* panel of the connection file and compare the templates there to the reference data in the Connect.log file. Make changes as necessary. See Chapter 16 for information about modifying filters.

Default Values for New Connection Files

When creating a new connection file, a few basic search attributes are entered by default. It is not guaranteed that these will work, as each database may only support its own subset of the Z39.50 attributes.

Consult the Z39.50 client configuration instructions from your information provider or your librarian to set up the connection file correctly for the remote database you want to access.

Default settings for a new connection file are:

Port ID: 210

Element Set Name: F (Full)

Record Syntax: USMARC

Text: ANSEL

Search Fields (Use Attributes): Any Field (1016), Author (1003), Year (31), Title (4), Keywords (21), and Abstract (62).

Filter: USMARC filter settings are used. All references import into the "Book" reference type. See "Filter Information" on page 465 to import into additional reference types.

Using Z39.50 Command-Line Syntax

NOTE: This section is intended only for people who are familiar with Z39.50 terminology and have access to the Z39.50-client configuration information for their remote databases. The advanced search strategies are documented here only for more technical EndNote users; this knowledge is *not* required for basic searching of remote databases.

These command-line searches do not work with PubMed or the ISI Web of Science.

It is possible to set up a search of a remote database that is not supported by the EndNote Search window or the connection file you are using. For instance, if you know about the Z39.50 attributes supported by the remote database, you can enter a Z39.50 search which EndNote passes directly to the server, without any translation. This lets you use searches that aren't already supported by your connection file and is useful for testing various search attribute combinations when creating or modifying a connection file.

These advanced searches are entered directly into the search item just as you would enter a search term. EndNote ignores the search menu for that item when it detects that you've entered an advanced search. If other search terms are needed, enter them into the subsequent search items and select the appropriate "And", "Or", or "Not" connectors (just like any other search).

An advanced search uses the following format:

`\\search term&/ATTRIBUTE TYPE/ATTRIBUTE VALUE`

The first two characters (\ \) tell EndNote this is an advanced search of a remote database. The next part, up to the ampersand, is the search term. The numbers of the Z39.50 attribute type and values follow. They are entered first with a slash and the number for the attribute type, then a slash, and the attribute's value. Repeat that pattern for as many attributes as you want to specify. Not all attributes need to be included. (See "Search Attributes" on page 463.)

The following is a common example that should work for most servers. This should find all references in which the title begins with "child."

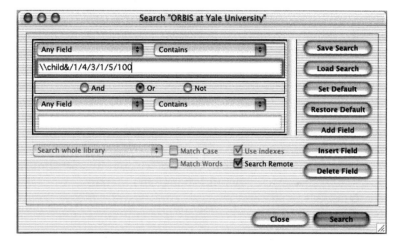

♦ A Use attribute (1) of 4 has been specified, so the search will be restricted to the Title for this database.

♦ A Position attribute (3) of 1 further narrows the search by having the search term be found as the first word in the field.

♦ A Truncation attribute (5) of 100 specifies no truncation at all so only "child" will be seen as a match, and words such as "children" and "childhood" will not.

Tip for Modifying Search Attributes

If you wanted to test how variations of the search attribute settings would impact your search, here's an easy way to do it—without having to edit your connection file.

1. With the connection already established, choose *Show Connection Status* from the *Window* menu. Keep the view set to *Status Messages*.

2. Start with a basic search using the Search window (without the command-line syntax). For example, search for "stress" in the Title field.

3. Look in the Status window, and you'll see which attributes are being used:

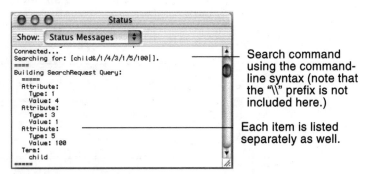

Search command using the command-line syntax (note that the "\\" prefix is not included here.)

Each item is listed separately as well.

Now, you can try out other attribute configurations to see how it would change the search.

4. You can copy the search command out of the Status window, and paste it into the Search window (remember to add the "\\" prefix to identify it as a command-line search), then add or modify the attribute values as necessary.

5. Click *Search* to try out your new combination of attributes.

6. When you have found a combination of search attributes that does what you need, edit your connection file and make those changes to the *Search Attributes* panel.

Chapter 18

Preferences, Toolbars, and Shortcuts

Chapter 18   Preferences, Toolbars, and Shortcuts

EndNote Preferences

The settings for configuring EndNote's display, formatting preferences, and other options are organized in the Preferences section of the EndNote program.

To access the EndNote preferences:

1. From the *EndNote* menu, choose *Preferences*.

2. A list of the available preference panels appears on the left side of the window. Click on the name of a panel in the list that corresponds to the setting you would like to change.

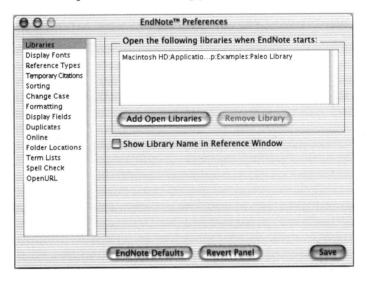

Saving or Discarding Your Changes

All of the preferences panels have the following options:

♦ *EndNote Defaults*: Reverts the settings for just the current panel to the original EndNote settings.

♦ *Revert Panel*: Removes any changes made to the current panel since it was last saved.

♦ *Save*: Saves the changes made to the current panel.

To close the Preferences window, choose *Close Preferences* (⌘-W) from the *File* menu or click the red close button in the upper left corner of the window. If you haven't saved your changes before closing the Preferences window, EndNote will alert you and give you the option to save the settings.

Library Preferences

Setting Default Libraries

Use the Libraries preferences section to specify which libraries should open by default when EndNote starts. To add a library to this list:

1. If the library is not already open, open it by choosing *Open* from the *File* menu, and selecting the desired library.

2. Return to the Library section of the Preferences dialog, and click the *Add Open Libraries* button to add all open libraries to the list.

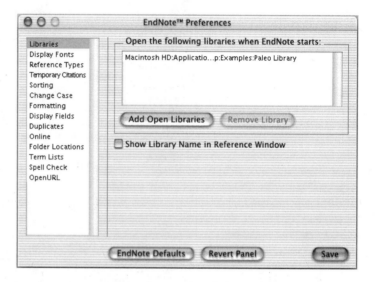

To remove a library from this list, simply select it in the Libraries panel, and click *Remove Library*.

Displaying the Library Name with Each Reference

Click the option to "Show Library Name in Reference Window" if you want the library name to appear at the top of each Reference window, as shown below.

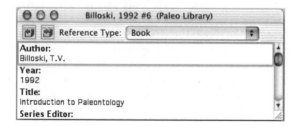

Display Fonts

The *Display Fonts* panel gives you the option of changing the font that EndNote uses to display much of the text throughout the program. The Library Display Font determines the font and size of the references listed in the Library window. The General Display Font changes the font used to display all other text that is typed into EndNote (such as in the Reference or Style windows). The General Display Font is also used for most of the previews and information panels in EndNote, as well as for bibliographies that are printed or copied directly from EndNote.

Changes made to the display fonts apply to all EndNote libraries opened on that computer. They do not affect the font used when you are formatting bibliographies in a word processing document. The normal font of the document is used for that.

To change the library display font:

1. From the *EndNote* menu, choose *Preferences*.

2. Click the *Display Fonts* option in the list.

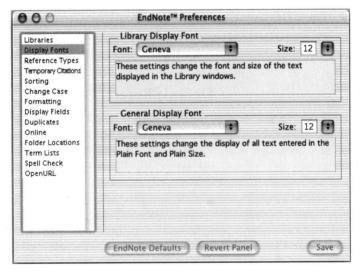

3. In either the Library Display Font or the General Display Font section: Select a different display font and/or size from the *Font* and *Size* lists.

4. Click *Save* to save the changes, and then close the Preferences window by clicking the red close button in the upper left corner.

Reference Types

Use the *Reference Types* preferences panel to customize your settings for the fields (such as Author, Year, and Title) and reference types (such as Journal Article or Book) that are used by EndNote. Any changes that you make in this panel apply to all of the libraries that open on the computer.

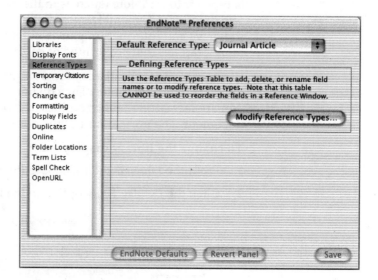

Default Reference Type

When you create a new reference in your EndNote library (by choosing *New* from the *References* menu), the new reference is set up for a journal article by default. If you would rather have new references automatically appear as books, patents, or some other reference type, change the "Default References Type" setting:

◆ Click the *Default Reference Type* list and choose from one of the available reference types.

If you need a reference type that is not in the list, you will need to create a new reference type for it and define it yourself (see "Adding and Deleting Reference Types" on page 351).

Defining Reference Types

If you need to modify any of EndNote's fields or reference types, click the *Modify Reference Types* button. This opens the EndNote Reference Types table where you can add, delete, and rename EndNote's reference types and fields.

See Chapter 14 for more information about reference types and how to customize them.

Temporary Citations

A "temporary citation" is an unformatted citation that EndNote inserts into your word processing document when you use the *Find Citation(s)* or *Insert Citation(s)* command from Word's *Tools* menu, or when you *Copy* and *Paste* a citation into a document. You can also type temporary citations into your document. The temporary citation is a placeholder that EndNote later changes to a "formatted" citation, such as "(Smith & Jones, 1999)."

By default a temporary citation includes the first author's last name, the year, and the EndNote record number, enclosed in curly braces:

```
{Smith, 1999 #24}
```

If necessary, you can change the temporary citation delimiters using the settings in this panel.

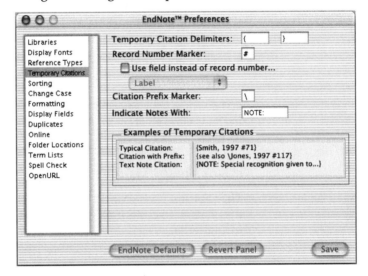

Temporary Citation Delimiters

Curly braces are used by default to indicate the start and end of each temporary citation. If you commonly use curly braces in your writing, you might want to select a different pair of markers for EndNote to use as Temporary Citation Delimiters.

Enter the desired markers into the appropriate boxes at the top of the Temporary Citations preferences panel.

NOTE: When EndNote 4 users upgrade to EndNote 7, the EndNote 4 default delimiters migrate to EndNote 7. The default delimiters in EndNote 4 were square brackets [].

Record Number Marker

The number sign (#) always precedes the record number in an EndNote temporary citation. You may change this by entering another character in the Record Number Marker box.

The EndNote record number is a unique number assigned to each reference as it is added to a library. The number is specific to that reference in that particular library. If you are collaborating with other writers who have their own EndNote libraries (or do not have an EndNote library at all), you might find it easier to replace the Record Number in the temporary citation with something that uniquely identifies the reference but isn't specific to your EndNote library. To do so, select the "Use field instead of record number" option and select from either the Accession Number field or the Label field.

♦ The Accession Number field is designed to contain the unique record number assigned to a reference from an online database.

♦ The Label field can be used to manually enter any unique code that you would like to use for each record.

NOTE: If you have selected the Accession Number field or Label field, and that field is empty in a particular reference, the Record Number will appear in the temporary citation.

Citation Prefix Marker

The Citation Prefix Marker separates prefix text in a citation from the citation itself. For example, if you wanted a citation formatted as:

        (see also Smith, 1999)

you would enter the text into the temporary citation as follows, with the "\" indicating the end of the prefix text and the start of the citation:

        {see also \Smith, 1999 #24}

If you prefer to use a different character as the Citation Prefix Delimiter, you may enter it in this preferences panel. Semicolons (;), letters, numbers, and characters already used as other delimiters may not be used for the Citation Prefix Delimiter.

NOTE: When you use Cite While You Write's *Edit Citation* command to add prefix text, the Citation Prefix Marker is automatically inserted as part of the temporary citation.

Including Notes in the List of References

Some journal styles (such as Science) permit you to include notes with the list of works cited at the end of the document. In such a system, the notes are numbered just like the citations, and included in the reference list in the order of appearance, just like the references.

To identify text to be included as a numbered note in the reference list:

1. Type the text into the body of your document where you would want the number for the note to appear.

2. Be sure to surround the entire section of text with your Temporary Citation Delimiters (curly braces by default), and begin it with "NOTE:". For example:

```
{NOTE: The authors would like to acknowledge
the support of...}
```

When the paper is formatted by EndNote using a numbered style, the text is assigned a number and listed along with the references at the end of the paper.

NOTE: With Cite While You Write, you can simply go to Word's *Tools* menu, go to the *EndNote 7* submenu, and choose *Insert Note*.

The way that these notes are identified may be changed in the Temporary Citations preferences. Enter a prefix that you'd like to use to signal that the text should be treated as a note.

Important Restrictions on the Use of the "NOTE" Feature

◆ This feature requires that a numbered style be used for the formatting; otherwise, the note will be left as it was entered in the body of the text.

◆ Enter text only. Do not attempt to insert graphics, equations, or symbols as note text.

◆ Do not use the temporary citation delimiters as part of the text of the note. Other markers, such as the record number marker and the prefix marker and the multiple citation separator may be used.

◆ These types of notes cannot be combined with regular temporary citations within the same set of brackets. They should be cited separately—each in its own set of brackets.

Sorting

When EndNote sorts author names and titles, you can identify what words or names to ignore for sorting purposes.

To add words to be ignored for sorting:

♦ Enter the term in the text box below either the "Author Fields" or "Title Fields" prompt, and click *Add*.

To remove a term from either list:

♦ Select the term and click *Remove*.

Click *EndNote Defaults* to revert both lists to the default settings.

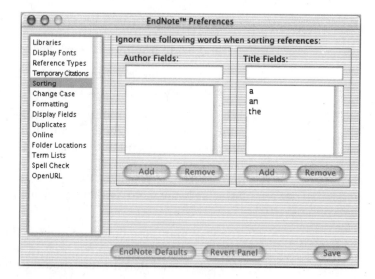

Authors

The Author Fields list is designed so that you may enter parts of author names that may be omitted for sorting purposes. For example, prepositions in names such as "von," "van," and "de" are included as part of the last name, but not considered part of the name for sorting purposes. The entries in the Author Fields list are case sensitive; that is, if you enter "von" it applies only to "von" and not "Von." These settings apply to the Generic fields for Author, Secondary Author, Tertiary Author, and Subsidiary Author. No names are entered by default.

Titles

When terms are added to the Title Fields list, the sorting routine ignores them when they appear at the start of the title. Capitalization does not matter for these words. That is, the word "the" can be entered (lowercase) and still apply to "The." These settings apply to the Generic fields for Title, Secondary Title (includes the Journal field), Tertiary Title, and Subsidiary Title. The words "a," "an," and "the" are entered as defaults.

Where is this information saved?

The lists of terms entered into the *Sorting* preferences panel are stored in the Users: [Your Folder]: Library: Preferences: EndNote *f* folder. The file is "EndNote Sort Words." For a quick way to duplicate the lists for another Macintosh running EndNote 7, copy this file to the same location on the other Macintosh. For another user account on the same machine, copy the file to the other user's EndNote *f* folder.

Change Case

The EndNote styles can be configured to change the capitalization of the author names or titles. Use the *Change Case* preferences to list the words that should not be modified when EndNote changes the case of titles or authors. This would commonly be used for special acronyms, equations, or compound names that require consistent capitalization.

To add words to the list:

♦   Enter the term in the text box at the top of the dialog, and click *Add*.

To remove an item from the list:

♦   Select the term and click *Remove*.

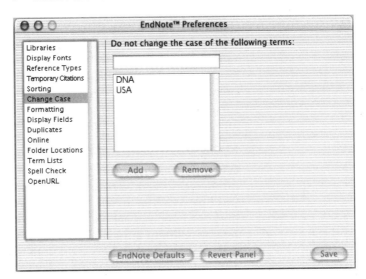

Where is this information saved?

The list of terms entered into the *Change Case* preferences panel is stored in the Users: [Your Folder]: Library: Preferences: EndNote *f* folder. The file is "EndNote Case Words." For a quick way to duplicate the list for another user running EndNote 7, copy this file to the same location on the other Macintosh. You can also copy it to another user account on the same machine.

Formatting

The Formatting preferences panel contains the following options:

Suggest formatting with EndNote's Cite While You Write/Add-in if the document type is supported

While the RTF Document Scan feature can be used on most word processor files, we recommend that you always use Cite While You Write for Word documents. It is much easier and allows more control and options to give you the exact output you want.

When this item is selected, and you attempt to use RTF Document Scan on a document that could be formatted with Cite While You Write, a message will appear recommending that you use Cite While You Write. You *can* still use RTF Document Scan if you wish.

Omit Author and/or Year from Formatted Citation if Removed from Temporary Citation

EndNote's default behavior is to remove the author or year from the formatted citation if you remove either of those items from a temporary (unformatted) citation. For example, "{, 1999 #24}" would format as just "(1999)" when using a style that creates (Author, Year) citations. If you prefer to type just the record number into your papers as the temporary citation, you should turn this preference off so EndNote will not remove the author and year from all of your formatted citations.

Merge Duplicates in Bibliography

When this option is selected, EndNote automatically omits duplicate references from a bibliography. It is a good idea to use this option if you are citing references from multiple EndNote libraries in one paper. In this situation, the same journal article reference might appear in two libraries and would have two different record numbers. EndNote will not identify the records as duplicates unless you have this option set to merge duplicates.

When this option is selected, EndNote checks the bibliography for duplicate references during the formatting process. If duplicates are found, they are removed. References are considered duplicates if they are the same reference type (such as Journal Article or Book) and the following fields are identical: Author, Year, Title, Secondary Title (Journal, Newspaper, Magazine, Book Title, Series Title, Conference Name, etc.), Volume, Issue, and Pages.

NOTE: The *Duplicates* preference settings do not apply to this feature. The criteria for determining duplicates is fixed for the "Merge Duplicates in Bibliography" setting.

Display Fields

Use the *Display Fields* preferences to choose which fields to display in EndNote's Library window. These settings apply to all libraries opened on the computer.

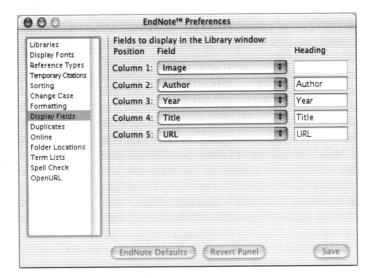

Choose the desired field from each *Field* list. You may select up to five fields to be displayed in the Library window. To show fewer than five fields, select *Unused* instead of a field name.

By default, the column heading in the Library window is the same as the Generic name of the field (except for the Image field, which is headed by a paper clip icon). If you would like to change the name for the Library window display, enter a new name in the Heading section next to the chosen field.

EndNote defaults to showing first a column indicating whether an image is attached to each record, then the first Author, Year, and Title in each record, and last the URL field.

Duplicates

The *Duplicates* preferences panel corresponds to the *Find Duplicates* command in the *References* menu (that command is described on page 190).

By default, EndNote identifies duplicate references in a library as references of the same reference type with matching Author, Year, and Title fields. Use this panel to customize the way EndNote identifies duplicate references.

♦ To select the fields that EndNote should compare when finding duplicate references, click in the check boxes to the left of the field names.

The "Generic" names of the fields are used here. For details about what the Generic field names correspond to for each reference type, see page 355. You may select as many fields as you want to make the duplicate detection more or less stringent.

Criteria

You may also set the "Criteria" to have EndNote compare the fields and look for an exact match or be more lenient in the comparison and ignore spacing and punctuation.

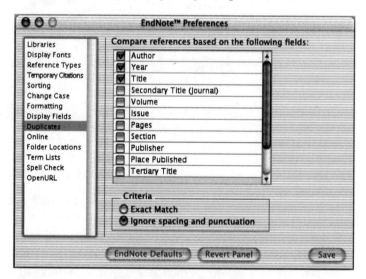

NOTE: These settings do not apply to the "Merge Duplicates in Bibliography" setting (page 482). That specific comparison of reference data is used only to remove identical references from bibliographies.

Online Preferences

Web Browser Settings

Use the *Online* preferences panel to select the Web browser that should open when the *Open Link* command is activated or when you click on an active URL (Internet address).

◆ To select a Web browser, click *Choose*, locate the Web browser on your hard drive, and click *Open*. (EndNote does not include a Web browser.)

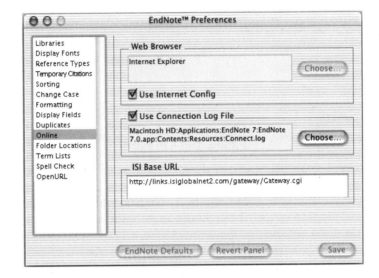

Click "Use Internet Config" to have EndNote use the browser settings stored in Internet Config (not included with EndNote).

Connection Log File

When you use the *Connect* command to connect to a remote database, EndNote keeps a copy of all of the retrieved references for that session in the connection log file (the file name is "Connect.log"). This happens by default, but you may turn this option off by unchecking the "Use Connection Log File" option.

We recommend keeping the option turned on because in the event that the references were not correctly retrieved or filtered into EndNote, you can always adjust the filter in the connection file, and import the Connect.log file instead of redoing the search and download (see page 144).

By default, the Connect.log file is stored in the same folder as the EndNote program. You may change the name and the location of the Connect.log file by clicking the *Choose* button. In the dialog that appears, enter a new name for the file (if desired), and select the new location for the file.

ISI Base URL

When you export references from the ISI Web of Science to EndNote, EndNote creates a "Go to ISI" link in the URL field of each reference. These links take you back to the ISI source record where you can find related references, times cited, and other information. If your institution uses a locally mounted version of Web of Science, you should enter the URL for that server here in EndNote's ISI Base URL preference. Otherwise, the links in references downloaded from Web of Science will take you to the main Web of Science server where you might not have access.

Folder Locations

The *Folder Locations* preferences panel is where you set the default location of your styles, import filters, and connection files. By default, EndNote sets these locations to be the Styles, Filters, and Connections folders in the EndNote folder.

All of the style, filter, or connection files stored in the chosen folders are displayed in the Style, Filter, and Connection Managers. These Managers allow you to select individual files that you use most with EndNote.

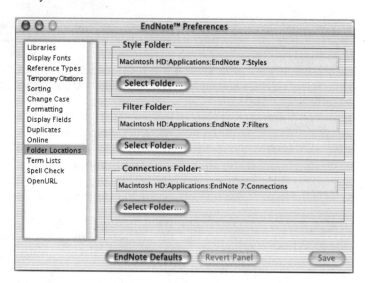

To change any of these folder locations, click the *Select Folder* button, select or open the folder that you would like to designate as the new Style, Filter, or Connection folder, and click *Choose*.

Term Lists

By default, every new EndNote library has three term lists associated with it: Authors, Journals, and Keywords. The term lists are automatically updated as you enter references into your library. The terms in these lists are also used to facilitate data entry using the "Suggest Terms as You Type" feature. This feature suggests terms as you type into fields with term lists linked to them. For example, as you type into the Author field, EndNote suggests author names from your Authors term list to help you with data entry. When you enter a new term that is not currently in the associated term list, it appears in red text to indicate that it is a new term. This can point out typing mistakes or the use of an incorrect keyword if you thought you were entering a name or a term commonly used in your library. More information about working with term lists is provided in Chapter 9.

Any of the term list settings described above can be turned off using the settings for the *Term Lists* preferences.

Suggest Terms as You Type (Auto-Completion)

When selected, EndNote will automatically complete matching terms when you are typing into a field that is linked to a term list (see page 215).

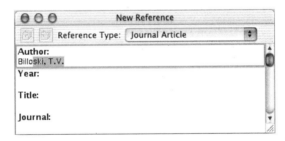

If you turn this feature off, you may still insert terms into a field by opening the desired term list from the *Tools* menu, or by typing ⌘ +1 and double-clicking the desired term.

Update lists when importing or pasting references

When this option is selected, the term lists are automatically updated as you import references (using the *Import* command from the *File* menu), drag-and-drop references, or *Paste* references in to your library. If you turn this option off, you can always manually update your term lists by selecting *Define Term Lists* from the *Tools* menu, highlighting a term list, and clicking *Update List* (see "Manually Updating Term Lists" on page 211).

Update lists during data entry

When this option is selected, the term lists are automatically updated as you type in new reference data. If you turn this option off, you can always manually update your term lists by selecting *Define Term Lists* from the *Tools* menu, highlighting a term list, and clicking *Update List* (see "Manually Updating Term Lists" on page 211).

Spell Check

On the Spell Check preferences panel, you can set general spell check *Options* and select or modify *Dictionaries*. For general information about how to start spell checking a record, see "Spell Checking" on page 122.

General Options

You can access these Spell Check Options from the EndNote Preferences Spell Check panel or from the dialog that appears when you run Spell Check. Click the *Options* button.

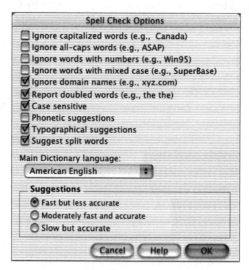

1. Select the check box next to each item you want to apply during spell checking.

2. Select a Main Dictionary language from the list of available dictionaries.

   For each language, EndNote uses a combination of dictionary files located in EndNotes's Spell folder. Select your primary language. If you want to apply additional language dictionaries, see the next section, "Modifying Dictionaries".

3. Decide how fast and accurate you want spell checking to work.

4. Click *OK* to save the changes.

NOTE: For a complete description of each item on the Options dialog, click the *Help* button on the dialog.

Modifying Dictionaries

You can access the Dictionaries preferences from the EndNote Preferences Spell Check panel or from the dialog that appears when you run Spell Check. Click the *Dictionaries* button.

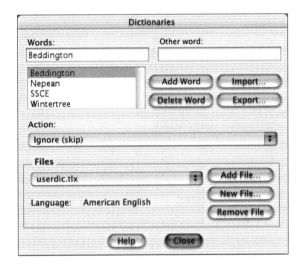

Use this dialog to view or edit the content of existing dictionaries, to add existing dictionaries for use, to create new dictionaries, and to remove dictionaries. The dictionaries listed under Files are currently in use (in addition to the Main Dictionary selected under Options).

NOTE: For a complete description of each option on the Dictionaries dialog, click the *Help* button on the dialog.

To modify dictionaries:

1. Under *Files*, select the dictionary file you want to view or modify.

   ♦ If it is already in the list, simply select it.

   ♦ If you need to locate an existing file to use, use the *Add File* button to locate the file on your computer and add it to the list. By default, dictionaries are kept in EndNote's Spell folder.

   ♦ To create a new dictionary, click *New File*.

   ♦ To remove a dictionary, display the file name in the list and click *Remove File*. This removes a dictionary from use, but doesn't delete the actual disk file.

2. The words in the selected dictionary appear in the top list.

   ♦ To add a word to the selected dictionary, type it under Words and click *Add Word*.

   ♦ To delete a word from the selected dictionary, select the word and click *Delete Word*.

   ♦ To change the Action applied to a word, select the word and then pick the new Action from the list.

Adding an Existing Dictionary

You may have selected English (or a different language) as your Main Dictionary Language, but want to apply an additional language during spell checking.

1. On the Dictionaries dialog, click the *Add File* button.

2. In EndNote's Spell folder, locate the dictionary file you want to use and Open it. The dictionary is added to the list under Files.

NOTE: For a list of supplied dictionaries with corresponding file names, see "Dictionaries Supplied with EndNote" on page 491.

Importing/Exporting a Dictionary

The Dictionaries dialog includes *Import* and *Export* buttons.

Use *Import* to locate and import a plain text file of terms into the current dictionary. The text file should contain a list of terms, with each term on its own line.

Use *Export* to save all terms from a dictionary to a plain text file, where each term starts on a new line.

Dictionaries Supplied with EndNote

These dictionaries are supplied with EndNote. When you select the main dictionary language, a combination of files are loaded, including files not listed here.

When you want to add additional languages, find the Dictionary you want to use from the left column, then look for the corresponding File Name. When you *Add* a dictionary, look for the appropriate File Name in EndNote's Spell folder.

Dictionary	File Name
User Dictionary: Contains English words that include non-ASCII characters	accent.tlx
User Dictionary: Contains common English misspellings and their correct replacements for auto correction	correct.tlx
User Dictionary: Sample user dictionary	userdic.tlx
American English	ssceam.tlx
American English Medical	sscema.tlx
British English	sscebr.tlx
British English Medical	sscemb.tlx
Danish	ssceda.tlx
Dutch	sscedu.tlx
Finnish	sscefi.tlx
French (European and Canadian)	sscefr.tlx
German	sscege.tlx
Italian	ssceit.tlx
Norwegian (Bokmal)	sscenb.tlx
Portuguese (Brazilian)	sscepb.tlx
Portuguese (Iberian)	sscepo.tlx
Spanish	sscesp.tlx
Swedish	sscesw.tlx

OpenURL

The *OpenURL Link* command on the *References* menu starts your default web browser and displays related record links in the browser window. It connects to an OpenURL standard syntax server and uses these OpenURL preferences along with data in your EndNote record to find related online references.

NOTE: This command has no relation to the URL field found in EndNote references or the *Open Link* command on the *References* menu.

The OpenURL preferences panel includes these settings:

Enable OpenURL: Select the check box to enable the OpenURL link option found on the EndNote *References* menu. The OpenURL Link command is available only when it is enabled here and a reference is open for viewing. By default, this feature is disabled.

The next two options on the OpenURL panel are available only when the Enable OpenURL box is selected.

OpenURL Path: EndNote supplies a default path for your browser, linking to an ISI server. If you have access to a different OpenURL server, you should enter that path here.

Arguments: We include a default argument to search for related online records. You can use this argument as a syntax example if you wish to enter your own arguments here.

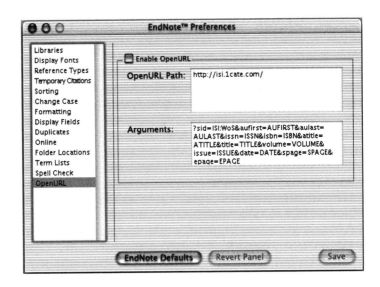

NOTE: Remember, you can revert back to the EndNote defaults at any time by clicking *EndNote Defaults*.

Cite While You Write Preferences

You can access the Cite While You Write preferences in one of two ways:

♦ From the *Tools>EndNote* menu in your word processor, select *Cite While You Write Preferences*

♦ From EndNote's *Tools* menu, go to the *Cite While You Write* submenu and select *CWYW Preferences*

Several EndNote preferences also directly affect Cite While You Write.

General Preferences

General preferences are useful when you always use your EndNote library along with your word processor, and you always use your word processor along with your EndNote library.

To access General preferences, go to your word processor's *Tools>EndNote* menu and select *Cite While You Write Preferences*.

Open EndNote When Starting Word

Select this item to always open EndNote when you start your word processor.

Close EndNote When Leaving Word

Select this item to always close EndNote when you leave your word processor. This works only when the EndNote program was launched with one of the Cite While You Write commands from your word processor's *Tools>EndNote* menu or if the *Open EndNote When Starting Word* preference is selected.

Return to Document After Inserting Citations

Select this item to always make your document the active window after inserting citations with EndNote's *Insert Selected Citation(s)* command. If this preference is turned off so that the Word document remains in the background, you will not see the inserted citation in the Word document until the document becomes the active window. This is because the display for the Word document is not updated in the background.

Enable Instant Formatting on new Word documents

This option is available for Cite While You Write. It turns Instant Formatting on or off for new Word documents. When you enable Instant Formatting, you can also determine how often EndNote scans for temporary citations and whether it checks for citation changes in existing citations.

To turn instant formatting on or off in an *existing* Word document, see "Instant Formatting" on page 263.

Keyboard Shortcuts in Word

Keyboard shortcuts for EndNote's Cite While You Write commands are available in Word.

To add or change a keyboard shortcut:

1. From Word's *Tools>EndNote* menu, select *Cite While You Write Preferences*.

2. Click the Keyboard tab.

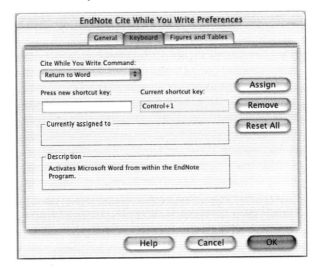

3. From the list of commands, select the command for which you would like to add (or change) a shortcut.

4. Under "Press new shortcut key," enter the new shortcut key combination on the keyboard.

   Keyboard shortcuts work in both EndNote and Microsoft Word.

   We suggest using a key combination that includes the COMMAND and CONTROL keys because they are not normally used together for Word commands.

   If you enter a key command that is already assigned to a Cite While You Write or EndNote Add–in command, EndNote will note which command it is currently assigned to. EndNote does not alert you if you assign a keyboard shortcut that was previously used by another Microsoft Word command.

5. Click *Assign* to assign the new shortcut.

Follow the same steps to remove an assigned shortcut key, except click *Remove* instead of *Assign*.

Click *Reset All* to remove custom key assignments.

Figures and Tables in Word

Use settings in the output style to determine whether images are placed in-text or at the end of the document, where captions and labels are located, and separation and punctuation around images and captions. See "Figure and Table Placement and Captions" on page 407.

The figures and tables settings in Microsoft Word override settings from the current output style. If your output style is set to print figures and tables in a list at the end of the document, the settings on this tab are ignored. However, if your output style is set to print figures and tables in-text, you can use this tab to override settings when you have moved figures around in your document and want to retain their placement.

To customize the in-text placement of EndNote figures and tables in Word.

1. From Word's *Tools* menu, select *Cite While You Write Preferences*.

2. Select the Figures and Tables tab.

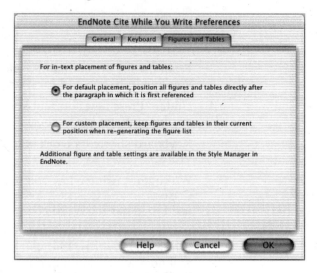

3. Select the appropriate radio button to:

   ♦ Place each figure or table directly after the paragraph where it is first referenced, or

◆ When re-generating figures, keep each figure or table in its current position. This allows you to move images around in your document and have them stay there when you Generate Figure List again.

Showing Word Processor Codes

The formatted citations and bibliography in your document are not plain text; they contain hidden data that make it possible for EndNote to unformat and reformat citations and bibliographies.

Microsoft Word's Field Shading

Formatted citations and bibliographies in Word documents are Microsoft Word fields. This gives EndNote the ability to uniquely identify them.

When you click on a field in Word (such as a formatted EndNote citation or the bibliography), it becomes shaded. You can change this behavior so that the fields are always shaded, shaded only when selected, or never shaded. To do so, choose Preferences from the *Word* menu and select the View item to see the options for field shading.

Related EndNote Preferences

Several other EndNote preferences directly affect Cite While You Write. To access EndNote preferences, go to the *Edit* menu in EndNote and select *Preferences*.

The related preference dialogs include settings for:

◆ *Temporary Citations*, described on page 477

◆ *Formatting*, described on page 482

These settings are stored with the EndNote program's preferences because they apply to formatting papers with either Cite While You Write or the EndNote Add-in.

Shortcuts to Make Using EndNote Easier

Contextual menus and toolbars can streamline your database building and citation processes.

To add or change Cite While You Write keyboard shortcuts in Microsoft Word, see "Keyboard Shortcuts in Word" on page 495.

Contextual Menus

As a convenience, EndNote provides contextual, or shortcut, menus for some of the most commonly used features. Contextual menus appear when you hold down the CONTROL key and click on something in the EndNote program (such as the Library window, or the Author field).

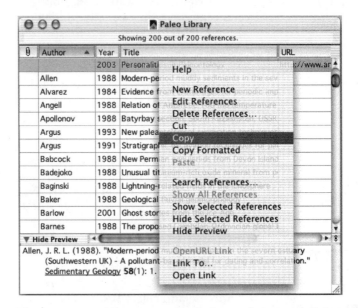

The contents of the menu depend on where you click and what options are available for that particular item. Only a subset of possible commands are displayed; these are intended to represent the most commonly used functions for the selected target. Choosing a command from the contextual menus has exactly the same results as choosing the command from the main menu or the toolbar.

A contextual menu appears wherever you click. It remains open until you choose a command from the list, click elsewhere, or press ESC.

Contextual menus are available for the following windows: references, libraries, term lists, search, retrieved references, and Managers (styles, filters, and connections).

Toolbars

Toolbars are available in EndNote to give you quick access to some of the commonly used commands. There are several toolbars (Main, Text, and CWYW); each is described below. To display a particular toolbar, choose *Show Toolbar* from the *Tools* menu, and select the desired toolbar to show. If a toolbar is currently showing, it will have a check mark next to its name in the *Show Toolbar* menu. At that point, choosing it from the *Show Toolbar* command will hide it.

Main Toolbar

Commands on the main toolbar include (from left to right): *New Library, Open Library, Print, Cut, Copy, Paste, Search, Sort References, New Reference, Connect, Open Link, Import, Export, Spell Check* (available when a record is open for editing), *Insert Picture, Insert Object*, a current style menu, and *Help*.

The style menu lists all the styles you have marked as "favorites" in the Style Manager, and displays the one that is currently selected to be used for the Library window preview, *Copy Formatted*, printing, exporting, or any formatting. If you do not see the style that you want in this menu, you can choose *Select Another Style* from the bottom of the menu to pick a new style. See also "The Style Manager" on page 364.

Text Toolbar

The text toolbar displays EndNote's text font and text size menus to change the font and size of the text in a reference or style. The buttons on the toolbar are (from left to right): *Bold, Italic, Underline, Plain Text, Superscript, Subscript,* and *Symbol* font. If a button is "pressed" that indicates that the text style represented by that button has been applied to the text that is selected (or where the cursor blinking).

CWYW Toolbar

The CWYW toolbar is available only when Microsoft Word is running and Cite While You Write support is installed. The commands on the toolbar are (from left to right): *Insert Citation(s), Format Bibliography,* and *Return to Word Processor*.

A complete CWYW toolbar is available within Word. See "The Cite While You Write Commands" on page 233.

Chapter 19

Using EndNote With Palm OS Handhelds

Chapter 19   Using EndNote with Palm OS Handhelds

Overview of Using EndNote with Palm OS Handheld Devices

The EndNote application for Palm OS® handheld devices uses a format that supports all of the reference types and fields used in the desktop EndNote application.

You can enter EndNote references into your desktop version of EndNote and/or into your handheld device. You can then synchronize files between your desktop EndNote library and your handheld EndNote library using standard HotSync® commands.

You can also beam individual references to another Palm OS handheld.

Installing EndNote for Palm OS

Installing your EndNote for Palm OS involves several steps. First, make sure you meet the hardware and software requirements. Then, follow the instructions for "Installing EndNote for Palm OS".

Hardware and Software Requirements

Requirements for running EndNote for the Palm Operating System include:

◆ Handheld device from Palm, Inc. (e.g. Tungsten series, Zire series, m series)

◆ Palm Operating System 4 to 5.2

◆ Communication port for HotSync operations

◆ 4 MB RAM

Installing EndNote for Palm OS

Installing your EndNote for Palm OS involves several steps. First, make sure you meet the hardware and software requirements listed in the previous section. Then, you must:

1. Check your HotSync connection to make sure it is working.

2. Install the EndNote Palm OS software.

3. Designate a single EndNote library for synchronizing.

4. Perform an initial HotSync operation to copy EndNote software to the handheld device, and then perform a second HotSync operation to copy the EndNote library to the handheld device.

First, check your HotSync connection:

Before you begin, make sure your Palm OS handheld application software is installed. Perform a HotSync operation to make sure you are able to send files between your Palm desktop application and your Palm OS handheld device.

Then, install EndNote Palm OS software:

It is best to install your Palm software (the application software that came with your handheld device) *before* installing or updating to EndNote 7. As you install EndNote, you will be asked whether you want to install the EndNote for Palm OS software.

NOTE: You may have already installed the Palm OS software when you installed EndNote! Look for the EndNote for Palm OS application on your Palm handheld device.

If you installed EndNote 7 and *then* installed your Palm application software, go to the folder Applications:EndNote 7:Palm, double-click on ENPalmInstaller, and follow the instructions to install the EndNote for Palm OS software.

In EndNote, designate a library for HotSync operations:

1. From the *Tools* menu in EndNote, select *Configure Handheld Sync*.

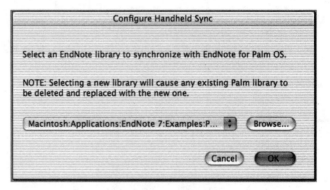

2. Select an EndNote library from the existing drop-down list or use the *Browse* button to locate your EndNote library.

3. Click *OK* to save the setting.

NOTE: You can update your Palm device with only a single library. If you perform a HotSync operation with a new library, any existing library on your Palm device will be replaced.

Use the HotSync Manager to set up your handheld device:

Perform an initial HotSync Operation to copy EndNote for Palm OS software to your handheld device. (For information about how to use the HotSync Manager, see the "Synchronizing Libraries" section that appears below.)

Then, perform a HotSync operation again to copy your EndNote library to your handheld device.

Synchronizing Libraries

Use standard HotSync instructions to synchronize your desktop EndNote library and your handheld EndNote library. For example, by pressing the HotSync button on a cradle or cable, or by using the HotSync application on the handheld:

A HotSync operation cannot be initiated from within EndNote. See your handheld device documentation for additional information about performing a HotSync operation.

The first time you synchronize your desktop EndNote library with your handheld device, the EndNote for Palm OS is copied to your handheld device. Subsequent HotSync operations synchronize the designated library.

NOTE: The handheld library must reside in main Palm memory; you cannot save a library to an expansion card.

Notes about Synchronization:

♦ You can synchronize your handheld library to a single desktop PC.

♦ You can designate a single EndNote library to synchronize with your Palm OS handheld. In EndNote, go to the *Tools* menu, select *Configure Handheld Sync*, and use the dialog to select a library.

♦ By default, a HotSync operation will synchronize the EndNote desktop library and handheld library, so that new references will appear in both libraries and edited references will be updated in both libraries. However, if you edit the same reference in the desktop library *and* the handheld library, neither record will be overwritten. A second, almost duplicate record will be created.

◆ You cannot copy only selected references to your handheld device; the entire designated library is synchronized. If you want to copy only a limited number of references to your handheld device, first copy those references to a smaller desktop EndNote library, designate that library in EndNote with *Configure Handheld Sync*, and then synchronize your handheld device with that interim library.

◆ If you want to enter references on your handheld, but not maintain the full desktop library on your handheld, use a smaller, interim library for synchronization. Enter your references on the handheld device, synchronize to the small desktop library, then copy the references from the small library to your full EndNote library. You can change HotSync settings to always overwrite the interim library with your Handheld library.

◆ Only the name of the image is displayed in an image field on your handheld device. The image name is locked (you cannot edit it) so that the file attachment in the desktop library will remain intact. Images cannot be added on the handheld. If you delete a reference with an image from your handheld device, synchronizing will delete both the reference and its corresponding image from the desktop library.

Starting EndNote for Palm OS and Displaying References

To start EndNote for Palm OS and open the EndNote library:

1. On your handheld device, list the Applications available and tap on the EndNote icon.

EndNote displays the name of the designated library.

2. Highlight the library name and tap *Open* to display the reference list (or select *Open* from the *EndNote>Library* menu).

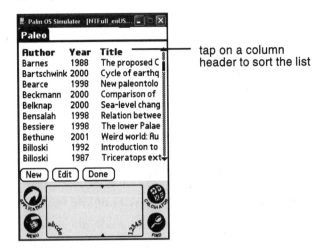

tap on a column header to sort the list

A reference list appears, displaying the first author's last name, the year, and the first title of each reference in the library.

Notes about the reference list:

◆ The title bar shows the name of the current library.

◆ The first author, year, and title are each truncated to fit within its column.

◆ Tap on a column header to sort the list by that column of information. Tap the same column header again to switch between ascending and descending order. This is a simple alphabetic sort that may not display in exactly the same order as your desktop library. Author names are not manipulated, and initial articles are not ignored in titles.

◆ To jump to a particular reference, enter characters with the Palm keyboard or text pad to scroll to that text in the current sort order. For example, in a library sorted by author, entering "DON" could scroll the list to "Donnelly."

◆ Tap on a row to select it. Select multiple rows by tapping on each one. Tap again to deselect a row. To deselect all rows, tap below the list of references, to the right of the *Done* button.

◆ To create a new reference, tap the *New* button.

◆ To open a reference for viewing or editing, tap twice on the row. Or, highlight the reference and tap *Edit*.

Viewing Library Statistics

To view statistics about the EndNote library on your handheld device:

1. Start the EndNote for Palm OS application on your handheld device.

2. Highlight the name of your library.

3. Tap the *EndNote* menu, then the *Library* menu, then *Info* to display statistics about the highlighted database, including the date created, the date modified, the file size, and the number of records found in the library.

Entering, Editing, and Deleting References

To enter a new EndNote reference on your handheld device:

1. Display the EndNote library reference list.

2. Tap *New* to display a New Reference template.

3. Use the drop down list to select a reference type.

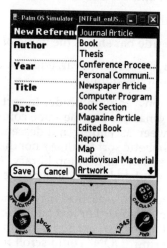

4. Enter your text into the appropriate fields. See "Notes about entering and editing references" on page 509 for more information about this display.

5. Tap *Save* to add the reference to your handheld EndNote library.

To edit or delete a reference on your handheld device:

1. With the reference list displayed, tap to highlight the reference you want to edit or delete.

2. Tap the library name in the title bar and display the *Reference* menu.

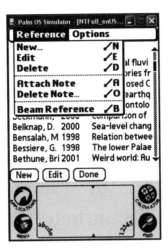

3. From the *Reference* menu, select:

   ◆ *Edit* to open the highlighted reference for viewing or editing

   ◆ *Delete* to delete the highlighted reference

   These additional commands are also available:

   ◆ *New* to create a new reference

   ◆ *Attach Note* to add text to the Note field of the highlighted reference

   ◆ *Delete Note* to delete text from the Note field of the highlighted reference.

Notes about entering and editing references:

◆ The title bar displays as much as possible of the first author's last name, year, and reference number.

◆ The drop-down list in the top right corner displays the current reference type. Tap on the arrow to show the complete list of reference types and select one.

◆ Use the up and down scroll arrows to scroll and/or navigate through records, depending on the setting under Preferences (See "EndNote Preferences" on page 511).

- Use the left and right navigation arrows to browse through references in the current sort order. (The navigation arrows are not available when you are creating a new record.)

- Up to three lines are displayed for each field of data. You can edit those three lines directly. However, if a field contains more than three lines of information, tap on the field to open a full-screen display (where you can view and edit the entire field).

- To access standard editing commands, first put the cursor within a field. Then, tap the library name in the title bar, then the *Edit* menu.

- Tap the *Note* button to easily add text to the Note field in the reference.

- To delete a note, tap the title bar, then the *Reference* menu, then *Delete Note*.

- The Palm OS "Private" record feature is not available.

Searching a Handheld Library

To jump to a particular reference in the reference list:

Enter characters with the Palm keyboard or text pad to scroll to that text in the current sort order. For example, in a library sorted by author, entering "DON" could scroll the list to "Donnelly."

To search by keyword:

1. Use the Find icon (magnifying glass) on your Palm device to search for keywords. With your EndNote reference list displayed, tap the Find icon to display the Find dialog.

2. Enter the keyword you wish to locate.

3. Tap *OK*, and the matching references appear in a list.

   - Tap a reference in the list to return to the full reference list with that single reference highlighted.

   - To return to the previous view, tap *Cancel*.

   - The search results are not saved when you leave the search results list. However, the Find feature retains your last search request so it is easy to run it again.

EndNote Preferences

Several preferences are available in EndNote for Palm OS. With your reference list showing on your handheld device, tap the library name in the title bar, the *Options* menu, and then *Preferences*.

Show Splash Screen at Startup

Use this option to enable or disable the splash screen display that appears when you start the EndNote for Palm OS application.

Default Reference Type

Use the list to select a default reference type to assign to new references added to your handheld. You can always change the reference type when entering or editing a reference.

Scroll button behavior in Edit View

Select the behavior of scrolling buttons while in Edit view:

- ◆ *Scroll*: The scroll button scrolls through the fields of the current reference.
- ◆ *Navigate*: The scroll button navigates forward and backward through references.
- ◆ *Scroll then Nav.*: The scroll button scrolls until the end of the current reference, then navigates to the next reference.

Beaming References Between Handhelds

You can beam a single reference or a group of highlighted references to another Palm OS handheld device.

NOTE: You cannot beam the EndNote for Palm OS application itself, and you cannot beam an entire library.

To beam a reference or group of references to another Palm device:

1. Make sure the EndNote for Palm OS application is installed on both Palm OS handheld devices.

2. On the handheld that contains the reference(s) you wish to beam, display the list of references in the List view.

3. Highlight the reference or references you wish to beam to another handheld.

4. From the *Reference* menu, select *Beam Reference*.

5. On the receiving handheld, tap *Yes* on the Beam Receive dialog to accept the reference(s).

   On the handheld that is accepting the beamed references, EndNote for Palm OS opens to the list view and highlights the new reference(s) in the list of references.

Appendix A

Making Backup Copies of Your EndNote Files

Appendix A   Making Backup Copies of Your EndNote Files

Backing Up Your EndNote Files

We strongly recommend that you keep several backup copies of your critical computer files, especially your EndNote libraries and papers that you are writing. There are many ways that a file can be damaged: CDs and hard disks can fail, viruses can erase or corrupt files, and, of course, there is always human error and the possibility of accidentally throwing away your thesis or grant proposal the day before it is due. If you have any kind of disaster, big or little, backup copies can save you hours or days of work.

The simplest way to make a backup is to use the Macintosh Finder to copy your files to a CD or Zip disk. This will work for your EndNote libraries until they are too large to fit on one of these.

To backup larger files, or automate the backup process, use a backup program. There are a number of commercial backup programs available that make regular backups easy and efficient. These programs can scan your disk for files that you designate as important, keep track of changes, and save you time by copying only the changed files. In addition, they can split large files, including EndNote libraries, among several disks. If you ever need those files, the backup program can "restore" them from the disks.

Important Files to Backup

The following list covers the important EndNote files to backup.

♦ **EndNote libraries**
The library is where all of your references are stored. Note that exporting data from your library is not a "backup." An export file is just a text document, whereas an EndNote library is a database.

♦ **Image files**
If images are included in your library, make sure you back up the DATA folder found in the same folder as your library.

♦ **Modified Styles, Filters, and Connection Files**
Modified styles are important to backup so that you do not have to recreate the bibliographic format if something happens to your customized style. Similarly, custom filters and connection files should be backed up so that you do not have to redo the work to get your references to import as you want them. If you haven't modified these files, it is not as important to make backups of them because you can always reinstall them with the EndNote Installer. The default

locations for these files are the Styles, Connections, and Filters folders in your EndNote 7 folder.

- **Word processing documents**
  The papers you have written that include EndNote citations should be kept with your EndNote backup files.

- **EndNote Preferences**
  Copy the EndNote Prefs file (located in the Users: [Your Folder]: Library: Preferences: EndNote ƒ folder). Each user account maintains its own EndNote preference file. This file contains the settings for most of the items in the EndNote Preferences, including modifications that you have made to your Reference Types table, display fonts, default library settings, online preferences, term list settings, and duplicates criteria.

  The list of words to be excluded from sorting (using the *Sorting* preferences panel) is stored in the Users: [Your Folder]: Library: Preferences: EndNote ƒ folder. It is called "EndNote Sort Words." The file that sorts the words from the *Change Case* preferences panel is in that same folder and is called "EndNote Case Words." If you have entered lengthy lists of terms into these preferences panels, you should also back up these two files.

Backup Suggestions

Keep at least two sets of backup disks, each at a different location. We recommend that you have sets for alternate days, so if you discover that something went wrong yesterday, you will have the day-before-yesterday's version.

Make archival sets of the files listed above whenever you finish an important document. An archival set should include all of the files that are needed to recreate a final formatted paper. Label the backup disks, lock them and keep them in a safe place far away from your computer (preferably off-site). If you ever need to recreate the document, you will have all of the necessary files.

Appendix B

Troubleshooting and Limitations

Appendix B   Troubleshooting and Limitations

Limitations of EndNote

Word Processor Compatibility

Using Cite While You Write

To Cite While You Write, you must use Microsoft Word X.

This is the fastest, easiest way to cite and format references and create a bibliography in a word processing document. Cite While You Write integrates EndNote references and instant formatting into Word via Word's *Tools* menu. For more information about Cite While You Write, please see Chapter 10.

Cite While You Write Limitations

Due to memory resources, EndNote can insert a maximum of 50 citations within a single set of delimiters. This example shows four unformatted citations within a single set of delimiters:

```
{Schwartz, 1990 #5; Smith, 2001 #250; Brown, 1999
#85; Greene 1999 #130}
```

If you try to insert more than 50 citations, EndNote issues a warning and asks whether you want to insert just the first 50. If you copy and paste more than 50 citations from EndNote to within one set of delimiters, Cite While You Write will not be able to format them.

Troubleshooting Cite While You Write

Installation Problems

No Word Startup Folder

The EndNote installer automatically copies word processor support files to your Word startup folder. The startup folder is typically created when you install Microsoft Word. For Word X, the path is: Microsoft Office X:Office:Startup:Word

There are various reasons why the startup folder could be missing. It could have been moved, renamed, or deleted; it's also possible that it was never created, especially if Word was copied onto your Macintosh and not installed using Microsoft's installer. You can create the Word startup folder and reinstall EndNote—or do a custom installation of EndNote to install just the word processor files.

If you have customized the name or the location of the startup folder, you may need to copy the appropriate word processor files to the designated startup folder. See "Manually Installing Support for Word X" on page 19 for information about manually copying the appropriate word processor files to your startup folder.

No Add-in Commands in Word's Tools menu

In Word X, EndNote commands should appear on the *Tools* menu in an *EndNote 7* submenu.

Verify that these Cite While You Write files appear in Word's startup folder (the default startup folder is: Microsoft Office X: Office: Startup: Word):

```
EndNote 7 CWYW Word X
EndNote 7 CWYW Commands
```

If you have changed the default startup folder for Word, you should move the files from your EndNote 7: Cite While You Write folder to the designated startup folder.

Once you have verified that the word processor files are installed in the correct folder, start Word to see if the EndNote commands appear in the *Tools* menu. If they are still missing, you probably need to reset the startup folder location from within Word:

1. From the *Word* menu in Microsoft Word, choose *Preferences*.

2. Select the "File Locations" item, highlight the *Startup* line, and click *Modify*.

3. In the dialog that appears, find the startup folder and click *Use Selected Folder*.

4. Close the dialog.

5. Choose *Tools>Templates and Add-ins*.

6. Select the CWYW files and click *OK*.

You should now see the EndNote commands installed in the *Tools* menu in Word. You should not have to repeat this process again, now that Cite While You Write is correctly installed.

No EndNote Manuscript Templates Available

EndNote Manuscript Templates should be available both from the *Tools* menu in EndNote and from the Project Gallery when you start Microsoft Word. To install the EndNote Manuscript Templates, do one of these:

♦ Reinstall EndNote.

♦ Do a Custom install of EndNote to install just the word processor files.

♦ Copy the template files from the EndNote 7: Templates folder to the Microsoft Office X: Templates: EndNote folder as described on page 19.

Cannot Find a Compatible Version of EndNote

If you choose any of the EndNote commands in Word's *Tools* menu and you get an error that a compatible version of EndNote could not be found, make sure you have a copy of EndNote 7 on your hard drive, and not an older version of the program. Install EndNote from the original CD if it is not installed, and remove any older versions of the EndNote application.

If you do keep an older copy of EndNote on your hard drive or on a mounted volume and it interferes with the Word command to start EndNote, you should start the EndNote program by double-clicking the EndNote program icon in the Finder.

If you have an older copy of EndNote on your Macintosh, Now Menus (one of the utilities included with the Now Utilities package from Now Software) can sometimes interfere when the Add-in tries to start the EndNote program. To get around this problem, either remove the old copy of the EndNote program from your hard drive or open the Now Menus control panel and remove the old copy of EndNote from the list of recently used applications.

If all else fails and Cite While You Write still cannot communicate with EndNote, you might need to rebuild the Desktop file on your Macintosh. To do this, simply hold down the COMMAND (⌘) and OPTION keys while the computer is starting up. Note that during this process, any comments that were entered into the Show Info window for a file are lost.

"Session Too Complex" Error

This Microsoft Word error is probably the result of having too many documents open at once, or formatting a long file series. The number of documents Word can open depends on many variables: the number of files, the size of those files, the number of programs running, the amount of available memory, etc. Headers, footers, and footnotes each count as separate documents. If you are formatting a file series that exceeds the limit, consolidate some of your files to reduce the number of files EndNote must open to format a bibliography.

Troubleshooting Connections

When connecting with a remote database, there are at least two computers involved in completing the tasks you wish to perform: yours and the database server. Most often, there are intermediary computers as well, such as Domain Name Servers (DNS), proxy servers, and firewalls.

With more than just your computer involved, things can get quite complicated. This section attempts to give you the understanding necessary to solve problems that arise with connections. If you do not find the information that you need here, please contact EndNote technical support.

The most basic problem you can encounter with connections is the failure to connect at all. There are four ways you may experience this problem:

♦ EndNote cannot connect to the Internet.

♦ EndNote cannot find the host.

♦ EndNote cannot connect to the host.

♦ EndNote cannot communicate with the host.

Problems Connecting to the Internet

In general, if you are able to use a Web browser or other Internet software, you should also be able to connect with EndNote. Try using your Web browser to make sure your Internet connection is working.

Dial-up Connections

Your computer system includes software to connect to the Internet through a modem connected to your telephone line. You need to set up the Network system preferences in order to connect with your Internet provider.

In most cases, trying to connect in EndNote will start up your dialup software automatically. Some networking packages require that you establish the dialup connection manually before trying to connect in EndNote.

Using America Online

If you connect to the Internet through America Online (AOL), you'll need to use an AOL Link connection to allow you to use non-AOL internet software through AOL. Contact AOL about setting up AOL Link.

Problems Finding the Host

There are a few possibilities for what could be wrong if EndNote cannot find the host:

◆ The domain name specified in the connection file is wrong.

◆ Your network software does not have the correct address for the Domain Name Server.

◆ Your Domain Name Server isn't working.

If the connection file has worked in the past, the problem may lie with the Domain Name Server. If you've just made the connection file yourself and it's never worked before, you probably entered the wrong Server Address.

If you suspect problems with the Domain Name Server, contact your network administrator.

Problems Connecting

Once the host is found, EndNote tries to connect. It sends a connection request to the host and waits for up to two minutes for a reply. It may receive none, or it may receive a refusal immediately. In the first case you'll see a time-out error message, and in the second case you'll see a "host refused connection" error message.

If you wait for two minutes and receive a time-out message, the remote computer is down for some reason. Try again later.

If you receive a refusal message, and this happens no matter which connection file you try to use, you are most likely behind a firewall.

Firewalls

One way to tell if you are behind a firewall is to ask your network administrator. A do-it-yourself way is to look in the configuration of your Web Browser. Look for "proxies" or "proxy server". (See your Web Browser documentation to locate proxy server settings, as the location changes depending on which version you are using.)

The configuration for a proxy server has two pieces of information: an address and a port. If your browser is configured to connect through a proxy server, you are behind a firewall.

To connect to a database from behind a firewall, you must ask your network administrator to allow communication through the firewall.

NOTE: If Internet Explorer is configured for use with a proxy server, EndNote will automatically handle the proxy server when accessing http-based connections (PubMed and *Web of Science*). If you do not use Internet Explorer, configure proxy settings with the Network System Preferences.

Before you contact your network administrator, check the connection file for the address of the server and the port specified.

To obtain the server address and port:

1. From the *Edit* menu, choose *Connection Files* and select *Open Connection Manager*.

2. Select the appropriate connection file and click *Edit*.

3. In the Connection File window, click on the *Connection Settings* option.

You will find the server address and the port on the *Connection Settings* panel.

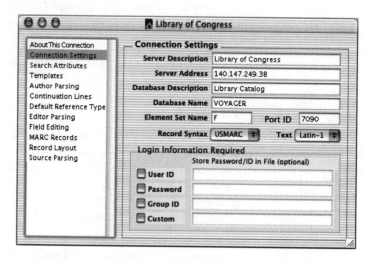

Depending upon the configuration of the firewall, the administrator may allow communication to all computers outside the firewall on the requested port, or communication to a specific server and port.

Communicating with Local Database Servers or Gateways

Many universities and organizations license Z39.50 databases for use on their own servers, or for access from a local gateway. The company providing the databases will include client software for accessing the databases. Some Z39.50 servers are designed to respond only to requests from this client software. In other cases, the server must be configured to allow requests from software other than the supplied client program.

If your organization maintains Z39.50 databases, but you are unable to connect to them with EndNote, ask your network administrator if the database server supports client software other than that supplied by the database provider.

Problems Communicating with the Host

Once you are connected, the most common problem in communicating with a host server is a password problem. Check your password and user ID. Check the upper or lower case requirements. If a password is rejected, you will see an error message that says something like "Server has rejected initialization."

The Connection Error Dialog

When searching a remote database, if there is a problem with the database, the search terms, or the connection file, EndNote presents an error message describing the source of the problem. The connection error dialog displays the original Z39.50 error message, if available, EndNote's translated version of that error, and any other message being sent directly from the server.

Errors Encountered While Retrieving References

For various reasons, some references do cause errors during retrieval. If EndNote encounters an error while retrieving references from a remote source, it stops the retrieval process. In order to get the rest of the references, it is best to submit the search again, and this time request the references start downloading with the one after the reference which might have caused an error. For example, if the error appeared while the tenth reference out of fifty was being retrieved, submit the search again, and when prompted, ask only for references 11 through 50 to be retrieved.

Problems With Retrieved Data

Blank Records

If blank records appear in your Retrieved References window, it could be due to a number of causes. One thing to check is whether your filter settings in the connection file match the format of the retrieved records. Open the connection file and view the *Templates* section. Also show the Connection status window, and change its view to show *Record Data*. The two formats need to match in order for the data to import.

Sometimes, when viewing the record data in the Connection Status window, you will notice that there is no bibliographic information for a reference that was retrieved. This happens sometimes where duplicate or blank entries remain in the remote database. These can be ignored.

Asterisks in Author Names or Titles

For some databases, diacritical characters in the author names and titles cannot be interpreted correctly when EndNote retrieves the references. In such cases, the diacritical characters are replaced with an asterisk (*). Use the *Change Text* command in the *References* menu to change the names with the asterisks to the name with the diacritical characters as they should be. See "Entering Special Characters" on page 116 for information about entering diacritics.

Understanding Mismatched Citations in RTF Files

When you are using the RTF Document Scan command, a citation matches window identifies unmatched and ambiguous citations.

This section applies only to the RTF Document Scan feature. When you use Cite While You Write, ambiguous citations are listed and resolved as they are inserted.

The Citation Matches Window

The Citation Matches window opens in the EndNote program after you format a paper (or if the formatting process is canceled). It lists all of the citations found in a document, in the order in which they appear in the paper.

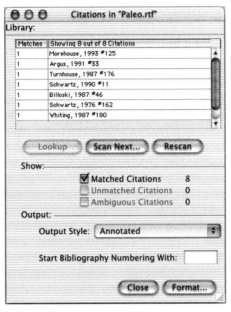

RTF Document Scan Citation Matches Window

In the Matches window, EndNote brings special attention to unmatched and ambiguous citations. You can choose from the check box options to show only the Matched Citations, Unmatched Citations, or Ambiguous Citations.

The Matches window lists all of the citations found in the document and displays the number of matching references for each citation.

If any number other than a 1 appears in the Matches column, the corresponding citation will be left unformatted in the document and will not be included in the bibliography EndNote generates.

Ambiguous Citations (Matches Greater than 1)

A number greater than 1 indicates that multiple references in the currently open library (or libraries) match the citation and EndNote does not know which reference to use. (EndNote automatically checks the matching references to see if any are duplicates. If so, they are not listed as separate possible matches.) To see which references are considered matches, highlight the citation in the Matches window and click *Lookup*. Reinsert the correct citation into the paper.

Unmatched Citations (A "Zero" Match)

A zero in the Matches column indicates that there is no matching reference in any open library for that particular citation. The Author, Year, and Record Number (if used in the temporary citation) must all match the Author, Year, and Record Number of a reference in the library in order for EndNote to consider it a match.

If text in your document is surrounded by citation delimiters (such as "{sic}"), EndNote will treat the text as a mismatched citation. You can ignore the warning about it being a mismatched citation, and EndNote will simply leave the text as it was before formatting. (See "Changing the Citation Delimiters" on page 531.)

Uncheck the "Unmatched Citations" box at the top of the Matches window to hide these items from view if you have numerous sections of bracketed text in your document and the corresponding unmatched citations are just cluttering the Matches window.

Correcting Mismatched Citations

Mismatched citations must be corrected either in the word processing document or in the EndNote library—whichever contains the incorrect information. Normally, the easiest way to fix a mismatched citation is to search the word processing document for the mismatched citation (use the *Find* command in your word processor's *Edit* menu), delete it, and then reinsert the citation from the library.

If there is a citation for which EndNote lists multiple matches, you can highlight the citation in the Matches window and click *Lookup*. EndNote displays the matching references in the Library window. You may then select the appropriate reference and reinsert it into the paper. Mismatches of this type are only possible when the record number has been omitted from the temporary citation in the text.

After you have corrected the mismatched citations and saved your changes to the paper, *Format* again. (The Matches window is still available after formatting if you want to see the list of citations.)

The best way to avoid citation mismatches:

♦ Keep all of your references in one main library.

♦ Copy and paste your citations from EndNote to your word processing documents instead of typing them.

There are several reasons why EndNote might not find exactly one match for each temporary citation in your paper. Listed here are typical problems and possible solutions. If a solution below involves changing a reference in your library, be sure to close or save all Reference windows before formatting to ensure that changes to your references are saved.

No Citations Found (Empty Matches Window)

♦ **Possible Cause:** No citations were found because the citation delimiters used in the paper no longer match the markers specified in the *Temporary Citations* panel of the *Preferences*.

Solution: Open the paper in your word processor and check which citation delimiters appear around the unformatted citations (for example, "{" and "}"). Then, switch back to EndNote and choose *Preferences* from the *Edit* menu, and select the *Temporary Citations* panel. Change the temporary citation delimiters in that panel so that they match the citation delimiters used in the paper. Rescan the paper and the citations should be found.

Unmatched Citations ("0" Matches)

A "0" in the Matches column means that EndNote could not find a reference in the library to match the temporary citation. You can still format your paper when there are zeros in the Matches column, however any zero match is ignored and left unformatted. If the unmatched reference is part of a multiple citation, *none of the entries in the multiple citation will be formatted*. If you used citation delimiters for text other than citations, the "0" match is not a problem and can be ignored.

♦ **Possible Cause:** Either the temporary citation or the EndNote reference has been modified so that there is a discrepancy between the two.

Solution: Find the reference in the library and open it. Look at the top of its Reference window, and verify that the reference's author, year, *and* record number are identical to the unformatted citation in your paper. Correct any discrepancies.

◆ **Possible Cause:** A citation marker has been used in a paper for something other than a citation, such as {3H} or {sic}.

Solution: If the "citation" that appears in the Matches window is just bracketed text, then ignore the "0." See also "Changing the Citation Delimiters" on page 531.

◆ **Possible Cause:** The reference you have cited has been deleted from the library.

Solution: Search for the reference in your library to verify that it is missing. If it is, create a new reference and re-enter the data into your library. The reference will now have a new record number. Reinsert the citation into the paper to replace the old citation.

Matches Greater Than 1

EndNote cannot format a citation that does not have a unique match to a reference in your library. If you see a number greater than 1 in the Matches column, EndNote was able to match more than one reference in the library to that citation, and it is therefore not unique.

◆ **Possible Cause:** You have typed incomplete citations into your paper, perhaps with just the author and the year and *not* the unique record number, and there is more than one citation that matches that author and year.

Solution: Highlight the citation in the Matches window and click *Lookup*. This will display the matching references. Copy the correct one, and then go back to the paper, delete the ambiguous one, and paste the complete temporary citation in its place.

◆ **Possible Cause:** A citation marker has been used in your paper for something other than a citation, and that text happens to match an author's name in your library.

Solution: If this occurs once in a while, temporarily change the notation in your paper that was mistaken for citation delimiters. For example change {Hall} to (Hall), then format the paper and redo the notation later. If this problem arises frequently, then it might be better to change the Citation Delimiters from "{" and "}" to "[" and "]". If you do this, you must also change the markers for all temporary citations in your paper. (See "Changing the Citation Delimiters" on page 531.)

Finding the Matches to a Citation

Highlight the ambiguous citation in the Matches window and click *Lookup* to display the Library window with all of the matching references showing. This helps you locate the intended reference so you can reinsert it into your paper.

To replace an ambiguous citation in your paper, select the reference you want to cite and choose *Copy* from the *Edit* menu. Open your paper, delete the ambiguous citation from the text of the document, and paste the correct citation in its place.

Changing the Citation Delimiters

By default, when EndNote scans your paper, it looks for citations enclosed in curly braces, "{ }". If you frequently use curly braces in your writing or incorporate backslashes into your citations, you can change the EndNote citation delimiters to other delimiters.

To change the citation delimiters:

1. Choose *Preferences* from the *Edit* menu, and click the *Temporary Citations* option.

2. In the Citation Delimiter section, delete the curly braces and type another set of delimiters such as "[" and "]" or "<" and ">". Beginning and ending citation delimiters must be different. Letters, numbers, semicolons, commas, and the number sign (#), and "@" cannot be used as citation delimiters. You can also change the citation prefix marker in this dialog (see page 477 for details). Citation Prefixes are described on page 255.

3. Click *OK*. Click *Save* and close the window.

The new citation delimiters are used when you copy and paste citations and when EndNote scans the paper.

If you change citation delimiters while in the process of writing a paper, you might create a situation where you have some citations using the old citation delimiters and some that use the new markers. This will cause a problem when EndNote formats the paper, since it will only find the citations that use the currently specified citation delimiters.

The EndNote Glossary

Boolean Operator
A Boolean operator is one of the connecting terms AND, OR, or NOT, used to combine search items. A matching reference must meet both of the conditions connected by the AND, so AND narrows the search compared to using either search item alone. OR is used to find records that match either of the conditions connected by the OR operator, and so widens the search. NOT is used to find any records that do not match the search item following it.

Cite While You Write
Cite While You Write software is installed with the EndNote program for use with Microsoft Word X. It integrates an *EndNote 7* submenu of commands into the *Tools* menu in Word for quick and easy insertion and formatting of citations, bibliographies, figures, and tables. Instant formatting and a traveling library that contains full reference information make Cite While You Write the easiest and most efficient way to cite references and create a bibliography.

Connection Files
Connection Files are EndNote files used to store the information necessary to connect to and search online databases. Connection Files are stored in the Connections folder in your EndNote 7 folder and can be browsed using the Connection File Manager (from the *Edit* menu, choose *Connection Files* and select *Open Connection Manager*). To establish a connection to an online database, go to *Tools>Connect>Connect* and select a service. Internet access is required.

Continuation Line
Continuation lines are second or subsequent lines of data belonging to a single tag, and are typically described in the context of a data file to be imported by EndNote. EndNote uses the indent level for continuation lines in order to distinguish text containing reference data from text containing instructions, prompts, and other miscellaneous text from your database's interface. Continuation lines need to be consistently indented the same number of spaces from the left margin. For example, the continuation lines below are indented four spaces from the left margin.

```
AB- A single-subject research design that used multiple baselines
    across behaviors compared traditional adaptations to adapted
    computer technologies.
```

Data File
A data file consists of the records captured or saved from a reference database, whether from an online database or from a CD-ROM. A data file must be a **text file** in order for its records to be imported by EndNote into an EndNote library.

Database
A database is a file consisting of one or more records, each containing one or more fields of information, such as the name of the author, title of publication, year of publication, and so on. In the context of EndNote, databases are typically collections of bibliographic data, and are referred to as libraries.

Default
A default is a value, action, or setting that a computer system or program will assume unless the user intervenes to override it.

Delimiters
Delimiters are punctuation that separates one term or field (or any piece of data) from another. Delimiters are used in the context of temporary citation markers (the curly braces are default delimiters that identify the temporary citations in the body of your text) and term lists.

Diacritics
Diacritics are phonetic variations, such as accents, associated with a letter. When using the *Sort References* command or formatting a bibliography, EndNote sorts diacritical characters according to the rules of the language that is selected on the Sort References dialog. Characters with diacritics are sorted differently in English, Spanish, Swedish, and other systems. Diacritical marks are significant in searches, as letters such as é, ü and î match only those letters exactly. Thus, a search for "résumé" does not find "resume."

Display Fonts
EndNote has a concept of "Plain Font," as well as "Plain Size," and "Plain Style." All references in your EndNote library should be stored in the plain font, size, and style, unless a specific change is necessary (such as the use of the Symbol font, or italics for emphasis of a word). The appearance of the plain font is determined by the General Display Font setting. This changes the font used to display the references, as well as being the font that is used when printing or exporting references directly from EndNote. The Library Display Font is the font used to display references in the Library window. Both display fonts may be changed using EndNote's preferences.

Field
A field refers to a part of an EndNote reference, such as the author, year, or title. In the EndNote Reference window, each field is displayed as its own section, containing a separate piece of information, such as author names or keywords. Fields are arranged in EndNote styles to show how the data should be formatted. They are arranged in EndNote import filters to show how the tagged data should be imported. EndNote allows for up to 40 fields in each reference.

Field Codes
Cite While You Write inserts hidden field codes around and inside your formatted citations in Word. These hidden codes contain reference information, and allow EndNote to format, unformat, and reformat citations within Word.

Filter
A filter is a file consisting of one or more **Reference Type templates** that instruct EndNote how to interpret and import data into the corresponding fields in EndNote. Filters are selected as import options when you choose the *Import* command from EndNote's *File* menu. EndNote comes with a variety of filters, each designed for a specific database. You may also create your own filters, or modify any of those supplied with the program. Filters

are stored in the Filters folder in the EndNote 7 folder; you may browse the list of filters by choosing *Import Filters* from the *Edit* menu and selecting *Open Filter Manager*.

Firewall
Firewalls are security measures that restrict access between computers and the Internet. In order to search **Z39.50** servers over the Internet, your network administrator may need to allow access to certain port numbers.

Generic Fields and Reference Types
The Generic reference type includes the complete set of 40 fields that are available in EndNote. It is "generic" in that it is not specialized for a specific type of reference (such as a book or a journal article). EndNote has a fixed set of "generic" fields that provides the basis for all specific fields used in the different reference types. The generic field names are not worded to be reference type-specific (for example, the generic field name "Author" is equivalent to "Reporter" for a newspaper article or "Artist" for the Artwork reference type). Generic field names are used throughout EndNote (for example, in the Sort References and Search dialogs) to refer to a similar category of fields that can be found in the different reference types. When you choose a generic field name in any of these dialogs, it refers to all fields in that row of the Reference Types table (see page 354).

Global Editing
Global editing commands allow you to make editing changes to a group of records at the same time, rather than having to edit each record individually. *Change Text* searches for text in your library, and either deletes that text or replaces it with other text that you specify. *Change Field* modifies any field in your library by either inserting text at the beginning or end of the field, replacing the contents of the field with different text, or deleting the contents of the field. *Move Field* provides a way to move the entire contents of one field to another field within a reference.

Information Provider
An information provider is a service that provides access to one or more databases, whether to an online or CD-ROM database. Examples of information providers include Ovid, ISI, SilverPlatter, and STN.

In-text Citation
An in-text citation is the brief citation to a reference that appears in the body of the text of a paper. Typically this is just the author name and year in parentheses, or a bibliography number.

Keyword
A keyword is a term that helps identify a record, and that is used for efficient searching. Also known as a descriptor, index term, subject term, or subject. Multiple entries (words or phrases) can be entered in the Keywords field of a reference.

Library
In the context of using EndNote, a "library" is the term for your EndNote database of references. It is a collection of records of reference material. When you choose *Open* from

EndNote's *File* menu, you open a library. The references are displayed in the Library window.

Literal Text
Literal text consists of any text in a data file that does not correspond to a **field** in EndNote. Literal text must be included in a filter in order for EndNote to parse multiple pieces of information found in a single tag in a record to the corresponding field or fields in EndNote. Examples of literal text include punctuation used to separate one piece of information from the next, as well as any identifying text, such as "vol." for Volume, or "pp." for Pages.

Log File
When using the *Connect* command to search and retrieve references from online remote databases, EndNote maintains a log file to record communication status messages with the remote database as well as a log of the references that were retrieved. The location of the log file can be determined (and changed) by choosing *Preferences* from the *EndNote* menu, and clicking the *Online* option.

MARC (MAchine Readable Cataloging)
MARC is a standardized format developed by the Library of Congress for producing machine-readable bibliographic records. MARC uses numeric tags such as tag 100 for Personal Author, and tag 245 for the Title.

Mnemonic Tag
A mnemonic tag is an abbreviated way of identifying the contents of the data that follows. Mnemonic tags frequently use the first two characters of the corresponding data, as in "AU-" for AUthor, "TI-" for TItle, or "SO-" for SOurce. Other mnemonic tags use a combination of the two naming conventions, as in "SO-<PY>" for the SOurce's Publication Year.

Output Style
An output style is a file that, in conjunction with the reference type for a particular reference, controls the output format of in-text citations, references in a bibliography, figures, and tables. Each output style that you use is stored in a separate file and can be used by more than one library. An output style contains instructions that tell EndNote which fields to print, in what order, and with what associated punctuation. It may also include additional font or style instructions. Output styles are often referred to simply as **styles**.

PubMed
PubMed is the National Library of Medicine's online public access version of their MEDLINE database. You can directly search PubMed and save records with the *Connect* command on EndNote's *Tools* menu.

Reference Types
An EndNote library can contain references from a variety of different sources, such as books, journal articles, and newspaper articles. We call these different sources **reference types**. EndNote provides built-in forms for these and other common reference types.

Remote Database
A remote database is the term used for databases available online using EndNote's *Connect* command. These are typically databases that are accessible on a Z39.50 server. They include library catalogs and other bibliographic reference databases. An Internet connection is required to access a remote database.

Retrieved References Window
The Retrieved References window appears when a connection to an **remote database** is established. This workspace displays the connection status as well as the references retrieved from your searches. Use this workspace to store retrieved references as you continue searching the remote database. When your searching is complete, copy the references from the Retrieved References window to the Library window to save them.

RTF File
RTF is an acronym for Rich Text Format, a standardized file format. You can save most word processor documents to this standard type of file while retaining formatting and styles. EndNote can Scan an RTF file in order to format in-text citations and generate a bibliography.

Sort
A sort defines how a set of references is ordered on a field by field basis, in either alphabetic or numeric order. Fields are sorted from left to right by character. Quotation marks, parentheses and other punctuation marks are considered during a sort, except when comparing title fields. In an alphabetic sort, punctuation comes first, then numbers, then the letters A-Z. Within a sort level, the sorting of diacritics (accented characters) is determined by the language setting. You may define a list of stop words that are ignored for sorting when they appear at the beginning of an author or title field.

Subject Bibliography
A subject bibliography is a bibliography with sorted references grouped under sorted Subject Headings. Typical headings group references by Keyword, Author, or Journal Title, but you can base headings on any EndNote field or combination of fields. You can even group references by reference type.

Styles
Styles are the files that EndNote uses to determine how to arrange references for a wide variety of bibliographic formats. Styles are typically for specific journals, though they can also be based on more general style guides such as the Chicago Manual of Style or the MLA Handbook. EndNote provides more than 1000 preconfigured styles in the Styles folder of your EndNote 7 folder. To preview and browse through these styles, choose *Output Styles* from the *Edit* menu, and select *Open Style Manager*. Styles are used to determine the format of references in the preview pane of the Library window as well as when you use the *Print, Export, Format, Format Bibliography,* and *Copy Formatted* commands. They are also referred to as **output styles**.

Subscription Databases

Subscription databases are online bibliographic databases which require payment or some form of authorization to enable you to connect (as opposed to "free" databases or library catalogs). For more information about these databases, contact the individual information providers.

Tagged Data

Tagged data consists of an identifier, typically a **mnemonic tag**, in the left margin of a **data file**, followed by text for one or more **fields** of information. Data must be consistently tagged if it is to be read by EndNote into the appropriate fields in EndNote.

Templates

Templates are used in both **styles** and **filters** to show EndNote how to output or import bibliographic data. The templates use field names to represent the actual bibliographic data as it should be arranged in a bibliographic entry (in the case of styles), or in a data file to be imported (in the case of filters). Typically, a different template is constructed for each **reference type**.

Manuscript templates are used to create Microsoft Word documents that conform to electronic publishing guidelines. You can select a predefined template from either EndNote or Word, which triggers a manuscript template wizard.

Term Lists

Each library has preconfigured term lists for authors, journals, and keywords. The term lists maintain a list of the names or words entered into the corresponding fields. They are used to help with data entry by suggesting terms as you type. The Journals term list can also be used to store various abbreviations of the journal names and later use those abbreviations as needed in bibliographies.

Text File

A text file consists entirely of characters that can be typed from a standard keyboard. A text file may contain any character from the English alphabet, punctuation marks, spaces, and numbers. A text file cannot contain any control characters or text styles used by a word processor to format text. EndNote can only import records captured or saved as text files, and cannot read files saved in a word processor format. EndNote can export references to a text file, but cannot apply styles within the text file.

Traveling Library

When you use EndNote's Cite While You Write commands in Word, each formatted citation in your document is saved with field codes that embed reference data in the document. The paper contains a "traveling library" of EndNote references cited. This makes it easy to use your document on other machines and share your document with colleagues.

URL

A URL, or Uniform Resource Locator, can be used to specify the location of any resource available on the Internet (typically for Web pages or FTP sites). A common format for a URL for a Web page is http://www.endnote.com.

Web of Science
The ISI Web of Science is the Web interface for access to the ISI Citation Databases, which cover over 8,000 international journals in the sciences, social sciences, and the arts and humanities. Through ISI Links, the Web of Science also offers navigation to electronic full-text journal articles, genetic information, and chemical and patent databases.

Search the Web of Science just as you would search any other remote database. Your search results are copied directly to the EndNote library of your choice.

Z39.50
Z39.50 is a NISO protocol that describes the search and retrieval of information from remote databases. It is primarily used for data retrieval from bibliographic databases.

Index

Symbols

H

hanging indents 398, 400
    in CWYW Word documents 265
hardware requirements 11
Headline case 437
HealthGate 158
Help file 3, 14
help! 5
Hide Connection Status command 143
Hide Preview 78
Hide Selected command 176, 180
hiding reference types 353
hiding found references 187
highlighting (See selecting)
Home key 28, 77
host refused connection error 523
HotSync operation 505
HTML 312
Humanities term list 14

I

Iberian dictionary 491
ibid 405
IBM PCs, transferring libraries from 90
icons, libraries 75, 87
identifiers, in filters 435
IGNORE field 424
Image field 111, 117, 349
images
    deleting 122
    editing 121
    including captions 121
    inserting 117
    replacing 122
    sharing 121
    storing 121
Import As Is, filter setting 432
Import command 151
    EndNote Library option 200
    Tab-Delimited import errors 164
import filters (see filters)
Import into Duplicates Library option 150
import traveling library 283
importing
    bibliographies 170
    changing case of imported text 436
    defining start of reference 439
    dictionaries for spell checking 490
    EndNote libraries 151

    errors 164
    excluding duplicates 150
    from multiple sources in one data file 435
    journal source data 441
    libraries 200
    MARC records 443
    options 150, 151
    tab-delimited files 162
    text translation option 151
indents
    (see also Continuation lines)
    bibliography layout 398
    in bibliographies 400
    in CWYW documents 265
independent bibliographies 309
    in a plain text file 311
        printing directly from EndNote 314
        using Copy Formatted 311
Index Medicus journal abbreviations 214
indexes for searching 188
Information Express 158
information provider 67, 536
Ingenta 160
INIST 158
initials
    (see also Author List panel)
    author names 396
    editors (see also Author List) 397
    from full names 396
Initials Only, filter option 431
Insert after field's text option 195
Insert before field's text option 196
Insert Item command (Search command) 185
Insert Note command, CWYW 249
Insert Selected Citation(s) command (CWYW)
    244
Insert Term command 216
inserting
    citations (CWYW) 241
    citations from multiple libraries (CWYW)
        247
    citations with drag-and-drop 244
    figures (CWYW) 271
    graphics 118
    images 117
    journal names into references 222, 224
    multiple citations 244
    multiple citations at once 298
    terms 216, 220

installation
    custom install 15
    EndNote for Palm OS 503
    files installed 14
    full install 13
    options 11
    problems, CWYW 519
instant formatting (CWYW) 263, 265
    enabling/disabling 494
international distributors 5
Internet address 4, 5
in-text citations (see citations)
Is Greater Than, as Search option 182
Is Less Than, as Search option 182
Is, as Search option 182
ISBN 109
ISI CD (Citation Indexes) 158
ISI ResearchSoft contact info 4
ISI Web of Science 158
ISI-CE import format (Web of Science) 152
ISSN 109
Italian dictionary 491
italic 112, 379

J

journal abbreviations 220, 386
    important points 222
    importing EndNote journals files 225
    removing periods 222, 388
    updating 223
    using EndNote's lists 214
    using when creating bibliographies 224
Journal Abbreviations command 222, 224, 386
    relationship to term lists 225
Journal Article reference type 355
Journal Article Source Tag 442
Journal field 106, 220
journal names
    abbreviating 386
    entering 106
    formatting 386
Journal Names Style panel 387
Journals term list 220, 348, 352, 388
    important points 222
    importing EndNote Journals files 225
    journal abbreviations 220
    updating 223
JPEG files, inserting 118
Jr., entering with author names 105

K

key commands 28, 77, 94, 113
keyboard shortcuts in Word 495, 496
keywords
    (see also term lists)
    cleaning up 192, 214, 217
    entering 110
    in manuscript template wizard 239
    indexing 190
Keywords field 110
Keywords term list 220
Knowledge Finder 158

L

Label field 109, 478
    in formatted references 399
Latin-1 151, 462
layout, bibliography 265, 398
less than 183
lessons to learn EndNote 25
Letter After Year option 390
libraries 536
    closing 87
    closing all at once 87
    compatibility 17
    default 84
    definition 75
    deleting 88
    icon 75, 87
    important points 75
    importing 200
    importing from Word 283
    limits 75
    locking 87
    making backups 515
    merging 200
    moving to different computer 343
    opening 86, 87, 297
    renaming 75
    repairing 88
    sending via email 89
    sharing on a network 87
    transferring from Windows to Macintosh 90
    using more than one per paper CWYW 247
libraries used
    in your Word document (CWYW) 265
library display font 80, 475